Sexuality and Memory in Early Modern England

This volume brings together two vibrant areas of Renaissance studies today: memory and sexuality. The contributors show that not only Shakespeare but also a broad range of his contemporaries were deeply interested in how memory and sexuality interact. Are erotic experiences heightened or deflated by the presence of memory? Can a sexual act be commemorative? Can an act of memory be eroticized? How do forms of romantic desire underwrite forms of memory? To answer such questions, these authors examine drama, poetry, and prose from both major authors and lesser-studied figures in the canon of Renaissance literature. Alongside a number of insightful readings, they show that sonnets enact a sexual exchange of memory; that epics of nationhood cannot help but eroticize their subjects; that the act of sex in Renaissance tragedy too often depends upon violence of the past. Memory, these scholars propose, re-shapes the concerns of queer and sexuality studies—including the unhistorical, the experience of desire, and the limits of the body. So too does the erotic revise the dominant trends of memory studies, from the rhetoric of the medieval memory arts to the formation of collective pasts.

John S. Garrison is Associate Professor of English at Carroll University, USA. He is the author of *Friendship and Queer Theory in the Renaissance* (2014) and *Glass* (2015). His essays have appeared in *Exemplaria*, *Literature Compass*, *Milton Quarterly*, and *Studies in Philology*. He has held fellowships from the American Philosophical Society, Folger Shakespeare Library, and National Endowment for the Humanities.

Kyle Pivetti is Assistant Professor of English at Norwich University, USA. He is the author of *Of Memory and Literary Form: Making the Early Modern Nation* (2015). His essays have appeared in the journals *Modern Philology* and the edited collection *Mapping Gendered Routes and Spaces in the Early Modern World* (2015).

Routledge Studies in Renaissance Literature and Culture

1. Stillness in Motion in the Seventeenth-Century Theatre
   P.A. Skantze

2. The Popular Culture of Shakespeare, Spenser and Jonson
   Mary Ellen Lamb

3. Forgetting in Early Modern English Literature and Culture
   Lethe's Legacies
   Edited by Christopher Ivic and Grant Williams

4. Luce Irigaray and Premodern Culture
   Thresholds of History
   Edited by Elizabeth D. Harvey and Theresa Krier

5. Writing, Geometry and Space in Seventeenth-Century England and America
   Circles in the Sand
   Jess Edwards

6. Dramatists and their Manuscripts in the Age of Shakespeare, Jonson, Middleton and Heywood
   Authorship, Authority and the Playhouse
   Grace Ioppolo

7. Reading the Early Modern Dream
   The Terrors of the Night
   Edited by Katharine Hodgkin, Michelle O'Callaghan, and S. J. Wiseman

8. Fictions of Old Age in Early Modern Literature and Culture
   Nina Taunton

9. Performing Race and Torture on the Early Modern Stage
   Ayanna Thompson

10. Women, Murder, and Equity in Early Modern England
    Randall Martin

11. Staging Early Modern Romance
    Prose Fiction, Dramatic Romance, and Shakespeare
    Edited by Mary Ellen Lamb and Valerie Wayne

12. The Uses of the Future in Early Modern Europe
    Edited by Andrea Brady and Emily Butterworth

13. Making Publics in Early Modern Europe
    People, Things, Forms of Knowledge
    Edited by Bronwen Wilson and Paul Yachnin

14. Representing the Plague in Early Modern England
    Edited by Rebecca Totaro and Ernest B. Gilman

15. Prophecy and Sibylline Imagery in the Renaissance
    Shakespeare's Sibyls
    Jessica L. Malay

16 Ecocriticism and Early Modern English Literature
Green Pastures
Todd A. Borlik

17 Narrative Developments from Chaucer to Defoe
Edited by Gerd Bayer and Ebbe Klitgård

18 Moral Play and Counterpublic
Transformations in Moral Drama, 1465–1599
Ineke Murakami

19 Family and the State in Early Modern Revenge Drama: Economies of Vengeance
Chris McMahon

20 Patrons and Patron Saints in Early Modern English Literature
Alison A. Chapman

21 Androids and Intelligent Networks in Early Modern Literature and Culture
Artificial Slaves
Kevin LaGrandeur

22 Shakespeare, Jonson, and the Claims of the Performative
James Loxley and Mark Robson

23 Making Space Public in Early Modern Europe
Performance, Geography, Privacy
Edited by Angela Vanhaelen and Joseph P. Ward

24 Friendship and Queer Theory in the Renaissance
Gender and Sexuality in Early Modern England
John S. Garrison

25 Blood and Home in Early Modern Drama
Domestic Identity on the Renaissance Stage
Ariane M. Balizet

26 Bodies, Speech, and Reproductive Knowledge in Early Modern England
Sara D. Luttfring

27 Rethinking the Mind-Body Relationship in Early Modern Literature, Philosophy and Medicine
The Renaissance of the Body
Charis Charalampous

28 Sexuality and Memory in Early Modern England
Literature and the Erotics of Recollection
Edited by John S. Garrison and Kyle Pivetti

Sexuality and Memory in Early Modern England
Literature and the Erotics of Recollection

Edited by
John S. Garrison and Kyle Pivetti

NEW YORK AND LONDON

First published 2016
by Routledge
711 Third Avenue, New York, NY 10017

and by Routledge
2 Park Square, Milton Park, Abingdon, Oxon OX14 4RN

Routledge is an imprint of the Taylor & Francis Group, an informa business

© 2016 Taylor & Francis

The right of the editors to be identified as the authors of the editorial material, and of the authors for their individual chapters, has been asserted in accordance with sections 77 and 78 of the Copyright, Designs and Patents Act 1988.

All rights reserved. No part of this book may be reprinted or reproduced or utilised in any form or by any electronic, mechanical, or other means, now known or hereafter invented, including photocopying and recording, or in any information storage or retrieval system, without permission in writing from the publishers.

Trademark notice: Product or corporate names may be trademarks or registered trademarks, and are used only for identification and explanation without intent to infringe.

Library of Congress Cataloging-in-Publication Data

   Sexuality and memory in early modern England: literature and the erotics of recollection / edited by John S. Garrison and Kyle Pivetti.
      pages cm. — (Routledge studies in Renaissance literature and culture; 28)
   Includes bibliographical references and index.
      1. English literature—Early modern, 1500–1700—History and criticism.
      2. Memory in literature. 3. Sex in literature. 4. Desire in literature.
      5. Literature and society—Great Britain—History. I. Garrison, John S., 1970- editor.
      II. Pivetti, Kyle, editor. III. Title: Literature and the erotics of recollection.
   PR408.M45S49 2016
   820.9'3538—dc23   2015027774

ISBN: 978-1-138-84438-4 (hbk)
ISBN: 978-1-315-73040-0 (ebk)

Typeset in Sabon
by codeMantra

This collection embodies the spirit of intellectual pursuit and collegiality imbued in both of us by our shared mentor, Margaret W. Ferguson. We dedicate this volume to her.

Contents

Introduction: The Erotics of Recollection   1
JOHN S. GARRISON AND KYLE PIVETTI

PART I
Legacies of Desire

1 Intimate Histories: Desire, Genre, and the Trojan War
  in *The Araygnement of Paris*   17
  JOYCE GREEN MacDONALD

2 The Will and Testamentary Eroticism in Shakespearean Drama   30
  DOUGLAS IAIN CLARK

3 Remembering to Forget: Shakespeare's Sonnet 35
  and Sigo's "XXXV"   43
  STEPHEN GUY-BRAY

4 "The stage is down, and Philomela's choir is hushed from
  pricksong": Revising and (Re)membering in Middleton's
  The Ghost of Lucrece   51
  DEE ANNA PHARES

5 Exemplarity and Its Discontents in Michael Drayton's
  Englands Heroical Epistles   66
  ANDREW FLECK

6 Guinevere's Ghost: Spenser's Response to Malory's Erotics   81
  KENNETH HODGES

PART II
Bodies, Remember

7 The Gallery of Erotic Memory in *The Faerie Queene*   97
  GORAN V. STANIVUKOVIC

x Contents

  8 False Muscle Memory in Marlowe and Nashe 112
      ROBERT DARCY

  9 Marlowe's Helen and the Erotics of Cultural Memory 120
      JOHN S. GARRISON

10 Strange Love: Funerary Erotics in *Romeo and Juliet* 129
      MARK DAHLQUIST

11 "The monument woos me": Necrophilia as Commemoration in Thomas Middleton's *The Lady's Tragedy* 144
      HEATHER WICKS

PART III
Intimate Refusals

12 Well-Divided Dispositions: Distraction, Dying, and the Eroticism of Forgetting in *Antony and Cleopatra* 159
      JONATHAN BALDO

13 Desiring Memory in Spenser's *Amoretti* and *The Faerie Queene* or "Is there Sex in the Library of Memory?" 177
      KYLE PIVETTI

14 Spenser's Erotic Refusals 192
      SU FANG NG

15 "Despisèd straight": Shakespeare's Observation of Semantic Memory Bias 207
      IAN F. MacINNES

16 *Hamlet* without Sex: The Politics of Regenerate Loss 220
      AMANDA BAILEY

      Afterword: "A Prescript Order of Life": Memory, Sexuality, Selfhood 237
      GARRETT A. SULLIVAN, JR.

      Contributors 245
      Selected Bibliography 249
      Index 269

Introduction
The Erotics of Recollection

John S. Garrison and Kyle Pivetti

"But isn't desire always the same?" When Roland Barthes poses the question in *A Lover's Discourse*, he inevitably raises problems of memory.[1] On the one hand, a raw impulse must always be the same, like thirst or hunger. On the other hand, desire is understood and recognized only in contrast to past experiences, including earlier moments of satiation. Barthes, certainly, recognizes the fraught tensions between sexuality and memory even if he gives no clear resolutions. *A Lover's Discourse* offers only fragmented reflections on romantic love and the languages through which love manifests, and when Barthes asks this question about desire, he struggles with the problem of absence. What happens when the object of affection doesn't show up? What happens when the lover leaves? "Sometimes I have no difficulty enduring absence," Barthes writes, "This endured absence is nothing more or less than forgetfulness. I am, intermittently, unfaithful."[2] Here, *getting over it* constitutes a sort of betrayal. The "faithful" alternative is to retain the beloved constantly in present memory in hopes of restoring the lost object of affection: "I waken out of this forgetfulness very quickly. In great haste, I reconstitute a memory."[3] Barthes, then, frames his romantic longing against the past, and his desire remains "always the same." Desire assumes that object is absent, and that raw impulse of wanting becomes the reconstitution of the past. Desire, in other words, depends upon memory.

Barthes is not the first to ponder the languages of longing, nor is he the first writer to cultivate suffering as some sort of masochistic pleasure. In Barthes' assertion that "endlessly I sustain the discourse of the beloved's absence," he echoes Ovid's classic meditation on absence in the *Heroides* (c. 25–16 BC).[4] The ancient collection imagines a series of mythological lovers writing letters that dwell on absence, and that theme, we discover, also turns to issues of personal and collective memory. In one late pair of letters, Ovid first assumes the perspective of Leander writing to his absent lover, Hero. Leander bemoans the ongoing bad weather that keeps him from swimming to Hero—and to her body. We know that he has made the trip across the Hellespont in the past; he gleefully retells the story to the very woman who would perhaps know it better than anyone. He writes,

> Meanwhile, while wind and wave deny me everything, I ponder in my heart [*mente agito*] the first times I stole to you. Night was but just

beginning—for the memory has charm for me [*namque est meminisse voluptas*]—when I left my father's doors on the errand of love.[5]

Leander goes on to narrate the whole account, from the escape to the swim to the "joys of that first night."[6] The memory, Leander insists, "has charm for me." By remembering the experience, Leander can discover a wholly new pleasure that will fill the time until he can actually meet Hero again.[7] At the moment, it seems that he writes neither to assure his legacy nor to convince Hero to give it another chance. Instead, he—like Barthes—experiences the erotics of remembrance.

When Hero responds, she indulges in her own recollections. She describes falling asleep, which then blends into equal parts fantasy and memory as she envisions Leander's return. She writes,

> For now I seem to see you already swimming near, and now to feel your wet arms around my neck, and now to throw about your dripping limbs the accustomed covering, and now to warm our bosoms in the close embrace—and many things else a modest tongue should say naught of, whose memory delights, but whose telling brings a blush [*quae fecisse iuvat, facta referre pudet*].[8]

Leander's promptings, it seems, provoke an exchange of both language and memory, grounded in the absence of the lover. Like Leander, Hero enjoys the particular erotics of recollection. Once the dream begins in its specific details of warm bodies and dripping arms, her readers can easily imagine for themselves what happened. The exchange, then, delights not just the couple but their wider audiences, including Ovid himself. After all, he is the one crafting the memories that provide such delight. He sustains the "discourse of absence" and allows others to partake, including writers of the late sixteenth century.

Readers of early modern English poetry know that the delights do not stop with Ovid's poetry. Christopher Marlowe looks to these same accounts when writing his own *Hero and Leander* (1598), which Robert Darcy's contribution in this collection will help us see as a poem of both impotence and delayed gratification. Marlowe was just as involved as Ovid in the erotics of recollection, in the images of dripping arms, as Hero. In this case, he finds in the literary legacy the delights of memory, of recalling stories told and retold even when modesty would suggest that they should be left unspoken. This instance reminds us, as Stephen Guy-Bray shows in both this collection and elsewhere, that acts of poetic influence across literary history share erotic valences.[9] Early modern England, in other words, functions as a site of erotic recollection: its writers re-appropriated literary desires to compose their own narratives of nation, religion, subjectivity, and desire.

This dynamic develops and extends an often-repeated truism of the period in English history, that it was a time of intense interest in recovering lost pasts. Philip Schwyzer summarizes that attitude nicely, remarking that "The idea of the past as segregated from the present by a powerful (if not insuperable) divide is … quintessentially early modern. It is not too much of an exaggeration to describe both the Renaissance and the English Reformation as projects devoted to recovering the essence of a long-last past, sundered from the present by great gulfs of ignorance and corruption."[10] Within these operations of loss and recuperation, we find similar problems to those of Barthes's abandoned lover. The thrill of recovery relies upon a previous experience of loss and the possibility that the lost object can never be fully recuperated. The sense of "great gulfs" that separate lovers or poets inspires the feelings of longing and attachment that signal the ways in which desire and memory are co-constituted.

But just as our volume examines literary appropriation as a mode of (eroticized) cultural memory, it also complicates the matter of sexual experience by seeking its relations to personal memory. Lina Bolzoni, in *The Gallery of Memory*, notes a common refrain across European works of the sixteenth century that heartache derives from an overactive memory: "It is commonly believed that the intensity of amorous desire causes the *phantasma*—that is, the image of the beloved—to concentrate within itself all the vital forces of the lover; it occupies the entire *vis imaginative*; it feeds upon incessant recollection; and it gathers the vital spirits together around it."[11] That overpowering consumption arises in a series of texts cited by Bolzoni—from Ovid's *Remidia amoris* to Ariosto's *Orlando furioso* to Giovanni della Porta's *Della Fisonomia dell'huomo*—and we could easily add Barthes as late-comer to that insight. This genealogy leads to a simple if briefly explored conclusion. She writes, "eros and memory are deeply related. With a much greater and more dangerous force than the images of memory, the *phantasmata* of eros occupy a space that opens up between body and psyche."[12] A study of memory, then, illuminates understandings of the body in the early modern period because they constitute one another. Knowing sex involves knowing something about its interplay with memory.

We therefore build upon the project set out by James Bromley and Will Stockton in *Sex before Sex*. That volume begins with a deceptively simple question about early modern England, "What is sex?"[13] That question, the editors admit, offers no easy answers and changes drastically across socio-historical contexts. Indeed, their title comes from the notion that "sex" does not refer solely to intimate physical encounters, especially when we talk about periods earlier than our own. Such confusions motivate the direction of our own study. We ask not what is sex, but how is sex understood as a thing of the past? How are erotic encounters remembered? And when does the act of remembering itself become erotic?

This focus means that we examine the physical acts of sex through its discursive representations that seek to recreate and imagine the body. Just as the languages of sexuality shape our understanding of sex acts themselves, the physical body is subordinate to the contexts that give it meaning. As the editors of *Sex before Sex* put it, "the wealth of extant work on early modern sexuality and sex often accordingly begins not with 'the agency of sex' but rather with discourses, such as sodomy, homoeroticism, lesbianism, friendship, and intimacy, that speak sex in ways that roughly anticipate, as the period's moniker implies, more modern forms."[14] This notion of "speaking sex" not surprisingly turns attention to the problems of representation, or the ways in which physical intimacies appear across of range of allusions, metaphors, and languages. Sex, as a number of scholars have shown, cannot be separated from the contexts that both give it meaning and even allow it to be mentioned in the first place. To give just two examples, a recent study by Melissa Sanchez traces the representation of sadomasochism and sexual violation to expose how Spenser and other early modern writers "use scenarios of erotic subjugation and suffering to ponder questions about sovereignty peculiar to their own moments in English history."[15] Such work productively reminds us that the terms of sexuality were applied in Renaissance contexts that might seem strange to a modern reader. In another vital study, Valerie Traub has shown how representations of female relationships in literary genres as well as medical treatises, maps, and other documents reveal that "lesbian"—itself an anachronistic term dependent upon our own contemporary context—emerges as a "representational image, a rhetorical figure, a discursive effect, rather than a stable epistemological or historical category."[16] In such cases, we learn that sex is at once specific to early modern contexts and related to modern day descriptions and categorizations. Like Sanchez and Traub, the authors in our collection diversely trace the terms of sexuality in literary texts to show how they operate alongside the terms of social and individual remembering.

This volume, then, explores the points of contact between issues of central importance for scholars of the early modern period. It suggests that memory and sexuality often work in concert, shaping one by means of the other. When Ovid assumes the perspective of Leander, he represents a sexual encounter, one that in turn molds the poetry of Christopher Marlowe. Yet the letter writing—and its literary legacies—always comes first. We pursue this insight. We seek out the ways in which the faculties of recall inform and construct the sexual experience. We search for not just *the recollection of erotics* but *the erotics of recollection*. Memory, we propose, reshapes the concerns of queer studies—including the unhistorical, the experience of desire, and the limits of the body. So too does the erotic revise the dominant concerns of memory studies, from the rhetoric of the medieval memory arts to the formation of collective pasts. We believe the present volume helps answer Carla Freccero's call for new work to "bring into relation desire and subjectivity with politics, sex, community, living, and dying."[17]

The essays collected here build upon but also complicate the resurgent interest in early modern attitudes toward memory. As Lina Perkins Wilder notes, "Much has been said in recent years about the Renaissance obsession with memory: memorials and the *memento mori* tradition, history and historiography, memory systems and emblems, representations of cultural memory," and we believe that the study of sexuality can bring new insight to this impressive, extant body of work.[18] The early modern "obsession" with memory bears out in any number of forms, including perhaps most directly through what Kurt Danziger describes as the "florid cultivation of memory during the sixteenth century" in works designed to teach skills of memorization to willing students.[19] What becomes clear is that memory bore enormous social importance as it involved not just individual lives but also issues ranging from nationalism to religion. Book-length studies such as Garrett A. Sullivan's *Memory and Forgetting in English Renaissance Drama*; William Engel's *Death and Drama in Renaissance Drama: Shades of Memory*; and Jonathan Baldo's *Memory in Shakespeare's History Plays* all demonstrate the degrees to which memory and its conceptualizations informed cultural productions of the period.[20] These works demonstrate the fraught contradictions running throughout early modern notions of memory, for they deal just as much with questions of forgetting, loss, and what Engel calls an "Aesthetics of Decline."[21] As Andrew Hiscock puts it: "in a culture that was obsessively concerned with the interpretation of the past, it comes as no surprise that early modern intellectuals frequently returned to the consideration of memory as a consuming source of vigorous, if ultimately irresolvable, debate."[22] That debate persists in the work of historians and literary critics alike who seek to understand how the consumers of the English literary culture recalled both the past and themselves. Essays in our collection do not simply participate in this rich critical conversation; they show that notions of sexuality drive the same pursuit of collective pasts and individual agency as does memory.

These new studies share a common inspiration in Frances Yates's *The Art of Memory*.[23] In the opening pages of her book, Yates outlines the ancient memory arts, a system of memorization that underlies any number of approaches to the subject. Through an imagined sequence of allegorical or emblematic images, Yates explains, ancient rhetoricians could memorize long sequences of material. They only needed to imagine those memory images as arranged in a memory place—an architectural structure that gave organization to the cues. That basic system, much discussed and debated, informs not just the works of Sullivan, Engel, and Wilder but also a number of essays contained in this volume. The impact of the memory arts is profound for the simple reason that they show a key insight into pre-modern thought. They show that memory itself was envisioned as a rhetorical device shaped and put to use through technical expertise and training. It can be used to move audiences, to shape etiquette, even to reveal transcendental truths.[24] Bolzoni recognizes that erotics played their role in this art: "If memory, by nature, plays an essential role in affixing and feeding the amorous phantasma, the art of memory proves to be keenly interested in reversing the process, in using it for its own ends."[25] Goran Stanivukovic, Su Fang Ng, Ian McInnes, and others will reveal the implications of that insight in the following essays. The manipulations of the skilled memory artist, they show, bring early modern sexualities into view. This volume's essays, in the end, suggest that sexuality and memory constitute one another, and that both undergird the fraught constructions of social identity in early modern England.

Legacies of Desire

Our first section addresses the legacies of desire permeating a "culture that was obsessively concerned with the interpretation of the past."[26] In some cases, our authors begin in the early modern period, looking back to classical depictions of sexuality. Opening the collection, Joyce MacDonald's "Intimate Histories: Desire, Genre, and the Trojan War in *The Araygnement of Paris*," examines George Peele's sixteenth-century play in which Paris faces the consequences of the infamous beauty contest, arguing that this mythological story informs the political identities of the sixteenth century. Our first section pursues such lines of inquiry through a number of materials and allusions. Turning our attention to how legal documents resonate with the erotic intentions of the previous generation, Douglas Clark's "The Will and Testamentary Eroticism in Shakespearean Drama" explores how desire cannot be disaggregated from property and genealogy. The essays in this section also move forward in time, as Stephen Guy-Bray focuses on modern adaptations of Shakespearean sonnets. In this case, the legacy of desire operates through languages and poetic forms that self-consciously repeat the past even as the content of the poems ruminates on the inevitability of repetition.

At the levels of both collective and personal memory, the past haunts the present. The phantom echo of sexual violation in history manifests as a ghostly figure in Middleton's *The Ghost of Lucrece*, a poem that Dee Anna Phares helps us understand as a meditation on literature's power to eroticize or de-eroticize past events by re-writing them. Andrew Fleck's "Exemplarity and Its Discontents in Michael Drayton's *Englands Heroical Epistles*" shows how Drayton negotiates complex registers of memorialization and eros as the poem shifts from Elizabethan memories of Lucrece's rape in antiquity to the medieval past to the poetic present. Ultimately, Fleck argues, the treatment of Rosamond's plight in *Englands Heroical Epistles* evokes the power of examples even as it confronts the limitations of exemplarity. The section rounds out with Kenneth Hodges' "Guinevere's Ghost: Spenser's Response to Malory's Erotics," which turns to the medieval romance to examine the reception of Guinevere in Edmund Spenser's *The Faerie Queene*, a text that several of our writers found to be a fruitful site where sexuality and memory intersect. Throughout this section, we find authors engaging in the same processes as Ovid and his fictional letter-writers. So it is with the legacies explored in these essays: the impulse to resuscitate the past brings with it old and new passions.

As a whole, the essays in this section show not only how new texts revivify past desires but also how these revivified desires become models for future forms of sexual expression. If such chronologies seem disjointed, they are purposely so. These essays contribute to an effort on the part of queer studies to sketch new historical narratives, including those that play with notions of teleology. In the phrasing of Madhavi Menon and Jonathan Goldberg, they share the pursuit of the "unhistorical," which functions "in opposition to a historicism that proposes to know the definitive difference between the past and the present."[27] Menon and Goldberg suggest we might pursue "homohistory," which would set aside the long-held understanding of history determined by difference, where what happened in the past is not what happens in the present.[28] As Margaret Ferguson notes in her description of the presidential theme for the 2015 Modern Language Society Conference, "sites of memory may also be found, or made, by certain uses of verb tenses and moods, as the body of recent and multilingual speculation on the 'futural past' attests."[29] Such considerations appear in essays such as those by Phares and Fleck, which emphasize that specters of the past are often invoked to shape the memories of future generations. These approaches share with other recent efforts in the study of early modern sexuality to evade "the tyranny of historicism and to do so from both ends."[30] Queer history, then, requires that readers and historians "[suspend] determinate sexual and chronological differences while expanding the possibilities of the nonhetero, with all its connotations of sameness, similarity, proximity, and anachronism."[31] In many ways, the essays in our collection answer Valerie Traub's recent call for scholars of sexuality to "read chronologically without straitjacketing ourselves or the past."[32] For the unhistorical reader, the past suddenly manifests in the present, perhaps even following what has yet to come. What should be left behind as the vestige of the past appears again, like Leander's arms wrapping around the lonely Hero.

Indeed, sexuality—constituted by anticipation, reaction, climax, retrospection, and repetition—has a crucial place in contemplations of personal and collective memory. Elizabeth Freeman nicely captures this in her concept of "erotohistoriography," which "does not write the lost object into the present so much as encounter it already in the preset, by treating the present itself as hybrid," and it allows "bodily responses, even pleasurable ones, that are themselves a form of understanding."[33] Queer historiography, erotohistoriography, and the unhistorical seek out those operations that trouble teleology, such as anachronism, hybridity, heterochrony, and homohistory. Shifting focus from the historical to the mnemonic, this collection illuminates the power of memory to embrace the anachronistic. Remembering inevitably brings the past to the present, treating it as an object of desire.

Bodies, Remember

According to Pierre Nora, the end of primitive society also promises the end of "real memory," its living, binding presence undone by the analytical formality of history. Modern "sites of memory"—monuments, national anthems, children's books—thus strive for that ancient phenomena of "emotion and magic."[34] Yet Nora's distinctions between pre-modern and modern visions of the past ignore the "living" site of memory common to both eras: the eroticized body. Our volume's second section examines this mnemonic and sexualized vessel at a moment of intersection in Nora's timeline, when the ancient and modern converge. The body, our authors suggest, poses several lines of inquiry that invoke collective and personal memory alike. Are erotic experiences heightened or deflated by the presence of memory? Can a sexual act be commemorative? Can an act of memory be eroticized? How is cultural memory codified or undermined by the presence of the erotic? If the private body is a site of erotic memory, how does it partake in a collective that is both sexual and national?

Like other authors in this volume, Goran Stanivukovic turns to Spenser's allegories of the body to explore how sensuality informs the operations of recollection. In "The Gallery of Erotic Memory in *The Faerie Queene*," he interprets the erotic iconography of the fountains in the episode of the Bower of Bliss before moving to an exploration of the tapestry involving Venus and Adonis that adorns the entrance to the castle of Malecasta. The essay concludes with an analysis of Britomart's ocular exploration of a series of erotic tales, all featuring their body parts, from antiquity woven into the tapestries that adorn the rooms in Busirane's castle. Ultimately, this essay argues, Spenser transforms the memory rooms from the early modern tradition and practice of *ars memoria* into erotic fictions of his romance epic. Robert Darcy then draws our attention to scenarios in which the body comes to terms with its needs, fears, and limitations through a combination of muscular and memorial response. "False Muscle Memory: Sexual Experience in Marlowe and Nashe" argues for an early modern literary advancement of false muscle memory—a dynamic by which recollection of prior sexual experiences can eroticize innocent bodies and even inanimate objects. John Garrison also turns to an early modern depiction of a beloved from classical antiquity. "Marlowe's Helen and the Erotics of Cultural Memory" finds that Faustus is ultimately disappointed by the appearance of Helen, who fails to measure up to her depiction in cultural memory. However, the manipulation of personal memory nonetheless heightens the erotics of the encounter and enables Faustus' own entry into cultural memory.

Connecting to themes in Stanivukovic's analysis, Mark Dahlquist's "Strange Love: Funerary Erotics in *Romeo and Juliet*" explores how Shakespeare's description of the plastic arts suggests that remembering the dead has an explicitly erotic dimension. Dahlquist develops the work of Ramie Targoff to argue that the play's *carpe diem* erotics necessitate imagining the beloved as a memorialized object in order to be regarded as desirable human person. Heather Wicks's "'The monument woos me': Eroticizing the Dead in Thomas Middleton's *The Lady's Tragedy*" shows us something quite different when taking the dead body as an erotic object. It demonstrates that not only is memory a poor substitute for the erotic experience, but the erotic experience also ultimately fails to satisfy his memory. The body, it would seem, incites erotic memory while it also places limits on memory's animating power.

These essays share the notion that body—whether living or dead, flesh or crafted in tapestry or sculpture—resonates as a vessel of remembrance. Our authors help us see that early modern texts presage a notion captured in Constantine Cavafy's "Body, Remember" (1916–18), which opens

> Body, remember just how much you were loved,
> not just the beds where you have lain,
> but also those longings that so openly
> glistened for you in the eyes.[35]

While the poem announces that the body can recall love, it also problematizes the seat of desire. It locates that impulse in the eyes of the lover, where it can be recognized and recalled. Thus, the memory of desire inhabits both the lover's body and the beloved's body, which express their longings through trembling voice and glistening eyes. Previous encounters are not lost to the past because the body still retains them. In fact, Cavafy's body even suggests pleasure remains in physical tissue, in similar ways to Hero and Leander's delightful recollections. In the pleading lyric "Come Back," the speaker concludes with a striking ellipsis: "Come back often, and take hold of me at night / When the lips and skin remember. ..."[36] We cannot know if the lover "comes back," but for a brief time "the lips and the skin" may do enough.

Cavafy's poems demonstrate the complexities of physical artifact and emotional memory. Like the many objects in this collection's essays—the tapestry, girdle, statues, dildo, soil, or written will—the body functions as both subject and object in the dynamics of remembrance, as it works as both the author of memory and the text upon which memories are inscribed.[37]

Intimate Refusals

While Hero enjoys her erotic memories in the *Heroides*, she recognizes that her visions might not please everyone. The lover comes to her in her sleep with memories of limbs and physical touch, but she also knows that she could say "many things else a modest tongue should say naught of."[38] To speak these details "brings a blush." Hero indulges her readers—namely, Leander—in one sense by inviting them to recreate the previous encounters between the two classical lovers. In another sense, she holds back from the full revelation of the memory because the "modest tongue" refuses. Even if she herself does not forget the details, she does not write them into her letter. Of course, we also know that she has probably said enough already. We do not have to be Leander to imagine what is being omitted in this telling. Her refusal speaks to the conflation of forgetting and remembering, a conflation that inspires the final section of our volume.

Barthes, although separated from Ovid by millennia, follows Hero in observing the push/pull dynamics of memory. We have seen him treat forgetting as faithlessness, but he also suggests the essential role of oblivion in the experience of sexual desire. Forgetfulness is "the condition of my survival, for if I did not forget, I should die. The lover who doesn't forget sometimes dies of excess, exhaustion, and tension of memory."[39] But just as Barthes proclaims forgetfulness, he also recommits to the memory of the beloved and his promise to "sustain the discourse of absence."

The active refusal to remember itself is an indulgence in memorialization. That problematic runs throughout the essays in our third and final section as they turn to distraction, chastity, or oblivion and generate only further indulgence in the mechanisms of erotic memory. Our authors showcase how operations of memory offer a way to manage instances when "sex" functions "as a site […] at which relationality is invested with hopes, expectations, and anxieties that are often *experienced* as unbearable."[40] What forms of erotic experience refuse to be forgotten? What happens when memory fails? Or what happens when lovers hope to foreclose the possibilities of erotic memory? Is it even possible to forget?

The opening essay by Jonathan Baldo examines the threats of distraction in Shakespeare's *Antony and Cleopatra*, suggesting that Cleopatra's efforts to distract reflect the outcomes of Shakespeare's stage more generally. Forgetting here proves its advantages, just as Ovid suggests. In a different vein, Kyle Pivetti studies the confluence of memory, eroticism, and nationalism in Edmund Spenser's *The Faerie Queene*, but he does so by placing the epic in dialogue with the sonnet sequence *Amoretti*. Spenser's efforts at bodily escape or indeed chastity, Pivetti reveals, cannot evade the erotic pleasures of telling the past. Su Fang Ng takes a different tack to engage the problems of memory in Spenser's canon. She simply asks, how can one forget the deceptive charms of Duessa, knowing that her erotic enticements are implicitly dangerous? That threat manifests in the girdle of Florimell, a mnemonic object subject to misuse and misappropriation.

Our final two essays explore how erotic desire shatters the links among memory, objectivity, and futurity. Ian MacInnes focuses his attention on Shakespeare's sonnets, where he finds the influence of semantic memory bias. In other words, the sonnets for MacInnes search for memory, but not true autobiographical accounts. The so-called "dark lady" poems foster the emotional affect of memory, delighting in what may not be true. Lastly, Amanda Bailey considers the early modern play most famously obsessed with memory, Shakespeare's *Hamlet*. Her insights, though, attack the play from questions of generation and futurism without the feminine. Memory, in this perspective, proceeds from the material earth, where asexual worms can foster a future from the past without giving birth.

The refusals rendered visible in these essays ultimately bring us back to the problems of memory. In each instance of forgetting, we find once again the rehearsal of the past. In this way, we return to the possibilities of the unhistorical. Overturning historical narratives never means forgetting. Instead, it means remembering—and reading—erotically.

Introduction 11

We leave with one last example from Ovid's *Heroides* that will lead us to the Trojan War and its destructive, erotic legacies. In another pair of letters, Ovid allows Paris to write to Helen, explaining the promises given to him by Venus. The letter pursues its rhetorical purpose: to convince Helen of the affair, to persuade her to give herself entirely to the Trojan lover. But for Paris, the affair is already consummated. He only needs to remember a chance encounter that predicts the pleasures to come. Paris confesses, "Your bosom once, I remember [*memini*] was betrayed by your robe; it was loose, and left your charms bare to my gaze—breasts whiter than pure snows, or milk, or Jove when he embraced your mother."[41] In this moment, Paris follows Hero and Leander by indulging the pleasures of erotic memory. No matter if the affair has yet to occur; Paris already remembers it.

Perhaps this volume ultimately suggests that memories such as Paris's do not belong to Paris alone. Ovid's readers, both early modern and contemporary, delight in the memory with not only the character but also the poet and his community of readers across time. Is this a form of fantasy or an experience of recollection? Perhaps the difference doesn't matter. Desire is always the same.

Notes

1. Roland Barthes, *A Lover's Discourse: Fragments*, trans. Richard Howard (New York: Hill and Wang, 1978, reprinted 2001), 15.
2. Ibid., 14.
3. Ibid., 15.
4. Ibid., 15.
5. Ovid, *Heroides and Amores*, trans. Grant Showerman (Cambridge: Harvard University Press, 1914, reprinted 1963), 249.
6. Ovid, *Heroides and Amores*, 251.
7. As Philip R. Hardie remarks in *Ovid's Poetics of Illusion* (Cambridge: Cambridge University Press, 2002), "Physical absence is compensated for by the vicarious pleasure of memory—Leander's narrative rehearsing of their first night together" (138).
8. Ovid, *Heroides and Amores*, 263.
9. In *Loving in Verse: Poetic Influence as Erotic* (Toronto and London: University of Toronto Press, 2006), Guy-Bray invites us to see Virgil's and Statius' influence on Dante, as well as Chaucer's influence on Spenser, as forms of male coupling rather than the more traditional analogue of parent and child that pervades discussions of literary genealogies.
10. Philip Schwyzer, "Shakespeare's Arts of Reenactment: Henry at Blackfriars, Richard at Rougemont," in *The Arts of Remembrance in Early Modern England: Memorial Cultures of the Post Reformation*, ed. Andrew Gordon and Thomas Rist (Burlington: Ashgate, 2013), 193.
11. Lina Bolzoni, *The Gallery of Memory: Literary and Iconographic Models in the Age of the Printing Press* (Toronto: University of Toronto Press, 2001), 145.
12. Ibid., 146.
13. James M. Bromley and Will Stockton, *Sex before Sex: Figuring the Act in Early Modern England* (Minneapolis: University of Minnesota Press, 2013), 3.

14. Bromley and Stockton, 8.
15. Melissa Sanchez, *Erotic Subjects: The Sexuality of Politics in Early Modern English Literature* (Oxford: Oxford University Press, 2013), 6.
16. Valerie Traub, *The Renaissance of Lesbianism in Early Modern England* (Cambridge: Cambridge University Press, 2002), 15.
17. Carla Freccero, "Queer Times," in *After Sex: On Writing Since Queer Theory*, ed. Janet Halley and Andrew Parker (Durham, NC: Duke University Press, 2011), 23.
18. Indeed, Wilder's focus on stage properties offers an excellent example of how combining memory studies with another field of study (i.e., new materialism) generates new understanding of both topics. Lina Perkins Wilder, *Shakespeare's Memory Theater: Recollection, Properties, and Character* (Cambridge: Cambridge University Press, 2010), 13. Andrew Gordon and Thomas Rist echo Wilder in their "Introduction: The Arts of Remembrance," in *The Arts of Remembrance in Early Modern England* (Aldershot: Ashgate, 2013), when they write, "'[A]rts of remembrance were omnipresent in early modern culture: manifest in tombs, statues and churches, but also in the décor of houses and arrangement of manuscripts, as well as in the literary construction of poetry and the performance practices of the theatre" (1).
19. Kurt Danziger, *Marking the Mind: A History of Memory* (Cambridge: Cambridge University Press, 2008), 98.
20. Garrett A. Sullivan, Jr., *Memory and Forgetting in English Renaissance Drama: Shakespeare, Marlowe, Webster* (Cambridge: Cambridge University Press, 2005); William E. Engel, *Death and Drama in Renaissance England: Shades of Memory* (Oxford: Oxford University Press, 2002); Jonathan Baldo's *Memory in Shakespeare's Histories: Stages of Forgetting in Early Modern England* (New York: Routledge, 2012). Other key studies in this vein include the collection edited by Grant Williams and Christopher Ivic entitled *Forgetting in Early Modern English Literature and Culture* (2004).Hester Lees-Jeffries' *Shakespeare and Memory* (Oxford University Press, 2013) relates debates on memory in the early seventeenth century to the developing theories of memory that emerge in contemporary neuroscience. A recent collection edited by Donald Beecher and Grant Williams, entitled *Ars Reminiscendi: Mind and Memory in Renaissance Culture* (Toronto: Centre for Reformation and Renaissance Studies, 2009), demonstrates the ongoing interest in the memory arts. For a performance studies approach see Peter Holland, ed., *Shakespeare, Memory, and Performance* (Cambridge: Cambridge University Press, 2006).
21. Engel, *Death and Drama in Renaissance England*, 2. Andrew Escobedo, in *Nationalism and Historical Loss in Renaissance England: Foxe, Dee, Spenser, Milton* (Ithaca: Cornell University Press, 2004), addresses a similar pervasive attitude of loss and separation.
22. Andrew Hiscock, *Reading Memory in Early Modern Literature* (Cambridge: Cambridge University Press, 2011), 8.
23. Frances A. Yates, *The Art of Memory* (Chicago: University of Chicago Press, 1966).
24. For a range of such claims that depend upon Yates's work with the memory arts, see Mary Carruthers, *The Book of Memory: A Study of Memory in Medieval Culture* (Cambridge: Cambridge University Press, 1990); Paolo Rossi, *Logic and the Art of Memory*, trans. Stephen Clucas (London: The Athlone Press, 2000); and Lina Bolzoni *The Web of Images* (Aldershot: Ashgate, 2004).

Introduction 13

25. Bolzoni, *The Gallery of Memory*, 146.
26. Hiscock, 8.
27. Jonathan Goldberg and Madhavi Menon, "Queering History," *PMLA* 120.5 (2005): 1609.
28. Menon develops the claims of "homohistory" in *Unhistorical Shakespeare: Queer Theory in Shakespearean Literature and Film* (New York: Palgrave Macmillan, 2008). Here, she takes aim at the "enabling premise" of "historical difference" (9).
29. Margaret W. Ferguson, "2015 Presidential Theme: Negotiating Sites of Memory," https://www.mla.org/2015_pres_theme (Retrieved June 8, 2015). Ferguson's inclusion of work on "futural past" (studies of how past cultures imagined their futures) emphasizes that visions of the future have a place in the study of memory. And queer theorists have recently emphasized that futurity has a close interrelationship with sexuality. For example, Lee Edelman has shown that gay identities are often framed as being outside the forward-looking spheres linked to reproductive futurism, and José Munoz has shown how queer sexuality is often characterized by remaining always speculative. Lee Edelman, *No Future: Queer Theory and the Death Drive* (Durham: Duke University Press, 2004) and José Esteban Muñoz, *Cruising Utopia: The Then and There of Queer Futurity* (New York: NYU Press, 2009).
30. "Queer Renaissance Historiography: Backward Gaze" (authors' introduction) in Vincent Joseph Nardizzi, Stephen Guy-Bray, and Will Stockton, *Queer Renaissance Historiography: Backward Gaze* (Burlington: Ashgate, 2009), 1. This approach depends on the "backward gaze"—the glance that treats literary texts as "alluring and strange" and collapses "textual and sexual pleasures" (4).
31. Golberg and Menon, 1609.
32. Valerie Traub, "The New Unhistoricism in Queer Studies," *PMLA* 128.1 (2013): 23.
33. Elizabeth Freeman, *Time Binds: Queer Temporalities; Queer Historiographies* (Durham and London: Duke University Press, 2010), 95–96.
34. Pierre Nora, "General Introduction: Between Memory and History'," *Realms of Memory: Rethinking the French Past Vol 1—Conflicts and Divisions*, ed. Pierre Nora and trans. Arthur Goldhammer (New York: Columbia University Press, 1996), 3
35. C. P. Cavafy, "Body, Remember ...," in *Complete Poems*, trans. Daniel Mendelsohn (New York: Alfred A. Knopf, 2012), 83.
36. Cavafy, "Come Back," *Complete Poems*, 47.
37. In many of the essays, objects play a key role in recalling past periods or storing memories for future generations. In this way, these objects fall into the category of what Jonathan Gil Harris terms "untimely matter." Acknowledging that the body can play a crucial role in commemoration, we suggest that it too might be considered part of this category where "'some other time' is not necessarily long ago, nor even waiting for us in the future. It is here now, if only we learn to recognize its folds." Jonathan Gil Harris, *Untimely Matter in the Age of Shakespeare* (Philadelphia: University of Pennsylvania Press, 2009), 187.
38. Ovid, *Heroides and Amores*, 263.
39. Barthes, *A Lover's Discourse*, 14.
40. Lauren Berlant and Lee Edelman, *Sex, Or The Unbearable* (Duke University Press, Durham and London: 2014), vii.
41. Ovid, *Heroides and Amores*, 21

Part I

Legacies of Desire

1 Intimate Histories
Desire, Genre, and the Trojan War in *The Araygnement of Paris*

Joyce Green MacDonald

George Peele's *The Araygnement of Paris* (1584) doesn't have much of a critical history. Its standing as an example of Elizabethan courtly entertainment was established by the end of the nineteenth century,[1] and discussion of the play well into the twentieth used its courtly status as a device to normalize its readily apparent formal messiness.[2] More recent historicist readings of the play also work to support a notion of its coherence, a coherence perceived as ideological and not formal. These views of the play's unity focus on its strongly gendered reproduction of the operations of royal patronage or on Queen Elizabeth's role as arbiter of justice. Both formalist and new historicist understandings of the play and the work it does insist on its consistency as it aims toward a single purpose. Whether unfolding a political allegory through its masque-like presentation aimed at equating "the social harmony of its ideal world with the actual hierarchy of the court,"[3] offering an extended meditation on the power of "healthy imagination"[4] in the morally conscious exercise of critical judgment, or delineating the terrible vulnerability of poets who sought literary patronage from the mighty[5], the *Araygnement* has been understood in absolutes, as a document of court culture centered on the imaginative or material presences of the Queen.

Both formalist and new historicist readings of the play assert that the *Araygnement* tells one story. This paper, though, begins from the recognition that it contains many stories, many kinds of stories, and tells those stories from various points of view. By drawing attention to its narrative and textual richness, I want both to revisit the notion of the play's closure and unification and to question whether the portrait it offers of royal authority and power in the public realm is as final and assured as both formalist and historicist critics have had it.

The play falls into three rough parts: the first three acts, unified around the mythological materials of Paris' choice of Helen as more beautiful than Diana, Juno, or Venus; most of act four, focusing on uncouth Vulcan's unsuccessful pursuit of one of Diana's nymphs and on the actual judgment itself; and the royal apotheosis of Act Five. Taking the busy contemporary courtiership of act five as its main subject requires us to overlook the self-contained quality of the first three acts, to which the last two were probably added at a later date.[6] By rereading the first three acts with their textual and generic affinities in mind, I want to emphasize the degree to which its representations of worldly authority are shaped by the relationship they bear to the experience of private individuals and to decenter the questions of its larger formal coherence that have dominated its criticism.

To insist that the play reconciles all contraries on its way to celebrating monarchical authority requires us to overlook its rich textuality—apparent in the variety of genres and texts it calls on to shape itself—and thus to ignore that narrative texture's role in the story it tells us. Rather than ignoring the gender of most women except the Queen and gendering authorship and courtiership as primarily male processes, it imagines women as poetic makers and speakers in negotiation for public authority. However much the play as a whole can be identified as a document of Elizabethan court culture, its first three acts self-consciously position themselves in relation to literary as well as mythological and historical pasts, personal as well as national histories, and invest this deep historicity with moods of erotic heartbreak. As it dramatizes the initiating event in the Trojan War, and thus the mythological origins of the British nation, *The Araygnement of Paris* insists on reminding us that public, epic events detailing the clash, fall, and rise of civilizations have their origins in the affective realm.

This paper thus imagines its literary subjects not only as the products of historical and political processes, but as equally constructed within the frequently contradictory and painful structures of desire. They cannot keep themselves from taking public, historical events personally because the power of their personal emotions is the frame through which they exist in and perceive the world. My belief in the formative power of the subjective and its resonance beyond the lives or experiences of individuals thus responds to a classic new historicist notion of what power is, how it operates, and what makes it visible in the lives of those subjected to it by insisting that we enlarge our analysis to pay critical attention to those literary places where manifestations of public political power and private erotic desires seem to cross.[7]

The beginning of a discussion of how deeply private feelings make themselves known in the ways in which Peele's goddesses and shepherds encounter an epic history of Troy is a good place to admit that in some ways the very notion of sharply demarcated private and public domains is merely an organizing fiction. Under the terms of this fiction, the domestic and personal notionally function as a kind of training ground for the development of a civic subject, whose participation in a Habermasian public sphere is recognized as one of the hallmarks of modernity.[8] The domestic is most significant as a kind of pre-qualification for public engagement and is primarily relevant in relation to it. But in tracing the expression of early modern political duties in terms of personal, intimate obligations within families and between husbands and wives, Melissa Sanchez insists that the division between public and private was much less distinct and hierarchical in that period. To talk about desire was often to talk about politics, and representations of political hierarchies and relationships were inevitably shaped by the waywardness of the erotic feelings that were understood to be their prototypes. Political life is thus constituted as both personal and relational—like love, becoming legible in terms of the nature of one's connection to others. Given the dominance of Petrarchan discourse as a way of talking about intimate connection, Sanchez notes that it was perhaps inevitable that ways of talking about love would be shaped by compulsion, loss, and pain and that the pain accompanying subjection—in her view, whether romantic or civic—was one of its characteristic emotional valences.[9] Shakespeare's Cleopatra assumes not only that love hurts—her skin is "black" (1.5.28) with bruises from Phoebus' rough sexual play—but that social experience becomes legible through this pain. Even fearful death is like "a lover's pinch, / That hurts, and is desired" (*Antony and Cleopatra*, 5.2.290–291).[10]

Sanchez connects her attention to the ways in which love was narrated to languages of politics and interpersonal relationship. Although not immediately concerned with the early modern, contemporary theories of affect and its place in civic life also offer valuable support for inquiries into the relationship between the personal and the public and the implications of applying the emotional structures of the first to the second. Intimacy strives toward "a narrative about something shared, a story about both oneself and others that will turn out a particular way," Lauren Berlant tells us.[11] However much we may want our love stories to "turn out a particular way," we have no assurance that they will, subject as such an organized, sustained imposition of narrative order must be to the wayward possibilities built into sharing life and space with the ones we love.

Another way of putting this, in terms more relevant to what I will be saying about *The Araygnement of Paris*, is that the stories lovers tell about their loves and the varied ways in which they tell them are complicated by contact not only with the public world of affairs, but with other kinds of stories others tell, even if those others are using the same tropes and textual tools. As we shall see, the poetic kinds in the first part of Peele's play—epic, pastoral, complaint, love, elegy—blur and mix together. Allusions to specific texts or bodies of texts and different ways of telling stories—or of retelling the same story—about the dangers and pleasures of intimacy jostle against each other, sometimes flowing together and sometimes springing apart. These allusions and cross-references historically contextualize Paris' choice within the epic "tragedie of Troie,"[12] thus providing a mythological and quasi-historical backstory for romantic lament. But the historical, epic import of his decision to accept Venus' bribe of sexual access to Helen shares narrative and generic space with the pastoral, elegiac tone the play reserves for the story of his love affair with the nymph Oenone—a love begun while he mistakenly believed he was only a humble shepherd and before he learned he was actually an abandoned prince of Troy. New accounts of sexual intimacy will support and inform Paris' newly revealed royal status, just as the play's sense of epic fate and historical dread is infused with broken and rejected pastoral in the first three acts. Emotions, prerogatives, genres all blur together.

The Araygnement of Paris connects ways of imagining intimacy and ways of imagining social identity, as well as ways of writing about love and ways of writing about imperial standing. But its lack of differentiation between what modern readers might regard as distinct registers of experience (and the narrative forms thought appropriate or those separate kinds) is typical of early modern literary practice. As historian Blair Worden reminds us, Renaissance poets "engaged not only with the literature and languages of the past but also, on broader fronts, with its history. Poets and historians were ... the same individuals."[13]

As both poet and popular historian, Peele himself participated in this categorical blurring. His *Farewell Entituled to the Famous and Fortunate Generalls of our English Forces*, a topical salute to Sir Francis Drake and Sir Thomas Norris as they set off to attack Spanish shipping after the failure of the armada, was first printed in a volume along with his *Beginning, Accidents and Ende of the Warre of Troy*, commonly known as the *Tale of Troy*, in 1589. Together the texts exemplify the process of conveying historical meanings through terms that are expressive, allusive, and comparative, rather than objective. Drake and Norris' job was to press the English military advantage as much as possible, up to and including installing an English-approved pretender on the throne of Portugal. Peele's account of their mission illustrates Sanchez's contention that political events were understood in emotional and sensual terms. The poem draws an implicit connection between the brave spectacle of the new English armada and the kinds of exotic shows available on the public stages of his day:

> Bid all the lovelie brittish Dames adiewe,
> That under many a Standarde well advanc'd,
> Have bid the sweete allarmes and braves of love.
> Bid Theatres and proud Tragedians,
> Bid Mahomets Poo and mightie Tamburlaine,
> King Charlemaine, Tom Stukeley and the rest
> Adiewe. ...[14]

Conflating the serious present occasion of the military counteroffensive with the shows staged by "proud Tragedians" as they sought to amaze and arouse their audiences, Peele finds the latter a fitting analogy for the former. The current military mission is like a particularly thrilling stage performance. Fiction and history melt together so that "mightie Tamburlaine" and Francis Drake become the same kind of hero, embarked on the same kind of imperial errand. The passage also contains another, equally striking analogy between apparently unlike things, this time set in the bedroom instead of at the waterside. Instead of or in addition to being akin to seeing a play, setting off to war is similar to when ladies challenge their lovers by soliciting sweet, private erotic combat. The heroic actions of warfare and nation-building feel just like sex, or martial aggression is remarkably similar to being put on the spot by a lady and peremptorily "bid" to perform.[15] In this latter formulation, women assume the active role, while valiant soldiers become the objects and servants of their desires. As it transfers the rules of intimacy to public engagements, Peele's exhortation to military greatness also "blurs or snags" gendered categories of experience.[16] The (unsettling? hot?) sexual memories he invites his readers to re-experience, the aesthetic pleasures he asks them to remember, begin as properties of individual perception but work together across gender and genre to stage acts of public collective political and military will.[17]

The *Farewell* takes sex and war, theater and reality as interchangeable, and the published volume in which it appears experiences no compunction in following Peele's salute to the heroes of the armada's defeat with an account of the origins of the Trojan War. Reading the two texts one after the other feels a little strange, although it probably shouldn't. Does binding them together imply that they are the same kind of story? Can it be right to identify Drake, the man of the hour, with Tamburlaine, who locked Bajazeth up in a cage like a bad dog? Following the story of Drake and Norris' success with a story about Troy seems wrong, too; after all, Troy fell. For Peele, though, Troy's ultimate fate is irrelevant. He seeks to elicit the same kind of response to Drake and Norris that his readers cherished about the grandeur of a Hector, giving the heroes of the current generation the historical stature they deserve: their "Countrymen, famed through the world for resolution and fortitude, may marche in equipage of honour and Armes, wyth theyr glorious and renowned predicessors the Troyans" (3).

The precision and consistency of his historical analogue is apparently not what matters to Peele here. No one in 1589 literally believed that the Trojans were the "glorious and renowned" ancestors of modern Britons. Instead, he exploits the power of literary example to invoke and revivify the "fortitude" of the ancients for the encouragement of present-day heroes. The kind of story, and the set of emotional responses it generated, matters much more than the accuracy of the details he invites us to memorialize. Emotional feeling escapes the private sphere to shape response to public historical event.

This impulse to mash up current events with myth, past with present, performance with reality—or to understand current events in terms of the theatrical, the performative, and the exemplary, rather than in terms of the objective demands of history—is only one way that Peele's *oeuvre* demonstrates the period's common tendency to shape its understanding of public events through the resources of story. The *Tale of Troy* also juxtaposes narrative forms and voices within itself, rather than only in relation to the *Farewell* with which it shares a published volume. As it seeks the proper tone to narrate Paris' choice among the goddesses and the tragic events his choice sets in motion, the poem first invokes a self-conscious medievalism:

Paris' father Priam was "surnamde the fortunate," and as for his mother, "Y-clypped Stately Hecuba was she" (8). The story of their large family summons nostalgia for a past golden age before the catastrophe to come but also locates them within a chivalric, courtly, and aristocratic milieu:

> The daughters lovely, modest, wise and yong.
> The sonnes as doth my story well unfolde,
> All knights at armes, gay, gallant, brave and bolde,
> Of wit and manhood such as might suffice,
> To venter on the highest peece of service. (8)

As the poem takes up Paris, however, it switches literary models from medieval romance to pastoral love elegy. Overcome with revulsion at what he will do to Oenone, Peele will now tell how Paris could "Nymphes and sheepheardes trulls beguile / And pypen songs, and whet his wits on bookes, / And wrap poor Maydes with sweet alluring lookes" (9). If she had never seen "His tycing curled haire, his front of Ivorie," (10) she would never have suffered. The tone and substance of Peele's new matter is familiar to us from Renaissance complaint, although (unlike the mass of Renaissance complaint poems) the *Tale of Troy* does not imagine a female speaker for its scene of ultimately imperial grief. Instead, the presumably male narrator, who began with the medievalist implication of a distant past, now takes the emotive, private woe of complaint as his own. Just as he emotionally supplements the current events of the Drake-Norris expedition with allusions to Tamburlaine and "Mahomet's Poo," cuing his readers on how to respond rather than simply informing them of what happened, Peele here dilates upon the *Tale of Troy*'s measured, distant opening by leaping to the emotional heart of the matter at hand.

Renaissance complaint has a literary history of appearing as pendant to sonnet sequences, as we see in Samuel Daniel's *Complaint of Rosamund*, published with his *Delia* in 1592, or *A Lover's Complaint*, first published in the 1609 edition of Shakespeare's sonnets.[18] There, complaint augments and feminizes the dilemma of the male speaker outlined in the sequence. Within the *Tale of Troy*, however, when the narrator switches to the complaint mode, he adds this typically female-voiced burden of sorrow and reproach to a very different kind of narrative: explicitly historical (as much as a story about the fall of Troy can be) instead of one already shaped by Petrarchan traditions of erotic pain and erotic sorrow. The outburst of complaint calls for a new reading practice, different from the one used for the measured medievalism of the opening.

The idea of a suffering Oenone, wronged and deluded by Paris, is not Peele's idea, of course, but Ovid's. She is the author of *Heroides* 5, the epistle from Oenone to Paris, and Paris mentions her in *Heroides* 16 as the deserving girl he forsook when he fell in love with Helen. She also appears in the narrative poem *Oenone and Paris* (1594), where she pleads in vain for him to return to her and heal the emotional damage he has caused: "finding thee, loe I have lost my selfe."[19] George Turberville translated the *Heroides* in 1579, while Michael Drayton takes them as his model in *Englands Heroicall Epistles* (1597), substituting women whose tragic loves affected the course of English history for Ovid's historical/mythological heroines. The *Araygnement*'s Oenone takes her speaking place among the flood of *Heroides*-inspired complaint poems that marked the 1590s, with their female speakers imitating Ovid's as they recount their tales of heartbreak. Peele's Oenone may emerge from a literary tradition enjoying new life in the 1590s, but her Ovidian quality is also visible in a kind of poetics that insists on bringing unlike things together (e.g., retaliatory war and male sexual performance), reproducing familiar events in unexpected vocabularies and tones as the story of a broken heart is revealed to lie at the center of a story about the Trojan War. Her story transposes love elegy into her own pastoral setting as well as into the epic events surrounding Paris.[20]

While we might not immediately think of Trojan warriors as successful military conquerors, Peele uses them to embody and perform an example of epic glory for contemporary soldiers. Similarly, in the *Araygnement*, Oenone's narrative intervention in a history that might otherwise be regarded as wholly epic or purely heroic does not change what we know about the outcome of the war. If, as I am arguing, Peele's versions of contemporary British history and culture depend on representations of the affect summoned by the nation's mythological Trojan roots rather than on any strict and exact historical analogue to make themselves visible, his play's awareness of *Heroides 5*—of an Ovidian history of empire and civilization—is a major conduit through which that affective representation proceeds. When Peele's Oenone vows to write her heartbreak, and when the play circulates both her intention and her grief as another example of the way her story and the stories of other suffering women were made known through the complaint tradition, the private becomes public, civic, imperial.

The letters written by Ovid's desperate heroines, and the particular epistle Peele alludes to here, exist as counter-narratives, different ways of knowing and feeling familiar events. Ovid's Oenone struggles as a pastoral heroine to make Paris remember and feel the love they shared together in the new realm of gods and heroes he chooses when he chooses Helen. She herself is not a native of the fragile world she shared with him. The daughter of a river god, she left her divine sphere to be with Paris, who was only a poor shepherd when they met. She gladly sacrificed status and dignity to be with him: "How oft have we in shadow one laine / Whylst hungry flocks have fed? / How oft have of grasse and greaves / Prepared a humble bed?"[21] She supported him through the harsh labor of a shepherd's life, helping him "to pitch / thy toyles for want of ayde," driving his hounds "to climbe the hilles / that gladly would have stayed" (27). Trying to make him remember and to return to the world they shared—the world she willingly entered with him—she emphasizes that her letter is for his eyes alone. Declining to write in the "Grecian fist" (26) that Helen could read over his shoulder and understand, Oenone insists that her words—like their love—are wholly private.

Yet Oenone's story does become known. Despite her sense of the difficulty of making Paris remember her—or rather, the difficulty she encounters in making him feel the power and value of their intimacy now that he has been presented with other options—we know that the love they shared does in fact survive somewhere outside her own grief. When they were together, he carved her name into a tree, and now

> The boysterous Beech Oenones name
> in outward barke dooth beare:
> And with thy carving knife is cut
> Oenon every wheare.
> And as the trees in tyme do waxe
> So doth encrease my name:
> Go to, grow on, erect your selves,
> Helpe to advance my fame. (27)

She and her story are "every wheare," existing alongside her own longing in a living counter-narrative to the perhaps more widely known of Paris' choice of Helen.[22] Obsessed by the past and by her thwarted desire in the present, she and her story nonetheless have a future that continually renews itself, organically surviving alongside the greater story of Troy.[23] It is different in tone and content from that other story of ill-fated love that drives the story of Troy's downfall and revival in the founding of Rome, but it is no less.

In her own inquiry into how to read the coexistence of various poetic and narrative forms within Renaissance texts, Diana Henderson also doubts that we should skip over the internal variety of the *Araygnement* on our way to celebrate the whole. Her work is one major modern exception to the critical impulse to normalize the *Araygnement*'s messiness, as she argues that the play's outbursts of pastoral in particular represent the "transfer of a female realm of authority from the erotic and poetic into the public and political domains of epic."[24] While I agree with Henderson that the play's formal discontinuities tell us something about the potential of its narrative styles and their purposes, and that this information is strongly gendered given the association of the privacy of erotic experience with the privacy of a feminized domestic world, I want to push her insights by pursuing the possibility that they can tend to disrupt categories of gendered experience as firmly as they deny the rigidity of categories of narrative order.

In comparison with Ovid's Oenone, who craves privacy and secrecy in her letter to Paris (a secrecy that the untamable organic growth of the tree into which he carved her name will belie), the character in Peele assumes a much greater degree of debonair control over her language and her power to command styles of speech and communication.[25] We last see her, wounded by Paris' falseness, vowing to go sit under a poplar tree "And write my answere to his vow, that everie eie may see" (667). But when she first strolls into the play with Paris, she asks him to play his pipe while she sings and offers him a choice of possible subjects for her contribution: from Cronos' division of the cosmos through a whole range of Ovidian transformations before the force of desire, concluding with the endless suffering labors of Prometheus, Ixion, and the daughters of Danaus. The frame she establishes for her accounts of tragic earthly loves is capacious enough to include both heaven and the afterlife (and even a sense of non-pastoral earthly majesty since the last of Danaus' daughters, Hypermnestra, became the ancestor of Perseus who founded Mycenae). Yet, after alluding to her vast and momentous historical archive, she settles on a "pretie sonnet" telling of the fates in store for those who "chaunge olde love for new" (282, 283). Denizen of her pastoral world, Peele's Oenone nevertheless speaks through a kind of historical knowledge that love hurts and resonates far beyond the slopes of Mt. Ida. The scene ends with Oenone asking Paris to remain faithful to her, "else thou doest her wrong." He vows that his love for her will never leave his "breathing hart," and they kiss (315, 317).

The literary choices of Peele's nymph range far beyond her pastoral setting and are informed by tragic as well as erotic potential. Rather, the erotic potential of the stories she brings up as possible subjects for her own invention and then discards in favor of love lyric is inseparable from their burden of loss and strangeness. Salmacis and Hermaphroditus; Medusa whom Athena transformed into a gorgon because she dared to have sex with Neptune in her temple; Proserpina suddenly snatched from her aboveground life as Ceres' daughter when Pluto kidnaps her—all these myths of transformation speak of desire as fateful and dangerous. All transport young women from one state into another—sometimes physically, sometimes emotionally—moving their bodies and their customary ways of experiencing them into unknown new territories.

As I note above, Peele's Oenone recognizes the transformation enforced on her by Paris' betrayal and leaves the play to find words to express it. Her sonnet, "Faire and fayre and twise so faire," is poised between her collection of possible erotic models from the historical and mythological past and an unknown future set into motion by the emotional choices lovers make in the present. Its own textual afterlife underlines the capacity of literary kinds to reach beyond their own formal natures to serve other purposes than those for which they seem to be formally designed, as it has been extracted from the play to stand alone in poetry anthologies.[26] In its own time, two very different lyrics from the play were published in *England's Helicon*. Both of them, one titled "Colin the enamoured Sheepheard, singeth this passion of love," and the other "Oenone's complaint in blanke verse," are songs of heartbreak.

Colin, one of a group of shepherds who enter the play at the beginning of act three, tells us about the indifferent Thestilis' coldness toward him:

O gentle love, ungentle for thy deede,
Thou makest my harte

A bloodie marke
With piercyng shot to bleede. (537–540)

Colin's wounded, bleeding heart is an image familiar to us from Petrarchan love lyric, a style that inscribes the pain of subjection into the male experience of love just as Ovidian complaint denominates this helplessness as feminine. Oenone, stunned by Paris' desertion, recognizes Colin as her fellow-sufferer: Thestilis "hath Colin wonne, that nill no other love: / And woo is me, my lucke is losse, my paynes no pytie moove" (599–600). The effect of the play's mixed genres not only invites us to reconsider the notionally rigid separation between the public genres of history and epic and the private lyric and lament, but also blur the generic origins of Colin's grief. He expresses his erotic victimization in recognizably Petrarchan and therefore male-focused terms, but, as he suddenly announces it amidst the dramatization of Oenone's pain, her female-focused style of complaint is the tool that shapes her (and our) recognition of his.

Peele's pastoral is thus large enough to contain both a company of anxious shepherds and Oenone's solitary sorrow. The literary valences of male and female pain coexist so that Oenone's private grief (which will nonetheless escape into the public world of growth and change) becomes the lens through which she can see and understand Colin's Petrarchan expression of inward, helpless longing. Masculinist new historicist readings of pastoral tend to read the form for the records it can contain of unsuccessful negotiations with the public structures of political authority, not necessarily fully appreciating the implications of the mutual entanglement of languages of love and languages of power. But in the *Araygnement*, Colin and Oenone share a vocabulary and a range of feeling. They suffer in the same way, yet only she succeeds in giving her private pain a public life in the world so that it survives as literature, and its traces make themselves known in the story of an empire's collapse. Peele's multiple representations of love's pain occur in overlapping stylistic worlds, one giving new life to the other. I have been suggesting that the habit of mixing narrative styles and forms and applying them to bodies of knowledge to which they might be regarded as unsuited is an important aspect of Renaissance poets' Ovidianism. So, too, is the play's willingness to unfix the genders attached to these styles and forms—perhaps especially in the case of Colin's heartbreak, which eventually kills him. Oenone, at least, survives to write.

The writerliness of Peele's Oenone, her capacity to summon and imitate and reproduce stories for her own purposes in proclaiming the value of her love for Paris, provides another thread of the self-conscious historical textuality within which the *Araygnement* forms itself. As Ovid looked to Virgil, Renaissance poets participated in the same kind of response and recreation when they wrote under the influence of Ovid. This intertextuality also appears when writers of Peele's generation measured themselves against each other. Strikingly, the elegiac pastoral of the *Araygnement* makes contact with the *Shepheardes Calender* when Colin and his friends Thenot, Hobbinol, and Digon apparently walk into Peele's play directly from Spenser, bearing the same names and the same concerns as Spenser's shepherds. The lyric that *England's Helicon* calls "Oenone's Complaint" begins by invoking the same muse—Melpomene, the muse of tragedy—whose aid Spenser's Colin seeks so he can properly mourn the death of his Dido in the November eclogue. Here, along with speaking in relation to her Ovidian prototype, Peele's Oenone establishes contact with a great contemporary poem, underlining her own standing as a poetic maker. The repeated invocation of Melpomene associates the private "woe" of his "sillie Nymphe" (612) with the magnitude of the catastrophe Spenser's Colin experiences:

> Shepheards, that by your flocks on Kentish downes abyde,
> Waile ye this wofull waste of nature's warke,
> Waile we the wight, whose presence was our pride,
> Waile we the wight, whose absence is our carke.
> The sonne of all the worlde is dimme and darke:
> The earth now lacks her wonted light,
> And all we dwell in deadly night[.][27]

Despite the play's embedding her in pastoral tropes and texts of retirement and play, Peele's Oenone somehow knows she is a citizen of literary and cultural worlds that Ovid's Oenone assumes from the start are closed to her. Like Ovid's Oenone, she writes, but her literacy and her lyricism distinctly mark her as Peele's own. Her command of story exists alongside and independently of the suffering she will undergo at Paris' hand and allows her to make her pain public in ways that her Ovidian model, relying on the emotional idiolect she shares with Paris and no one else, cannot. That Peele gives her the authority to conduct the stylistic negotiation between complaint and pastoral suggests her subject and her way of talking about it are not necessarily properly confined to one realm.

The first three acts of *The Araygnement of Paris* think of pastoral not only in terms of the erotic pain it can record, but also in terms of its capacity to manage and narrate other kinds of experiences. They insist on the erotic, the affective, the bodily, as important registers of a range of experiences that we might otherwise think of as merely historical or only political. Sensitive to the powers of narrative and of narrativity itself to make us fully perceive phenomena whose layered meanings would otherwise remain unknown to us, the *Araygnement*'s Oenone takes the power and significance of her archive for granted. She perceives a significance that reading for courtly authority without accounting for the places where worldly power must yield to sex would make us miss.

Notes

1. Felix Schelling, "The Source of Peele's *Arraignment of Paris*," *MLN* 8.4 (1893): 103–104.
2. See, for example, Andrew Von Hendy, "The Triumph of Chastity: Form and Meaning in *The Arraignment of Paris*," *RenD* 1 (1968): 87–101; and Henry G. Lesnick, "The Structural Significance of Myth and Flattery in Peele's *Arraignment of Paris*," *SP* 65,2 (1968): 163–70.
3. Von Hendy, 98.
4. Susan T. Viguers, "Art and Reality in George Peele's *The Araygnement of Paris* and *David and Bethsabe*," *CLA Journal*, 30, 4 (1987): 496.
5. Characterizing the *Tale of Troy* as a kind of failed gift aimed at eliciting crown patronage, Louis Adrian Montrose, "Gifts and Reasons: The Contexts of Peele's *Araygnement of Paris*," *ELH* 47, 3 (1980), notes that Peele never received it: "Peele's gift went unrequited. Within a few months he was dead" (457).
6. See R. Mark Benbow in his introduction to his edition of *The Araygnement of Paris* in *The Dramatic Works of George Peele*, gen. ed. C. T. Prouty, vol. 3 of 3 vols. (New Haven: Yale University Press, 1970), 12.
7. In seeing action on personal feelings as having inescapably public resonances, I am influenced by psychoanalytically informed readings of sexuality and gender in early modern literature such as Carla Freccero's *Queer/Early/Modern* (Durham: Duke University Press, 2006) and Valerie Traub's *The Renaissance of Lesbianism in Early Modern England* (Cambridge: Cambridge University Press, 2002). Stephen Guy-Bray's *Homoerotic Space: The Poetics of Loss in Renaissance Literature* (Toronto: University of Toronto Press, 2002) traces how literary forms and their histories can be particularly linked to expressions of male same-sex desire, thus providing a cultural record of the erotic.
8. For a useful brief review of these matters, see Lauren Berlant, "Intimacy: A Special Issue," in her introduction to the special issue of *Critical Inquiry* she edited entitled *Intimacy* (Chicago: University of Chicago Press, 2000), 3–6.
9. *Erotic Subjects: The Sexuality of Politics in Early Modern English Literature* (New York: Oxford University Press, 2011).
10. I take all Shakespeare quotations from *The Oxford Shakespeare: Complete Works*, gen. eds. Stanley Wells and Gary Taylor (Oxford: Clarendon Press, 2005).
11. "Intimacy," 1. Although she is not an early modernist, Berlant's body of work is deeply concerned with the implications of applying the forms of domestic, private emotion to shared civic life; see especially *The Queen of America Goes to Washington City: Essays on Sex and Citizenship* (Durham: Duke University Press, 1997).
12. I cite Benbow's edition, which numbers lines consecutively through the play; here, line 29. Future references appear parenthetically in my text.
13. "Historians and Poets," *Huntington Library Quarterly* 68, 1–2 (2005), 71–72.
14. A3; I will provide future references parenthetically in my text. "Poo" means "poll," or "head". Matthew Dimmock notes that Mohammed was commonly represented as a giant brazen head, often covered in flames or fireworks, in his discussion of theatrical representations in *Mythologies of the Prophet Muhammad in Early Modern English Culture* (Cambridge: Cambridge University Press, 2013), 101–48.
15. The OED notes that one definition of "bid" is specifically to challenge someone to battle, with an example of period usage taken from *2 Tamburlaine*.

16. Victoria Rimell, *Ovid's Lovers: Desire, Difference, and the Poetic Imagination* (Cambridge: Cambridge University Press, 2006), 3. Her discussion of *Heroides* 16, 165–70, in which she sees Paris as a character out of the *Amores* reveling "in his own ... pleasure-pain," (169) is relevant both to my sense of the mixed-up genders in Peele's history and to my larger argument that feelings about intimate connection bleed into representations of civic or public engagements.
17. On the construction of such "affective economies," where personal feelings are articulated and amplified through social circulation, see Sara Ahmed, *The Cultural Politics of Emotion* (New York: Routledge, 2004); she uses the phrase on her p. 8.
18. On links between *A Lover's Complaint* and Shakespeare's sonnets, see Katherine Duncan-Jones, ed., *Shakespeare's Sonnets*, rev. ed. (A & C Black: London, 2010), 89–96; and John Kerrigan's edition of *'The Sonnets and A Lover's Complaint' and The Sonnets* (New York: Penguin Classics, 1986).
19. D2v.
20. On intertextuality in the *Heroides*, see Paul Allen Miller, "The Parodic Sublime: Ovid's Reception of Virgil in *Heroides* 7," *Materiali e discussioni per l'analisi dei testi classici* 52 (2004): 57–72; Megan O. Drinkwater, "Which Letter?: Text and Subtext in Ovid's *Heroides*," *American Journal of Philology* 128,3 (2007): 367–87; and Sara Lindheim, "*Omnia Vincit Amor*: Or, Why Oenone Should Have Known It Would Never Work Out (Eclogue 10 and *Heroides* 5)," *Materiali e discussioni per l'analisi dei testi classici* 44 (2000): 83–101.
21. George Turberville, *The Heroycall Epistles of Publius Ovidius Naso, in English Verse* (London, 1567), 27. Subsequent references will appear parenthetically.
22. I thank Garrett Sullivan for this insight.
23. It lacks the historical aspect I note in Oenone's story, but here one might compare the action of the brokenhearted shepherdess of *A Lover's Complaint*. Trying to forget her unfaithful lover, she throws the gifts he gave her, and her own letters to him "sadly penned in blood" (47) into a flowing river—but just as Oenone's tree renews itself and carries her fame into the future, the river carries the shepherdess' tokens of loss onward into a wider sea.
24. *Passion Made Public: Elizabethan Lyric, Gender, and Performance* (Urbana: University of Illinois Press, 1995), 7. Her discussion of *The Araygnement of Paris* is her chapter two, 85–119.
25. On the female authors of the *Heroides*, see Efrossini Spentzou, *Readers and Writers in Ovid's Heroides: Transgressions of Genre and Gender* (Oxford: Oxford University Press, 2003); Laurel Fulkerson, *The Ovidian Heroine as Author: Reading, Writing, and Community in the Heroides* (Cambridge: Cambridge University Press, 2005); and Sara Lindheim, *Mail and Female: Epistolary Narrative and Desire in the Heroides* (Madison: University of Wisconsin Press, 2003).
26. It appears, for example, in *An Anthology of the Poetry of the Age of Shakespeare*, ed. W. T. Young (Cambridge: Cambridge University Press, 1910), 64; and the *Oxford Book of English Verse, 1250–1900*, ed. Arthur Quiller-Couch (Oxford: Clarendon Press, 1919), 141–42.
27. *The Shepheardes Calender conteyning twelve aeglogues proportionable to the twelve monethes* (1579), fol. 45.

2 The Will and Testamentary Eroticism in Shakespearean Drama
Douglas Iain Clark

In recent years, critics ranging from Mary Carruthers to Lina Perkins Wilder have shown that a range of materials and intellectual practices constituted early modern memory and, in turn, helped to define the relationship that the individual subject had to the social world.[1] We learn that the commonplace book, wax tablet, and even the theater itself cultivated the art of memory in Shakespeare's England. However, such studies have not yet addressed how notions of the will helped to represent and preserve memory in early modern drama. It would be pertinent, then, to explore another important way that "material objects function as memory tokens in early modern culture and Shakespeare's plays" by examining how the will, as both faculty and legal testament, was used to depict the dangers and anxieties associated with the commemoration of human endeavors.[2] More specifically, this essay seeks to convey how wills and testaments are employed as dramatic devices in *Hamlet*, *Julius Caesar* and *Troilus and Cressida* to memorialize the impulses of the human will, however deviant, dangerous, or erotic those impulses are.

Taming the Will in the Last Will and Testament

Commenting on the nature of the will and its operation within the human subject is a key facet of the moral and natural philosophy of the period. Many early modern philosophers, theologians, and essayists aim to provide a distinct theorization of the will, although they often struggle to categorize its nature and placement within the soul because of its inherent instability as a faculty.[3] Regardless of its imputed power to affect our salvation, the will's status as a prominent, if corrupted, faculty is generally conceived to act as a rogue agent in the rational soul, problematizing the ethical operation and structure of being because it may function to fulfill sinful desires.

Thomas Wright, for instance, directs the reader of *The Passions of the Mind in General* to consider how "the chiefest castell" of man's "soule" is comprised of "wiite and will."[4] Proposing a conception of the soul based upon a metaphor (this "castell") would suggest order, hierarchy, and structural integrity, but the characteristics that Wright ascribes to the will actually undermine the soul's integrity. The will, after all, may be drawn "unto inordinate appetites," moved by "waves and billows of apparent reasons,"

The Will and Testamentary Eroticism in Shakespearean Drama 31

which would draw the will from its high state to appease the "sensitive appetite."[5] Being divided by two contrary inclinations, "the one to follow reason, the other to content the senses," the will's "libertie and freedom" is directly impinged.[6] So, just as the reasonable soul is divided in its powers, the will itself is divided in its own potential operation. Wright further emphasizes the will's vulnerability when he describes how it acts as a female "governesse of the soule."[7] Although the title of governess may imply rule and order, the will may receive "some little bribe of pleasure" from the passions that would undo its control over the senses.[8] Immoderate passion dissolves internal order, and our intemperate, womanly wills perturb our soul, allowing it to "swell with pride and pleasure."[9] Wright, then, attempts to link the will to the rational power of the soul, yet he cannot do so without witnessing the base, lustful attractions that may interfere at any point. In the attempt to theorize the nature of the will, Wright demonstrates the powerful and unruly role the will takes in the governance of the human soul.

Early modern essayists like Wright sought to highlight the dangers associated with the operation of the will, yet in spite of its prominent connection to ethical intemperance, the will was still conceived of as directly informing how the human subject was to be memorialized in death. Henry Swinburne gives a clear example in his legal instruction manual *A Briefe Treatise of Testaments and Last Wills* (1590). He writes, "*testamentum est voluntatis nostre insta sententia, de eo quod quis post mortem suam sieri voluit.* A testament is just sentence of our will; touching that we would have done after our death."[10]

The arrangement of wills as a social practice in Elizabethan and Jacobean England did indeed "seek to preserve affiliations beyond the grave—to reproduce social alliances through the distribution of objects, space, property," although the prominence of these affiliations was only made possible by the implementation of the Statutes of Uses (1536) and the Statue of Wills (1540) enforced during the reign of Henry VIII.[11] The statute of 1536 reformed medieval common law to stop land owners who were trying to "escape the burdens of feudal tenure" and the payment of royal revenues by apportioning their legal estate to feoffees.[12] Four years later, the Statute of Wills (1540) was offered as a compromise and allowed "the majority of landowners" to have "the right to devise their freehold land as they wished," free from the restrictions of previous inheritance laws that limited the passing of lands and associated chattel property to immediate family.[13]

Succeeding these legal reforms, many church ministers, in accordance with the 1549 *Book of Common Prayer*, stressed that "menne must be ofte admonished that they sette an ordre for theyr temporall goodes and landes, whan they be in health."[14] From the suggestions given in the *Book of Prayer*, ministers were encouraged to make the unprecedented attempt of removing "will-making from its traditional deathbed setting."[15] In particular, John Hooper, a devout reformer and bishop of Gloucester and Worcester, suggested that all his ministers

> were to exhort their parishioners, four times a year, to make their last wills while they were in good health and perfect memory. ... Such a precaution would not only give them quietness of mind, but [it would] also ensure their own control over their will-making and lessen the risk of disputes after their deaths.[16]

Although Hooper's example was "seldom imitated by later bishops ... the advice was taken up in sermons and other works of Christian counsel that called for the settlement of worldly affairs well before death."[17] The rise of professional will-making can be traced, for example, in Thomas Phayer's *A Booke of Presidents* (1586). In this text, a last will and testament stresses the condition of the testator's "whole minde" and "good & perfect remembrance;" Henry Swinburne equally notes that "our farewell to the world, the memorial of our immortality" should be made by one "of perfect mind & memory;" William Gouge offers a similar proposal, stating that the fit time for making a will was "while his understanding is good, and his memorie perfect."[18] Such precautionary measures were given in order to make sure that a will and testament was created in accordance, as Swinburne suggests, with the use of "reason" to reflect the internal "will" of a testator in a manner that was Godly and just and avoided "wicked" matters opposed to "iustice, pietie, equitie, honestie."[19] An exemplary and just transposition of the internal will of a testator was, therefore, to limit waywardness and corruption that the faculty of the will could stimulate within the human subject. Instead, perfect memory, moral temperance, and religious piety should shape the "memorial of our immortality" of the last will and testament.[20]

Although wills may ostensibly provide a lucid insight into a testator's personality and religious preferences, interpretative caution must be employed when analyzing the preambles of wills. In respect to the creation of and stipulations contained within preambles, wills may "tell us more about the external constraints on testators than they do about shifting private belief."[21] As Duffy argues, the increasing use of formulaic wills in the course of the Reformation may be understood as an expression of expediency and prudence to the "possible and the approved."[22] It may then be the case that in some instances the preambles of wills reflect the willingness of testators to conform to scribal authority and templates of approved piety, rather than conveying the unadulterated last wishes of individuals at liberty to convey the particular idiosyncrasies of their individual wills. In this way, wills and testaments may still actually represent the will of their testators in the form of willed self-censorship. Thus, where the memorialization of one's life is constrained by the expected and the expedient, the "perfect memory" of an individual may happen to forget, or merely forgo, the inclusion of sexual or malicious desires in their wills. A great number of plays in the period do, however, actively engage with examining the consequences of the erotic and deviant impulses that may inform the creation, manipulation, and execution of the last will and testament.

Performing Testamentary Erotics

The advice of the 1549 *Common Book of Prayer*, that a will should be made in good health and perfect memory, is taken on board in John Webster's *The Duchess of Malfi* (c. 1614).[23] The Duchess creates her will in good health and "in perfect memory" (1.1.375), commenting that it would be better to make her will "smiling ... than in deep groans and terrible ghastly looks" because such illness would lead her to part with her "gifts" in "violent distraction" (1.1.376–9). Although she conforms to the advice of church ministers and of writers like Swinburne, Phayer, and Gouge, the Duchess avoids employing a member of the clergy or even a lay-scribe to help form her will.[24] She, rather, uses the moment as an opportunity to seduce Antonio, utilizing him as an "overseer" of her testation, eventually bequeathing herself to him in marriage (1.1.382). Notably, the Duchess is punished for attempting to pursue her will for Antonio by allowing him to form her will and testament as a token of her desire for him. Her personal will informs the formation of her legal will in this respect, yet the realization of her erotic desires will also spur on her brothers' villainous deeds. As Ferdinand laments in a moment of final clarity, "Whether we fall by ambition, blood, or lust / Like diamonds, we are cut with our own dust" (5.5.71–2); the Duchess falls victim to a system of power that facilitates the satisfaction of male lust but commonly acts to subjugate and punish willful women.

Ben Jonson's *Volpone* (1607) also depicts the connection between the last will and testament and sexual desire. The action of Jonson's play centers around how Volpone derives personal pleasure, as well as profit, from duping Voltore, Corbaccio, and Corvino into believing that each has been chosen to be the sole heir of Volpone's estate. Various scams are executed by Volpone's servant, Mosca, who presents himself as a witness to the writing or oral execution of Volpone's will. Following Mosca's advice, Corbaccio redrafts his own will to disinherit his son so that Volpone would be the "sole heir" of his fortune (1.4.95). Further to ruining this male line of inheritance, Mosca dupes Corvino into believing that Volpone, in the last strength he had to utter speech, named him as the recipient of his inheritance: "Whom should he would have his heir? 'Corvino'" (1.3.45–47). While Mosca gains Corvino's confidence, Volpone slips off to attempt to seduce Corvino's wife, Celia. Indeed, Mosca's deviousness and Volpone's unapologetically false will-making boldly highlight some of the practicalities, as well as the fears, surrounding oral and scribal modes of will-making in the period.

The anxieties associated with the execution of wills can also be traced in *The Merchant of Venice*. A will and last testament shapes the narrative of courtship that Portia is forcibly made part of. As Portia describes, "the word choose" is not one that indicates liberty, but rather signals how her particular desires are superseded by the conditions of her father's last will: "I may neither choose who I / would nor refuse who I dislike; so is the will of a living daughter curbed by the will / of a dead father" (1.2. 20–22). The imposition of male control over female sexual desire was a common feature of the plays of the period, and the instruction that Portia's father gives for a casket lottery to determine her husband seems a pertinent example of such sexual inequalities. Here, we find Portia being forced to conform to the demands of a deceased father who is memorialized in the caskets and riddles left in his wake—tokens of male legacy that act to shape and control her future sexual life—all the while being made to remember the "virtuous" qualities of her father by Nerissa (1.2.24). The only hope Portia seems to have to achieve her own desires is to employ her own "will and skill," associated with "surety, contrasting it with the risks of male (ad)venture," to maneuver within the strictures of law that frame the nature of her identity as a possession of her father and her future husband, Antonio.[25]

Depicting the sexual anxieties and pitfalls surrounding the memorialization of wills and the passing of personal and familial legacies seems to be a common feature of early modern plays.[26] In spite of Portia's success in laying some claim of agency over her will, the erotic features of testamentary memorialization are often shown to be shaped by the vagrant and corrupt nature of the faculty of the will in a way that leads to moral, mortal, or existential crises. Such circumstances are depicted in *Hamlet* when Claudius describes the Prince's pitiable state, his "impious stubbornness," as an "unmanly grief" that "shows a will most incorrect to heaven, / A heart unfortified, a mind impatient," and an "understanding simple and unschool'd" (1.2.94–7). Claudius proposes that Hamlet's will is "incorrect" because it enables him to retain the memory of his father, which apparently demonstrates excessive "filial obligation" (1.2.91). Hamlet's preeminent education should have taught him how to forget this affection; however, this "will" to recollect his love for his father only spurs him to unite this memory to an image of "incestuous sheets" (1.2.157). Urging Hamlet to forget seems to engrain the memory of his father more prominently into his mind: an act facilitated by the thought of Gertrude and Claudius' transgressive sexual practices and one that is reemphasized by Old Hamlet's renowned patrimonial imposition "remember me" (1.5.91).

Certainly, Hamlet's "lethargic, non-performance of the Ghost's commands" seems to suggest, in line with Laertes' portentous word of caution to Ophelia, that his "will is not his own" (1.3.16–17).[27] In this respect, the imposition of Old Hamlet's will appears to stimulate the volatility associated with the will of young Hamlet. Thus, Hamlet's grief causes "a sigh so piteous and profound / As it did seem to shatter all his bulk / And end his being" (2.1.94–96), and as Polonius states when consoling Ophelia, "the very ecstasy of love / Whose violent property fordoes itself / And leads the will to desperate undertakings" (2.1.102–104). Old Hamlet's will seems to have disturbed young Hamlet's mind to the point where the subjectivity produced from Hamlet's pledge to "erase from his memory all pre-existing matter" may allow for his very sense of "being" to be unraveled, as evidenced by the "desperate undertakings" of his desires.[28] This confluence of wills informs Hamlet's erotically volatile public persona as well as his inward,

The Will and Testamentary Eroticism in Shakespearean Drama 35

existential quandaries about the "undiscovered country" that "puzzles the will" (3.1.78–80) and leads to personal destruction.

Although Portia and Hamlet negotiate the wills of their fathers to different degrees of success, the potency of their parents' last wishes relies equally upon a metonymic representation of absence: Portia is reminded of the rights she must go through and fulfill by the caskets bequeathed to her by her father, and Hamlet comes face to face with the full scope of his patrilineal obligations via the shade of Old Hamlet. Symbolic of both death and duty, the casket and the shade transpose each parent's will *without* the presence of the last will and testament itself. What distinguishes *Julius Caesar* and *Troilus and Cressida* from these aforementioned plays is their particular investment in the eroticization of absence through the use of a will and testament as a dramatic device.

Eroticizing Absence

Disgruntled at being "under" Caesar's "huge legs" as "he doth bestride the narrow world / Like a colossus" (1.2.134–36), Cassius and his co-conspirators displace their wounded pride and perceived powerlessness into homicidal tendencies. Caesar's colossal "will" seems to be the cause of his enemies' displeasure: it completely eclipses the fame and political authority that his rivals may hope to enjoy, leaving them to reflect upon the ignobility of their status as "underlings" (1.2.140) and the possibility that they are destined only to find "dishonourable graves" (1.2.137). Cassius' hyperbolic description of Caesar's power is, therefore, not merely an effective piece of rhetoric as it also fittingly foreshadows the potency that is posthumously attributed to Caesar's will and prefigures how the commemoration of his legacy is construed in decidedly erotic terms.

The eventual enactment of Caesar's will (realized through the conditions of his last will and testament) occurs because he poses a threat to the Roman republic. As Brutus expresses: "Crown him that / And then I grant we put a sting in him / That at his will he may do danger with" (2.1.15–17).[29] Brutus' description of Caesar, here, emphasizes the danger of licensing Caesar's will with the authority of a crown. This collective desire for Caesar's death is actualized, appropriately, through the manipulation of Caesar's will.

CAESAR: Decius, go tell them Caesar will not come.
DECIUS: Most mighty Caesar, let me know some cause,
  Lest I be laughed at when I tell them so.
CAESAR: The cause is in my will. (2.2.69–71)

Caesar is initially defiant in coming to the senate but changes his mind when Decius offers an altered interpretation of Calpurnia's portentous dream. The awful significance and accuracy of Calpurnia's prophesies are inverted by the imposition of male influence over the representation of memory: Decius' rhetoric directly affects how her dream is reinterpreted by Caesar, manipulating Caesar's will in order to lead him to his demise.[30] Nevertheless, I would propose that Caesar's death does not merely confirm the ineffectiveness of his will in comparison to his conspirators'. Rather, in Antony's hands, Caesar's will, enforced through his testamentary bequests, is shown to exert tremendous influence in the course of the play.

In describing the posthumous, testamentary will of Caesar, Antony renews Caesar's power through an erotic reappropriation of Caesar's memory:

> But here's a parchment, with the seal of Caesar.
> I found it in his closet. 'Tis his will.
> Let but the commons hear this testament—
> Which, pardon me, I do not mean to read—
> And they would go and kiss dead Caesar's wound,
> And dip their napkins in his sacred blood,
> Yea, beg a hair of him for memory,
> And, dying, mention it within their wills,
> Bequeathing it as a rich legacy
> Unto their issue. (3.2.129–38)

Antony describes Caesar's will as to be *so* moving that the plebeians present would be incited by it to appropriate both Caesar's body and memory as property that they would bequeath in their own will's as a "rich legacy" for their own progeny. In such an act, Antony is able to manipulate his audience's collective remembrance of Caesar to perpetuate his nobility by imparting it within the plebeians' own wills. The certainty of this prospective, united will-making is based upon an erotic connection made between the lips of the commoners and the bloody body of Caesar.

Antony fittingly puts his own mouth to use in memorializing Caesar's legacy. Although Antony feigns that he would lack the skill to employ "sweet Caesar's wounds, poor poor dumb mouths" to "speak" for him (3.2.218–19), when urging the crowd to inspect Caesar's corpse, he more than adequately demonstrates how effective he is at putting "a tongue in every wound of Caesar" (3.2.221). By exhibiting the pierced mantle of Caesar, Antony manages to import the holes in Caesar's cloak with meaning, doing so by actively reimagining the events that took place for his enraptured audience:

> Look, in this place ran Cassius' dagger through:
> See what a rent the envious Caska made:
> Through this, the well-beloved Brutus stabbed,
> And as he plucked cursed steel away,
> Mark how the blood of Caesar followed it. (3.2.173–76)

Antony entices his audience to memorialize Caesar by interpreting a memory of his death that neither party was privy to. Creating such a memory is fittingly enacted by using the absent spaces in Caesar's mantle: each new hole acts as a space in which to emphasize and reemphasize the injustice of Caesar's fate. The heavily erotic imagery of tonguing, kissing, and penetration all serve to "stir up" the plebeians "in a sudden flood of mutiny" (3.2.204), cultivating *pathos* in order to crucially imbue Caesar's will with a power in which to convince his audience of the merits of the fallen Roman. This act, as Gail Paster proposes, "reinvests Caesar's body with a portion of its original phallic power," although his wounds more overtly display their affective power in this speech as bodily orifices that signify a fetishized "female silence."[31] However, it may be that Caesar's "'will' ... his maleness," as figured by the internal drive that informs his last will and testament, plays a greater role in renegotiating the landscape of the Roman body politic within the play than Paster accounts for.[32]

Such is the potency of Antony's memorialization and his attempt to inflame their passions that he proposes that the plebeians "have forgot the will I told you of" (3.2.231). Ironically, the excessive eroticization of Caesar's will, generated through the symbolic use of his feminized body, leads the excited crowd to forget the very source of their excitement. Issuing this reminder allows Antony to reemphasize the value that the will and testament holds in commemorating the body and memory of Caesar and is finalized by providing details about the nature of Caesar's last bequest. As Antony explains, Caesar has left

> His private arbours and new-planted orchards
> On this side Tiber. He hath left them you
> And to your heirs for ever: common pleasures
> To walk abroad and recreate yourselves. (3.2.240–42)

The last portion of this will ostensibly offers up these pastoral walking spaces for the enjoyment and recreation of all citizens of the republic, though the "common pleasures" of Rome's people may also be interpreted as signifying the act of re/procreation itself. It is this testamentary bequest that encourages the plebeians to indulge in the regenerative, and possibly generative, power of "recreation," allowing for the wills of Cassius and Brutus to be curbed and for Antony to enshrine the popular memory of Caesar in the phrase: "This was a man!" (5.5.76). Caesar's original, internal power of will is depicted as being vulnerable to external influence, yet in the oration of Caesar's testament, Antony cultivates the significance and influence of the original internal drive that shapes the content of Caesar's testamentary will. In death, Caesar's will is attributed with a potency that is inaccessible to him in life: a power of posthumous willing realized, crucially, through acts of erotic memorialization. As such, Caesar's will both offers new erotic "recreation" for Rome's common masses and recreates his memory as a figure of humility and generosity through Antony's sexualized performance of his will.

Renegotiating the attributed force and function of the faculty of the will and the testamentary legacy in erotic terms is also a crucial element of the dramatic structure of *Troilus and Cressida*. However, this play places a more concentrated focus on how the power of the will may, in accordance with moral discourses of the period like Thomas Wright's, problematize normative visions of order, power, agency, identity, and reality for many of the play's characters. Furthermore, it would appear that *Troilus and Cressida*'s role in addressing the "difficulty of sustaining a transcendental vision of monarchical order" as well as the "natural and social order" is directly informed by the threat that the will poses to various characters throughout the play and is appropriately concluded by Pandarus' own failed attempt to memorialize his own licentious existence.[33]

Ulysses' exposition on how universal chaos is generated provides an initial illustration of the will's destructive influence:

> Then everything includes itself in power,
> Power into will, will into appetite;
> And appetite, an universal wolf,
> So doubly seconded with will and power,
> Must make perforce an universal prey
> And last eat himself up. Great Agamemnon,
> This chaos, when degree is suffocate,
> Follows the choking. (1.3.119–26)

When the proper degree and reason are ignored, the monstrous power of the will is unleashed. Ulysses' use of anadiplosis ("power into will, will into appetite") establishes the will as the central rhetorical component to his rationalization of the human subject's potential to invert personal and collective hierarchies of power. The will empowers this wolfish, autophagous aspect of our being, although as Ulysses' warning suggests, its nature is paradoxical: allowing the will to operate without restraint actually limits its function—it is so excessively potent that it functions to destroy itself. Without order, appetite and will would enable the individual to cannibalize its own identity, power, and self-worth in a contradictory act of *dis*empowerment. Thus, the will may fuel the desire for infinite action or sin, but our own limitations and the defective nature of the will stop us from meeting the full extent of its demands.

The will is figured as necessitous *to* but incredulous *of* the proper arrangement of psychic and moral order for Greek and Trojan alike. Pandarus' epilogue, consequently, provides a particularly fitting conclusion to the play as it reemphasizes the destructive role the will has taken within the narrative.[34] Echoing Troilus' exposition on love—that "the will is infinite and the execution confined; that the desire is boundless and the act a slave to limit" (3.2.78–80)—Pandarus exclaims that the "poor agent is despised" in the world because "our endeavour be so desired and the performance so loathed" (5.11.35–39). This lament originates from Troilus' curse that Pandarus should have to live in "ignomy and shame" of his indecent behaviour (5.11.33). Troilus constructs a deleterious legacy for Pandarus by yoking his name to illicit attributes: he wishes Pandarus be remembered because of his deviant erotic habits.

Accepting his fate and the ignominy that his name would now signify, Pandarus attempts to conclude the drama by offering the audience some prediction of what his future should hold—but he cannot do so. He instead promises to finalize his own legacy in "some two months hence" when "hence my will shall here be made" (5.11.52). The promise to perform his will at a *later* date is an act that primarily attempts to validate his role in the play's conclusion: his intent to produce a testamentary will in a proposed sequel of *Troilus and Cressida* would suggest that he wields the authority to provide a formal conclusion to the current play and insinuates that its sequel would serve to represent a testamentary record of the outcome from the "diseases" he feels in his "aching bones" (5.11.56 and 35). Be it shame, a lack of personal restraint, or actual venereal malady, Pandarus' disease is, however, kept alive and afforded no cure in this open-ended epilogue. By stating his resolve to author a legacy for himself in a dramatic future that will never come to pass, Pandarus inadvertently memorializes the ineffectiveness of his will. This act also, ironically, serves to commemorate the association of his name with deviant sexual behavior. Hence, *Troilus and Cressida* concludes to reiterate how the "poor" human agent is "despised" on account of its sullied relationship to the will, and that it must perish because of this bond.

Tracing the erotic memorialization of the will illuminates an intriguing facet of the will's realization in early modern literature: it may be employed as a tool for shaping identity as well as altering the basis of signification, but it is also conceived as a faculty of the individual that operates to create a legacy for itself. However, as depicted in *Julius Caesar* and *Troilus and Cressida*, the testamentary will's depicted function—to preserve the memory of Pandarus and Julius Caesar—relies upon eroticizing states of absence or annihilation. Testamentary remembrance is depicted in these plays to derive meaning from moments of destruction. Sensuality and eroticism simultaneously enforce and undermine the will's significance, as well as its power to shape modes of memorialization.

As this essay has demonstrated, it is apparent that a number of early modern plays took time to reflect upon the status and significance of last wills and testaments. Such dramas seem to exploit the association that the written will has with the faculty will, often representing the last will and testament as a manifestation of a testator's power of will in accordance with Henry Swinburne's sentiment that the legal will and testament is "a just sentence of our will."[35] Moreover, the dramatic representation of will-making and the execution of wills touches on the numerous anxieties associated with the creation of legacies, their legitimacy, and the social and sexual politics associated with inheritance. Fulfilling the demands of last wills highlights both the vulnerability of the internal will to external influence and the potentially volatile and corrupt operation of an individual's will. Whether represented in metonymic form, through manipulated oral testation, or through the physical document itself, wills and testaments are depicted as thoroughly erotic sites of remembrance in these Shakespearean plays.

Notes

1. Mary Carruthers, *The Book of Memory* (Cambridge: Cambridge University Press, 1990); William Engel, *Death and Drama in Renaissance England: Shades of Memory* (Oxford University Press, 2002); Hester Lees-Jeffries, *Shakespeare and Memory* (Oxford: Oxford University Press, 2013); Garrett A. Sullivan, *Memory and Forgetting in Renaissance Drama: Shakespeare, Marlowe, Webster* (Cambridge: Cambridge University Press, 2005); Lina Perkins Wilder, *Shakespeare's Memory Theatre: Recollection, Properties, and Character* (Cambridge University Press, 2010).
2. Lees-Jeffries, *Shakespeare and Memory*, 7.
3. See John Case, *Speculum Moralium Quaestionum* (Oxford, 1585); Haly Heron, *A New Discourse of Moral Philosophy* (London, 1579); Richard Hooker, *Of the Lawes of Ecclesiastical Politie* (London,1604); William Jewell, *The Golden Cabinet Of True Treasure: Containing the Summe of Morall Philosophy* (London,1612); Franz Lambert, *The Mind and Judgment of Master Frances Lambert of Avenna of The Wyll of Man* (London,1548); William Perkins, *A Treatise of Man's Imagination Shewing His Naturall Euill Thoughts: His Want of Good Thoughts: The Way to Reforme Them* (Cambridge,1607); Guillarme Du Vair, *The True way to Virtue and Happiness* (London,1623); Thomas Wright, *The Passions of the Minde in General* (London, 1621).
4. Thomas Wright, *The Passions of the Minde in General* (London, 1621), 5.
5. Wright, *The Passions of the Minde*, 58.
6. Wright, *The Passions of the Minde*, 58.
7. Wright, *The Passions of the Minde*, 58. The Latin feminine noun *voluntas* may also have a hand in figuring the will in this way.
8. Wright, *The Passions of the Minde*, 58. Describing the will in these gendered terms also features in Phillipe de Mornay's searching treatise of man's subjectivity, *The True Nature of Man's Owne Self*: 'The affections are not moderated by the judgement, deliberation, or honest councell: the will, as mistresse of the affections, forbids the *motive power*, that she transport not the members to perpetuate unreasonable or pernicious things' (Phillipe de Mornay, *The True Nature of Man's Owne Self*, London: 1602), 146. As the mistress of the affections, the will is responsible for the "infinite multitudes of mishaps" that can befall the self, but it is a role that is in constant danger of being redirected by itself (the wants of the body and mind) to the degradation of the soul and body alike (Mornay, *The True Nature of Man's Owne Self*, 38).
9. Wright, *The Passions of the Minde*, 59. It may come as no surprise to those familiar with early modern instructional tracts that the uncertainty attributed to the operations and nature of the will, alongside the perception of its detrimental effect upon subjectivity and order, is connected to femininity by Wright. As he describes, women are "extremely addicted to follow their owne desires" with

The Will and Testamentary Eroticism in Shakespearean Drama 41

passions so strong as to be "crossed of their willes," and that "we may well conclude, that Passions desires keepe neither sense, order, nor measure" (Wright, *The Passions of the Minde*, 74–75).

10. Henry Swinburne, *A Briefe Treatise of Testaments and Last Wills* (London: 1590), 3v. *A Briefe Treatise* is an exemplary legal handbook of the period—one that offers an extremely thorough account of how to correctly compose a will in accordance with ecclesiastical and civil law.
11. Jeffrey Masten, *Textual Intercourse: Collaboration, Authorship, and Sexualities in Renaissance Drama* (Cambridge: Cambridge University Press, 1997), 4.
12. E.W. Ives, "The Genesis of the Statue of Uses," *The English Historical Review* 82.325 (Oct., 1967): 674.
13. E.A.J. Honigmann and Susan Brock. *Playhouse Wills 1558–1642: An Edition of Wills by Shakespeare and his Contemporaries in the London Theatre* (Manchester: Manchester University Press, 1993), 13.
14. Houlbrooke, *Death, Religion, and the Family in England 1480–1750* (Oxford: Clarendon Press, 1998), 82.
15. Houlbrooke, *Death, Religion, and the Family*, 82.
16. Houlbrooke, *Death, Religion, and the Family*, 82.
17. Houlbrooke, *Death, Religion, and the Family*, 82. This type of provision was still seen to be prudent throughout the reign of Mary I, Elizabeth I, and James VI and was notably emphasized in a number of legal manuals and handbooks that were constructed to conform to a type of professional standardization. See Honigmann and Brock, *Playhouse Wills 1558–1642*, 18.
18. Thomas Phayer, *A Book of Presidents* (London, 1586), 175r; Henry Swinburne, *A Brief Treatise of Testaments and Last Wills*, 8r; and William Gouge, *Of Domesticall Duties* (London, 1622), 571. See also William West, *Symbolaeographia* (London, 1592).
19. Swinburne, *A Brief Treatise of Testaments and Last Wills*, 8r and 5v.
20. Swinburne, *A Brief Treatise of Testaments and Last Wills*, 8r. The wisdom purported in these texts, however, did not seem to be implemented by the laity of early modern England in the manner expected of them. As suggested in his essay "Attitudes to Will-Making in Early Modern England," Marsh proposes that "many testators were sick when they made their wills," although they were at least 'sound of mind' when giving their testation (Christopher Marsh, "Attitudes to Will-Making in Early Modern England", in *When Death Do Us Part: Understanding and Interpreting the Probate Records of Early Modern England*, ed. Tom Arkell et al. Oxford: Leopard's Head Press, 2000, 164).
21. Eamon Duffy, *The Stripping of the Altars: Traditional Religion in England 1400–1580* (New Haven: Yale University Press, 1992), 507. It would be unwise, then, to judge a testator's last will and testament as an uncensored expression of individual faith.
22. Duffy, *The Stripping of the Altars*, 523.
23. The issue of timeliness and will-making is also depicted in *The Merry Wives of Windsor* (1602). In 3.4, Slender constructs a pun that makes light of the recommendation that wills should be made early, rather than on one's death bed. Responding to Anne Page's question of 'What is your will?' Slender exclaims the following: "My will! 'od's heartlings, that's a pretty jest indeed! I / ne'er made my will yet, I thank God; I am not such a sickly / creature, I give God praise" (3.4.53–56). Where Slender's attitude to will-making is made in jest, Languebeau Snuffe's warning to the baron Montferrers in Act Two, Scene One of Cyril

Tourneur's *The Atheist's Tragedy* (1611) is presented in all seriousness: "you shall do well if you be sick to set your / state in present order. Make your will" (Tourner, *The Atheist's Tragedy, or, The Honest Man's Revenge*, 2.1.135–36). The dialogue of these characters, though made in very different circumstances, attests to the creation of wills in sickness, rather than in health.

24. It has also been suggested that lay scribes took "an increasingly large share of the business of will-writing" from clergy members, marking a shift in the technical production and composition of written wills (Houlbrooke, *Death, Religion, and the Family in England 1480–1750*, 125).
25. Natasha Korda, "Dame Usury: Gender, Credit and (Ac)counting in the 'Sonnets' and 'The Merchant of Venice'", *Shakespeare Quarterly* 60.2 (Summer 2009): 140.
26. Male anxieties over the passing of legacies can also be traced in a number of early modern plays. Where Jonson's *Volpone* and Ulpian Fulwell's *Like Will to Like* (1568) dramatize the problems caused by the falsity of written or oral wills, Middleton's *The Phoenix* (c.1603) and the anonymously authored *The London Prodigall* (1607) emphasize the problems of prodigality for matters of inheritance. Both plays explore the familial politics surrounding the passing of titles and estates onto sons who are initially deemed unworthy of their father's legacy. Each comedy, however, is resolved by showing how each son actually deserves to receive his inheritance: *The London Prodigall* depicts the reformation of the prodigal son, Matthew Flowerdale, who repents utterly for his wanton ways; Prince Phoenix's actions prove his inherently virtuous nature to his father, thus ensuring his inheritance of his father's Dukedom. Consider also the consequences of Lear's division of his lands made through a vow his "constant will to publish / Our daughters' several dowers" (1.1.41–42).
27. Sullivan, *Memory and Forgetting*, 43.
28. Sullivan, *Memory and Forgetting*, 13.
29. Brutus' description of this 'sting' of Caesar's is later used to describe Antony's use of language at Philippi in 5.1.32–38.
30. The ease in which Caesar's will is manipulated here is echoed in Cinna's, the Poet's, reflection on the power that his dreams have over directing his own will: "I dreamt tonight that I did feast with Caesar, / And things unluckily charge my fantasy. / I have no will to wander forth of doors, / Yet something leads me forth" (3.3.1–4). Although ominous memories may serve to warn of impending doom, both Caesar's and Cinna's wills are shown to be easily swayed by their own curiosity.
31. Gail Kern Paster, *The Body Embarrassed: Drama and the Disciplines of Shame in Early Modern England* (New York: Cornell University Press, 1993), 110–11.
32. Paster, *The Body Embarrassed*, 112.
33. David Norbrook, "Rhetoric, Ideology and the Elizabethan World Picture", in *Renaissance Rhetoric*, ed. Peter Mack (MacMillan Press: London, 1994), 158.
34. The will's association with a debilitating sense of limitation, seen in Ulysses' speech, pervades the rest of the drama and is often connected to erotic actions. For instance, Hector admonishes Paris and Troilus for indulging the "hot passion" of their "distempered blood": a corruption of integrity that affects everyone who would indulge "their benumbed wills" beyond proper degree (2.2.169 and 179). Hector's accusation that Paris is not able to make "free determination / 'Twixt right and wrong" is based upon the fact that his will has not been desensitized to the influence of excessive passion (2.2.170).
35. Swinburne, *A Briefe Treatise of Testaments and Last Wills*, 3v.

3 Remembering to Forget
Shakespeare's Sonnet 35 and Sigo's "XXXV"

Stephen Guy-Bray

Love and memory are habitually intertwined. In fact, we could say that love can be understood as a particularly intense form of memory, but then so is hate. I want to begin my discussion by looking at a famous classical example of the connection of these emotions. In the long scene in the *Aeneid* in which Aeneas takes leave of Dido, he promises always to think well of her: "*nec me meminisse pigebit Elissae / dum memor ipse mei, dum spiritus hos regit artus*" ("nor shall it pain me to remember Elissa, as long as I remember myself, as long as my spirit rules these limbs").[1] These are beautiful and dignified words, but just how ineffective they are is soon made clear by Dido's blistering curse:

> *Sequar atris ignibus absens*
> *et, cum frigida mors anima seduxerit artus,*
> *omnibus umbra locis adero*
> (Absent, I shall follow you with dark fires; and when cold death has divided my limbs from my soul, I shall be present everywhere as a ghost).[2]

For Aeneas, the memory of their loves will be a pleasant companion that will last as long as he lives, but Dido predicts a future in which her ghost will become, in effect, Aeneas' memory, a companion who is a constant torment.

In their bringing together of memory, love, and hate, and in their pairing of emotional and linguistic memory, these passages provide a paradigm for the kinds of romantic memory I discuss in the rest of this paper. Perhaps most important, the two passages do not present us with a choice in which there can be either a happy memory or an unhappy one: both kinds of memory will continue to exist, as Aeneas' meeting with the still aggrieved Dido in the underworld demonstrates. But while it seems clear that for Dido the memory will always be bitter and for Aeneas the memory will always be sweet, in practice, as we shall see, erotic memories tend to be bittersweet. It is impossible to be either like Dido or like Aeneas with any consistency. What is also important (and especially so for poetry) is that memory is not only mental or emotional; it is also linguistic. In the passages I have quoted, we can see this in the way Dido's use of "artus" remembers Aeneas' use of the same word. In the case of the poems that are my main concern here, we shall see that memories of various kinds inhere in the literary form itself.

I want now to look briefly at Sir Thomas Wyatt's translation of Petrarch's line (it is the first line of the sonnet) "Passa la nave mia colma d'oblio," as "My galy charged with forgetfulness." That Wyatt's sonnet is seen as one of the inaugural texts of the English Renaissance creates an interesting contrast between the memory inherent in the very idea of a renaissance as well as in the very idea of translation and the forgetting that is foregrounded in the poem. Of course, this contrast is an essential part of the poem itself, which focuses on the contrast between the speaker's memories of love and the total forgetfulness of that love on the part of his beloved. For my purposes, what is most important is Petrarch's odd image of a ship full of forgetfulness, an oddness that is emphasized in Wyatt's version. The English word "charged" means full, as does the Italian "colma," but the English word also has the meaning of having been selected to perform a certain task, a meaning not available to Petrarch because of the different semantic range of the Italian word. Thus for Wyatt forgetfulness is not only the cargo of the metaphorical ship but also the duty of that ship. Wyatt usefully introduces the idea of forgetfulness—in a specifically romantic context—as active rather than as a merely passive slipping away. Now the sonnet, especially as a kind of poem that talks about love, has become one of the things we remember most about both Petrarch and Wyatt.

At more or less the same time Wyatt translated Petrarch's sonnet, the Earl of Surrey adapted the poem's opening image in his poem "O happy dames":

> In ship, freight with rememberance
> Of thoughtes and pleasures past,
> He sailes that hath in governance
> My life, while it wil last.[3]

For Petrarch and Wyatt, forgetting is both the problem, insofar as the beloved woman neither heeds nor remembers the speaker's love, and—although this possibility is not explicitly mentioned—the solution, because if the speaker could truly forget his love he could, perhaps, be happy again. For Surrey, memory is really only the problem, as it forces upon the speaker the contrast between the happy past and the painful present. For Surrey's speaker (and, to a lesser extent, for Petrarch's and Wyatt's speakers as well), forgetting would be preferable in some ways as it would mean the end of the painful memory most forcefully expressed by Dido. The poems I discuss in the rest of this essay demonstrate the impossibility of erotic forgetting and the extent to which forgetting and remembering are inevitably both active forces within a relationship and both structuring elements within a sonnet: the dialectic of remembering and forgetting and the contrast between pleasant and painful memories are highlighted by the kind of oscillation I have commented on so far.

We tend to think of forgetting as something that happens despite ourselves and to see it primarily as loss. Indeed, in terms of a now largely old-fashioned literary history, the Renaissance is a particularly intense kind of remembering, a protest against what Samuel Daniel (in reference to Stonehenge) called "The misery of darke forgetfulnesse."[4] But some critics have argued that forgetting is not only active but even desirable: to forget something may be to do something better. As Garrett Sullivan has argued, "Forgetting entails not merely the loss of memory traces, it also clears a space for and initiates a fresh act of judgement; it is the precondition of something *new* being done."[5] Sullivan also suggests that "forgetting is generative of certain subjective possibilities within its own time, of alternatives to claims made by memory."[6] But if forgetting is an activity in itself, the question of how we can actively forget naturally arises. In a recent discussion of Renaissance popular culture, Natália Pikli argues that "Writing … may even paradoxically be a means of forgetting."[7] Pikli's specific concern is very different from mine, but her formulation usefully presents writing not as an aid to memory, which is one of the commonest ways in which writing is presented, but rather as something that helps one to disrupt memory.

I want now to turn to Shakespeare and to look at how he balances memory and forgetting in an erotic context. He adapted Surrey's adaptation of Petrarch when he came to write the first two lines of Sonnet 30—"When to the sessions of sweet silent thought / I summon up remembrance of things past."[8] When C.K. Scott Moncrieff needed a title for his translation of one of the greatest works on erotic memory ever written he turned to this poem. Thus, the chain of literary associations (of cultural remembering) is carried into the twentieth century. Shakespeare's version of the phrase emphasizes the redundancy that is only latent in Surrey's "rememberance / Of thoughtes and pleasures past." In Surrey's poem, the word "past" heightens our sense of the contrast on which the poem, which is the contrast between happy memories and an unhappy present. In Shakespeare's sonnet, however, the word "past" can really only be said to stick out, as if he wished us to remember that we can only remember what is past and thus that to remember is always to look back. Furthermore, as is generally the case with a tautology, this looking back may be neither necessary nor—within the narrative of a sonnet sequence—advisable. Like so many, and probably too many, of Shakespeare's sonnets, Sonnet 30 presents us with a situation in which 12 lines or remembering more or less abject misery are followed by a final couplet that remembers a joy that may, perhaps, compensate for all that pain: "But if the while I think on thee, dear friend, / All losses are restored and sorrows end." The two roles of memory in erotic life, so sharply distinguished in the speeches of Aeneas and Dido with which I began, coexist (in strife rather than in peace) in many of Shakespeare's sonnets. Shakespeare's desire to emphasize this coexistence may perhaps explain the fact that so many of his sonnets are built on the pattern of 12 unhappy lines and two happy ones. Perhaps his sonnet sequence demonstrates the extent to which a certain obsessive and erotic remembering is built into the sonnet form.

In the remainder of this essay, I shall be concerned with Sonnet 35 and with "XXXV," the recent recension of this sonnet by the queer native poet Cedar Sigo. Sonnet 35 is one of a group of sonnets (much less numerous than the kind of sonnet described in the previous paragraph) in which the lover's memory of his bad behavior causes him to be unhappy. The hapless speaker begins by attempting to console his lover:

> No more be griev'd at that which thou hast done:
> Roses have thorns, and silver fountains mud,
> Clouds and eclipses stain both moon and sun,
> And loathsome canker lives in sweetest bud (1–4).

Memory is at work in two ways in this opening quatrain. It is not merely that the lover remembers his appalling behavior, but also that the speaker presents the lover's memory of how the natural world operates as something that should comfort him or, at least, as something that should let him put his sins in context: this memory (collective rather than individual) will help him to forget and thus will help both of them to greater happiness by putting their personal problems into a larger context in which imperfection is an inescapable fact of life rather than the result of one person's perversity. As so often with Shakespeare, the development of the metaphors—here, the things in the natural world to which the lover's faults can be compared—changes as the poem progresses, so I want to look at this quatrain in somewhat greater detail.

In these four lines, we move from things that may be unpleasant but are inescapably part of things we consider beautiful (the thorns of a rose and the mud of a stream) to things that are extrinsic to the things we consider beautiful (the other heavenly phenomena that interfere with our appreciation of heavenly bodies) to the idea that a beautiful object (the rose) contains its own downfall (the canker). I think this is an important progression: after all, while a rose is beautiful despite its thorns, and while all roses have thorns, a canker destroys the beauty of the rose and, crucially, not all roses have cankers. Like many other metaphors in Shakespeare (perhaps the best example are the metaphors in the parallel quatrains of Sonnet 73), these metaphors approach narrative status. From my point of view in this essay, we could say that the speaker's different comparisons for what his lover has done—first, your faults coexist with your beauty; second, your faults come from external sources; third, your faults are a sign of your particular bad nature and will destroy you—are prompted by his memories of the various bad things his lover has done and, one gathers, of the bad people with whom he has done these bad things.

After this first quatrain, the speaker turns in line 5 from his emphasis on the particular nature of his lover to a more general consideration ("All men make faults") that is immediately followed in the second half of the line by a return to concentrating on himself ("And even I in this"). The attempts in the first quatrain to console the lover ("No more be griev'd at that which thou hast done")—to make him forget—are now explained "Authorizing thy trespass with compare" (6). Rather than exonerate the lover, the rest of the sonnet focuses on the speaker's own faults. What is more, in the line "Such civil war is in my love and hate" (12), the speaker returns to the theme of the coexistence of happy and sad erotic memories. I wrote earlier that Sonnet 35 was one of a group of sonnets that dealt with the lover's unhappiness (rather than the speaker's), but while this is partially true, it is also the case that Sonnet 35 is, yet again, a sonnet concerned chiefly with the speaker's own unhappiness. To a great extent, the point that Shakespeare's sonnets make about erotic memory—or, at least, the point relevant to my discussion here—is that erotic memory is essentially the memory of oneself, of one's own thoughts, feelings, and experiences. The other person is really just a prop, whether a pleasant one (as in Aeneas' vision of a future in which the memory of Dido will be a pleasing companion) or an unpleasant one. To put it a slightly different way, the other person is a mechanism like a sonnet: something that enables one to remember things about oneself.

Sigo's version of Sonnet 35 is part of a recent book called *The Sonnets: Translating and Rewriting Shakespeare*, in which contemporary poets produce new versions of each of the sonnets. The subtitle presents us with two versions of the work of these poems: in translating Shakespeare, the contemporary poets concentrate on remembering him; in rewriting Shakespeare, they concentrate on forgetting him, although admittedly the remembering and the forgetting are impossible to separate. The project as a whole is obviously concerned with cultural memory and, by implication at least, with the extent to which our memory of Shakespeare's version of romantic love—or of what we perceive to be his version—influences our love affairs here and now. I think that the extent in question may be greatest for gay men, who until recently have had very few literary examples of same-sex love. Shakespeare's sonnets have a long and distinguished (if frequently mawkish) history of serving as foundational texts in gay men's sense of themselves as romantic beings. The subject, then, is not especially fresh, but I think Sigo's take on it is fresh, and I think it is worth our while to pay attention to the way he deals with forms of memory. Like Adrienne Rich in one of the best contemporary examples of the cultural memory of Renaissance poetry (I refer, of course, to her poem "A Valediction Forbidding Mourning"), Sigo could say that he wants "To do something very common, in my own way" (18).[9]

A very close comparison of the poems would provide an excellent example of what I believe is one of Sigo's basic points: that to remember something is inescapably to change it—we could even say that "XXXV" demonstrates that remembering may itself be a kind of active forgetting. For instance (and most obviously) the dignified statement with which the sonnet begins has turned into "Fuck off with your crippling guilt" (1). The difference is unmistakable, to put it mildly, but there is a sense in which what Sigo wrote is exactly what Shakespeare meant—except that in his sonnet, the guilt is primarily presented as being crippling for the speaker rather than for the man who has reason to be guilty. In Sigo's poem, this question is unresolved, although it seems likely that it is the other person who is crippled by guilt. In the next two lines of the poem, we see the natural objects of Shakespeare's first quatrain turn into things completely under human agency: "The earth has edges, boys get thrown in fountains / Dusk is painted over the moon, the sun grows black in your sleep" (2–3). The earth does not really have edges, for instance, and the moon and the sun here are no longer celestial bodies but rather seem merely to be part of a painted backdrop. As well, underlying the semantic change in the word "fountain" from Early Modern to Modern English (a change from fountains as a feature of the landscape to fountains as something humans construct), Sigo finds his equivalent for the mud that is always part of streams (English streams, anyway) in what seems more like a high-spirited and possibly even romantic prank.

In this part of Sigo's poem, I am especially interested in what he does with the image of the canker and the bud. As I pointed out above, one of the most significant things about that image in Shakespeare's poem is that not all flowers have cankers and that Shakespeare has thus moved from a statement that everyone might conceivably be at fault to a statement that suggests that perhaps only his lover is at fault. Sigo's equivalent for this flower is a lotus: "peel back your lotus to its bloody root" (4). The most iconic Indian flower substitutes for the most iconic European flower, the rose that appears so frequently throughout Shakespeare's sonnets. The patent substitution indexes some latent ones: the lotus is a symbol of purity in Indian religion, whereas here its bloody root corresponds to the thorns of the second line of the sonnet as a symbol of the coexistence of beauty and imperfection. The lotus is a symbol of purity because its beautiful blossom is rooted in mud: here we have a hidden equivalent to the mud of the second line of the sonnet. I would also argue that the suppressed rhyme of "bloody" (how Sigo describes the lotus's root) and "muddy" (how the lotus's root could accurately be described) points to a further substitution: Sigo replaces Shakespeare's rhymed and regular poetic form for what is chiefly free verse.

There is a further substitution in these lines, and it is one that points to another form of memory. Sigo follows the reference to the lotus with the statement that "No one is beyond reproach except the indians" (5). This might seem to continue the reference to the lotus—as I have pointed out, the iconic Indian flower—except that the lotus is Indian in the sense of being from India, whereas Sigo is Indian in the sense of being a North American native; I think that his decision to spell "indian" with a lower case letter is intended to stress the inaccuracy of this appellation. That North American natives are still often called Indians is an especially good example of the way our memories and the expectations we form based on them—in this case, on a world historical scale rather than on a romantic one—color and distort how we remember things. Also at play here, of course, is the speaker's memory of the history of North American natives, a history in which they were not at fault—and, to put it in the terms of this essay, a history in which white people tried to forget that the land was not really theirs at all. While the statement that the Indians cannot legitimately be reproached may make sense as a judgment on North American history and, in the present day, on the question of land claims and access to resources, it does not really work as a statement in an argument about romantic matters between lovers. The line conflates two very different arenas of right and wrong, just as the use of the term "Indian" to refer to North American natives conflates two very different parts of the world.

Up to this point, my discussion of Sigo's poem has looked chiefly at its content, which has seemed to be the most important link to Shakespeare's sonnet. I want now to turn to its form and to consider how in this respect as well Sigo remembers (and forgets) his poetic original. The sonnet form would seem to be something that Sigo does not remember—in fact, his writing the poem might illustrate Pikli's idea of writing as forgetting—except that he does. Most of the poem is written in free verse, but toward the end, as Sigo approaches the terminal lines permitted by the sonnet, the sonnet form returns. Lines 13 and 14 of Sigo's poem can be read as the rhyming couplet that Surrey made an essential part of the English sonnet (that this sonnet is often called the "Shakespearean" sonnet is a good example of the importance of forgetting to literary history): "You're so fine I still play dumb / A zombie dust inside your lungs." The lines do not quite rhyme and they do not quite scan, but they are obviously closer to rhyming (as a couplet) and to scanning (they are trochaic tetrameter, and the first of the two lines is acephalous). We could say that the "zombie dust" is the dust of ages that is still, somehow, living rather than merely dust and that produces a rhyming couplet at the end of a poem that had up to this point refused to become a sonnet—that is, the zombie dust is the particular kind of survival after death that we can see in the persistence of poetic form.

But in fact these lines are not quite at the end of the poem. Sigo concludes the poem with a fifteenth line, as if to underline his resistance to the zombie form of the sonnet. Interestingly, however, this extra line is, unlike all the other lines of "XXXV," regular iambic pentameter: "Draw me in deeper with deceit and smoke." In fact, not only is this a completely normal line of English poetry—not just for its iambic pentameter but also for the trochaic substitution in the first foot—but it also has alliteration and assonance. Sigo's poem ends in a veritable orgy of poetic regularity. While the existence of a fifteenth line forgets the sonnet form, the regular scansion of the lines remembers this form. Except, of course, that it doesn't. Sigo adds another statement to his pentameter line and thus turns the ten syllables of the standard unit of English poetry into a line with as many syllables as a sonnet has lines: "let's go again." Despite all the conflict of the poem, it ends with an invitation to sex that is also an appeal to memory. Ultimately, Sigo's poem shows that Aeneas' happy memories and Dido's unhappy memories are not necessarily the paradigm for love affairs: a love affair may combine both remembering and forgetting as well as happiness and unhappiness.

While we might have wondered in the course of Sigo's poem whether this relationship could be saved, the sexy ending—the sexiest ending of any poem ever, I think—reveals that erotic memories triumph over more prudential considerations, including, perhaps, the desire to forget, as well as even the desire to remember accurately. Memory may apparently be painful, as it has led to the "crippling guilt" of the first line, but it's not just painful, or, at least, its painfulness is not the only thing about it. The appeal to go again is an invitation to continue the love affair, and in the context of this essay we can understand this as a suggestion that the following with which Dido threatens Aeneas may be erotic rather than punitive (or, at least, rather than only punitive). We can also take it as an appeal to continue writing poems and, in particular, to continue writing sonnets, a kind of poem that typically focuses on erotic memory. The speaker of Sigo's poem is willing to forget the bad things that have happened and begin again; the poem will also begin again. Earlier, the speaker had said "I talk myself out of the song" (10), but the ending of the poem suggests that this is not possible. The literary memory that characterizes "XXXV" as a version of a much older poem that itself remembers even older poems prevents either the love affair or the poem from ending. We could perhaps even say that for a poet, and for many readers, the primary erotic memory is the sonnet form itself.

Notes

1. Virgil, *Aeneid* in *Opera*, ed. R.A.B. Mynors (Oxford: Clarendon, 1969), IV.335–6. Translations are my own.
2. Ibid IV.384–6.
3. Henry Howard, Earl of Surrey, "O happy dames," in *Poems*, ed. Emrys Jones (Oxford: Clarendon, 1964), 8–11.
4. Samuel Daniel, "Musophilus," in *Poems and a Defence of Ryme*, ed. Arthur Colby Sprague (Cambridge, MA: Harvard University Press, 1930), 352.
5. Sullivan, *Memory and Forgetting in English Renaissance Drama*, 47.
6. Ibid, 136.
7. Natália Pikli, "The Prince and the Hobby-Horse: Shakespeare and the Ambivalence of Early Modern Popular Culture," *Journal of Early Modern Studies* 2 (2013): 122.
8. All quotations from Shakespeare are from the *Riverside Shakespeare*.
9. Adrienne Rich, "A Valediction Forbidding Mourning," in *Poems: Selected and New, 1950–1974* (New York: W.W. Norton, 1975), 18.

4 "The stage is down, and Philomela's choir is hushed from pricksong"
Revising and (Re)membering in Middleton's *The Ghost of Lucrece*

Dee Anna Phares

Helen of Troy's famous countenance may have been "the face that launched a thousand ships / And burnt the topless towers of Ilium,"[1] but it was Lucrece's violated body that served as the inspiration for a series of important dramatic and poetic works in the late sixteenth and early seventeenth centuries. These two women stood as opposing poles in early modern England: one, a symbol of duplicity and sensuality, and the other, an icon of patriotism and purity because "The rape of Helen led to the fall of Troy; the rape of Lucrece leads to the rise of the Roman republic."[2] As Coppélia Kahn suggests, "The story of Lucrece ... is one of the founding myths of patriarchy."[3] It not only depicts a wife so committed to her husband, and to a system that ties female honor to male reputation, that she embraces suicide to maintain that ideology, it also demonstrates how the memory of rape and death are effective tools for seizing and maintaining power.

Many versions of the tale follow the lead of the classical sources—Book 2 of Ovid's *Fasti* and Livy's *History*—by de-emphasizing Lucrece/Lucretia and her rape in order to concentrate on how Lucius Junius Brutus exploited the event to end the tyranny of the Tarquins. In essence, these texts seek to enshrine a narrative focused on male agency and justice, instead of one based on female vulnerability and eroticism. Most, in fact, rapidly move through the story: Collantinus (Collatine) proudly proclaims, and then proves, his wife's virtues by taking the king's son, Sextus Tarquinius (Tarquin), and other lords to witness Lucrece's chaste industriousness—she spends her evening weaving; Tarquin later returns to Collantinus' home and abuses his hospitality and his wife; Lucrece discloses the rape to her husband and father, Lucretius, and demands they swear a vow to avenge her; she kills herself and then Brutus uses her body and her story to foment a popular uprising to overthrow the Tarquin monarchs, which ultimately leads to Roman republicanism. The rape is only glanced at as it is presented as little more than a sign of Tarquin corruption and the occasion for insurrection. But there can be no communal memory of the Roman republic without the rape, and so even an evasion of that central fact only reinforces its inherent eroticism. The most celebrated and well-known version of the story is keenly focused on the body of the ravaged matron—memorializing her beauty as much as her chastity and shifting the discourse about her place in the popular imagination.

Shakespeare's 1594 narrative poem *Lucrece*—later known as *The Rape of Lucrece*—offers nearly 2000 lines of agonizingly detailed description of the thoughts, feelings, and actions of both violator and victim before and after the rape. As Karen Bamford reminds us, "the poem is distinguished from previous treatments of the theme not only by its length but also by its eroticism."[4] Much of the erotic charge grows from the work's presentation of Lucrece as both pornographic and mnemonic object. As Michael Hall points out, the rapist, Tarquin—as well as the narrative itself—is so fixated on Lucrece's "physical attractiveness that even her virtue is physicalized and eroticized."[5] Throughout the poem, Tarquin's gaze and his poetic blazon envisions an anatomized woman made of sexualized parts, while at the same time constructing Lucrece as a disembodied ideal—a "virtuous monument"[6] who is more "tomb effigy than a living woman."[7] Even before the actual rape, Lucrece is presented as both eroticized living victim and sacralized lifeless memorial to stolen virtue.[8] At the end of the poem, Lucrece occupies an even more vexed rhetorical and historical space: her beauty and chastity become fetishized so that her defiled/revered body commemorates the rape itself. Shakespeare's poem, then, operates as *monumentum*—a work of art that "stimulates remembrance of a person or event"[9]—which means that rape and Lucrece become synonymous in the collective memory.

In the preface to the 1937 edition of Thomas Middleton's rarely read and seldom-praised poem, *The Ghost of Lucrece* (1600), editor Joseph Quincy Adams suggests that "its merits as verse" are less important than "its significance for the study of two great Elizabethan men of letters," referring to Middleton's contribution as a "contemporary continuation of Shakespeare's popular *Lucrece*."[10] Quincy's words mark Middleton's text as little more than an inferior sequel to Shakespeare's poetic masterpiece. While few would argue that *The Ghost of Lucrece* is as aesthetically pleasing and nuanced as *The Rape of Lucrece*, it is not entirely fair to dismiss the former as simply a "continuation" of the martyred matron's story. It also complicates Shakespeare's presentation of the heroine and her attacker, as well as the reader who consumes her story. Quincy's emphasis on "two great Elizabethan men" ignores *The Ghost of Lucrece's* power to not only remember/re-member the rape but to overwrite and override the rapist's sensualized narrative that figures so prominently in Shakespeare's poem.

In *The Ghost of Lucrece*, Shakespeare's heroine is exhumed and her spirit called back by a conjuring poet intent on unsealing Lucrece's "virtuous monument" and forcing her not simply to remember, but to relive and to re-articulate the rape. However, the ghost of Lucrece is not as malleable as Shakespeare's wifely paragon; the ghost attempts to take control of her narrative—figuring Tarquin, the poet, and the male readers as greedy nurslings who are nourished by her infamy. Constructing herself as a wrathful mother-figure, this shade of Lucrece endeavors to de-eroticize the collective memory of her violation through infantilization of her rapist and castigation of those who fetishize her chastity.

The ghost's efforts to evoke maternal imagery as a means of neutralizing the libidinousness of her story actually intensify the eroticism by focusing attention on the maternal body and the sensuality of the mother-child relationship. Despite her attempts to revise the way that both Tarquin and readers remember her, Middleton's ghost of Lucrece operates as an object for male scopophilic enjoyment—just as Shakespeare's Lucrece does. The ghost's voluble misery in Middleton's version, however, places even greater emphasis on the victim's recollection and communication of corporeal and psychical pain, providing the conjuring-poet—and the male audience—with a measure of audio-erotic pleasure that ensures that the memory of Lucrece and her rape will always be eroticized and always be reiterated.

The opening lines of *Ghost* are about "making knowledge visible" or accessing the memory of Lucrece and her story through the presentation of her form on a metaphorical stage.[11]

> ... Awake, Rhamnusia!
> Call upon the ghost of goréd Lucretia.
> Thrice hath the trumpet of my pen's round stage
> Sounded a '*Surge!*' to her bloody age.[12]

Middleton's poet-narrator seems dedicated to exposing Lucrece's "goréd"[13] body and her shame in a manner similar to that employed in *The Rape of Lucrece*. In Shakespeare's poem, the narrator rhetorically undresses and anatomizes the would-be victim, exposing her to the reading audience by utilizing Tarquin's vision of Lucrece:

> Her breasts like ivory globes circled with blue,
> A pair of maiden worlds unconquèred.[14]

The male speaker also declares that

> What [Tarquin] beheld, on that he firmly doted,
> And in his will his willful eye he tired.
> With more than admiration he admired
> Her azure veins, her alabaster skin,
> Her coral lips, her snow-white dimpled chin.[15]

Noting the use of the blazon-like description of the sleeping matron in Shakespeare's poem, Lee A. Ritscher points out that "Lucrece is something-to-be-seen," a thing to be visually consumed before she is sexually consumed.[16] By utilizing Tarquin's painterly eye, Shakespeare's text presents an image of "an object which is capable of being raped."[17] Lucrece is an eroticized body on which voyeurism and sexual violence are enacted, and she is a name that invokes the memory of both. Ironically, the ghost of Lucrece—an incorporeal shade of the Roman matron—is *embodied* and potentially granted subjectivity through what Donald Jellerson refers to as a "kind of reverse blazon [in which] Lucrece is pieced back together by the poet's Orphic breath."[18] She is literally re-membered through recollection of her story. By shifting from the language of *ekphrasis* (Shakespeare) to metaphors of drama (Middleton), Lucrece is given an opportunity to move from object to actor as her ghost is staged for both spectator and audience. Yet, this presentation is not empowering. Just as in *The Rape of Lucrece*, the audience "participate[s] in the voyeuristic exercise whereby the body is ... dehumanized"[19] through reading, imagining, and remembering. In *The Ghost of Lucrece*, however, that voyeurism and recollection stem not from the deployment of the "Petrarchan blazon," but from the exhibition of Lucrece as performer whose body and text are controlled by a poet/playwright, an audience, and even a lead actress who cannot entirely erase the lingering memory of Shakespeare's eroticized heroine.

The memory of Shakespeare's Lucrece looms large in the opening moments of *The Ghost of Lucrece* as Middleton's poet uses "the trumpet of [his] pen's round stage"[20] to encourage the ghost to remember and reenact the misfortunes presented in Shakespeare's narrative poem:

> Sad spirits, soft hearts, sick thoughts, souls sod in tears,
> Well-humoured eyes, quick ears, tear-wounded faces,
> Enrollèd vestals, Dian's hemispheres,
> Rape-slaughtered Lucreces, all martyred graces,
> Be ye the audience, take your tragic places.
> Here shall be played the miseries that immures
> Pure diamond hearts in crystal covertures. (ll. 37–43)

The references to "eyes," "ears," and "audience," as well as to the notion of playing, highlight the theatricality of the scene that is to follow—resembling the Prologues of *Romeo and Juliet*, *Henry V*, and *Troilus and Cressida* more than *The Rape of Lucrece* or other narrative poems. But whereas the audiences at the Globe or the Rose were comprised of a broad cross-section of the English population, Middleton's imagined audience consists of "Rape-slaughtered Lucreces"—women violated and marked by violence, just as Lucrece has been. In reality, of course, the primary readers of the poem would have actually been male.[21] The poet's call for the victims to "take [their] tragic places" reinforces the idea that women are inextricably linked to the memory of their tragedies; it is their positioning as tragic victims that defines them and makes their stories worthy of staging. Yet, at the same time, these females are denied individuality and personal remembrance of their particular traumas: only Lucrece's experience is staged; only it *matters*.

The disinterred spirit of a sexualized woman, pondering her fallen state, was not uncommon in Middleton's time. The copious complaint poems of the late sixteenth and early seventeenth centuries—which featured ghosts

"The stage is down, and Philomela's choir is hushed from pricksong" 55

who briefly return to lament and repent for their sins—focused on women whose lives and afterlives married them to unchastity and ignominy: women like Elstred, Rosemond, and Jane Shore.[22] Lucrece, as a paragon of chastity, problematizes *Ghost's* status as a complaint poem, because as Laura Bromley points out, "women in complaint poems usually plead with a poet to help them find recognition and forgiveness."[23] The audience of "Rape-slaughtered Lucreces" are voiceless and cannot ask for forgiveness if they even wish to; their recognition only comes from the staging of *the* ghost of Lucrece—and her spirit longs not for pity but for vengeance. Bromley views the text as more of a satire than a complaint and sees Middleton—and by extension, the narrator/poet—utilizing Lucrece to expose the immorality and corruption of Elizabethan society, a strategy common in the verse satires of the 1590s.[24] The theatrical language also suggests a need to go beyond the limitations of works such as John Marston's *The Scourge of Villanie* (1598)—which featured two-dimensional and insensitive misanthropes—to the kinds of more well-formed satirist/revengers found in Jacobean drama: Malevole in Marston's *The Malcontent* (1603) and Vindice in Middleton's *The Revenger's Tragedy* (1607).[25] *Ghost's* poet/narrator, then, exploits the conventions and language of contemporary theater as well as the collective memory of a simultaneously erotic and sympathetic heroine to highlight not only Tarquin's vice but England's vice as well. As in the verse satires, the lines between purity and prurience are incredibly thin—those who purportedly expose iniquity too often proliferate it.

This construction of narrative poem as stage tragedy—and Lucrece's ghost as player—reinforces vice by making spirit flesh and memory speech. In fact, the Prologue also presents the *dramatis personae* of the "play" by calling forth,

> Black spirits, hard hearts, thick thoughts, souls boiled in lust,
> Dry fiery eyes, dull ears, high bloody looks
> Made of hot earth, moulded in fire and dust,
> Desire's true graduates read in Tarquin's books,
> Be ye our stage's actors. Play the cooks:
> Carve out the daintiest morsel—that's your part—
> With lust-keen falchion, even in Lucrece's heart.[26]

In this passage, Tarquin is portrayed as playwright, as master thespian, and as playscript from which the "stage's actors" must takes their cues. As Garret A. Sullivan points out, in seventeenth-century England, "remembering is about praxis ... it is an action taken in response to a call to behave in a certain (more or less precisely designed) fashion."[27] At this moment in *Ghost*, the "Black spirits" are asked not only to "read in Tarquin's books," or learn from his example, but also to act as he acts: so that each of these "true graduates" becomes a Tarquin who recalls raping a Lucrece. Here, the poet encourages the performers to eviscerate the subject of the play—Lucrece—inviting them and, by extension, us to consume her as a theatrical and sexual object that we have exhumed from her monument. Furthermore, the narrator's earlier construction of himself as the playwright, whose "pen's round stage" demands the ghost's entrance, suggests that he too is a Tarquin who wants to relive the rape, not only by *hearing* and *seeing* Lucrece again, but by watching and listening to the reactions of the "Rape-slaughtered Lucreces" in attendance.

This staging of the violation at the heart of the narrative is, on one level, simply a more elaborate form of the scopophilia than that present in Shakespeare's poem; the stage direction to "Play the cooks" with Lucrece's heart suggests a sadistic, even pathological, kind of stage management of a ghastly scene. But the conjuring poet-prompter is not wholly in control of what is performed. Jellerson points out that "Middleton's Lucrece, back from the dead, knows precisely how her reputation has been read,"[28] and so seeks to revise that text, but as Lina Bolzoni reminds, in the early modern period, "memory play[ed] an essential role ... in the production of something new."[29] In other words, in order to re-envision the past, one must first excavate the memory. However, new narratives that grow from old memories are palimpsests, and traces of the original text bleed through, especially in *Ghost*, with its two competing memories of the Roman matron: one individual/private and one communal/public. The pervasiveness and eroticism of the popular memory of Lucrece complicates the ghost's ability to overwrite how she has been memorialized. To produce "something new," the ghost of Lucrece must craft a revised version of her tragedy that is more compelling than Livy's or Shakespeare's. She takes the stage, forcing the audience to watch and listen: to see the assault as more than a catalyst for political change, a competition between men, or the natural result of Tarquin following a "hot heart,"[30] and to ensure that we observe not Lucrece's eroticized body, but see "Lucrece with a trine of eyes, / Quenching the fire of lust with tears and blood" through her construction as a powerful and correcting mother figure.[31]

The invocation of maternity in *Ghost* is far from accidental and demonstrates how this text and "Shakespeare's earlier poem tell the same story in very different ways."[32] *The Rape of Lucrece* offers provocative suggestions that Tarquin's assault has left Lucrece both dishonored and pregnant, which have further eroticized communal recollections of the martyred matron. After the rape, an inconsolable Lucrece questions why it is that "cuckoos hatch in sparrows' nests"[33]—obliquely referring to cuckoldry (cuckoo) and the potential consequences of an illicit union: a husband unwittingly rearing another man's child.[34] Lucrece refuses to allow Collatine to bear the double-shame associated with adultery and bastardy, even if both were the result of violent coercion. She declares:

> 'Well, well, dear Collatine, thou shalt not know
> The stainèd taste of violated troth,
> I will not wrong thy true affection so,

> To flatter thee with an infringèd oath.
> This bastard graff shall never come to growth:
> He shall not boast who did thy stock pollute,
> That thou art doting father of his fruit.[35]

The allusions to "graff," "stock," and "fruit" invoke the images of propagation and controlling issue. In patriarchal cultures, whether in ancient Rome or early modern England, roots matter—and grafting tainted stock can ultimately infect and destroy family trees by giving legitimacy, title, and property to a "bastard graff." Deleuze and Guattari note how the notion of the tree is crucial to understanding Western history, ideology, and ontology, declaring, "there is always something genealogical about a tree," which is concerned primarily with "tracing and reproduction."[36] Building upon Deleuze and Guattari, Miranda Wilson explains:

> With the 'family tree,' each generation emerges as an outgrowth of preceding generations, even as it forms a base for those to come. In this formulation, Collatine, not Lucrece, serves as the stock. As a wife, Lucrece should occupy the position of a shoot, slip, twig, or scion—that section of stem cut off from another plant and inserted into a cut in the stock plant during grafting. This common representation of marriage marks Lucrece as dependent upon her husband, enfolded and invigorated by him, just as the grafted slip is contained and nurtured within the cleft of the stock.[37]

Furthermore, Lucrece's use of the adjective, "This," to describe the "bastard graff" indicates that she believes herself to be pregnant and that she must take action to ensure that a child "shall never come to growth." In her mind, suicide is the only course of action that will allow Lucrece, Collatine, and her father, Lucretius, to maintain their dignity, their genealogical purity, and their reputation[38]—or as Wilson puts it, "Lucrece imagines that by uprooting herself, she can save Collatine from the unprofitable and shameful position of the cheated gardener."[39] Yet, it is not only Collatine's shame that concerns Shakespeare's Lucrece. Given that early modern English medical and legal discourse suggested that conception was only possible if there was mutual enjoyment of the sex act, pregnancy was believed to be an unmistakable sign of consent.[40] Jocelyn Catty points out that while Lucrece does maintain that she never gave her consent to Tarquin, her body may have betrayed her. Shakespeare's Lucrece declares,

> Though my gross blood be stained with this abuse,
> Immaculate and spotless is my mind:
> That was not forced, that never was inclined
> To accessary yieldings, but still pure
> Doth in her poisoned closet yet endure.[41]

Catty draws attention to Lucrece's "ambiguous allusion to her body's 'accessory yieldings' [which] might, like the 'yielding' of the portals, indicate merely the (involuntary) opening up of the body, but it might alternatively suggest sexual arousal during the rape: potentially implicating her further."[42] I would argue that this possibility of unintentional "yieldings" is how Lucrece herself accounts for her pregnancy even though her mind is "Immaculate and spotless." It also explains why Lucrece "force not argument a straw, / Since that my case is past the help of law."[43]

Catty reminds that "*The Lawes Resolvtions* records that if a woman conceives, 'there is no rape; for none can conceiue without consent.' Shakespeare's *Lucrece* is to suggest the possibility that a genuinely resisting woman may be betrayed by her body's responses."[44] In Renaissance renderings of Lucrece, she is either chaste or she is pregnant, but not both—and the only way for Shakespeare's Lucrece to cut through the Gordian knot of consent is to stop her body before her body is (mis)read by others. However, the very fact of the allusions to that pregnant body invites readers to view her suicide not only as an act of valor and wifely virtue, but potentially as an act of evasion and prevarication.[45]

In *The Ghost of Lucrece*, the violated matron endeavors to re-write Shakespeare by turning any mention of fertility and pregnancy to a charge against Tarquin, not herself. Lucrece's ghost employs the language of child-bearing and nurturance to divorce herself from literal pregnancy and its associations with vitality and abundance. Because she lacks a physical body, and therefore the ability to bring life into the world, the shade can only bring forth destruction. Right after her "entrance," Lucrece's ghost declares that "Hecatë's triform / Weans my soul, sucking at revenge's dugs, / To feed upon the air."[46] In a perverse inversion of traditional maternity, Lucrece is fed on the poisonous milk of vengeance so that she can then force-feed Tarquin, the poet, and us her version of the tale. Pointedly calling out the narrator who took her "from the virgin paradise of death / [and] Conjures my ghost with poetizing breath," Lucrece rails against the man who "Blew [her] dissevered limbs into this form."[47] The poet's desire to not simply memorialize her, but to also re-member her, rips Lucrece from paradise as his "poetizing breath" reignites the "candle of [her] shame."[48] But, instead of simply playing the part of the martyred matron, and bemoaning "This helpless smoke of words [that] doth me no right" as Shakespeare's heroine does,[49] Middleton's Lucrece burns her audience with a "venereal flame."[50]

The ghost of Lucrece collapses the fire of sexual consummation, sin, hell, and pregnancy into one as she imagines the metaphorical progeny of "fiery blood and luxury."[51] Lucrece denies a literal bodily conception, instead suggesting that,

>Shame was the tinder, and the flint desire
>That struck in Tarquin's bosom and begot
>A child of fire, a firebrand, and hot

"The stage is down, and Philomela's choir is hushed from pricksong" 59

    That it consumed my chastity to dust,
    And on my heart painted the mouth of lust.[52]

In this passage, it is Tarquin, not Lucrece, who is impregnated. But it is Lucrece who is forced to suckle this "child of fire" with her heart's blood, an idea further reinforced by the succeeding stanza:

    Was I the cradle, O my chastity,
    To rock and lull this bastard firebrand,
    Nursed with my blood, weaned with my tragedy,
    Fed at my knife's sharp point upon my hand,
    Born and reborn where'er my spirits stand?[53]

While these passages obviously allude to the rape itself—and to the suicide that follows it—the interrogatory nature of the lines 94–98 suggests that Lucrece is actually rejecting the charge that the allure of her chastity was "the cradle" of "this bastard firebrand" or that she assented to the attack. In fact, Lucrece's announcement, "now is my tide of blood," evokes not only her fatal self-wounding, but also calls to mind menstruation—further reinforcing the notion that she is not literally pregnant. Instead, she is filled with the memory of her violation. Lucrece invites Tarquin and the poet, who are "spirit[s] of fire, bred in a womb of blood," to "quaff thine own fill" of her shame.[54]

In the phantom's speeches, milk is transformed into blood and tears, so that her breasts function neither as "ivory globes" to be circumnavigated and conquered[55] nor as a "virtuous monument" that feels no pain. Her command that Tarquin "suck till thy veins run over / And such a teat which scarce thy mouth can cover,"[56] reminds him and the audience that her body, opened by brutal penetration by phallus, knife, and narrative exploration is not easily contained.

By constructing herself as wraith-like mother, the ghost of Lucrece seeks a rhetorical and psychological advantage over the memory of the rape. She labors to disempower Tarquin, the poet, and the poem's readers by infantilizing them and negating the erotic vigor of womb and breast by replacing flesh with fire and milk with blood. She is at once trying to return the male audience (including Tarquin and the narrator) to a state of sexual innocence while also trying to instill in them a fear of their inherent vulnerability in the hands of a punishing mother. This strategy, however, is fundamentally flawed and actually helps reinforce her position as erotic mnemonic object.

To the reader, the maternalized ghost of Lucrece cannot help but invoke images of other classical examples of murderous mothers—especially Medea and Clytemnestra. But as Luce Irigaray points out, the *Oresteia's* Clytemnestra is not only a mother and revenger, she is also a "passionate lover."[57] Irigaray outlines the ways in which patriarchal cultures seek to "repress the desire of / for the mother"[58]—but such repression does not actually discourage the erotic possibilities of the maternal body or the erotic possibilities of a punishing mother; it also fails to preclude the notion of an eroticized child. Building on and problematizing the work of Irigaray, Kyoko Taniguchi suggests that, "To talk about the eroticism of that which is maternal, then, is to see the mother both as the object of erotic fantasy and the subject who is doing the fantasizing in a bidirectional field. ... constantly oscillating at multiple levels."[59] In this schema, both mother and child possess not only erotic desire but also the potential for aggression, even violence toward one another.[60] The ghost's power over a child-like Tarquin only works if he actually is innocent and incapable of enacting his own violence. As Kathryn Bond Stockton points out, "It is a mistake to take innocence straight. To believe the benign publicity [about childhood], as it were," because children are neither asexual nor inherently immune from enjoying the suffering of others.[61] Tarquin, the poet, and the poem's readers are not children, and even if they were, they cannot be denied a measure of erotic power.

The ghost's revisions to the popular memory of Lucrece actually intensify the erotics of her story by staging the rape and its consequences—birth and nursing—elements that are absent from Shakespeare's poem. The theatrical metaphors and the ghost's potent descriptions of herself as ravaged and leaky mother effectively materialize her while reducing her to a series of members (womb, breast, heart) and fluids (milk, blood, bile) with "each part of her body ... cathected and decathected" by a predominantly male audience.[62] In essence, then, her edited text ends up de-emphasizing her chastity and fixing greater attention to her raped body.

Individual memory is private, singular, and therefore finite; communal memory, because of its public nature, on the other hand, has the capacity to proliferate and endure. In this calculus, personal remembrance is always subsumed by shared remembrance that continues beyond the lifespan of any single person who is past knowing or caring how he or she is thought of. Mercedes Moroto Camino notes that "stories [of famous females] and their characters are 'images' of masculine history," but Shakespeare's Lucrece is "unaware that memory, or the memory that has served history, has rendered woman's words and deeds obsolete and given them a masculine 'image' instead."[63] Middleton's ghost of Lucrece, however, does understand how she has been imagined in masculine history and desires the opportunity to re-imagine herself, using a "pen of blood" to emend the record.[64]

Near the end of Middleton's narrative, the wronged wraith demonstrates her awareness that she and her image have been constructed and manipulated by men—specifically Tarquin and the poet. She declares,

> Lo, under that base type of Tarquin's name
> I cipher figures of iniquity.
> He writes himself the shamer, I the shame,
> The actor he, and I the tragedy.

> The stage am I, and he the history,
> The subject I, and he the ravisher.
> He, murd'ring me, made me my murderer.[65]

The ghost of Lucrece reveals herself as a kind of empty space that is filled by the male author and actor—both female bodies and the stage are mnemonic *loci* to be accessed by men. As Camino suggests, "Lucrece's text bears Tarquin's impresa."[66] While in the popular memory she has always been acted upon—"The stage am I"—ghostly Lucrece attempts to conjure up her generative power to create a new story for herself with a pen "Thrice steeped and dipped in Phlegethontic flood," proclaiming "Then shall I stamp the figure of the night / On Tarquin's brow Tarquin's brow."[67] Lucrece now wants Tarquin to wear *her* impresa, to hear her memory of the rape and its aftermath—and then she wants to rest beneath a new monument whose epitaph is inscribed by her.

The remainder of Lucrece's narrative focuses on separating the victim from the rapist's supposed motivations—the attractions of her beauty and chastity—until at last the ghost announces,

> Bleed no more lines, my heart. This knife, my pen,
> This blood, my ink, hath writ enough to lust.
> Tarquin, to thee, though very devil of men,
> I send these lines. Though art my fiend of trust.
> To thee, I dedicate my tomb of dust.
> To thee I consecrate this little-most
> Writ by the bloody fingers of my ghost.[68]

In essence, Lucrece is not only reinterring her body, she is also reconstructing her funeral effigy and her epitaph to depict herself as actor and playwright—as productive body, not empty monument inscribed with the words of Tarquin, Collatine, Brutus, or even Shakespeare and Middleton. Her closing remarks, that "The stage is down, and Philomela's choir / Is hushed from pricksong," allude to her own power to transform her personal memory of rape to a history of her feeling and experiences, which should be sung to a wide audience.[69] As the *OED* notes, "pricksong" refers to a "melody to be performed in counterpoint" or "Music sung from notes written or pricked, as opposed to music sung from memory or by ear; written or printed vocal music." The blood that flows from Lucrece's breast becomes the ink with which she "pricks" her story, moving from recollection to a permanent record of the atrocities that she and the women in Philomela's choir have had to endure. She "writes [herself] the shamer" of Tarquin, Tereus, the poet, and all the other villains who silenced their victims through violence and objectification by making her individual memory available to the wider community.

However, while Lucrece yearns to write her own epitaph and then seal her monument once and for all—to cease "the stream of tragic blood and fire"—the poet who initially conjured the Roman matron's spirit has the final say, as once she is re-interred, Lucrece no longer has the power to speak.[70] The epilogue begins by eulogizing a Lucrece who is presented as a cunning lawyer pleading her case "at the bar of hell" and using "a tongue of tears and bloods," but focus in the next stanza shifts.[71] The narrator abandons the image of Lucrece that the ghost constructed in her own narrative—of rebuking maternal power and creativity—and instead embraces the image crafted by Tarquin: a Lucrece whose beauty and chastity arouse the desire for conquest. The conjuring poet not only declares that Lucrece "was as chaste as fair, as fair as chaste,"[72] he re-institutes the Petrarchan blazon of Shakespeare's poem:

> Her hair, which win Arachne's finest loom
> Was kissed with silver shuttles, O that hair
> Which made Collatium shine in spite of Rome,
> Combing her tresses like Jove's golden heir—[73]
> Her eyes, the curious fabric of her world,
> Apollo's touchstones where he tried his beams. ...[74]
> Her tongue, which Orpheus tuned before he died. ...[75]
> Her breath, which had a violet perfume
> Tempered with rose all verdure, O her breath. ...[76]
> Her teats, twixt whom an alabaster bridge
> Parts each from other, like two crystal bowls
> Standing aloof upon the body's ridge. ...[77]

As Patricia Parker notes, the tendency to inventory the female body is related to the desire to control the female body.[78] And yet, at the close of this poem it seems to be doing more—it is erasing the memory of the ghost's speech. It reverses and negates Lucrece's revisions, except for her own inadvertent enhancement of the erotic. The final couplet even obliterates Lucrece's name, so that again she is nothing but "stage" and "subject" to a more powerful Tarquin/poet: "First Tarquin-life clad her death's array. / Now Tarquin-death hath stol'n her life away."[79] Lucrece's efforts to de-eroticize collective memory are thwarted by the narrating poet who chooses to immortalize the sensualized body "now stained by death, before by ravishments."[80]

Mary Carruthers notes that memory is not simply a matter of "individual authoring or composing," but also a "matter of authorizing, which is a social and communal activity"[81]—in other words, personal memory is not necessarily communal memory. The poet/narrator in Middleton's text reasserts communal memory over individual memory, returning to the *monumentum* of Livy, Ovid, and Shakespeare—but with greater emphasis on the suffering maternal body. In the end, Lucrece loses all agency, because while *The Ghost of Lucrece* employs the trope of the theater with its flesh-and-blood actors, the medium of poetry cedes all power to the poet who pricks/prints the song of his choosing—and he wishes to dis-member rather than re-member the woman behind the rape and beneath the "tomb of dust."

"The stage is down, and Philomela's choir is hushed from pricksong" 63

Notes

1. Christopher Marlowe, *Doctor Faustus: The A-Text*, in *Doctor Faustus and Other Plays*, ed. David Bevington and Eric Rasmussen (Oxford: Oxford University Press, 1995), 5.1.90–91.
2. William Shakespeare, *The Rape of Lucrece*, in *The Sonnets and Other Poems*, ed. Jonathan Bate and Eric Rasmussen (New York: Modern Library, 2009), xiii. All quotations from Shakespeare's *Lucrece* are from this edition unless otherwise stated.
3. Coppélia Kahn, "*Lucrece*: The Sexual Politics of Subjectivity," in *Rape and Representation*, ed. Lynn A. Higgins and Brenda R. Silver (New York: Columbia University Press, 1991), 141.
4. Karen Bamford, *Sexual Violence on the Jacobean Stage* (New York: St. Martin's Press, 2000), 65–66.
5. Michael Hall, "Lewd but Familiar Eyes: The Narrative Tradition of Rape and Shakespeare's *The Rape of Lucrece*," in *Women, Violence, and the English Renaissance Stage: Essays Honoring Paul Jorgensen*, ed. Linda Woodbridge and Sharon Beehler (Tempe, AZ: Arizona Center for Medieval and Renaissance Studies, 2003), 66.
6. Shakespeare, *The Rape of Lucrece*, l. 391.
7. Joyce Green MacDonald, "Speech, Silence, and History in *The Rape of Lucrece*," *Shakespeare Studies* 22 (1994): 79.
8. For a discussion of Early Modern funeral effigies and epitaphs, see Scott L. Newstock, *Quoting Death* (New York: Palgrave, 2009); Nigel Llewellyn, *The Art of Death: Visual Culture in English Death Ritual c. 1500-c.1800* (London: Reaktion Books, 1991); Peter Marshall, *Beliefs and the Dead in Reformation England* (Oxford: Oxford University Press, 2002); and Peter Sherlock, *Monuments and Memory in Early Modern England* (Aldershot: Ashgate, 2008). John Weever's *Antient Funeral Monuments* (London: W. Tooke, 1631), offers a fascinating contemporary discussion of practices related to entombment and their connection to memory.
9. Andrew Butterfield, "Monument and Memory in Early Renaissance Florence," in *Art, Memory, and Family in Renaissance Florence*, ed. Giovanni Ciappelli and Patricia Lee Rubin (Cambridge: Cambridge University Press, 2000), 135.
10. Joseph Quincy Adams, ed., *The Ghost of Lucrece*, by Thomas Middleton (New York: Charles Scribner's Sons, 1937), vii. See Sarah Carter, *Ovidian Myth and Sexual Deviance in Early Modern English Literature* (Basingstoke, United Kingdom: Palgrave Macmillan, 2011), 67–68 for a discussion of *Ghost's* indebtedness to Shakespeare's poem.
11. Lina Bolzoni, *The Gallery of Memory: Literary and Iconographic Models in the Age of the Printing Press* (Toronto: University of Toronto Press, 1995). See Bolzoni's chapter, "Making Knowledge Visible: The Accademia Venziana" (3–22) for a discussion of the compilation of the *Somma*—a universal catalogue of human knowledge that uses visuals patterned on artificial memory systems to organize and represent information.
12. Thomas Middleton, *The Ghost of Lucrece* in *The Complete Works of Thomas Middleton* (Oxford: Clarendon Press, 2010), ll. 33–36. All quotations are from this edition of the poem unless otherwise stated.
13. Ibid., l. 34.
14. Shakespeare, *Rape of Lucrece*, ll. 407–408.

15. Ibid., ll. 416–20.
16. Lee A. Ritscher, *The Semiotics of Rape in Renaissance English Literature* (New York: Peter Lang, 2009), 56.
17. Rischer, *The Semiotics of Rape*, 59.
18. Donald Jellerson, "Haunted History and the Birth of the Republic in Middleton's *Ghost of Lucrece*," *Criticism* 53, no. 1 (Winter 2011): 54.
19. Mercedes Maroto Camino, '*The Stage Am I*': *Raping Lucrece in Early Modern England* (Lewiston, NY: Edwin Mellen Press, 1995), 19.
20. Middleton, *Ghost of Lucrece*, l. 35.
21. See Wendy Wall, *The Imprint of Gender: Authorship and Publication in the English Renaissance* (Ithaca, NY: Cornell University Press, 1993).
22. See Donald Jellerson, *Ghost Complaint: Historiography, Gender, and the Return of the Dead in Elizabethan Literature* (PhD diss., Vanderbilt University, 2009), 10–12.
23. Laura G. Bromley, "The Lost Lucrece: Middleton's *The Ghost of Lucrece*," *Papers on Language and Literature* 21 (1985), 268.
24. Ibid., 264, 270.
25. Ibid., 270. Bromley discusses how Middleton's ghost is an early analogue of Vindice.
26. Middleton, *Ghost of Lucrece*, ll. 44–50.
27. Garrett A. Sullivan Jr., *Memory and Forgetting in English Renaissance Drama: Shakespeare, Marlowe, Webster* (Cambridge: Cambridge University Press, 2009), 9.
28. Jellerson, "Haunted History," 58.
29. Bolzoni, *The Gallery of Memory*, xv.
30. Shakespeare, *Rape of Lucrece*, l. 314.
31. Middleton, *Ghost of Lucrece*, ll. 51–52.
32. Jellerson, "Haunted History," 56.
33. Shakespeare, *The Rape of Lucrece*, l. 849.
34. See Philip David Collington, *"O Word of Fear": Imaginary Cuckoldry in Shakespeare's Plays* (PhD diss., University of Toronto, 1998) for an exhaustive discussion of cuckoldry and the punning on cuckoo—a bird which lays its eggs in another bird's nest.
35. Shakespeare, *The Rape of Lucrece*, ll. 1058–64.
36. Gilles Deleuze and Félix Guattari, *A Thousand Plateaus: Capitalism and Schizophrenia*, trans. Brian Massumi (New York: Continuum, 2003), 8, 12.
37. Miranda Wilson, "Bastard Grafts, Crafter Fruits: Shakespeare's Planted Families," in *The Indistinct Human in Renaissance Literature*, ed. Jean E. Feerick and Vin Nardizzi (New York: Palgrave Macmillan, 2012), 104.
38. Melissa E. Sanchez, *Erotic Subjects: The Sexuality of Politics in Early Modern English Literature* (Oxford: Oxford University Press, 2011), 100–101.
39. Wilson, "Bastard Grafts," 104.
40. Joseph Solman, *Aristotle's Master-piece: or The Secrets of Generation Displayed in all the Parts Thereof*, 1694 (London: Garland, 1986), 177.
41. Shakespeare, *Rape of Lucrece*, ll. 1655–59.
42. Jocelyn Catty, *Writing Rape, Writing Women in Early Modern England* (Basingstoke, United Kingdom: Macmillan, 1999), 67.
43. Shakespeare, *Rape of Lucrece*, ll. 1021–22.
44. Catty, *Writing Rape*, 16.

45. See Roy W. Battenhouse, *Shakespearean Tragedy: Its Art and Its Christian Premises* (Bloomington: Indiana University Press, 1969), 3–41. Like St. Augustine before him, Battenhouse views Lucrece's suicide as a way of blotting out her guilt for secretly desiring Tarquin.
46. Middleton, *Ghost of Lucrece*, ll. 60–62.
47. Ibid., ll. 64–65, 63.
48. Ibid., l. 66.
49. Shakespeare, *Rape of Lucrece*, l. 1027.
50. Middleton, *Ghost of Lucrece*, l. 75.
51. Ibid., l. 77.
52. Ibid., ll. 89–93.
53. Ibid., ll. 94–98.
54. Ibid., l. 115, 129.
55. Shakespeare, *Rape of Lucrece*, l. 407.
56. Middleton, *Ghost of Lucrece*, ll. 141–42.
57. Luce Irigaray, "The Bodily Encounter with the Mother," in *The Irigaray Reader*, ed. Margaret Whitford (Oxford: Blackwell, 1991), 36–37.
58. Ibid., 36.
59. Kyoko Taniguchi, "The Eroticism of the Maternal: So What If Everything Is about the Mother?" *Studies in Gender and Sexuality*, 13 (2012), 125.
60. Ibid., 124–25.
61. Kathryn Bond Stockton, *The Queer Child, or Growing Sideways in the Twentieth Century* (Durham: Duke University Press, 2009), 12, 4–5.
62. Irigaray "The Bodily Encounter with the Mother," 38.
63. Camino, 'The Stage Am I,' 71.
64. Middleton, *Ghost of Lucrece*, l. 414.
65. Middleton, *Ghost of Lucrece* ll. 395–401.
66. Camino, 'The Stage Am I,' 32.
67. Middleton, *Ghost of Lucrece*, l. 415–17.
68. Ibid., ll. 563–69.
69. Ibid., ll. 593–94.
70. Ibid., l. 591.
71. Ibid., ll. 603–604.
72. Ibid., l. 612.
73. Ibid., ll. 613–16.
74. Ibid., ll. 620–21.
75. Ibid., l. 627.
76. Ibid., ll. 634–35.
77. Ibid., ll. 641–43.
78. Patricia Parker, *Literary Fat Ladies: Rhetoric, Gender, Property* (London: Methuen, 1987), 131.
79. Middleton, *Ghost of Lucrece*, ll. 653–54.
80. Ibid., l. 652.
81. Mary Carruthers, *The Book of Memory* (Cambridge: Cambridge University Press, 1990), 234.

5 Exemplarity and Its Discontents in Michael Drayton's *Englands Heroical Epistles*

Andrew Fleck

On the penultimate page of his account of Henry II's reign, Raphael Holinshed appends a brief memorial of Rosamond Clifford, the desirable young woman on whom the Plantagenet king doted late in life. He follows a long line of historians who mention Rosamond, but even as he marginalizes her as an afterthought, Holinshed enhances the account of her exemplary character and incomparable beauty. He declares that "for hir passing beautie, propernesse of person, and pleasant wit, with other amiable qualities" he considered her "verelie a rare and peerelesse peece."[1] He notes that her tomb bore the Latin epitaph "*Hic iacet in tumulo, Rosamundi non Rosa munda, / Non redolet, sed olet, quae redolere solet*," and directs those seeking the English "meaning" of these lines to "Graftons large chronicle, page 77" (115). The intrepid reader who does consult Richard Grafton's *A Chronicle at Large* finds that the mid-Tudor historian mentions the couplet, explains that it was "Englished by Fabian in meter," and includes his predecessor's florid translation:

> The Rose of the worlde, but not the cleane flowre,
> Is here nowe grauen: to whom beautie was lent.
> In this graue full darke, now is her Bower,
> That by her life was sweete and redolent.
> But now that she is, from this life blent
> Though she were sweete, now fowly doth she stinke,
> A myrrour good for all that on her thinke.[2]

The early Tudor chroniclers fashion a gaudy rhyme royal stanza from the simple balance of the Latin couplet.

The memory of Rosamond Clifford and her submission to Henry II also appealed to Holinshed's contemporaries, who embellished her story even more significantly. At the end of the sixteenth century, English poets competed to imaginatively fill the gaps in the chronicle histories' narratives of Henry and Rosamond.[3] William Warner invented an episode exploring her seduction in *Albion's England*. Samuel Daniel ventriloquized her tale in a lengthy and subsequently enlarged *Complaynt*. Thomas Deloney composed a melodramatic, *Mournfull Dittie, on the death of Rosamond, King*

Henry the seconds Concubine. Michael Drayton placed the imagined correspondence of Rosamond and Henry II at the head of his paired, Ovidian letters in *Englands Heroicall Epistles*. In Drayton's popular text—he published eleven, sometimes revised and expanded editions between 1597 and 1619—the poet places Rosamond in her famous, labyrinthine tower in Woodstock, reflecting on the "foule Offence" she and Henry have committed.[4] She makes the same pun that the chroniclers enjoyed, "Rose of the World, so doth import my Name, / Shame of the World, my Life hath made the same," and begs Henry for death and oblivion (RH 129–30). Her letter participates in the Elizabethan vogue for complaint, indebted to Ovid's *Heroides* and their apostrophic address to absent lovers.[5] Drayton, however, takes a step further than Ovid and imagines the distressed letter writers receiving a response. In his reply Henry II, absenting himself from her embrace in order to quell his sons' rebellion, sentimentally begs Rosamond not even to "whisper of thy Death," and promises to make the memory of her submission into something positive (HR 200). Their epistolary exchange involves the writing and rewriting of their liaison, attesting to the instability, biases, and mutability of erotic memory. They remember the nature of their desires and particularly the exemplarity of Rosamond differently. As he transforms Ovid's epistolary complaints, Drayton gives the king the last word and seems to inscribe the royal, optimistic interpretation of Rosamond's meaning as final.[6] Yet the juxtaposition of competing memories of erotic exchange finally serves to destabilize the exemplarity of Rosamond Clifford.

Medieval legends about Rosamond Clifford and Henry II grow out of a few scanty details. Early in the thirteenth century, Gerald of Wales, the earliest historian to mention her, alludes to Rosamond only in passing when he describes Henry II's decision to live in "manifest" adultery after his final estrangement from Eleanor of Aquitaine.[7] For Gerald, this episode illustrates Henry's wickedness, his brazen pursuit of his unbounded desires, so that even though "*quoniam 'componitur orbis regis ad exemplum,' non solum facto quinimmo longe magis offendit exemplo*" (166). Gerald gives Henry negative exemplarity as a willful king who brazenly embraces his offensive example. Roger of Howden, writing at about the same time as Gerald, offers a more sentimental treatment of Rosamond. Although he does not narrate anything of her life, he does describe her magnificent tomb. Roger recalls that St. Hugh, as bishop of Lincoln, visited the various religious foundations in his see, including the abbey at Godstow near Woodstock. There he found a tomb "covered with cloths of silk, and surrounded by lamps and tapers," and asked the abbey's nuns about it.[8] They told him "this was the tomb of Rosamond, who had formerly been the mistress of Henry, king of England ... and that he, for love of her, had shown many favours to that church" (257). Unlike Gerald, who used Rosamond to blacken the memory of Henry II, Roger recalls that an indignant St. Hugh required the reburial of Rosamond outside of the church so that "other women, warned by her example, may abstain from illicit and adulterous intercourse" (257). Together, Gerald and Roger provide the basis for the ambivalent reception of Rosamond's example. From one perspective, a lecherous Henry II pursues adulterous gratification with a simple country maid; from another, a seductive Rosamond bewitches the king and leads him astray.

The titillating episode of the king's adultery appealed to subsequent historians who further embellished it. Ranulf Higden draws on both Gerald's *De Principis Instructione Liber* and Roger's *Chronica* and adds new material. In his *Polychronica*, Higden returns to Gerald's chiding of the king who had been "pryuely a spouche breker" until he imprisoned Eleanor, after which time he "lyued now openly in spousebrekyng and is not ashamed to mysuse the wenche Rosamond."[9] Before abridging Roger's description of Rosamond's tomb "in the chapyter hows at Godestow," Higden inserts a new detail. In order to satisfy his desires, the king installs Rosamond in a "chamber of wonder crafte slyly made by dedalus werke" in Woodstock. The historian implies that the king hid his paramour in a baffling retreat, "leste the Quene sholde fynde and take Rosamund" (357 r). Higden invents both the wonderful dwelling and the rationale for its existence. After all, Henry had imprisoned the rebellious Eleanor, as Higden notes a few lines earlier, and she did not enjoy her liberty again until after the king's death 16 years later.[10] Influenced by the hazy memory that Henry imprisoned Eleanor at about the same time that Rosamond died, Higden and his adherents implied that jealous Eleanor posed a danger to her erotic rival.[11] Higden's version of events, which includes another wonder, a "lytel Coffre" on which, ekphrastically, "it semyth that geantes fyghten beestes startlyn foules fleyn and fysshes leepe withoute ony mannes moeuynge," provides the basis for Fabyan, Grafton, and later Tudor accounts of Rosamond (357r). Only John Leland, in his investigations under Henry VIII, attempted to verify the details contained in the medieval chroniclers, noting that Rosamond's monument, "taken up a late," had born the inscription "*Tumba Rosamondae*," and that a "crosse hard by Godstow" bears a reference to her.[12] Although Leland's less romantic notes did not appear in print until much later, he does at least claim to have seen the location of Rosamond's final resting place.

Holinshed and his Tudor predecessors treated Rosamond as exemplary, but they drew different and competing lessons from her example. Grafton and Fabyan's ambiguous figuration in their rhyme royal epitome of Rosamond—included in John Stow's *Annals* as well—as a "myrrour good" for those who "thinke" about her allows for slippage in the meaning to be derived from her.[13] Perhaps readers should seize the day as they consider her brief, "sweet and redolent" life in the arms of the king, finding in her an example of a fortunate but fleeting happiness. She might also serve as a *memento mori*, teaching readers of the consequences of an immoral and ambitious existence, with her decaying corpse that "now fowly doth stinke" serving as moral retribution for her temporary ascendency and as a reminder that carnal pleasures pale next to the eternity of the grave.

Holinshed, however, offers Rosamond as an unambiguous paragon whose flower, like one pressed in a book, has lost its enticing scent over the centuries. He delicately avoids his sources' emphasis on the stench that accompanies the putrefaction of the dead. Holinshed's reluctance to spell out the distasteful point of the cruel reminder that this Rose of the world has not only lost its aroma but now rots and "stinke[s]," embodies a broader Elizabethan ambivalence about Rosamond Clifford. She was, after all, the adulterous paramour of a king at odds with his wife, Eleanor of Aquitaine. Rosamond may have struck Holinshed as an unparalleled model of beauty and grace, but her submission to the private lust of the monarch turned this fallen woman into a monitory example as well.

The rationale for compiling and preparing historical treatments of elite figures received new emphasis shortly after the initial publication of Holinshed's *Chronicles*. Thomas North, relying on the French intermediary of Jacques Amyot, completed his English translation of Plutarch in 1579. Amyot had doubly justified his undertaking by referring to the power of historical examples, first, to prepare readers for action in the uncertain circumstances of the present, and second to guide readers toward virtue and away from vice. He asserts that because "memorie is the storehouse of mens conceits," a "historie is the very treasury of mans life" that "preserued [great deeds] from the death of forgetfulnes."[14] Historians battle the power of oblivion to erase the memory of influential actors. Making the humanist argument for the importance of history, Amyot defends the commemoration of historical figures because the recollection of "examples past, teacheth vs to iudge of things present, & to foresee things to come" (*iii v). Moreover, for Amyot, history has a moral purpose, in addition to this political one, because "examples are of more force to moue and instruct, than are the arguments and proofes of reason, or their precise precepts, bicause examples be the very formes of our deedes, & accompanied with all circumstances" (*iiii r). Inspired by Amyot's own recourse to exemplarity, North commends the reading of Plutarch to all of Queen Elizabeth's subjects, since by "adding the encouragement of these exsamples to the forwardnes of their owne dispositions," her subjects will find inspiration to undertake great deeds "for their worthy Queene" (*ii v). To his regular English readers, North commends the reading of exemplary history as more morally instructive "than to read it in the Philosophers writings" (*iii r). Amyot and North rehearse the value of history's exemplary figures in terms that the era's poets would adopt as well.

Elizabethan poets also pressed the claims of exemplarity into a justification for their art. Sir Philip Sidney most famously argued that poetry could supply the defects of philosophy and history. Whereas "the one [philosophy] giveth precept, and the other [history] the example" (84), poetry perfects them both in creating a speaking picture that moves its readers in ways that neither obscure doctrine nor flawed examples can.[15] When George Puttenham turns to the value of "poesy historical" and argues that it surpasses all other forms of writing, he justifies his claim by elaborating on the power of exemplarity. Praising memory in terms similar to those Amyot employs, Puttenham considers the sources that supply memory as it "examin[es] and compar[es] the times past with the present" and concludes that "no kind of argument in all the oratory craft doth better persuade and more universally satisfy than *example*, which is but the representation of old memories and like successes happened in times past."[16] Historical poetry, of the sort that Drayton and his rivals produced, should offer "good and exemplary things and actions of the former ages," for the political and moral instruction of readers (129). Sidney and his fellow poets praised historical verse of the kind Drayton and Daniel produced at the end of the century because in their hands the historical example could ideally offer both political and moral instruction. The ambiguous narrative surrounding Rosamond, however, would ultimately point to the limits of exemplarity's utility.

Elizabethan poets appropriated and shared the story of Henry II's adultery with Rosamond Clifford with some ambivalence. They took up Rosamond's plight and interpolated it into the tradition exemplified in the *Mirror for Magistrates*. They took the bare details described by Gerald and Roger or Stow and Holinshed—in which a lustful Henry consummates his desire on Rosamond and sequesters her in a labyrinthine tower at Woodstock where she dies and is interred in an opulent tomb—and transformed them into a more dramatic complaint (in Puttenham's sense of "love forlorn or ill-bestowed" [136]) of a bashful Rosamond's reluctant submission to her king's desire. In part they accomplish this by making Rosamond speak for herself.[17] Her Ovidian complaints, in which she speaks the truth of her erotic encounter with her royal master, allow these poets to surpass their predecessors among the historians—who were limited by the few available details—by creating a more complex and vivid example. Their desire to imagine Rosamond's plight, however, ultimately mars her utility as a straightforward moral example. For instance, when Thomas Delony turned to Rosamond's story, consulting Holinshed and possibly inspired by other late-Elizabethan poets' treatment of her, he heightened the melodrama of the episode by focusing on Rosamond's despair at Henry's departure.[18] When the king's sons break into rebellion, the king must take his leave of Rosamond, the "fairest Rose in all the world / to feed my fantasie" (51–52). He promises to carry the rosy memory of his beloved Rosamond "in my heart while hence I am" (63), but she courageously offers, "like a Page, / your shield and Target [to] bear" in the field rather than remain in England (93–94). Henry persuades her to embrace the safety of the "Woodstocke Bower" and departs. In the final few stanzas, the enraged Eleanor discovers Rosamond's hiding place and forces her to drink poison.

Although Henry's treatment of Rosamond typically reflected poorly on the royal adulterer in the chronicle tradition, the tale's ability to humanize the monarch may have compelled verse historians to include the episode for this reason. In the second edition of his verse chronicle *Albion's England*, for instance, William Warner initially prefers to focus on the English king's important resistance to foreign, papal tyranny. Having treated the king's responsibility for Becket's murder at some length, Warner briefly teases his readers with the promise of the story of "The Kings fayre Leiman Rosamund, and how his Sonnes rebell," only to declare immediately his determination to "ouer-passe" those episodes in favor of the story of Henry's successor, Richard I.[19] The popular tale of Henry's involvement with Rosamond had passed from one chronicle to the next, so Warner's decision to tease his audience with the prospect of this tawdry tale and then refuse to narrate it must have disappointed his readers. In the third edition of *Albions England*, despite his professed desire to pass over Henry II's adultery almost in silence, Warner provides his version of Henry's seduction of innocent Rosamond, her seclusion in an "intricate and great" bower, and Queen Eleanor's horrible vengeance on Rosamond, "the Quintessence of Beauty."[20] He casts the story as one of true love and figures Eleanor's attack on Henry's beloved as the cause for Henry's historical alienation from his powerful, rebellious family.

Warner's elaboration of this scandalous episode appeared in print at the same time as Samuel Daniel's first version of *The Complaynt of Rosamond*, itself a text that treats this tale and its heroine with some misgivings.[21] An ambivalence of remembering and forgetting the scandalous example also troubles Daniel's complaint. At the narrative's outset, the ghost of Rosamond sues the Elizabethan poet, Samuel Daniel—author of the sonnets that precede her complaint in the 1592 quarto—appealing to him to help her spirit find peace.[22] Denied access to the healing oblivion of the river Lethe, Rosamond explains that "Caron denies me waftage / ... And says my soule can never passe that River / Till Lovers sighes on earth shall it deliver."[23] In order to inspire this pity, Rosamond must trade on "my shame that never sleepes" (3) and tell her tale to Daniel again, since "Time hath long since worne out the memorie, / Both of my life, and life's unjust depriving" (17–18). The poet creates competing interests to justify his verse narrative: on the one hand, Rosamond would explicitly prefer to erase the memory of Henry's forcing himself upon her, but on the other hand she must revive that traumatic memory in public in order to ease her ghost. Her melancholy tale lacks the devotion Deloney attributes to her or the comedic seduction Warner invents. Daniel's rustic Rosamond carries her blushing beauty to the court and learns the corrupting dissimulation of the elites' erotic affairs. When the king sees her, Rosamond's beauty causes him to "forget himself" and condescend to her. She defends her honor, but a bawd, "A seeming Matrone, yet a sinfull monster," urges her to make the most of her erotic vitality (216). Ultimately, she cannot reject the king's advances and submits to his demands. The king places her in a palace at Woodstock, but Eleanor discovers her, penetrating the secret of the "Laberinth ... by that threed / That seru'd a conduct to my absent Lord" (575–76), a detail found in Warner's account and suggested by the story of Theseus and Ariadne in the original Cretan labyrinth, and forces her to drink poison. In subsequent editions of the *Complaynt*, Daniel expects some amount of oblivion in his readers or implicitly acknowledges the mutability of memory when he embellishes the episode of the melodramatic scene of Eleanor's confrontation with Rosamond with an additional 150 lines. Rosamond laments that she has "beene registred / In the blacke booke of the unfortunate" examples of seductresses (547–48), but she must traumatically experience that unhappiness again and again under Daniel's pen and his readers' gaze if she is ever to cross the river Lethe into oblivion. There is a history, and it involves an erotic scandal. She might prefer to forget that aspect of her life and yet the logic of her complaint requires her and her poetic amanuensis to commemorate that event in verse.

The problem of commemorating seduction, adultery, and sin that might be better forgotten crops up around the historical record Daniel and others evoke in their recollection of Rosamond. A central figure of this ambivalent memory in Daniel's poem is the tomb Rosamond's doting, royal lover erects in order that "posterity shall know, / How faire thou wert above all women kind," so that later ages "monuments shall find, / Shewing thy beauties title not thy name" (689–92). Of course a monument to Rosamond's exemplary beauty also commemorates the dangerous temptation of her beauty and its sinful consequences. In Daniel's poem, this opulent, papist shrine suffers under the reproving hands of the bishop of Lincoln, and the desperate ghost of Rosamund worries that "now scarce any note descries / Vnto these times, the memory of me" (705–706). Fortunately, the young Elizabethan poet creates a poetic monument and places it in the hands of his readers, fulfilling Rosamond's hope that her plight will generate the necessary sighs and pity to, paradoxically, arrive in oblivion. The king's paradoxical monument to beautiful, tempting Rosamond figures in Michael Drayton's complex retelling of Daniel's version of the chroniclers' commemoration of the erotic interlude as well.[24]

Drayton uneasily negotiates the tension between the creative demands of his poetry and his contemporaries' appreciation for historical poetry. In his address to the reader he imagines that some will want to know "why I haue annexed notes to euery Epistles end."[25] After each of the letters of *Englands Heroicall Epistles*, Drayton includes "Notes of the Chronicle History" that gloss some of the preceding poem's lines.[26] In the case of Rosamond's verse letter, she puns on her name, "Rose of the World / Shame of the World," as every chronicler before her had done, and Drayton glosses this line at the end of her epistle before moving on to Henry's reply. He explains that the "Rose of the World" alludes to the inscription on the historical tomb "at Godstow, where this Rose of the World was sumptuously interred," and recalls that this shrine to adultery had offended the sensibility of "a certain Bishop, in the Visitation of his Diocesse, [who] caused the Monument which had been erected to her Honour, utterly to bee demolished" (EHE 139).[27] He explains that he makes these references to the chronicles "because the worke might in truth be iudged brainish, if nothing but amorous humor were handled therein," and he has therefore "inter-wouen matters historicall, which vnexplaned, might defraud the minde of much content" (A2 v). Hearkening back to the justification of poetry as offering something more than simply frivolous, "brainish" matter, Drayton anchors his imaginative epistolary erotic exchanges in the serious memorials of the chronicles.

This gesture threatens to capsize one of Drayton's other purposes in publishing *Englands Heroicall Epistles*. He dedicates each pair of letters to a potential patron. In the case of the exchange of Rosamond and Henry, for instance, Drayton writes to Lucy Russell, the Countess of Bedford.[28] But, as we have seen, Rosamond offers an ambiguous example, and Drayton risks offending Bedford and other patrons with his erotic complaints. In his justification of himself to the reader at the outset of his book, he contorts his work in order to explain that he "sorted the complection of the Epistles, to the character of theyr iudgement to whom I dedicate them" but quickly asserts that the match of patron and epistles does not extend to the ambiguous morality of some of the complaints. He sees the alignment of patron and subject "excepting onely the blamefulnes of the persons passion, in those poynts wherein the passion is blameful" (A2v). Beginning *Englands Heroicall Epistles* with the challenging example of Rosamond, Drayton confronts the difficulty of marshaling exemplarity to suit his complimentary ends.

Modeled on Ovid's *Heroides*, Drayton's *England's Heroical Epistles* present the letters of women in distress. Like Penelope writing to Ulysses or Dido addressing Aeneas, Rosamond writes to the absent Plantagenet king from her desolate abode in the labyrinthine "mounting Towres" (RH 76) of Woodstock that Henry has built both to constrain her and to keep her safe from his jealous wife. Drayton's Rosamond in her secret, defensive structure most closely resembles Ariadne writing to Theseus in the tenth epistle of Ovid's *Heroides*, in which the abandoned woman curses the fateful "twisted clewe" that revealed the labyrinth's secret.[29] Unlike Ovid's example, however, Drayton imagines the desperate letters of his heroines receiving replies. In fact, in this initial pair of letters, Drayton makes it clear that Henry has carefully read Rosamond's complaint. The king's reply to Rosamond recasts her lamentations, figuring them with positive interpretations.[30] From the start, Rosamond insistently draws a meta-textual analogy between herself and the formerly blank paper now stained with ink that carries her history to an absent royal reader.[31] She modestly craves that Henry will "endure / These tainted Lines, drawn with a Hand impure" (RH 1–2). Henry will hold the letter in his hands as he reads it, and "This scribbled Paper which I send to thee, / If noted rightly, doth resemble me" (RH 11–12). Once she was as virginal "As this pure Ground," but having committed adultery with her king she is now "blotted with this foul Offence" (RH 13, 15). Significantly, she transfers the polluting agency of the hand from the start of her letter, when the impure hand was hers, the one making letters on the page, to the stain imparted onto "this pure Ground, whereon these Letters stand," which was as blank as she was until "stayned by thy Hand" (13–14). This first letter of

Englands Heroicall Epistles, having come into the hands of the campaigning Angevin king as Rosamond had herself come into his hands, gets recast by its imaginative royal reader. He denies at first that the "blotted Paper should Thy Selfe resemble," but, referring to Rosamond's paper now in his hands, he eventually accepts Rosamond's conceit and reimagines it (HR 24). If Rosamond were paper her beauty would so surpass the white paper in his hand that "The Gods thereon their sacred Lawes would write / With Pens of Angels Wings" (HR 26–27). Significantly, the text of Rosamond's affair with Henry II must always come to Elizabethan readers mediated by inky stains. No blank, virginal sheet can convey her history. Drayton's readers hold in their hands the common and not especially white paper on which black ink allows them to read a printed facsimile of Rosamond's and Henry's epistles and shame. Drayton's book gives the lie to the king's romantic rewriting of Rosamond's gesture to a common trope of stained innocence. As the late Elizabethan effort to provide a voice for this paramour of the king attests, the literary memory of Rosamond must always be mediated by fantasies that rewrite their story.

Rosamond's mutable recriminations and Henry's recasting of them embody the competing remembrances of their relationship in this epistolary exchange. Rosamond describes her futile pastime of angling in the brook that meanders near her tower as exemplifying the shame in her affair with the king. Whenever she "cast[s] in my Bait," the fish in this stream "flye th'inticing Gin" (RH 119, 121). She fails to catch anything. Rosamond treats this failure as evidence of the taint she has acquired and imagines the crystal brook chiding her with a complaint that her presence "should pollute that Native puritie" (RH 128). Henry responds to this representation of her blemished nature with an optimistic interpretation. Her virtuous beauty stuns the creatures in the stream. The fish refuse to feed on her baits because they "all amazed lye, / So daunted with the lustre of thine Eye" (HR 151–52). The brook may murmur loudly, but it does not chide Rosamond for her encounters with the king. Rather, the stream, "finding, that the envious Bankes restrain it" directs its complaints at the earth that holds it back from "offer[ing] up some small Drops at thy Feet" and "T'excuse it selfe, doth in this sort complaine it" (HR 144–46). Drayton creates the illusion that the king has carefully read Rosamond's letter and responds to specific complaints carried within it. Because his epistle replies to Rosamond's, he has the advantage of reinterpreting her complaints.

Rosamond particularly regrets that others now see her as a monitory example. From her tower, she observes those who scornfully "cast their Eyes at mee" (RH 79). Some of these are "maried Women" who "curse my hatefull Life, / Wronging a faire Queene, and a vertuous Wife" (RH 83–84). As the woman committing adultery with England's married king, Rosamond knows that she has done wrong and that most women will consider her a negative model, a morally compromised woman who leads a (royal) husband astray, with the political implications piled onto the simple domestic transgression of being the other woman. As a beautiful young woman, the unmarried Rosamond also serves as a cautionary tale. The adulterous attention she has drawn from a married man scares other innocent young women, who may shun the example of this wicked girl with her premature knowledge of sexual experience. Fearing the implications of desirability, these "Maidens wish, I buried quicke may die" (RH 85). Considering her surroundings in the "Labyrinth" constructed to protect and contain her, Rosamond acknowledges that she has become a "Monster," both the traditional, fearful guardian of the maze in Ovid and the fearful example contained in the etymology of the word *monster*. Responding to these complaints, Henry again seeks to recast the negative associations Rosamond ascribes to herself and her state in an optimistic, romantic light. The wives and unmarried maidens who look upon Rosamond must either with "Eyes with Envie lowre" at Rosmond (HR 133), wishing they could be like her, or they "prayse thine owne" eyes "which be so cleere, / Which from the Turret like two Starres appeare" (HR 135–36). He goes on to express his expectation that "some famous Poets Song," perhaps Drayton's *Englands Heroical Epistles* itself, will serve to make the name of Rosamond into a powerful and positive example. Then "with the very sweetnesse of that Name, / Lyons and Tygers Men shall learne to tame" (HR 154–56). Unlike the envious wronged wives and innocent maidens, the "carefull Mother, at her pensive Brest, / With ROSAMOND shall bring her Babe to Rest" (HR 157–58). Once again, Henry prefers to imagine the object of his affection in the best possible light, as a good and admirable, rather than monstrous, example.

For all of Henry's optimistic attempts to recast Rosamond's feelings of shame, he can only finally overcome the most shocking aspect of her letter with silence. Rosamond cannot quite bring herself to discuss her relationship with Henry as a rape. In fact, all of the poets who treat this incident must tiptoe around the issue. The Rosamond who justifies herself to Samuel Daniel, for instance, had lamented the situation in which she found herself. The very fact that the most powerful man in England has devoted himself to her enticing beauty will dishonor Daniel's Rosamond and "Whether I yeelde or not I liue defamed / ... And if I yeeld, tis honorable shame, / If not, I liue disgrac'd, yet thought the same" (338, 342–43). Further complicating Rosamond's choice, the man who pursues her "is my King and may constraine me," a conflation of gender and political authority that finally compels Rosamond to accept his dishonorable advances.[32] Drayton's Rosamond expresses a similar ambivalence, as we have seen in her characterization of the staining "hand" of the king and of her now-polluted hand.

Rosamond recalls her liaison with England's monarch with a mixture of regret and pleasure, shame and satisfaction. Her memory of their time together represents a crisis of identity, one that concludes with her begging her royal correspondent for death.[33] At one point, Rosamond disowns volition in Henry's pursuit of his "unlawfull Pleasure" (RH 29). Her "Bodie was inforc'd" she writes, but "my Soule yet ne'r consented to" the act

(RH 33–34). She reiterates that their copulation occurred against her will since "'Twas not my Minde consented to this Ill" (RH 31). And yet, later in the poem, Rosamond concedes that she takes pleasure in her affair with the king and cannot deny that it appeals to her, even as she loathes her sin.[34] Expressing her efforts to blot out the memory of the event, Rosamond recounts the tears she has shed in hopes of washing away the record of her infamy but finds that these pitiful signs only make her name and herself shine more clearly. She confesses that "Once did I sinne," but concedes that "Memorie doth cherish" their time together (RH 71). Her coupling with Henry was an "offense" and a sin, but she cherishes the affair, although she suffers infamy. She then mentions the wronged wives and anxious maidens who gaze on her in her tower before turning to one final exemplary woman: Lucrece.

Retiring from the accusatory eyes of wives and maidens, Rosamond passes time in her secluded tower's picture gallery. Walking among these images, Rosamond and her attendant come across "Chaste Lucrece Image," and her naïve maid "desires to know, / What shee should be, her selfe that murd'red so?" (RH 97–98). Rosamond attempts to relate the exemplary story of "that Roman Dame" but finds herself unable to proceed, overcome as she is by the suggestive contrast with "mine owne Guiltinesse" (101). Chaste Lucrece, who ended her own virtuous life once the son of Rome's tyrant, Tarquin, raped her, had served as a political exemplum for almost two thousand years. Shakespeare, whose poem on the subject Drayton seems to evoke, had made her story current again shortly before the publication of *Englands Heroical Epistles*, and as Melissa Sanchez argues, Lucrece's example also figures in the vulnerable position of the "male political subject who cannot legitimately rebel against his ruler" (95).[35] Rosamond finds herself in a similar position to Lucrece, although she accepts life and dishonor rather than an honorable death. Lucrece serves as a silent reproach to Rosamond for her decision.

Despite his efforts to recast Rosamond's complaints, Henry can find no way to reimagine his paramour's evocation of Lucrece. Other classical exemplars in Rosamond's letter—she regrets that she did not draw the proper lessons from the marvelous "Casket, of souch wond'rous cost" (RH 153), adorned with images of Neptune and Jove that Henry sent her before visiting her—give Henry a chance to praise Rosamond's beauty again. But in those examples a mortal woman submitted to a deity's force. The example of Lucrece signifies in more significant but less ambiguous ways. The violation of her chastity by a royal rapist in ancient Rome had sparked the ire of Rome's citizens and led to Tarquin's banishment and the foundation of a republic in opposition to monarchy. There is no representational slippage that Henry can exploit to recast this exemplum to ameliorate Rosamond's shame. Drayton's king, who carefully responds to each of Rosamond's other complaints, must, like Warner or Drayton himself, strategically decide to overpass this point of his lover's epistle.

Like several of his contemporaries, Drayton appropriates the example of Rosamond's submission to Henry II to explore the heightened stakes of a man's adultery when that adultery is committed by a king. Like his predecessors, Drayton figures Rosamond as defending her spiritual purity and preserving her chastity until the power of a monarch compels her to submit. Like those who treated Rosamond before him, Drayton confronts the ambiguity of her example: she is both an unparalleled beauty and a party to adultery, to speak of her in one register is to import the other register, and despite the moral censor's desire to tear down the deluxe stone monument to her memory, the poem creates a lasting monument in verse. Unlike Daniel or Warner, however, Drayton invents a means for Rosamond's complaints to receive a reply and in doing so he creates an example with greater power to challenge royal authority. Rosamond may not have the strength to resist a determined man; she may not have the political standing to resist the compulsion of her king. Despite her doting king's attempts to excuse their immoral behavior and perhaps even his culpability in the act, when Rosamond casts herself as a moral example of a political violation, a negative example to pair with the example of Lucrece, Henry must pass over the unambiguous, threatening example of an incitement to rebellion without comment. For Drayton, the limits of exemplarity are reached when moral exemplum shades into political application.

Notes

1. *Chronicles*, vol. 3 (London, 1587), 115.
2. *A Chronicle at Large* (London, 1569), 76–77.
3. Georgia Brown argues that the vogue for complaints in the late sixteenth century allowed lyric poets to contest the epic narratives of official chronicle history. *Redefining Elizabethan Literature* (Cambridge: Cambridge UP, 2004), 182.
4. "Englands Heroicall Epistles," in *Works of Michael Drayton*, ed. J. William Hebel, vol. 2 (Oxford: Blackwell, 1961), line 15. Rosamond's Letter to Henry will be cited in text as RH and line number; Rosamond's reply to Henry will be cited in the text as RH and line number; I will refer to other paratextual matter as EHE and page number. It is worth remembering that this standard edition of Drayton relies on the 1619 edition of *Englands Heroicall Epistles*. When I cite some of the material from earlier editions, I will refer to those specific editions.
5. Duncan F. Kennedy argues that the verse epistles Ovid creates serve as substitute presence for the physically absent addressee. "Epistolarity: The *Heroides*," in *The Cambridge Companion to Ovid*, ed. Philip Hardie (Cambridge: Cambridge UP, 2002), 221.
6. See, for instance, Kavita Mudan Finn, *The Last Plantagenet Consorts: Gender, Genre, and Historiography 1440–1627* (New York: Palgrave, 2012), 181. I read this contest for meaning in light of Melissa Sanchez's reading of political and erotic submission and powerlessness in the literature of early modern England. As she argues about this issue in Wroth's *Urania*, narratives of political and erotic submission present the possibility that "political subjects will so enjoy the moral and erotic authority associated with victimization that they will

remain loyal to their sovereign not in spite of his abuse, but because of it." *Erotic Subjects: The Sexuality of Politics in Early Modern English Literature* (Oxford: Oxford UP, 2011), 117.
7. Giraldus Cambrensis, *Opera*, ed. George F. Warner, vol. 8 (Wiesbaden: Kraus Reprints, 1964), 164. Gerald recounts that after imprisoning Eleanor, the king's serial adultery, which had previously been "occultus," now became "manifestus," but rather than naming Rosamond, he puns on her name: "non mundi quidem rosa juxta falsam et frivolam nominis impositionem, sed immundi verius rosa vocata palam et impudenter abutendo." Later he names her, asserting that "post mortem Rosomaundae puellae," Henry II went on to ruin many other young women (232). Virgil B. Heltzel traces the development of chronicle treatments of Rosamond. *Fair Rosamond: A Study of the Development of a Literary Theme* (Evanston: Northwestern University Studies, 1947), 2.
8. *The Annals of Roger de Hovedon*, trans. and ed. Henry T. Riley, vol. 2 (New York: AMS Press, 1968), 257.
9. [*Polychronicon*] ([Westminster, 1482]), 357 recto. This is John of Trevisa's English translation of Higden, published by Caxton in early Tudor England. It includes the earliest reference to the Latin couplet and offers a more literal translation of the Latin than Fabyan's rhyme royal stanza.
10. For Henry's stubborn refusal to forgive Eleanor for supporting their sons' rebellion and her imprisonment during the rest of his life, see Ralph V. Turner, *Eleanor of Aquitaine: Queen of France, Queen of England* (New Haven: Yale UP, 2009), 230.
11. Heltzel suggests the power of this coincidence in the public's imagination. *Fair Rosamond*, 3.
12. *The Itinerary of John Leland*, ed. Lucy Toulmin Smith, vol. 1 (Carbondale: Southern Illinois UP, 1964), 328–29.
13. *Annales of England* (London, 1592), 220.
14. *The Lives of the Nobel Grecians and Romanes* (London, 1579), *iii verso.
15. "The Defence of Poetry," *Miscellaneous Prose of Sir Philip Sidney* (Oxford: Clarendon, 1973), 84.
16. *The Art of English Poesy*, ed. Frank Whigham and Wayne A. Rebhorn (Ithaca: Cornell UP, 2007), 128, my emphasis.
17. As Michel Foucault notes, the truth of sex comes not from the act but from the discursive meaning ascribed to the act. *The History of Sexuality*, vol. 1, trans. Robert Hurley (New York: Vintage, 1990), 59.
18. Deloney probably had his Holinshed open as he wrote his ballad. He asserts that "Most peerelesse was her beauty found," an echo of Holinshed's "peerelesse peece." "A Mournfull Dittie, on the death of Rosamond, King Henry the seconds Concubine," in *The Works of Thomas Deloney*, ed. Francis Oscar Mann (Oxford: Clarendon, 1912), line 5.
19. *The First and Second Parts of Albions England* (London, 1589), 104.
20. *Albions England: The Third Time Corrected and Augmented* (London, 1592), 179, 181.
21. Although he focuses particularly on the early modern stage, Jeffrey Masten's notion that male early modern writers engaged in collaborative textual production produce "a female body as textual corpus" might be usefully applied in the context of these poets who ventriloquize Rosamond's voice as they pass her from one male poet to another. *Textual Intercourse: Collaboration, Authorship, and*

Sexualities in Renaissance Drama (Cambridge: Cambridge UP, 1997), 60–61. Goran Stanivukovic updates these notions around the queerness of intertexts in "Beyond Sodomy: What is Still Queer about Early Modern Queer Studies?" *Queer Renaissaince Historiography: Backward Gaze*, ed. Will Stockton, Stephen Guy-Bray, Vincent Nardizzi (Farnham: Ashgate, 2009), 61.

22. Stephen Guy-Bray argues that unlike the reluctant writers of Ovid's *Heroides*, Daniel's complaining Rosamond takes control of her textuality in this exchange. "Rosamond's complaint: Daniel, Ovid, and the Purpose of Poetry," *Renaissance Studies* 22.3 (2008), 341. Wendy Wall treats the complaint's self-consciousness as a way for Daniel to authorize his work. *The Imprint of Gender: Authorship and Publication in the English Renaissance* (Ithaca: Cornell UP, 1993), 253.
23. "The Complaint of Rosamond," in *Poems and a Defence of Ryme*, ed. Arthur Colby Sprague (London: Routledge and Kegan Paul, 1950), lines 12–14.
24. Daniel D. Moss, in fact, argues that Drayton ultimately engages most closely with Daniel, at the expense of Drayton's overt gestures to Ovid and the *Heroides*. *The Ovidian Vogue: Literary Fashion and Imitative Practice in Late Elizabethan England* (Toronto: U of Toronto P, 2014), 133.
25. Because I will be referring to prefatory material that changes slightly in the 1619 edition, I cite *Englands Heroicall Epistles* (London, 1597), A2r.
26. Lindsay Ann Reid sees these glosses as evoking the glosses of E. K. in Spenser's *Shepheardes Calendar*, marking the topical relevance of the poems and signaling Drayton's indebtedness to Spenser. *Ovidian Bibliofictions and the Tudor Book: Metamorphosing Classical Heroines in Late Medieval and Renaissance England* (Farnham: Ashgate, 2014), 172.
27. As Bart van Es argues, Drayton's annotations do not simply anchor his poem in the chronicle tradition; they evince his own desire to make a more creative, literary contribution, even as they gesture to verifiable history. "Michael Drayton, Literary History, and Historians in Verse," *RES* 59 (2007), 261.
28. Danielle Clark considers the possibility that Drayton more often addresses female patrons when a female character pens the first letter of his paired epistles. "'Signifying, but not sounding': gender and paratext in the complaint genre," in *Renaissance Paratexts*, ed. Helen Smith and Louise Wilson (Cambridge: Cambridge UP, 2011), 147.
29. *The Heroycall Epistles*, trans. George Turberville (London, 1567), [I5v].
30. Barbara C. Ewell traces the underlying "unity" to be found in the "radically different shapes," Henry and Rosamond impose on "the same reality." "Unity and the Transformation of Drayton's Poetics in *Englands Heroicall Epistles*: From Mirrored Ideals to 'The Chaos of the Mind,'" *MLQ* 44 (1983): 238.
31. Kennedy observes that Ovid's heroines made similar self-reflexive gestures. "Epistolarity," 224. Reid sees these gestures throughout *Englands Heroicall Epistles* as foregrounding Drayton's intertextual engagement with is contemporaries. *Ovidian Bibliofictions*, 173. Alison Thorne reads the many anxious references to the act of writing in the women's epistles as illustrating a concern that to disclose their desires in letters is to risk a kind of "self-betrayal." "'Large complaints in little papers': negotiating Ovidian genealogies of complaint in Drayton's *Englands Heroicall Epistles*," *Renaissance Studies* 22.3 (2008): 373.
32. On the conflation of political loyalty and erotic submission, see Sanchez, *Erotic Subjects*, 33.

33. Garrett Sullivan treats the power of erotic memory to create a crisis of identity for Romeo, Antony, and particularly for Helena in Shakespeare's works. *Memory and Forgetting in English Renaissance Drama: Shakespeare, Marlowe, Webster* (Cambridge: Cambridge University Press, 2005), 48.
34. Danielle Clark notes the difficulty of addressing erotic desire, even in order to reject it, in the wronged virginal figures of Drayton's *England's Heroicall Epistles*. "Ovid's *Heroides*, Drayton and the articulation of the feminine in the English Renaissance," *Renaissance Studies* 22.3 (2008): 395.
35. Meghan C. Andrews argues that Drayton drew extensively on Shakespeare, not only on his *Lucrece*, but also on his history plays, in writing *Englands Heroicall Epistles*. "Michael Drayton, Shakespeare's Shadow," *SQ* 65 (2014): 299.

6 Guinevere's Ghost
Spenser's Response to Malory's Erotics

Kenneth Hodges

> One day, to pass the time in pleasure,
> we read of Lancelot, how love enthralled him.
> We were alone, without the least misgiving.
> More than once that reading made our eyes meet
> and drained the color from our faces.
> Still, it was a single instant overcame us:
> When we read how the longed-for smile
> was kissed by so renowned a lover, this man,
> who shall never be parted from me,
> all trembling, kissed me on my mouth.
> A Galeotto was the book and he that wrote it.
> That day we read no further.
>
> —Dante[1]

As Paolo and Francesca discover to their sorrow, memories of Launcelot and Guenevere are dangerous, the line between exquisite service and damnable sin almost invisible. Instead of an inert object, the book that records their deeds becomes a character in its own right, a Galeotto bringing lovers together, transforming memories into present temptation and sin. Sir Thomas Malory's *Le Morte Darthur*, printed just as the Middle Ages blurred into the Renaissance, made the seductive story of Launcelot and Guenevere widely available to English audiences. For Malory, too, their memory was an incitement to love, but unlike Dante, Malory endorses their love:

> [I]t gyueth vnto al louers courage, that lusty moneth of May. ... For thenne alle herbes and trees renewen a man and a woman, and in lyke wyse louers callen ageyne to their mynde old gentilnes and old seruyse and many kynde dedes that were forgeten by neclygence. For lyke as wynter rasure doth alway arase and deface grene somer, soo fareth it by vnstable loue in man and woman. ... But the old loue was not so: men and wymmen coude loue togyders seuen yeres and no lycours lustes were bitwene them; and thenne was loue trouthe and feythfulnes. And loo in lyke wyse was vsed loue in Kynge Arthurs dayes.

82   Kenneth Hodges

> Wherfor I liken loue nowadays vnto somer and wynter, for lyke as the one is hote and the other cold, so fareth loue nowadays. Therfore, alle ye that be louers, calle vnto your remembraunce the moneth of May lyke as dyd Quene Guenever, for whome I make here a lytel mencyon, that whyle she lyued she was a true louer, and therfor she had a good ende.[2]

This passage insists that true love is a matter of memory: fickle lovers forget; true lovers remember. However, this passage raises more questions than it answers about how sexuality properly interacts with love and religion. Malory may praise Guenevere here, but his story of the Grail appears to condemn sexuality. He allows no easy answers.

The memory of Launcelot's and Guenevere's erotic relationship haunts Edward Spenser's *Faerie Queene*. While the legend of King Arthur was an attractive vehicle to discuss English national identity, it was dangerously erotic, especially since the story of Launcelot and Guenevere marks how easily the relation between queen and knight could be corrupted. The frame of the poem, after all, involves Arthur's quest for the Faerie Queene who, as Spenser tells Raleigh, represents Queen Elizabeth.[3] While never appearing, Guenevere's memory shadows *The Faerie Queene*, a sexual ghost beside the virgin queen. One object Spenser uses to evoke and to manage the memory of Malory's work is a miraculous girdle. During the Grail quest, Galahad receives the "Sword with the Strange Girdles," whose magical girdle can only be replaced by a royal virgin who must stay virgin all her life; the spindles of the sword memorialize positively Eve's penitence and her loss of virginity and negatively Cain's murder of Abel. Spenser transforms this into Florimell's girdle, which marks not virginity but chastity, and whose history of mythological transition is switched to Venus and her transition not from virgin to mother but from loyal wife to adulteress. The girdles' shifting functions mark how the relation of eroticism with knightly and national identities has changed post-Reformation. The paired girdles' erotic entanglements show that Spenser was far more engaged with Malory's memory than criticism has realized. *Le Morte Darthur* is not a passive source text of a few marvels; it is a rival text, very much present in early modern England and with which *The Faerie Queene* actively engages to achieve its effects.

Despite our tendency to label it medieval, Sir Thomas Malory's *Le Morte Darthur* was influential in the early modern period. William Caxton printed it in 1485, about a month before Richard III fell at Bosworth Field and Henry VII established the Tudor dynasty. It was reprinted in 1498 and 1529 by Wynkyn de Worde, in 1557 by William Copland, and in the 1580s by Thomas East. However, under Elizabeth, using the Arthurian legend to model Protestant service for a virgin queen was difficult because Malory persistently intermingles knightly service with erotic love. Queen Elizabeth's tutor Roger Ascham famously blasted the morality of Malory's work, saying, "the whole pleasure of which booke standeth in two special poyntes, in open mans slaughter, and bold bawdrye. ... Yet I know, when Gods Bible was banished the Court, and *Morte Arthure* receiued into the Princes chamber."[4] His condemnation comes despite the fact that Malory's complex text includes a powerful critique of earthly engagements: the Grail quest condemns killing and most forms of sexuality, including Launcelot and Guenevere's affair. However, sixteenth-century Protestants could not simply embrace this condemnation of Guenevere's adultery, as the Grail quest primarily teaches Roman doctrines of transubstantiation (with the Grail having held both the wine of the Last Supper and Christ's blood from the crucifixion) and celebrates monastic asceticism. For Protestant readers, the Grail quest's rejection of the flesh was at least as bad as Launcelot and Guenevere's wanton enjoyment of it. In his introduction to a collection of John Calvin's sermons, Nathaniel Baxter complains about "that infamous lege[n]d of K. Arthur (which with shame inough I heare to be newly imprinted) with the horrible actes of those whoremasters, Launcelot du Lake, Tristram de Liones, Gareth of Orkney, Merlin, the lady of the Lake, with the vile and stinking story of the Sangreal."[5]

Instead of denouncing *Le Morte Darthur*, Edmund Spenser sought to reform the Arthurian legend.[6] Instead of denying the erotic and religious themes so deeply embedded in the cultural memory, he tried to redirect them into acceptable Protestant forms. Book 1 of *The Faerie Queene* uses the legend of Red Crosse to rewrite the Grail legend, diverting the Catholic quest for the pure Eucharist into a Protestant story of personal sin and repentance.[7] Problematic memories of medieval erotic love receive his attention next. Guyon destroys a garden that recalls the *Roman de la Rose*. Britomart becomes the avatar of a fecund chastity in which eroticism is linked to marriage and to dynasty, but which is entwined with memories of Malory. That she is an answer to Launcelot is apparent in theme and in some suggestive echoes.[8] Her character is defined not just *per se* but in relation to other characters, such as the fearful, fugitive Florimell; the passive, suffering Amoret; and the virginal Belphoebe; but this definition by triangulation of erotic chastity goes beyond characters present in *The Faerie Queene* to include the memory of characters in Malory, and these memories are invoked by the girdle Spenser stole from Malory.

Florimell's girdle that tests chastity echoes in many ways the girdle that tests virginity, which Perceval's sister weaves for Galahad's sword. Michael Leslie has already established the general connection between Florimell's girdle and the belts or baldrics used to carry swords, frequently used as symbols of chastity,[9] but the specific connection between the two girdles shows Spenser's careful *pas de deux* with Malory's text. Perceval's sister's girdle is part of a suite of significant objects that confront the Grail knights on the Ship of Faith, as they were assembled long before by the prophetic wife of King Solomon: King David's sword, hung on a plain hempen girdle, and a bed with mysterious spindles. Following prophecy, Perceval's sister replaces the old girdle with a new one, woven from her own hair. Gold and silver letters on the scabbard of King David's sword—known as the "Suerd with the Straunge Gyrdels" (1:499; XVII.7)—warn that the old girdle can only be replaced by a dedicated virgin:

> [N]one be soo hardy to doo awey this gyrdel, for it oughte not to be done away but by the hands of a mayde, and that she be a kynges doughter and quenes, and she must be a mayde alle the dayes of her lyf, bothe in wylle and in dede. And yf she breke her vyrgynyte, she shalle dye the moost vylaynous dethe that euer dyd ony woman. (1:485; XVII.4)

Florimell's girdle is less extreme: it is tied to virtuous wifehood, not virginity, and the penalty is not villainous death but social shame:

> That girdle gaue the virtue of chast loue,
> And wiuehood true, to all that did it beare;
> But whosoeuer contrarie did proue,
> Might not the same about her middle weare,
> But it would loose, or else a sunder teare. (IV.v.3)

However, the difference between Malory's celebration of virginity and Spenser's celebration of chastity is not as great as it first appears. Both girdles are put in a context of divine approval of licensed sexuality. In Spenser, the girdle originally belongs to Venus, made for her by Vulcan, but lost when she began her affair with Mars (IV.v.3–6). In Malory, the spindles on the bed that accompany the Sword of the Strange Girdle come from a miraculous tree. Eve brought out of Paradise the branch of the apple tree that was her downfall, and she planted it in penitence. It grew white, because a virgin planted it. But then "God came to Adam and bad hym knowe his wyf fleshly as nature requyred" (1:486; XVII.5), and its seedlings turned green. The treatment of Eve, emphasizing not sin but penitence, is surprisingly sympathetic. The whiteness of the wood that marks her virginity fits well with the Grail quest's celebration of virginity, but her loss of virginity is also celebrated: she is following divine will, and the green fertility of the tree responds to her sexuality. So, while Perceval's sister's girdle celebrates virginity, the associated spindles acknowledge and praise married sexuality. Both girdles then are linked to an Old Testament context: in Malory, the ship, bed, sword, and old girdle are prepared by Solomon and his wife; in Spenser, Satyrane brings Florimell's girdle to the tournament in an "arke / of gold, that bad eyes might it not prophane" (IV.iv.15), recalling the Ark of the Covenant that resided in Solomon's temple. The link to King David (like Arthur, one of the Nine Worthies), Solomon, and the temple help establish the royal importance of regulated sexuality; it also moves from originary sexuality to a period of sexuality constrained by biblical law.

The girdles, in linking Florimell to Perceval's sister, reveal a cluster of other similarities, none of them absolute allusions but together creating a constellation of similarity against which differences in theme can be seen. Perceval's sister is repeatedly linked to ships and the sea; so, too, is Florimell, with her love of Marinell and her time with Proteus. Both have their carnality threatened by forms of consumption that go beyond the sexual. Florimell, after her visit to the witch's hut, is pursued by the hyena "that feeds on wemens flesh, as others feede on gras" (III.vii.22). Perceval's sister, after leaving the Ship of Faith, is attacked by knights who serve a lady whose illness can only be cured by the blood of a royal virgin and have therefore been demanding blood from passing women for years (1:491–93; XVII.10–11). The women's relations to their bodies are highlighted by the persistence of soulless bodies, perhaps suggesting the absurdity of treating a merely physical chastity as a virtue. Perceval's sister, who dies after voluntarily being bled to heal the sick lady, leaves a body that is put to sea, where it accompanies Launcelot for over a month (1: 494; XVII.13), before it finally drifts to Sarras, where she is buried beside Galahad (1:505; XVII.23). Her dead body becomes an object of reverence and a means of instruction. In Spenser, of course, Florimell does not die, having taken refuge in the sea, but the death of her horse and the loss of her girdle make others think she is dead. To assuage the sorrow of her loutish son, the witch makes the snowy Florimell, described as a "carcas dead" (III.viii.7). This snowy body then becomes an object of desire and controversy. Florimell and Perceval's sister, considered together, map a complicated topography of forms of sexual purity.

The passion of Perceval's sister is partly inherited from Guenevere, and the dead virgin is a reflection on the adulterous queen. Eroticism, in other words, is not simply the product of individual moments but of intertextual memory. Malory creates genealogical links tying Guenevere to Perceval's sister.[10] When Arthur meets Perceval's father Pellinore, Merlin prophesies to Arthur that "ye shal be right glad to yeue him your sister to wedde" (1:60; II.25). Pellinore's sons are then included in a list of Arthur's nephews when they enter a tournament (1:187; VII.27). Since *sister* in Middle English could mean either *sister* or *sister in law*, Pellinore has married either Arthur's sister or Guenevere's; for a variety of reasons, chiefly the widely known and admired love affair between Pellinore's son Lamorak and Arthur's half-sister Morgause, it is most likely that Pellinore's wife is Guenevere's sister. That would make Perceval and Perceval's sister her nephew and niece by blood (and Perceval's aunt, who gives Perceval religious advice at the start of the quest would also be a sister of Guenevere's). Her kinship to Guenevere, reinforced by her own namelessness, offers Perceval's sister as an inviting stand-in for a religious consideration of the queen's sexuality and spirituality. Perceval's sister's girdle, a product of pure virginity, is entangled with divine histories of married sexuality in the stories of Eve and Adam, Solomon's wife and Solomon, in ways that make more sense if we recognize that Perceval's sister is being used to comment on Guenevere.

The presence of Launcelot's kin on the Grail quest illuminates the state of his soul and his dissipated holiness. Two of the three Grail knights are kin to Launcelot. Bors is Launcelot's nephew (or cousin). Galahad is forcefully tied to Launcelot: not only is Galahad Launcelot's son and the one who wrests the title of best knight from him, but the two are linked by repeated prophecies and comparisons. The recognition that Guenevere's kin are also present in large numbers in the Grail quest, though, reveals that Malory was not concerned simply with Launcelot's soul. Instead, mirrors of both lovers provide perspectives on the intersection of love and holiness. In particular, the pairing of Galahad and Perceval's sister reflects the pairing of Launcelot and Guenevere. Martin Shichtman has pointed out the intense undercurrent of eroticism as Galahad and Perceval's sister discuss the sheathing of his sword in her girdle in the chamber dominated by a mystic bed. He writes:

> Virginity becomes eroticized in the relationship between Galahad and Percival's sister. Matched well in their holiness, in their saintly certitude, the two participate in what might be read as a symbolic wedding ceremony, with a symbolic consummation—their very chastity setting off sparks.[11]

Certainly Malory's prose when read with an ear for double entendre is suggestive, with Galahad's phallic sword, first gripped by him before she touches it, and his claim that it is hers as much as his, then in the ecstatic aftermath their pledges to each other:

> Thenne they sayd to Galahad, in the name of Ihesu Cryste, we praye yow that ye gyrd you with this suerd whiche hath ben desired so moche in the realme of Logrys. Now lete me begynne, sayd Galahad, to grype thys swerd for to gyue yow courage. But wete ye wel, hit longeth no more to me than it doth to yow. And thenne he gryped aboute hit with his fyngers a grete dele, and thenne she gyrte hym aboute the myddel with the swerd. Now rek I not though I dye, for now I hold me one of the blessed maydens of the world, whiche hath made the worthiest knyght of the world. Damoysel, sayd Galahad, ye haue done soo moche that I shalle be your knyghte alle the dayes of my lyf. (1:489; XVII.7)

The pleasure in seeing these two help satisfy each other's deepest desires comes not just from the familiar medieval mystical claim that the desire for the closeness of God is greater and offers more joys than any other human drive. There is also relief. The sexual energy here is not sinful or in any way forbidden: it is something the characters embrace and rejoice in. *Erotic* is not a word either Spenser or Malory is likely to have heard: the *Oxford English Dictionary* records the first usage in 1668, after Richard Burton used *erotical* in 1621 in his *Anatomy of Melancholy*.[12] But, if we understand *erotic* to be not just a synonym for *sexual* but rather a word that celebrates the pleasures of the sexual, then this is certainly an erotic (if unambiguously virginal) scene.

The scene echoes Guenevere's gift of a sword to Launcelot at his knighting. As Launcelot reminds King Arthur:

> I ought of ryghte euer to be in your quarrel, and in my lady the quenes quarrel, to do batail. For ye ar the man that gaf me the hyghe ordre of knyghthode, and that day my lady your quene dyd me grete worship, and els I had ben shamed. For that same day ye made me knyghte, thurgh my hastynesse I lost my suerd, and my lady your quene fond hit, and lapped hit in her trayne, and gafe me my suerd when I hadde need therto, and els had I ben shamed emonge alle knyghtes. And therfor, my lord Arthur, I promised her at that day euer to be her knyghte in ryghte outher in wronge. (1:514; XVIII.7)

Many elements are the same: the gift of the sword, the woman's intimately wrapping it in something closely associated with her, the knight's grateful promise of lifetime service. Chronologically, Launcelot and Guenevere's exchange comes first, long before Galahad's birth; narratively, however, it is only recounted after, letting each scene provide context for the other. Galahad and Perceval's sister reveal the secular context of Launcelot and Guenevere's relationship, and if there is less overt eroticism (at least in Launcelot's account of it to Guenevere's husband), Launcelot's promise to serve the queen in right or wrong has a slightly ominous ring to it. Clearly, Malory's Grail quest can be used to reject adultery and indeed sexual activity in general; however, the erotic elements persist in the intense engagement of knight and damsel for the pleasure and inspiration of both. Furthermore, Perceval's sister ensures that when earthly sexuality is rejected, women are not rejected along with it in favor of an all-male world where (hetero)sexual temptation could be avoided. Instead, Malory presents us with a religious, virginal woman who participates in many of the adventures of the Grail quest.

By linking Florimell to Perceval's sister, Spenser creates an intertextual web connecting Guenevere, Perceval's Sister, Britomart, Amoret, Belphoebe, The Faerie Queene herself, and others so that *chastity* is defined by a complex set of comparative contrasts. In the "Letter to Ralegh," Spenser speaks of "the loue of Britomart, the ouerthrow of Marinell, the misery of Florimell, the vertuousnes of Belphoebe" (718). Virginity may be the path of serene virtue, Britomart's chastity may be protected by strength and high purpose, but Marinell's overthrow and Florimell's misery are acceptable parts of chaste human sexuality.[13] Florimell's girdle helps mark the nuances that distinguish Malory's rebuke of Guenevere (emphasizing ascetic virginity) from Spenser's (emphasizing temperate chastity). This wide-spread web complicates binary readings of the poem. Lauren Silberman suggests that Florimell's "girdle represents female genitalia" and that it serves as a sort of visible hymen, marking a woman's sexual state.[14] She goes on to argue that the girdle must be understood as part of a putative Elizabethan sexual binary that praised virginity and condemned its loss, to the extent that the focus on the hymen "excludes post-hymeneal, married chastity from the universe of discourse."[15] She supports this by noting the judges award the girdle to the false Florimell despite Amoret's being the one who can actually wear it, showing an inability to recognize married chastity.[16] Spenser may indeed be critiquing the exaltation of virginity, but the girdle cannot be reduced to the representation of virginity or of the hymen. Instead of representing one extreme end of the sexual spectrum, as Pereceval's sister's girdle (which tests both physical purity and mental intent) does, Florimell's girdle occupies the middle. Furthermore, it is a familiar middle, very much part of the inherited discourse.[17] The idea of a mantle that proves chastity, not virginity, has a long medieval history in romances, *fabliaux*, and ballads.[18] Malory includes a chastity test for wives: Morgen le Fay creates a drinking horn that only a chaste wife can drink from without spilling, which creates chaos when it reaches the court of Cornwall (1:233; VIII.34). This drinking horn may invoke (male) sex organs, but obviously it tests the wives' ability to handle a horn decorously, not whether or not they are virgins. Spenser, in transforming this mantle into a girdle, creates a contrast to Perceval's sister's girdle precisely to explore the difference between chastity and virginity. This, in turn, forces one away from purely physical readings of the girdle. The loss of chastity, unlike the loss of virginity, is not marked on the body. When Andrew Marvell has the ghastly image of worms testing his lover's long-preserved virginity in "To His Coy Mistress," he marks the danger that virginity might lead to an irrational exaltation of the flesh without attention to the state of the virgin spirit. Perceval's sister's unblemished body continues to circulate long after she is dead, but Spenser is less interested in such relics, and the decision to award the girdle to the soulless body of the false Florimell is clearly a failure to understand what the girdle represents. The false Florimell's failure to wear the girdle may represent, as the cynical Squire of Dames assumes, physical sexual misconduct; however, one wonders if, even if the snow maiden were still maiden, the girdle might register the absence of the spiritual commitment to chastity that the soulless artefact cannot have. Artegall's final restoration of the girdle to Florimell for her wedding re-establishes married chastity as a positive virtue, not simply the absence of virginity and the absence of extra-marital lovers, and celebrates her new status as wife that decisively distinguishes her from her double who can mimic her only when love is a matter of pursuit and dispute, not loving marriage.

Focusing not on the physical traces of chastity but on the psychological or spiritual sides of it starts to shed light on Florimell's relation to the sea. Perceval's sister's virginity, actively desired and demanded by her faith, is marked by an allegorical relation to the sea. When Perceval's sister leads the knights to the Ship of Faith, and then when her dead body is put to sea in a rudderless boat, she participates in a trope repeated in a number of stories, including Chaucer's *Man of Law's Tale*, in which miraculous, undirected sea voyages are a marker of providence and the saintly worth of the boat's occupant.[19] For Perceval's sister, the sea is where she has her passionately pure encounter with Galahad; it is at sea where her corpse spends time as a silent instructress of Launcelot; it is the sea that finally brings her body to Sarras where her body can be laid by the side of Galahad and her brother Perceval. Her submission to the sea, following not her will but her faith, is tied to her purity.

The sojourn on the Ship of Faith marks a narrative separation in Malory's Grail quest, dividing those who are pure in faith from those who are not. Initially, the story follows the Grail knights but also Gawain and others who are too sinful ever to achieve the Grail. After the time in the ship, the narrative focuses only on Bors, Galahad, Perceval, and Launcelot, who at least sees a glimpse of the Grail. At the same time, the sea comes to connect Britain to the roots of its religious heritage: unguided ships take the Grail knights and Perceval's sister back to the Middle East, back whence the Grail came, back to the lands where Jesus died. In doing so, they connect the British present to the religious past.[20] The journey of ships to Britain, guided or not, mapped the roots of cultural inheritance: Diocletian's daughters, Brutus and his men, Custance bearing the gospel. The return of a religious figure from Britain to the Mediterranean completes a cycle and shows British maturity as an established community claiming equality with its progenitors. Perceval's sister's personal purity connects her not simply to God but to a religious community extending across time and oceans, helping define Britain's place in the world and history.

Like Malory, Spenser uses the waters for nationalist purposes, as when the Thames and the Medway marry (their wedding brings the chastened Marinell to hear Florimell's lament, tying their individual story to a political allegory) but the oceans are not the convenient pathways protecting the faithful or tying the British church to continental origins. Petrarch taught early modern readers to read the sea as the stormy site of human passion. In love, a rudderless boat is not a ship of faith where an unnamed sister of Perceval's can unexpectedly be granted the spiritual authority to instruct Galahad; instead, it represents the lover's psyche, vulnerable and lost without a trusty pilot, buffeted by emotions. In this externalization of the psychology of the two women, Malory's and Spenser's oceans are treated very differently, suggesting that while married chastity may have many of the same religious elements as virginity, it differs in its engagement with the tempestuous landscape of erotic human relations.

Britomart, just before she meets Marinell, laments:

> Huge sea of sorrow, and tempestuous griefe,
> Wherein my feeble barke is tossed long,
> Far from the hoped hauen of reliefe,

> Why doe thy cruel billowes beat so strong,
> And thy moist mountains each on others throng,
> Threatning to swallow vp my fearefull lyfe?
> O doe thy cruell wrath and spightfull wrong
> At length allay, and stint thy stormy stryfe,
> Which in thy troubled bowels raignes, and rageth ryfe.
>
> For else my feeble vessell crazd, and crackt
> Through thy strong buffets and outrageous blowes,
> Cannot endure, but needs it must be wrackt
> On the rough rocks, or on the sandy shallowes,
> The whiles that loue it steres, and fortune rowes;
> Loue my lewd Pilott hath a restless minde
> And fortune Boteswaine no assuraunce knowes,
> But saile withouten stares, gainst tyde and winde:
> How can they other doe, sith both are bold and blinde?
>
> Thou God of windes, that raignest in the seas,
> That raignest also in the Continent,
> At last blow vp some gentle gale of ease,
> The which may bring my ship, ere it be rent,
> Vnto the gladsome port of her intent. (III.iv.8–10)

While Britomart's ending prayer recalls the ship of faith, she substitutes Aeolus and Neptune for the Christian God, and these are more turbulent and changeable deities.

The difference between the seas in Malory and Spenser is tied to the different presentation of girdles. For Perceval's sister, a small ship upon the sea is a place of safety and authority: it is here that she presents her girdle to Galahad, the physical sign of their spiritual love. Her surrendering to the power of the sea is figured as faith surrendering to the love of God. In Spenser, however, the sea is the realm of Proteus, Florimell's opponent. Proteus is the source of the misunderstood prophecy that keeps Marinell from loving her. He then becomes her captor, offering in his infinite variety of shapes the seductive appeal of inconstancy. Florimell goes to sea in a small ship out of desperation when she attempts to escape the hyena. At first, it seems like Perceval's sister, Chaucer's Custance, and so many other innocent women, Florimell will be guided and protected in the small boat as the fisherman sleeps and the boat is unpiloted:

> For being fled into the fishers bote,
> For refuge from the Monsters cruelty,
> Long so she on the mighty maine did flote,
> And with the tide droue forward carelesly,
> For th'ayre was milde, and cleared was the skie,
> And all his windes *Dan Aelous* did keepe,

From stirring vp their stormy enmity,
As pittying to see her waile and weepe;
But all the while the fisher did securely sleep. (III.viii.23)

Unfortunately for her, this does not last. The fisherman wakes and attempts to rape her, and when Florimell springs into the sea to escape, she becomes prey to Proteus himself. Given the troublesome passions of the ocean, it is not surprising, perhaps, that she loses her girdle on the shore, just before she gets onto the boat. Perceval's sister's virginity may thrive in the space of faith upon the waters; Florimell's chastity is imperiled by the limitless power of passion that the sea represents.

The difference in the sea, in turn, makes the shore a different place in Spenser than in Malory. In Malory's Grail quest, where the sea so often represents faith, the shore can be a space of unwelcome compromise. In a small, damning detail that shows Launcelot's inability to sustain the heights of religious fervor, Malory reports that, after sailing on the rudderless ship for some time and sustained by manna provided by the grace of God, Launcelot "on a nyghte he wente to playe hym by the waterside, for he was somewhat wery of the ship" (1:494; XVII.13). In Spenser, though, the shore initially seems a more promising space.[21] Florimell loves Marinell of the Rich Strond, a figure that inhabits the boundary between the restless ocean and the stable land (Spenser has Britomart use the suggestive word "Continent").

Yet the shore does not bring them together in a continent union mixing the best of the rich, passionate ocean and the stable land. Marinell initially rejects women's love because Proteus had prophesied that "A virgin straunge and stout him should dismay, or kill" (III.iv.25) and his mother took this as a warning against love. This illustrates the dangers (to all concerned) of a chastity based on misogyny rather than on positive virtue.[22] This is an echo of Malory: at the start of the Grail quest, the prophet Nacien commands "that none in the queste lede lady nor gentylwoman with hym, for hit is not to do in so hyghe a seruyse as they labour in" (1:433; XIII.8). After that warning, both Bors and Perceval have encounters with fiends disguised as women who try to seduce and destroy them. Thus, when Perceval's sister, described at first as merely a gentlewoman, knocks on the door of the hermitage where Galahad is staying and asks him to follow her, a reader is not primed to recognize her as a holy figure. When, in her discourse, she treats Eve sympathetically (1:486; XVII.5), rebukes Solomon for his antifeminism (1:487; XVII.5), and makes Solomon's wife the prime mover in the preparation of the ship with its sword and bed, she corrects the potential misogyny of the male knights' asceticism; this rejection of misogyny allows the sublimated eroticism of her interaction with Galahad to emerge as a positive force ennobling both of them. In Spenser, the potential misogyny is clear in Marinell's mother's misinterpretation of Proteus' prophecy, corrected violently by Britomart's spear. Marinell's injury draws Florimell from the court: like Britomart's, her chastity is coupled with an honest desire for her lover.

Unlike Britomart, she is painfully vulnerable, and she is pursued for most of the rest of the text. In *The Faerie Queene*, at least, men are at least as likely as women to function as threats to chastity.

However, the meeting of Marinell and Florimell revises our understanding of her relation to the ocean. Just as, contrary to what Proteus' prophecy led Marinell's mother to believe, Florimell actually becomes the agent of healing, so Florimell's flight to the sea actually provides the mechanism for her union with Marinell. After Marinell finds her in Proteus' prison, he cannot figure out how to get her out, so he pines away. His mother finally finds the remedy in Neptune, god of the sea, and she does so by the legalistic argument that, as Marinell has claim to all the treasures that fall into the sea, Marinell should have rightful claim to Florimell (IV.xii.31). Her entrusting herself to the small boat thus leads her to the right place (Proteus' palace, where the wedding of Thames and Medway is celebrated) and gives her the right claim (her status as a cast away) to achieve her love. Symbolically it makes sense that she finds married chastity not by avoiding but by braving the turbulent seas of love; in terms of the shadow of Perceval's sister, whose travels on the Grail quest lead to her physical death but spiritual salvation, this is a successful translation of many recognizable elements of Malory's Catholic, ascetic, virginal discourse into Spenser's exploration of erotic chastity.

Literary memory thus affects later presentations of eroticism and virtue. The seductive power of Launcelot and Guenevere's love shaped literature long after Dante acknowledged it. The Grail quest was an attempt to manage the erotic energy by channeling it into religious mysticism. Perceval's sister and Galahad invoke the memory of the adulterous love in order to model a passionate virginity. Perceval's sister's girdle, lovingly woven for Galahad out of her own hair, becomes the vehicle to connect the Arthurian love story to older biblical stories as well. Spenser, carefully trying to rework the Arthurian material to celebrate a virgin queen, uses the girdle as the explicit point of contact to Malory, linking his work on chastity not directly to Guenevere but to her virgin double. He brings with the girdle a suite of images, so that his story of Florimell interlocks with Perceval's sister's on a number of levels, creating meaning through a promiscuous series of intertextual entanglements. He may reject Malory's bold bawdry and erase Guenevere from the narrative, but he preserves the religious eroticism and weds it to a more literal human sexuality.

Notes

1. Dante, *Inferno*, trans. Robert Hollander and Jean Hollander (New York: Anchor Books, 2002; originally New York: Doubleday, 2000) V.127–38.
2. *Caxton's Malory*, ed. James W. Spivak and William Matthews (Berkeley: University of California Press, 1983) 1:537; XVIII.24. Spenser and the Elizabethans would have known only editions based on Caxton's printing, and so it is Caxton's edition I shall cite throughout. For convenience in consulting other

editions of Malory, I cite both by page number and by Caxton's book and chapter numbers.
3. Edmund Spenser, "A Letter of the Authors ...," *The Faerie Queene*, 2nd edn., ed. A. C. Hamilton, Hiroshi Yamashita, Toshiyuki Suzuki, and Shohachi Fukuda (Harlow: Pearson, 2001), 716. All citations of *The Faerie Queene* will be to this edition.
4. Ascham, *The Scholemaster*, in *The English Works of Roger Ascham*, ed. William Aldis Wright (Cambridge: Cambridge University Press, 1904), 231.
5. Baxter, "Epistle Dedicatorye," in John Calvin, *The Lectures of Daily Sermons, of that Reverend Diuine, D. Iohn Caluine, Pastor of the Church of God in Geneua, vpon the Prophet Ionas* (London: J. Charlewood for Edward White, 1578), A2v-A3r. Accessed through Early English Books Online, 24 Oct. 2013.
6. For Malory's influence on Spenser, see Mark Lambert, "Malory, Thomas" in *The Spenser Encyclopaedi*, ed. A. C. Hamilton et al. (Florence, KY: Routledge, 1990), 450–51; Andrew King, *The Faerie Queene and Middle English Romance: The Matter of Just Memory* (Oxford, 2000); Paul Rovang, Refashioning 'Knights and Ladies Gentle Deeds': The Intertextuality of Spenser's *Faerie Queene* and Malory's *Morte Darthur* (Madison, NJ: Fairleigh Dickinson University Press, 1996); and David Summers, Spenser's Arthur: *The British Arthurian Tradition and The Faerie Queene* (Lanham, MD: University Press of America, 1997).
7. Kenneth Hodges, "Reformed Dragons: Bevis of Hampton, Sir Thomas Malory's *Le Morte Darthur*, and Spenser's *Faerie Queene*," *Texas Studies in Literature and Language*, 54.1 (2012): 110–31; and "Making Arthur Protestant: Translating Malory's Grail Quest into Spenser's Book of Holiness," *The Review of English Studies* 62.254 (2011): 193–211.
8. In III.i.31, Britomart comes to Castle Joyous, whose name is suggestive of Launcelot's castle Joyous Gard, and the unfortunate drama of two people of the same sex ending up in bed together and the fighting that occurs there when Malacasta invites herself into Britomart's bed is loosely reminiscent of Launcelot's experience with Belleus.
9. Leslie, Spenser's *"Fierce Warres and Faithfull Loves": Martial and Chivalric Symbolism in The Faerie Queene* (Cambridge, UK: D. S. Brewer, 1983), 169–78.
10. For a fuller argument, see Dorsey Armstrong and Kenneth Hodges, *Mapping Malory: Regional Identities and National Geographies in Le Morte Darthur* (New York: Palgrave, 2014), 45–71.
11. Shichtman, "Percival's Sister: Genealogy, Virginity, and Blood," *Arthuriana* 9.2 (1999), 16.
12. "erotic, adj. and n." OED Online. December 2014. Oxford University Press. http://www.oed.com/view/Entry/64083?redirectedFrom=erotic& (accessed January 23, 2015).
13. Spenser's use of vulnerability and suffering is complex: for an account of it, see, Joseph Campana, *The Pain of Reformation: Spenser, Vulnerability, and the Ethics of Masculinity* (New York: Fordham University Press, 2012), 163–203.
14. Silberman, *Transforming Desire: Erotic Knowledge in Books III and IV of The Faerie Queene* (Berkeley: University of California Press, 1995), 101–102.
15. Silberman, *Transforming Desire*, 103.
16. Silberman, *Transforming Desire*, 104.
17. See for instance Joanna Thompson, *The Character of Britomart in Spenser's Faerie Queene* (Lewiston, NY: Edward Mellen Press, 2001), 27–60.

18. Francis James Child, *The English and Scottish Popular Ballads*, 5 vols., (New York: Dover, 1965; originally Boston: Houghton, Mifflin, and Company, 1884–98) 1: 257–71.
19. See, for instance, Helen Cooper, *The English Romance in Time: Transforming Motifs from Geoffrey of Monmouth to the Death of Shakespeare* (Oxford: Oxford University Press, 2004), 106–26; Geraldine Heng, *Empire of Magic: Medieval Romance and the Politics of Cultural Fantasy* (New York: Columbia University Press, 2003) 180–237.
20. Armstrong and Hodges, *Mapping Malory*, 101–32.
21. The tradition of reading the marriage of Marinell and Florimell as a marriage of sea and land enhances the value of the Rich Strond as a meeting of oceanic passion and stable continence. See for instance Thomas P. Roche, Jr., *The Kindly Flame: A Study of the Third and Fourth Books of Spenser's Faerie Queene* (Princeton: Princeton University Press, 1964), 189–94 and "Marinell," *The Spenser Encyclopedia*, ed. A. C. Hamilton et al. (Toronto: University of Toronto Press, 1990), 453; David O. Frantz, "The Union of Florimell and Marinell: The Triumph of Hearing," *Spenser Studies* 6 (1985), 124.
22. Silberman is surely right that his behavior exhibits "gynophobia," not just the narcissism and potential homosexual desire that Nohrnberg describes and calls a "specious chastity." See Silberman, *Transforming Desire*, 27; James Nohrnberg, *The Analogy of The Faerie Queene* (Princeton: Princeton University Press, 1976), 431.

Part II
Bodies, Remember

7 The Gallery of Erotic Memory in *The Faerie Queene*

Goran V. Stanivukovic

Readers of Edmund Spenser's *The Faerie Queene* (1590) are familiar with the depiction of memory as an antiquarian called Eumnestes. He is a keeper of old books and manuscript scrolls, preserving records of the past from forgetting and perishing. Spenser's description of antiquity frames the House of Alma (Book II, canto 9, stanzas 54–60) as "an account of the relations among memory, history, discipline and heroic action."[1] Although in the first instance this connection of memory with books and scrolls "invites us to consider memory in relation to early modern textual practices"[2], Eumnestes' chamber also links Spenser's depiction of memory with the mnemonic system as described in the rhetorical system in the early modern period. This essay argues that Spenser's renewed interest in artificial memory determines the stylistic and conceptual medium for his erotic writing. In this essay 'erotic writing' refers to the "literary quality that deals in a fundamental way with human physical sexual activity."[3] Extending this understanding of eroticism to *The Faerie Queene* to the mnemonic system, we can say that Spenser's poem is not just a great epic of Elizabethan national history but also a key text of erotic literature built on the classical foundation of natural and artificial memory.

The author of the rhetorical treatise *Ad Herennium*, composed in the 5th century BCE and sometimes attributed to Cicero, writes that

> artificial memory includes backgrounds and images. By backgrounds I mean such scenes as are naturally or artificially set off on a small scale, complete and conspicuous, so that we can grasp and embrace them easily by the natural memory—for example, a house, an intercolumnar space, a recess, an arch, or the like. An image is, as it were, a figure, mark, or portrait of the object we wish to remember.[4]

This description of memory as a cognitive place that shapes un-forgetting provides the conceptual model for Spenser's writing about the past. Spenser follows the classical idea of arranging places and images within imagined houses and different architectural forms like caves and rooms as sites for allegorical digressions in his poem. Eumnestes' "ruinous and old"[5] (55) chamber of memory in the House of Alma is only one of the rooms in the second book crafted in the tradition of *Ad Herennium*. In this room, the past is revived allegorically through the images, classical figures, myths, and stories of erotic nature that represent a strong counterpoint to the heroic narrative.

Some of Spenser's recent critics have argued that the "model of natural memory," especially as it is manifested in "a peculiar national memory," underpins the political implication of the memory scene in the House of Alma.[6] Yet this model of memory represents only one side of a more complex scene of memory in the House of Alma. In this house, memory works across several thematic layers and blends two models of memory, natural and artificial. While natural memory is the ability to recollect images and places, or to memorize, resulting from the practice of rote learning, artificial memory represents a way of structuring a speech around previously identified places; artificial memory helps "speakers to remember their speeches during delivery."[7] Spenser would have been familiar with the mnemonic system conceptualized as both natural and artificial memory from his training in classical rhetoric that he received in The Merchant Taylors' School in London. Artificial memory provides a more structured but no less diverse way of organizing recollection into a specific textual form, making memory sites constituent segments in the architectonic of Spenser's poem. Within the stanzas[8] of individual cantos and books of Spenser's romance epic, the places (*loci*) and images of artificial memory are arranged in such a way that they reinforce the allegories upon which the houses and rooms are built. This rhetorical commonplace of arranging places to correspond with ideas in a system of memory was familiar to Spenser's contemporaries. In an echo of *Ad Herrenium*, John Willis, a seventeenth-century English translator of his own Latin original of a treatise of memory entitled *The Art of Memory. So far forth as it dependeth upon Places and Idea's* [sic] (1621), writes:

> The Art of Memorie, so farre foorth as it dependeth upon Places and Idea's [sic], consisteth of two parts. *Reposition* is that part, whereby things to be remembred, are layd up in minde by their Ideas, bestowed in the places of *Repositories*. A *Repositorie* is an imaginary house or building.[9]

The classical system of *ars memoria* is "based on the association of specific sounds, words, ideas, or arguments with a physical space—a wall, or part of a building—divided into a matching number of compartments."[10] Frances Yates has amply demonstrated that artificial memory was fully embraced in the sixteenth century.[11] The prevalence of rooms and castles as structural forms of narrative composition within Spenser's 1590 and 1595 *The Faerie Queene* registers the prevalence of artificial memory as the compositional and cognitive strategy of Spenser's erotic writing. Following the rules of humanist theory of memory and Petrus Ramus's reform of the rhetorical system, Spenser uses such rooms and houses as spaces of artificial memory

The Gallery of Erotic Memory in The Faerie Queene 99

within ekphrastic writing. Writing about the role of ekphrasis in classical romances, Margaret Anne Doody states, that *"ekphrasis in a fictional text not only recalls to us myth, legend, history, but also, and cardinally, reminds us that we have a moral, aesthetic, and intellectual duty not only to perceive [...] but also to interpret the entire work at hand."*[12] Ekphrasis in Spenser is one of the main forms of writing and representation through which myth and history are remembered. It is also the main conduit for erotic and sexual knowledge in a text otherwise routinely associated with heroic, political, and nationalistic endeavors.

The text of *The Faerie Queene*, as Simon Shepherd has noticed, "assumes a male readership, in that it offers points of identification available to men only and objects of desire culturally designated for men rather than women."[13] Ekphrasis highlights the poem's deep interest in eroticism, especially the relationship between sexuality and female chastity, temperance of the heroic man, the danger sex and rape posit to the commonwealth, and the representational nature of sexuality. But Spenser is also alert to the difficulties and dangers that male sexual desire creates for women, and his epic romance pays tribute to that literary affect especially in sites of erotic ekphrasis. Questions raised in the process of interpreting the visual and verbal writing about desire and sexuality in Spenser's poem are not merely whether such sites of memory disturb or transgress the heroic narrative, but what possible range of ideas emerge in such a reading. The link between memory and eroticism in Spenser is most apparent in moments when his erotic writing is enhanced through vivid pictorialism. In those moments Spenser's poetry becomes, what Philip Sidney calls "speaking picture,"[14] echoing Horace's *Ars poetica*. Spenser's visual poetry of desire involves pagan gods and goddesses caught in the sexual action and in acts of sexual violence. The sensual world of *The Faerie Queene*, in which "rape is sometimes strangely transmuted,"[15] suggests that the building of a new national commonwealth, like the female body, is under threat by male sexuality. Page after page, *The Faerie Queene* reveals the extent to which sex is inextricable from, if repressed within, national history. If Spenser's erotic ekphrasis, as one critic has observed, "focuses at least as much on the seductive power of women as on the sexually predatory violence of men,"[16] then ekphrasis reveals itself as a form through which Spenser represents the complex interplay of politics, eroticism, and violence in the gendered bodies of both men and women in his poem. The erotic ekphrasis in Spenser attempts to preserve eroticism from historical forgetting. It is also a site of pleasure and a source of pleasure for Spenser's readers. What sex and the past share is that they are both subject to representations.

The connection between memory and eroticism in *The Faerie Queene* has consistently eluded critics who have otherwise written perceptively about eroticism in Spenser's poem. From G. Wilson Knight's assertion, in 1939, that Spenser's "poem is concerned heavily with man's erotic and sensuous nature"[17] to a recent elucidation of the "narratives of sexual violence"[18] in *The Faerie Queene*, scholars have treated eroticism as either a major topic of agency, or as a constituent element of political discourse. Yet, what kind of "erotic knowledge"[19] does Spenser's poem remember in the spaces of memory? This essay's central contention is that where memory speaks through pictures laden with erotic meaning from classical antiquity, Spenser's ekphrasis makes memory rooms and houses, not sites of mystic fantasy but places of verbal and visual representations of sexuality. As memory is a faculty that turns places and images into meaning-producing forms, memory's erotic chamber is neither merely an ornament nor just a repository of classical knowledge. Rather, the erotic ekphrasis is a dynamic place. It is a site of agency, prescribing "particular modes of behavior and specific kinds of action."[20] Memory that brings back from the archives of the mythical erotic iconography the images and stories of sexualized nature appeals to interiority and affect, reminding us of what Richard Burton says about memory. "Memory", Burton says, "lays up all the species which the senses have brought in, and records them as a good register, that they may be forthcoming when they are called for by phantasy and reason."[21] For Burton, memory is produced by affect, but it also appeals to reason. The meaning of the erotic ekphrasis, then, emerges in our perception of the interplay between the cognitive and the affective energies that Spenser exploits. In that, erotic ekphrasis in Spenser is a reminder that, like any history, sexuality is always the subject of, and is produced by, memory. Memory, that is, helps fight forgetting that always threatens sexual agency with oblivion and repression.

"Castle Ioyeous," a place of delight in Book III (Canto 1) is one such place where memory saves erotic joy from the oblivion of time. The inside of the castle is covered with a tapestry representing the story of Venus and Adonis, with "cunning hand ... pourtrahed" (stanza 34). The emphasis on artistic workmanship and the work of imagination relate eroticism to representation. Adonis' transformation is depicted as "A worke of rare deuice, and wondrous wit" (34). In his tapestry of memory, each stanza captures the fantasy of seduction, voyeurism, and aggression. Rendered a speechless object of Venus's desire, Adonis submits to her allure and is taken "into a secret shade ... Where him to sleepe she gently would perswade, / Or bathe him in a fountaine by some couert glade. (III.1.35). As prey of Venus's desire, Adonis is both displayed to the reader's eye and made an object of Venus's voyeuristic gaze and sexual intentions. The poem oscillates between representing sexuality as a drive threatening to women in episodes involving rape and displaying it as an imprisoning force for men, as in the episode of Venus's seduction of Adonis.[22] Venus's sexual power is made more evident in the next stanza, where she draws her desiring hands down each of Adonis' limbs (III, 1.36, line 6). The details in Spenser's erotic writing not only invent, in the strictest rhetorical sense as imagine and construct, desire as representation, but also make that representation central to the memory's re-invention of the past. A famous erotic story of the cultural past has become a repository of ideas about modern sexuality. Details in this carefully crafted representation of female rapacious desire and masculine timorous self-control reads like a place in a classical memory chamber. Quintilian formulates this process in the following way: "We require, therefore, places, real or imaginary, and images and symbols, which we must, of course, invent for ourselves."[23] In the tapestry of Venus sexual past is made alive through a representation of aggression that is the erotic obverse of numerous scenes of heroic aggression and power elsewhere in the poem. *The Faerie Queene* is one of the most erotic non-dramatic texts in early modern English literature, and Spenser is a poet who writes about eroticism with unrestrained relish. Spenser turns the tapestry representing the story of Venus and Adonis into something more than a story of "sexual enticement and fatal separation."[24] Love in the castle of joy is love of the erotic body; joy is that of sexual desire.

The four stanzas that narrate the story of Venus and Adonis form a poetic version of the four walls in a room "appareled / With costly clothes of *Arras* and of *Toure*" (34), where each stanza, like each wall covered with a panel of tapestry, represents a place or image associated with an idea related to sexual agency. Thus in stanza 39, Redcrosse knight sees:

> … round about [the chamber] many beds were dight,
> As whilome was the antique worldes guize,
> Some for vntimely ease, some for delight,
> And pleased them to vse, that vse it might:
> And all was full Damzels, and of Squires,
> Dauncing and reueling both day and night,
> And swimming deepe in sensual desires,
> And *Cupid* still emongst them kindled lustful fires. (III.1.39)

The revelry in stanza 39, which culminates in the "caroling of loue and iollity" of the "wanton sort" (40), that is, of the young men and women, is a warning to the Redcrosse Knight about his fragile temperance. He leaves the site of erotic seduction loathingly. Yet having just left the room of erotic joy, he is tempted by the erotic power of the proud Persian Queen in stanza 41. The inescapability of sexual challenge to heroic masculinity is central to the erotic story in the ekphrasis. That significance surrounds the Redcrosse Knight as his eyes move over each of the panels in the room housing the tapestry of Venus, tapestry that is a memory site where the classical gods as well as "Damzels" and "Squires" are engulfed by "lustful fires" (39), in other words, where sexuality of the pagans gives meaning to contemporary eroticism, where sexuality is presented as much as a godly activity as a noble one. The mnemonic effect of the classical story of seduction and surrender shows how the erotic ekphrasis simulates action in literature and how it can be employed in bridging the distance between sexuality and the past and between the past and the present. The erotic danger of the past is only separated from the present by a door, indicating the threshold between heroic and erotic discourses in the formation of chivalric masculinity in the poem, the threshold that Redcrosse Knight is eager to pass. The passing of this threshold represents a symbolical step that divides heroic temperance and sexual temptation. The crossing of that threshold puts the erotic male body at risk of sexuality. Adonis' planned escape from the lustful arms of Venus is presented, in classical mythology, in both Ovid's narrative version of the myth and in Spenser, as an illusion of freedom from female sexuality. As Spenser reminds us of the classical myth, the boy will soon be "Deadly engored of a great wild Boore" (38). It has been suggested that this is the closest we get to a rape in this episode.[25] Yet, if we read this image within the erotic ekphrasis as sexual violence only, this rape of a boy is then aligned with the rape of women.

The epic, the romance, and the visual arts of the North-Western Renaissance abound in images of the rape of women. They do not register many places in which boys are raped by men—unless the subject is Adonis and the boar. We thus lose sight of the specific gender politics with which this death, be it accident or not, has entered the Western iconography of Adonis. Adonis raped by a boar is a victim of sodomitical rape by a symbol of hyper-masculine sexual force. When Adonis is "transmew[ed]" (38; transformed) into "a dainty flower" (38) through Venus's magic art, Spenser's readers are reminded that the flower woven into the tapestry that continues to grow is not just about a life that grows out of death, but of a body of youth raped by another male that is not allowed to wither as a result of sodomitical violence. Like Shakespeare in *Venus and Adonis*, Spenser zooms in, if briefly, on the image of a raped boy, juxtaposing the sexual aggression of women with the erotic violence of men. The erotic ekphrasis, therefore, does not let us forget that often-forgotten ending in the clash of erotic bodies. In that ending, each erotic body, Venus's, Adonis', and the boar's, finds its end by seeking its object of sexual yearning.

Verbal pictorialism of these stanzas combines cognitive and sensuous aspects of representation within a familiar place of memory, the story of Venus and Adonis. In ekphrasis, language and picture do not compete as mediums of expression. Rather, they complement each other in an attempt to overcome any disadvantage that either words or pictures may have as "arbitrary arts."[26] In the broadest sense, ekphrasis gives form to "broad allegories of this relationship"[27] between the visual and the verbal. The relationship between the verbal and the visual in Spenser's poetry has been said to be distant because it brings together two different, if not un-related, media through which matching ideas are expressed or corresponding images crafted.[28] The reason for this distance lies in the fact that, like sex and the past, language and picture are representational. They stand at some distance from the object or idea to which they refer. But the distance between language and picture in ekphrasis is even greater than in any other kind of poetic pictorialism because ekphrasis is an allegorical narrative in its own

The Gallery of Erotic Memory in The Faerie Queene 103

right, whose meaning is shaped by the surrounding textual milieu. Mnemonic ekphrasis is a structure larger than image, for it is itself made up of a series of images; it is a visual composition of dense and multilayered symbolism. Therefore, the seduction story of Venus and Adonis is brought alive not only through the verbal representation of tapestry, but also because the woven images in it have shaped the knowledge of and the ideologies at the heart of the paradox of the erotic politics of early modern men and women. Women, represented as sexually rapacious but cold, conflict with men, who are meant to be sexually dangerous if rational beings. The verbal and the visual in the erotic ekphrasis double the paradox of this ideology, by telling a story in the visual medium that was thought, too, to fashion the subject it represents according to its own feigning laws. To echo Ben Jonson on the relationship between poetry and picture: "they both invent, feign, and devise many things, and accommodated all they invent to use, and service of nature."[29] What is natural in a verbal picture is not what is lifelike but what imitates and therefore stylizes the world it shows. The way in which places in the memory scene of Venus and Adonis are arranged in order to lure, even arouse, the knight errant (and the early modern reader-viewer) into the seductive web of the story told by the tapestry of Venus, as well as to warn him against the danger of that seduction, turns Spenser's erotic and mnemonic ekphrasis into both a mini-narrative and a macro-stylistic strategy of verbal and visual immediacy. The "antique worldes guize" (39) is a key to an understanding of Spenser's use of ekphrasis, which he deploys both as a mythological screen that hides pleasures that come out from the recognition of sexual pleasures of the classical stories and as a site of sexual agency that is inseparable from the historical narrative. The erotic licentiousness of Book II will be tamed and sublimated by the generative and dynamic energies that stream through the Garden of Adonis toward the end. But desire will erupt again when we turn to Book III. It will appear in the form of the erotic ekphrasis, when a history of sexuality intersects with a history of heroic endeavor. If the mnemonic ekphrasis in the tapestry of Venus introduces mainly female eroticism as a form of active libidinal agency, if not of sexual fulfillment,[30] Book III does that with masculine desire, also in a series of erotic ekphrases.

Erotic ekphrasis in Book III deepens the relationship between the picture, or place, and erotic significance that accompanies it by representing different kinds of sexual knowledge and erotic experience. In Book III, David Lee Miller writes, "we descend into gestation and parturition, allegories not of sublimation but of embodiment."[31] As we have seen, this descent into allegories of embodiment has already started in the previous book, yet in Book III, Spenser connects these allegories of embodiment to the memory of a gallery of gods. Clio, the Muse of History, under whose guidance the poetry of the body in this book is written, is "Daughter of *Phoebus* and of *Memorie*" (III.3.4). At the heart of Book III, in the House of Busyrane (Canto 11), we come to another house of erotic memory in which a tapestry tells a story of desire and sexual aggression. Spenser's model for the House of Busyrane may have been a Renaissance mansion house. The walls of early modern mansion houses were adorned with expensive tapestries and painted hangings representing stories and motifs of mythological nature and national iconography in succession.[32] The castles, chambers, and houses in Spenser's erotic ekphrasis could be said to be poetic versions of this architectural and decorative history. These poeticized physical spaces are a reminder of a connection of Renaissance poetry with the material world at a conceptual level. In the House of Busyrane, Spenser arranges a series of ekphrases consisting of the images of erotic allegories that connect Jupiter's and Neptune's erotic powers with the erotic politics of the poem deeply rooted in Spenser's classicism.

Upon entering the first room in the House of Busyrane, the heroine Britomart sees a richly woven tapestry ("goodly arras of great maiesty" [28]), embroidered with portraits representing amorous and lustful scenes ("all of loue, and all of lusty-hed" [29]), arranged against the background of vicious wars of love waged by Cupid. At this point, the pageants in which emotions and sexual violence mix are visually executed as separate stories told as individual places of memory, involving metamorphoses of Jupiter. Narrowly following Ovid, who in Book VI of *Metamorphoses* describes some of Jove's transformations, Spenser first depicts him as changed into a bull and seducing Europa (30), then transformed into a golden shower and introduced to Danaë (31), and finally turned into "a snowy Swan, / To win faire *Leda* to his louely trade" (32). The next set of panels shows jealous Juno inflicting deathly punishment on Semele for her clandestine affair with her husband, Jupiter (33). It then moves to show Jupiter transformed into a "soaring Eagles shape ... / ... when as the *Troiane* boy so faire / He snatcht from *Ida* hill, and with him bare: / Wondrous delight it was [34]). This stanza invokes the story of same-sex seduction, of Jupiter turned into an eagle seducing Ganymede in the air. These are earthly delights ("Whiles thus on earth great *Ioue* these pageaunts playd" [35]). Then, Cupid is presented sitting in Jupiter's heavenly throne ("The winged boy did thrust into his [Jupiter's] throne" (35)] and taking delight in occupying the place of the god of the heavens. These movements from the panels involving scenes of sexual aggression to sites of homoerotic dalliance are represented with elaborate artistry that "all the world with flashing fier bent, / So like, that all the walles did seeme to flame" (38). The Sidneian credo that poetry is a "living picture" brings to life stories of the past in yet another tapestry, the "faire arras" (39) of the House of Busyrane, now moves from heaven to sea. The world of this erotic ekphrasis is a masculine world, a world brimming with sexually violent supreme gods. But this world of erotic energy also parallels in intensity, danger, and threat the heroic world of men's political mission in the poem. In a poem so often read through the prism of Elizabethan nationalism and the reformation ideology, to privilege a reading of some of the most disturbing details of Spenser's representation of sexual desire means to erase the hierarchy between national and erotic meanings of that poem.

The attempt to read Jupiter's pageants as a series of memory places and as an ekphrasis is to interpret the discourse of memory as a discourse of sexuality. Images within the erotic ekphrasis reveal Spenser's gift of using pictures to speak about erotic acts. One could say that the literary needs images to reinforce the idea it develops because "a text cannot explain itself without a picture" and that ekphrasis reveals the fact that "language momentarily cedes authority to image" in the close relationship in which word and image are brought closely together in early modern art and literature.[33] On the other hand, I would argue that Spenser's erotic ekphrasis also reveals that the link between image and text in erotic ekphrasis shows not so much the text's incapacity to "explain itself" but the fact that the manner and intensity in which Spenser represents sexuality transgresses social and cultural norms that contain and control it. Thus Spenser's erotic ekphrasis becomes both the hiding place for sexual transgression and a site that openly celebrates sexual liberties. Spenser's erotic ekphrasis is a "particularly shifty trope"[34] because it can be seen as both a place of literary imitation and a space of erotic satisfaction, where the poet negotiates aesthetic and ethical principles. For instance, the sea-horses that snort and send streams of briny waters through their nostrils ("from their nosthrilles blow the brynie streame" [41]) simulate ejaculation. The immediacy of such details naturalizes sexual acts as pleasurable and, as the next set of memory places show, dangerous as well. The set of pageants featuring Neptune, a god to whom his brother Jupiter has given the reign of the sea, is the next place in the mnemonic chamber in the House of Busyrane. Metamorphosed into "a Dolphin fayre / And like a winged horse" (42), Neptune seduces Amphitrite; transformed into the horse Pegasus, he takes pleasure with Ceres ("like a winged horse he tooke his flight, / To snaky-locke *Medusa* to repayre, / On whom he got faire *Pegasus*, that flitteth in the ayre" [42]). The last of Jupiter's pageants is devoted to Saturn, turned into vine, and exhausted and emptied of manly seed, imagined as a withering twig of grape vine drying out on the white bosom of Philliras ("He [Saturne] turned himself into a fruitfull vine, / And into her faire bosome made his grapes decline" [43]). The first gallery of erotic pageants shaped as memory sites is dominated with pictures representing sexual violence, masculine aggression, fornication, and homosexual seduction. Stanza after stanza, Spenser suggests that, like Jupiter's empire of heaven, Elizabethan England, the new commonwealth of the Faerie Land, is a realm in which sexual and political powers are inseparable. The erotic ekphrasis captures a new cultural scenario of the romantic and erotic age of Elizabethan England by juxtaposing contemporary with classical representations of erotic subjects. In stanza 46, Scudamour sees

> Kings Queenes, Lords Ladies, Knights & Damzels gent
> Were heap'd together with the vulgar sort,

> And mingled with the raskall rabblement,
> Without respect of person or of port
> To shew Dan *Cupids* power and great effort: (III.9.46)

If the scene represented in this stanza appears to us tame in comparison to Jupiter's lascivious pageants of the previous stanzas, it is only to show the randomness of mixing lovers from different classes, including those from the social margin like base commoners and rascals. This ekphrasis presents a world in which Cupid's "lustful fires" (39) kindle desire between people regardless of their rank and social status, making classical and early modern times one period. The alluring power of the ekphrasis, however, seems limited. Britomart seems not to be touched by the erotic ekphrasis of Jupiter's pageants as she moves through the House of Busyrane. The erotic milieu in which Britomart finds herself in the House of Busyrane reminds us that, in narrative terms, ekphrasis is a place set apart from the narrative of nationalism; that it counters the narrative of nationalism, even if it is made part of it. The ekphrasis, therefore, suggests that the erotic world Spenser depicts is a separate world, experienced more through the senses, even if its mnemonic mode implies cognitive as well as affective composition. As a mode of expression, ekphrasis facilitates recall of the unfamiliar; it re-creates and remembers the forgotten.

Characters in *The Faerie Queene* who look at the world of ekphrasis, as Britomart does when she walks through the House of Busyrane, are not bidden to remember the past. Rather, the past is remembered for them in the ekphrases composed of the stories of antiquity that would have been familiar to the class of male readers, Elizabethan noblemen, targeted by the poem. Commenting on the ekphrasis of Jupiter's pageants, Harry Berger has argued that "[Jupiter's] tapestries celebrate the mythic moment when erotic monotheism or monomania overcomes nonerotic and cosmic polytheism: Jove, Phoebus, and Neptune are shown as diverted from the heavens, the sun, and the ocean."[35] They do that, but Spenser's poetry also connects that shift, to paraphrase Berger, from a nonerotic cosmos to an erotic monomania with a moment in the Christian world of chivalry and aristocratic rule. In that world, men and women, from the top to the bottom of the social ladder, are brought together through erotic desire. It appears, then, that eroticism, not nationalism, is the force that erases class boundaries and eliminates social hierarchy. *The Faerie Queene* insists again and again on coupling, even, and especially, when coupling comes as a result of "dangerous attractiveness,"[36] as shown in the ekphrases in Books II and III. Cupid is unselective in choosing his victims, but sexual coupling, not nationalistic fervor only, is the foundation of a state ruled by an absolutist monarch without progeny.

The examples of the Venus and Cupid tapestries are two of the most representative and complex instances of the erotic and somatic stylization of memory, reminding us that the operation of memory affects both the mind and the body, that, as Garrett A. Sullivan has argued, "memory is both internal and external, cerebral and bodily."[37] Spenser's erotic ekphrasis expands Aristotle's idea that memory is a "state of affection" (716) experienced spiritually "occurring in the soul" (716), by making it both a mental and sensual faculty, a view common in the early modern period. The rhetorician Thomas Wilson adds a dose of realism to his description of memory when he says that "memorie is to the mind, that life is to the body," in his 1560 *The Arte of Rhetorique*. The ekphrasis of the House of Busyrane not only appeals to the mind, by urging it to interpret the allegorical composition in order to draw a moral lesson and protect the heroic body from sexual temptation, but it also imbues that body with sensual life, life that is yet unfamiliar. Ekphrasis does double work as a form in Spenser's poem: erotic ekphrasis at once warns against eroticism and entices the onlooker to succumb to the libidinal energies it displays. The work of ekphrasis, however, does not end up with the last panel of Jupiter's pageants in Cupid's tapestry, when Britomart is about to leave the House of Busyrane.

Cupid's tapestry comes before an altar in the next room. If pleasure is the main affect threaded through the woven story in the tapestry showing Jupiter's pageants, its obverse, falsehood and absence of pleasure, are symbolically embodied in the forms adorning the altar. Although made of precious metal ("rich metal" [51]) the altar presents monstrosity and falsehood: "A thousand monstrous forms therein were made, / Such as false love ..." (51). The altar in this room of falsehood and of the spoils of war mix eroticism and political history, bringing the classical and the contemporary together. Spenser depicts the room as a place in which "warlike spoils" (52) of old victories, showing "wastefull emptinesse" (53). It is a site of decline and failure: spears are broken, haberdashers split, laurel garlands crushed. From the erotic ekphrasis in the first room, the poem moves to the ekphrasis of weakening heroism in this room, recollecting that which is forgotten in a heroic world—the fragility of heroic power, the fragility of heroic masculinity, and how easily power can crumble to a mass of broken arms. The ekphrasis on the altar engages the mind, not just the eyes, and Britomart, "beholding earnestly" the scene of decay caused by the "cruell loue" of once "mighty Conquerours and Captaines strong" (52), is made to draw a lesson of restraint and moderation for the reign she symbolically represents. Spenser's engagement with memory at historiographic, iconographic, visual, and textual levels never loses sight of the close connection between cognition and remembering. This affiliation also comes out of a culture deeply invested in interpreting the past.

Yet the link between memory and eroticism is only one possible connection between the faculty of remembering the unfamiliar or the forgotten and the past. The association of memory with eroticism is part of a larger body of early modern knowledge, which in the early modern period was concerned with "the body's ability to remember"[38] as well as with anatomy and anatomical writing, as sites of knowledge. In his study of memory in early modern England, Andrew Hiscock has documented in detail the sixteenth- and seventeenth-century writing about humoral states of the body, as predispositions for the faculty of memory.[39] If, as Hiscock argues, the English humanist rhetoricians and theorists resisted taking on systematically the classical writing about memory, writers of imaginative literature were more receptive to the fertile tradition of the ideas about memory. They were quick to turn the rhetorical theory of memory into the creative practice of literary composition, in turn playing with, and resisting, theoretical precepts. In doing so, they were closer to their Italian contemporaries and immediate predecessors. Documenting the history of the close relationship between eroticism and memory in the print culture of Italian humanism, Lina Bolzoni has argued that, "If memory, by nature, plays an essential role in affixing and feeding the amorous *phantasma*, the art of memory proves to be keenly interested in reversing the process, in using it for its own end."[40] The art of memory, understood here to refer to the technology of artificial memory, became related to the creative imagination. Drawing attention to the distinction between natural and artificial memory, Bolzoni further draws attention to the fact that artificial memory became a vehicle for the shaping of erotic meaning in early theoretical texts on *ars memoria*. "Sexual references," Bolzoni continues, "are common among the examples of images of memory given by the treatises [of memory]"[41] in the practices associated with memory in the early modern period. They were not so in classical antiquity.

Spenser not only delved deeply into the late medieval and humanist Italian epic as models when he composed *The Faerie Queene*[42] but evidently made extensive use of the art of memory for us to read his epic romance as a sustained poem of memory. One of the features of mnemonic writing in the early modern period is both the diversity and the intensity of erotic representations that were part of the memory system. Mary Carruthers has argued that the link between memory and eroticism prevails in "shocking images, depicting violence, scatology, and sexuality that come up in some works of medieval literature."[43] Spenser's writing about the eroticism of memory is an extension of this earlier tradition, building on the medieval tradition and on the flourishing of memory in the humanism of the Elizabethan period.

Spenser also wrote his erotic ekphrases both against the background of and as a reaction to the reformed rhetorical system promoted by Petrus Ramus, the agent of this "clean sweep ... of the old art of memory," who effectively "abolished the artificial memory."[44] Although Spenser adopts some of the elements of natural memory, for example, by potentially making his erotic rooms external projections of cultural and character's forgotten or repressed impulses, he structures those rooms according to the precepts of artificial memory. In handling the art of memory as *art*, that is, as a construction of the mind and imagination, not merely a natural faculty of an individual, Spenser adjusts the art of memory to the situations and characters in his poem, which are allegorical constructions created within the boundaries of epic conventions. In adjusting the classical idea of artificial memory to a new notion of natural memory, Spenser is not alone among the humanist writers in England. An early contemporary of Spenser's, the rhetorician Thomas Wilson wrote in his 1560 edition of *The Art of Rhetoric* that, "the same is memorie to the mind, that life is to the bodie."[45] Wilson's comparison suggests that memory is the lifeblood of the mind, while making memory closer to the body as well. Spenser's mnemonic allegories of sexuality occupy a position between the mind and the body, in that they guide the mind to interpret, not as a mere technical exercise but a model for life, or a cautionary tale, the effect of memory on the body. Not giving up entirely on the old form of memory while also not fully embracing the emerging model of natural memory, Spenser displays his classicism and his indebtedness to classical learning, which would have included the rhetoricians who wrote on memory such as Aristotle and Cicero.[46] In *The Faerie Queene*, Spenser turns the art of memory into the erotic narrative within which the past remembers itself through sexual liberty, seduction, ejaculation, rape, and homosexuality. Through erotic ekphrases Spenser not only displays his knowledge of the general principles of how memory was organized as a tool of narrative composition but also reveals eroticism as a constituent discourse of the national epic.

Another way to acknowledge Spenser's indebtedness to memory is to recall Maurice Evans's succinct statement that "the art of memory gave Spenser both methods and materials which he exploited more comprehensively than any other Renaissance poet."[47] Spenser's galleries of erotic imitation and the erotic memory rooms are metanarratives, within which the narrative of memory of the erotic past remembers itself through ekphrasis. As a site of memory, the erotic ekphrasis represents another mode of writing in Spenser, highlighting his persistent interest in sex (and love) and expanding our awareness of the repertoire of his style. Recently, David Scott Wilson-Okamura has observed perceptively and correctly: "There is a lot about Spenser's style, and about Renaissance style in general, that we still don't know."[48] Wilson-Okamura alludes to the lack of formalist analysis of Spenser's verbal art and to the relative neglect of scholarship about the relationship of style and larger concerns in Spenser's writing. Because of its elaborate composition and attention to stylistic and symbolic detail, the erotic ekphrasis of Spenser's epic writing is also something to which critics writing about eroticism in the literary historiography of the Renaissance should return with a renewed interest.

Notes

1. Alan Stewart and Garrett A. Sullivan, Jr. "'Worme-eaten, and full of canker holes': Materializing Memory in *The Faerie Queene* and *Lingua*," *Spenser Studies* 17 (2003), 216.

2. Ibid., 218.
3. Ian Frederick Moulton, *Before Pornography: Erotic Writing in Early Modern England* (Oxford: Oxford University Press, 2000), 5.
4. [Cicero], *Ad Herennium*, ed. Harry Caplan (Cambridge, MA: Harvard University Press and London: William Heinemann, 1989), III, xvi, 29.
5. Throughout the essay, I quote Spenser's text from *The Faerie Queene*, ed. Thomas P. Roche, Jr. (London: Penguin, 1987).
6. Christopher Ivic, "Spenser and Interpellative Memory," *Ars Reminiscendi: Mind and Memory in Renaissance Culture*, ed. Donald Beecher and Grant Williams (Toronto: Centre for Reformation and Renaissance Studies, 2009), 290.
7. Wilbur Samuel Howell, *Logic and Rhetoric in England, 1500–1700* (Princeton: Princeton University Press, 1956), 85.
8. It is worth remembering that the Italian word for "room" is *la stanza*. Thus the notion of closed space can be linked to the original meaning of stanza as a poetic form as "stantia," which in Vulgar Latin meant "standing, stopping place." The meanings of room as "la stanza" and stanza as "la stantia" form a conceptual link with the notion of a confined space, completed and filled with meaning. See www.etymonline.com. Accessed on 2014/12/27.
9. John Willis, *The Arte of Memory. So far forth as it dependeth upon Places and Idea's* (London: W. Jones, 1621), sig. 2r. STC (2nd ed.) 25479.
10. Brian Vickers, *In Defence of Rhetoric* (Oxford: Clarendon Press, 1988), 65.
11. Frances A. Yates, *The Art of Memory* (London: Pimlico, 1992), 232.
12. Margaret Anne Doody, *The True Story of the Novel* (New Brunswick, NJ: Rutgers University Press, 1996), 138. Emphasis in the original.
13. Simon Shepherd, *Spenser* (Atlantic Highlands, NJ: Humanities Press, 1989), 58.
14. Sir Philip Sidney, *An Apology for Poetry*, ed. Geoffrey Shepherd (Manchester: Manchester University Press, 1973), 101.
15. Ibid., 70.
16. James A. W. Heffernan, *Museum of Words: The Poetics of Ekphrasis from Homer to Ashbery* (Chicago and London: The University of Chicago Press, 2004), 70.
17. G. Wilson Knight, "The Spenserian Fluidity," quoted from *Edmund Spenser*, ed. Paul J. Alpers (Harmondsworth: Penguin, 1969), 225.
18. Melissa E. Sanchez, *Erotic Subjects: The Sexuality of Politics in Early Modern English Literature* (Oxford: Oxford University Press, 2011), 59.
19. Lauren Silberman, *Transforming Desire: Erotic Knowledge in Books III and IV of* The Faerie Queene (Berkeley, Los Angeles and London: University of California Press, 1995). I borrow the phrase "erotic knowledge" from the title of this book.
20. Garrett A. Sullivan, Jr., *Memory and Forgetting in English Renaissance Drama: Shakespeare, Marlowe, Webster* (Cambridge: Cambridge University Press, 2005), 7.
21. Robert Burton, *The Anatomy of Melancholy*, ed. Holbrook Jackson (New York: New York Review of Book, 2001), Part I, Section 1, 160.
22. As a site of charged erotic energy and sexual indulgence, the Bower of Bliss (II. xii) is the climax of the imprisoning force of sexuality coming from female characters.
23. Quintilian, *Institutio Oratoria*, tr. H. E. Butler (Cambridge, MA, and London, England: Harvard University Press, 1993), XI, ii, 21.

24. Heffernan, *Museum of Words*, 70.
25. *Ibid.*, 70.
26. Murray Krieger, *Ekphrasis: The Illusion of the Natural Sign* (Baltimore and London: The Johns Hopkins University Press, 1992), 13.
27. Stephen Cheeke, *The Aesthetics of Ekphrasis* (Manchester and New York: Manchester University Press, 2008), 13.
28. John B. Bender, *Spenser and Literary Pictorialism* (Princeton: Princeton University Press, 1972), 23.
29. Ben Jonson, "Explorata: Or Discoveries," *The Complete Poems*, ed. George Parfitt (Harmondsworth: Penguin Books, 1974), 419.
30. As Simon Shepherd has shown, in Book IV, Spenser explores "the possibility of active female desire." Shepherd, *Spenser*, 66.
31. David Lee Miller, *The Poem's Two Bodies: The Poetics of the 1590 'Faerie Queene'* (Princeton: Princeton University Press, 1988), 223.
32. Mark Girouard, *Elizabethan Architecture* (New Haven and London: Yale University Press for The Paul Mellon Centre for Studies in British Art, 2009), 354–57.
33. Leonard Barkan, *Mute Poetry, Speaking Pictures* (Princeton and Oxford: Princeton University Press, 2013), xiv.
34. *Ibid.*, xv.
35. Harry Berger, Jr., *Revisionary Play: Studies in The Spenserian Dynamics* (Berkeley, Los Angeles, London: University of California Press, 1988), 177.
36. Stephen Greenblatt, *Renaissance Self-Fashioning: From More to Shakespeare* (Chicago and London: The University of Chicago Press, 1984), 172.
37. Sullivan, Jr., *Memory*, 11.
38. Andrew Hiscock, *Reading Memory in Early Modern Literature* (Cambridge: Cambridge University Press, 2011), 14.
39. *Ibid.*
40. Lena Bolzoni, *The Gallery of Memory: Literary and Iconographic Models in the Age of Printing Press*, trans. Jeremy Parzen (Toronto: University of Toronto Press, 2001), 146.
41. *Ibid.*
42. A detailed account of Spenser's indebtedness to Italian epic tradition is provided in Veselin Kostić, *Spenser's Sources of Italian Poetry: A Study in Comparative Literature* (Beograd: Filološki fakultet, 1969). Also, David Scott Wilson-Okamura, *Spenser's International Style* (Cambridge: Cambridge University Press, 2013).
43. Mary Carruthers, *The Book of Memory: A Study of Memory in Medieval Culture*, 2nd ed., (Cambridge: Cambridge University Press, 2008), 162–72.
44. Yates, *The Art of Memory*, 229.
45. Thomas Wilson, *The Art of Rhetoric*, ed. G. H. Mair (Oxford: Benediction Classics, 2006), 241.
46. Spenser's classical learning and the books he would have had access to, an owned, are discussed in detail in Andrew Hadfield, *Edmund Spenser: A Life* (Oxford: Oxford University Press, 2012), 224–29.
47. Maurice Evans, "Memory," *The Spenser Encyclopedia*, gen. ed. A. C. Hamilton (Toronto and Buffalo: University of Toronto Press; London: Routledge, 1992), 468, 467–68.
48. Wilson-Okamura, *Spenser's International Style*, 17.

8 False Muscle Memory in Marlowe and Nashe

Robert Darcy

Lacking any real scientific expertise, I don't come at memory from a psycho-biological position of inquiry, but I'm curious about how the memory of muscles might have worked in the late sixteenth century.[1] I am particularly interested in the collapsing of personal visual and tactile experiences into memory. Muscles, and their surrogates, specifically in the form of the phallus, offer good candidates for investigation. Sexual musculature is easy to imagine crossing historical boundaries, whatever those boundaries may be, and so I'm interested in exploring muscle as a generator of erotic excitement and as a repository for memory. Marlowe's "Hero and Leander" performs a pseudo-ekphrasis of Leander's body—of its musculature alongside its softer parts, Leander's white belly and edible shoulder (ll. 66–65).[2] It also references the penile muscle as popularly understood—the "thing," as it were, that Neptune fondles in the Hellespont. It is the muscle that is and is not a muscle, one that necessarily can and does exist both in presence and in memory. It's there, and it's not. It's a limb, and yet it's not. The Schroedinger's cat of muscles, this phantom fifth limb can appear and disappear as Marlowe disposes of Leander's body. I'll get to the problem of that disposal a little later.

This chapter suggests that a memory of muscle is a memory in jeopardy, because at any given time the source of that memory may persist or fade away. When it's not there, its absence belies our memory of what was, the feeling of being cheated out of a bargain—a thing of memory that the world won't reproduce. But retreating from false memory engenders the possibility of its reincarnation by means of a surrogate. In Nashe, the falsehood's surrogate is present in the dildo, when the absent presence is substituted by the need for meaningful gratification. In Nashe's "Choise of Valentines," Tomalin climaxes too soon and leaves his prostitute girlfriend to fend for her own sexual gratification. When the performing phallus is there but wilting away, there remains the possibility, by means of the dildo, of its still standing as a phantom limb detached from the body—even when that body is otherwise present. Bear with me here—what I'm building is a bit abstract, but I'll shortly follow with specifics.

How do we remember muscle? It would seem that sexual awakening makes us first aware, not of the body, but of the body's potential contour.

Muscles are a secondary sexual characteristic contingent on gender and age. We almost never ascribe muscles to women or to the old, despite the physical potential of all bodies, gendered or aging, to build or maintain visible muscle. For example, Marlowe's poem never grants us a glimpse of young Hero's muscles. Even when she's nude at the end of the poem, her nudity is not described or otherwise by us discovered, but we see Leander in glorious form within the opening hundred lines:

> His body was as straight as Circes wand,
> Jove might have sipped out nectar from his hand.
> Even as delicious meat is to the tast,
> So was his neck in touching, and surpast
> The white of Pelops shoulder, I could tell ye,
> How smooth his brest was, & how white his bellie,
> And whose immortal fingars did imprint,
> That heavenly path, with many a curious dint,
> That runs along his backe, but my rude pen,
> Can hardly blazon foorth the loves of men. (61–71)

In part, we contribute our own memory to making this description possible. That is, we're told that Leander's naked, and having his nudity described conjures memory of the naked male we can see and remember from a variety of sources, in sculpture, art, and elsewhere. The narrator encourages us to conjure our own memories of the male muscled body, through the description of naked Leander—especially if we're men whose "loves of men" (l. 70) so blazoned are evoked by such a sight. In counterpoint to Hero's embroidered robe, muscles, it would seem, are described and remembered as male and male only, despite the anatomical falsehood of that.

Part of my argument depends upon a sympathy with early modern minds, a sympathy perhaps unfairly informed by twenty-first century pornography. Images of the chiseled male body are abundantly available to us today. And by that I mean there is no dearth of access to it for any of us using modern media. Leander is young, with molded flesh, a back "dinted" with the lower dimples of an active athlete. We today—those of us who have looked—can conjure this equivalency to mind from memory. Marlowe, and for that matter Nashe, did not presumably have anything like the degree of easy access to the range of images and depictions that we have, even if they did know the classical body. Nonetheless, their poetic depictions offer something that resonates as familiar to us.

Despite this body knowledge, I'm addressing a particular muscle not prepared in the gym, through hard labor, or on the athletic field. The sculpted male body still has yet to produce that other piece of evidence of virulence, the erection, which it probably will but may not be able to do. "Hero and Leander" is rarely talked or written about as a poem concerning impotence.[3] It's obviously a poem about young love and first times, and maybe something like a clumsy after-prom encounter, but when Leander strips and dives into the Hellespont, there is tumescent promise and excitement. Does such promise materialize? Leander's aim is clear; his nudity, merely described at the foreground of the poem, is at last established in the flesh: "With that hee stript him to the iv'rie skin, / And crying, Love I come, leapt lively in" (ll. 637–38). What he hopes to achieve at the end of his swim is glistening and abstractly familiar in human terms—union with Hero, a reasonable progress. Yet his earlier visit to Hero's tower is curious. After winning her long-awaited assent, Leander is stymied:

> Like Aesops cocke, this jewell he enjoyed,
> And as a brother with his sister toyed,
> Supposing nothing else was to be done,
> Now he her favour and good will had wone.
> But know you not that creatures wanting sense,
> By nature have a mutual appetence,
> And wanting organs to advance a step,
> Mov'd by Loves force, unto each other lep?
> Much more in subjects having intellect,
> Some hidden influence breeds like effect.
> Albeit Leander rude in love, and raw,
> Long dallying with Hero, nothing saw
> That might delight him more, yet he suspected
> Some amorous rites or other were neglected. (ll. 535–48)

Leander is both Aesop's cock and no cock at all. He is as unlike animals as "subjects having intellect" in his sexual instinct. He likes Hero's body, but only as a brother does a sister's, as a rooster does a pearl, and he suspects that something else is missing in his approach. This suspicion of something else may in fact represent a struggle, a kind of psychomachia internalized by Leander as a proxy for Marlowe's contemporary male reader: "Renaissance poets like Marlowe derive from Ovid a sense of feminine identity as fundamentally split, as a discursive site onto which patriarchal desire projects its own contradictory impulses and behaviors."[4] Hero is a sister who may also be a lover, triggering a naïve and ephemeral psychological solution toward making that incongruity impossible, and in so doing, irrepressibly haunting, as "love resisted once, grows passionate" (l. 623).

Leander apparently doesn't know—or does not want to know—how to have sex. This lack of knowledge might suggest an absence of memories of any kind of past experience or even transmitted information about how sex works. Has Leander heard shared memories of sex? Have those memories failed to translate? Or does Leander possess a memory of information about sex that has lodged erroneously in his young mind, leaving him improperly informed? The particular question regarding Leander at the intersection of memory and sexuality revolves around what he has learned, or inferred, up to this point of adolescence. What is his foreknowledge and memory of sex? Is he remembering sex that didn't happen during his first night with Hero—the "suspected" rites "neglected" (ll. 547–48)—triggering a vague sense of what could have or should have happened? His dive into the Hellespont may involve tentative foreknowledge based on a phantom memory, the product of a phantom phallic limb, a Derridean hauntology/ontology of what's there but also missing.[5] He may know where his swim will lead him, but he may also hope that the swim alone might deliver a sexual experience toward something presently climactic. Swimming naked, after all, is at least for some an erotic activity. If Leander is swimming naked to "get off," to use adolescent terms, the act of swimming and the idea of Hero as both knowledge and memory are his ostensible motivation. The poem offers a fantastical narrative of that swim, involving the god Neptune, whose watery hands pour over young Leander's body as the god sees the boy in motion:

> He clapt his plumpe cheeks, with his tresses playd,
> And smiling wantonly, his love bewrayed.
> He watcht his armes, and as they opend wide,
> At every stroke, betwixt them would he slide,
> And steale a kisse, and then run out and dance,
> And as he turned, cast many a lustfull glance,
> And threw him gaudie toies to please his eie,
> And dive into the water, and there prie
> Upon his brest, his thighs, and everie lim,
> And up againe, and close beside him swim,
> And talke of love: Leander made replie,
> You are deceav'd, I am no woman I. (ll. 665–76)

I propose this story does not require mythology to tell. I propose we're invited to watch the psychology of excitement and trepidation processed through the mind of a naïve adolescent on a swim toward his first night of sex. Leander develops a memory of his body in the Hellespont, one that is "no woman." He feels the attention that water pays to his "every limb." His knowledge of his body gives him a frame of reference to what was out-of-frame earlier with Hero. The "delight" he "suspected" "neglected" is confirmed in naked isolation, belying the narrator's deeply ironic quip, "Of that which hath no being, doe not boast, / Things that are not at all, are never lost" (ll. 275–76). In this respect, context generates memory. The forecast or expectation of an event can change the pre-memory of it, attached to events in the past, even those that did not happen. Leander can form memories in the present based on his anticipation of what's to come and his anxiety over what did not previously occur.

If it's fair to break the fiction of the poem, to imagine it as a non-mythological account, we might see a much more common story—one involving boy meeting girl—though it needn't be a girl. Boy meeting boy is just as good. I imagine, in terms of the appearance and disappearance of the imaginary phallus, girl meeting girl is also just as good. The permutations abound in the psycho-sexual world of LGBTIQ. (At my school, I think to our credit, we've called this conglomeration at various times "Alphabet Soup" and most recently "Common Ground.")

Psychically the ideation of a sexual experience that hasn't happened but is believed to be imminent has several possible implications. The readiness of the body to meet another body is either superficial or profound in every instance (sometimes both) and potentially unknowable in advance. Leander's experience of Neptune in the Hellespont may well be characterized as a memory. His muscle-draining swim left him hurt and weary. Why he conjured the idea of a male god is curious. Or rather why Marlowe had his male narrator think of a male god pursuing Leander is curious. Leander might be imagined tapping into the collective memory of the sea deity to draw strength during a treacherous swim. The narrator may conjure a same-sex erotic encounter as a reasonable pre-cursor to a heterosexual encounter, an incidence of adolescent experimentation circulating in the personal memories of many of Marlowe's readers. The struggle to swim to Hero is, in any case, overdetermined as male—a male on male, on male, on male, encounter—imagined though previously unexplored and likely confusing to a sexually inexperienced adolescent.

What emerges here is a portrait of male sexual suffering in a psycho-social context and of the way that suffering gets expressed toward others. Hero's surprise on opening the door to naked Leander is worth noting:

> … seeing a naked man, she schriecht for feare,
> Such sights as this, to tender maids are rare.
> And ran into the darke her self to hide … (ll. 721–23)

Leander has been harmed—not by Neptune—but by an experience of nakedness essentially of his own making. By way of his swim, he has passively fondled himself without knowledge of that. I'm not talking about masturbation. I'm talking about a prior lack of knowledge, or possession of knowledge proving untrue, about what nakedness can mean erotically. Leander is acting as his own Sex-Ed teacher to his own body, cast as reluctant student. He's initiating himself into exploring what's missing, the phantom aspect of his memory. What is and is not, what should and should not be—especially sexually—are unclear to an adolescent youth whose world is otherwise structured and defined. Hero sees in naked Leander at her door that which she did not see before, that which he earlier did not have the capacity to offer.

How from there do we choose a prom date or a valentine? Nashe's "Choise of Valentines" is companion to Marlowe's poem in that both poems figure an awkward sexual encounter. Each concerns muscled limbs that are or aren't there. On seeking out his favorite prostitute—one he's previously frequented and who swears to him, on purchased time, a lover's devotion—Tomalin first imagines the experience being over before it has begun. The sight of Francis's enticing body "makes the fruites of love oftsoone be rype / And pleasure pluckt too tymelie from the stemme / To dye ere it hath seene Jerusalem" (ll. 118–20).[6] The ignition of desire leads to an immediate remorse for its conclusion—figured as premature, a shipwreck on the way to the Crusades. Oddly, the effect is a temporary impotence; despite Tomalin's kissing, clapping, feeling, and viewing, "Yett dead he lyes" (l. 130). His remembered member will not reappear, having died already. If Francis's rubbing and chafing cannot revive the missing muscle, she wishes herself "dead" "ten thousand times" (l. 136). The verbal play here, where "dead" can signify physical death or "the little death" of orgasm, emphasizes that the non-responsive member may contribute to the titillation that will feed the subsequent encounter of the dildo. We can thus imagine the encounter with the flaccid penis as a form of what Karmen MacKendrick has termed *counterpleasures*, "pleasures that run contrary to our expectations of pleasure in so many ways."[7]

Here is a more mature and experienced pair than Hero and Leander. Tomalin is already in a position to remember a post-coitus state and to dread it from a pre-coitus position. Francis trades promises of many deaths to inspire the return of the lover's phallus. Tomalin's dread is a memory of experience that is equated with death. Hers is a failure to find "meanes … that maie availe to his recoverie" (ll. 137–38). The operating concern for both Tomalin and Francis is the readiness of the phallus. It may become erect or else remain flaccid. It may deliver a sufficient duration of pleasure or else die too soon. Nashe's reference to Ovid here offers one more link between his poem and Marlowe's, this time at the level of a cultural memory of Ovid. Nashe writes, "lyke one with Ovids cursed hemlock charm'd," Francis focuses too much on expectation or future-memory, and as a result, his limbs "spend their strength in thought of hir delight" (ll. 124–26). Ian Moulton suggests that Tomalin's "lack of control is provoked by excessive female desire."[8] I link this claim about sexuality to issues of memory by underscoring that his knowledge of her desire is based on memories of past encounters and on his desire to make future memories. Still, it all comes back to muscle. Everything about the moment seems to hinge on the outcome of whether the muscle will flex and remain flexed, or not.

Tomalin does rise to the occasion, but not for long enough, and by climaxing before she needs him to, Francis responds in her disappointment by resorting to the dildo. The presence of orgasm makes Nashe's poem all the more radical. As Sarah Toulalan notes, early modern depictions of dildos reinforced that these objects could bring pleasure but also underscored that semen was necessary to engender female orgasm. However, "the nearer we get to the likeness of a penis that can ejaculate, the nearer was the possibility of complete female satisfaction."[9] Perhaps powerful memories of past sexual encounters with Francis, in combination with the bodily memory of the semen from his premature ejaculation—not fantasies of potential encounters—bridge the gap and bring her sexual experience to fruition. Without disparaging the dildo, I propose that psychically Leander and Tomalin share an experience of being tossed away. Tomalin watches as his shrinking penis is replaced by something superior, as Francis declares:

> My little dildo shall supply their kinde:
> A knave, that moves as light as leaves by winde;
> That bendeth not, nor fouldeth anie deale,
> But stands as stiff as he were made of steele (ll. 237–40)

Francis has a ready alternative to the unreliable human phallus, and her body remembers pleasure in either case. Nashe's lovers leave the scene of the encounter, and the poem leaves us its readers, satisfied and complete, if only by proxy.

The Hellespont, with its pampering god, nevertheless allows Leander to leave it and its watery hands. They give him up to a future he doesn't know, on shores where previous versions of his story find him dead. That Marlowe's poem ends at line 818 is evidence, I think, of a poet shrinking from the story's outcome. There are so many ways and permutations for what might have occurred as a Marlovian variation on a story whose end Chapman felt he knew with certainty, one perhaps purposely unexplored by Marlowe. Nashe offers a joke, but one with teeth: that memory of love and desire is not enough to satisfy the beloved one hopes to hold. Just as Andrew Nicholls suggests we can "take queer pleasure in the failure of heterosexual desire, but no malice is intended," I suggest that we can view these poems as playful offerings where memory and desire flirt with each other but perhaps do not go home together.[10] We witness in both poems a memory of loss from both ends, from naivety and experience. Their muscles, we may find, are as easily remembered as forgotten.[11]

Notes

1. Although I do not explore it here, performance studies in Shakespearean drama has been interested for some time in muscle memory from an early modern and modern actor's perspective, most recently in Peter Holland, *Shakespeare, Memory, and Performance* (Cambridge, UK: Cambridge University Press, 2006). See especially the chapter by Carol Chillington Rutter, "'Her First Remembrance from the Moor:' Actors and the Materials of Memory" (168–206), citing choreographer Jeff Friedman's use of this chapter's operative term in his "Muscle Memory: Performing Embodied Knowledge," ed. Richard Candída Smith, *Art and the Performance of Memory* (London, UK: Routledge, 2002): 156–80.
2. All citations to "Hero and Leander" are to *Hero and Leander by Christopher Marlowe: A Facsimile of the First Edition, London 1598*, ed. Louis L. Martz, (Johnson Reprint: New York, 1972). I have slightly modernized the spelling for readability.
3. An exception is Helga Duncan, "'Headdie Ryots' as Reformations: Marlowe's Libertine Poetics," *Early Modern Literary Studies* 12.2 (2006): par. 30–31,

where she reads Leander as afflicted by a poet-Marlowe's assault on productive virulence. Chloe Preedy also traces impotence in Nashe and Marlowe, ultimately asserting Leander's recovery from a brief setback, "'I Am No Woman I': Gender, Sexuality, and Power in Elizabethan Erotic Verse," *E-Pisteme* 2.2 (2009): 46–57.
4. Bruce Boehrer, "Ovid and the Dilemma of the Cuckold in English Renaissance Drama," in *Ovid and the Renaissance Body*, ed. Goran V. Stanivukovic (Toronto: University of Toronto Press, 2001), 172.
5. Jacques Derrida, *Specters of Marx: The State of the Debt, the Work of Mourning, and the New International* (London: Routledge, 2006).
6. Nashe, Thomas. *The Choise of Valentines: Or the Merie Ballad of Nash His Dildo*. Ed. John S. Farmer. London, 1899. A reprint edition of Farmer's transcription is also available from Dodo Press, 2007.
7. Karmen MacKendrick, *Counterpleasures* (Albany, NY: SUNY Press, 1999), 2.
8. Ian Frederick Moulton, *Before Pornography: Erotic Writing in Early Modern England* (Oxford, UK: Oxford University Press, 2000), 177. On the poem's pornographic nature in the context of gender, see also Moulton's "Transmuted into a Woman or Worse: Masculine Gender Identity and Thomas Nashe's 'Choice of Valentines,'" and Michael Stapleton's reprinted "Nashe and the Poetics of Obscenity: *The Choise of Valentines*," both in *Thomas Nashe*, ed. Georgia Brown (Surrey, UK: Ashgate, 2011), pp. 29–48, 49–88; Jeffrey Kahan, "Violating Hippocrates: Dildoes and Female Desire in Thomas Nashe's 'The Choice of Valentines,'" *Paradoxa* 2.2 (1996): 204–16; and Bruce Thomas Boehrer, "Behn's 'Disappointment' and Nashe's 'Choice of Valentines': Pornographic Poetry and the Influence of Anxiety," *Essays in Literature* 16.2 (1989): 172–87.
9. Sarah Toulalan, *Imagining Sex: Pornography and Bodies in Seventeenth-Century England* (Oxford, UK: Oxford University Press, 2007), 77. There has been much recent work on Nashe's poem, the dildo, and the sexual prosthesis in the early modern consciousness. See Melissa Jones, "Spectacular Impotence: Or, Things That Hardly Ever Happen in the Critical History of Pornography," *Sex before Sex: Figuring the Act in Early Modern England*, ed. James M. Bromley and Will Stockton (Minneapolis: University of Minnesota Press, 2013), 89–110; Liza Blake, "Dildos and Accessories: The Functions of Early Strap-Ons," and Will Fisher, "'Had It a Codpiece, 'Twere a Man Indeed': The Codpiece as Constitutive Accessory in Early Modern English Culture," both in *Ornamentalism: The Art of Renaissance Accessories*, ed. Bella Mirabella (Ann Arbor, MI: University of Michigan Press, 2011), 130–55; 102–29.
10. Andrew Nicholls, "Venus and Adonis Frieze," in *Shakesqueer: A Queer Companion to the Complete Works of Shakespeare*, ed. Madhavi Menon (Durham and London: Duke University Press, 2011), 415.
11. I am especially indebted to John Garrison and Kyle Pivetti for helping me develop this chapter into its present form. They are gracious, generous, and insightful editors.

9 Marlowe's Helen and the Erotics of Cultural Memory

John S. Garrison

The depiction of Helen in Marlowe's *Doctor Faustus* (1604) offers a particularly intriguing case study for exploring the intersection between recollection and romantic longing. This figure seemingly summoned from classical antiquity at once emblematizes a shared cultural memory of the classical world and functions as an archetype for erotic desire, given her status as a legendary possessor of supreme female beauty. Faustus' reaction to her sudden presence in his study, "Was this the face that launched a thousand ships / And burnt the topless towers of Ilium?" might surprise us, then (5.1.90–91). One might think that a figure of such preternatural loveliness would be immediately recognizable, in terms of either profound aesthetic appeal or a powerful surge of attraction on Faustus' part.[1] In this moment, he seems to believe that erotic attraction might serve as confirmation of cultural memory: if he finds her unquestionably attractive, she is the divine beauty that inspired the Trojan War. Taking his hesitation as a starting point, this essay explores how the dynamics of expectation and disappointment inherent in erotic longing tie closely to both personal and collective memory.

How could Faustus hope to recognize a figure about whom he has neither personal memory nor any concrete description to which he can compare her? How *could* one recognize a historical or literary figure from classical antiquity? Received wisdom from the ancients about the specifics of Helen's appearance is notably scant, and such a paucity of description may be tied to the power of her beauty. In tracing the absence of details about Helen's features in Homer's and Virgil's accounts, Laurie Maguire puts nicely the problem of depicting Helen, "If Helen is indisputably the most beautiful woman in the world, as soon as you provide details you make her beauty disputable."[2] Indeed, Faustus' inability to confirm Helen upon sight points to a dilemma faced by adapters and directors of the play. Who do you cast or how do you choose to depict one "whose heavenly beauty passeth all compare," as she is described by one of the scholars in the play (5.1.29)? If making a film version in 1967, does one cast Elizabeth Taylor as the paradigmatic female beauty? Does her appearance opposite Richard Burton confirm her status as ultimately desirable in the eyes of her desiring subject? Stage performances have dealt with the problem of Helen's beauty in diverse ways—ranging from shrouding the actress in a black veil to portraying her as a corpse to presenting Mephistopheles in drag—to depict diversely how we might imagine this encounter.[3] These attempts in performance to "re-member," to piece together the most beautiful woman in the world, underscore the impossibility of recalling such a figure in a universally desirable body.

Faustus' question, though, may signal not only his uncertainty but also his disappointment. He may be disenchanted by Mephistopheles' conjuring, either because he senses this to be a demon in the guise of Helen or because he experiences the disappointment inherent in the process of divorcing fantasy from actual, sensory experience. That is, the expectation of an erotic encounter with a partner embodying ultimate beauty—indeed, a first erotic encounter with any partner really—sets one up for the lived experience not matching the imagined experience. Disappointment with Helen is both a personal disappointment as Faustus confronts his conjured paramour and a disappointment with the legacy of antiquity if the paragon is not perfect.

Imperfection in person may dialectically collide with the fantasy of a perfect Helen in order to generate sexual excitement. John Lyly's *Euphues* (1578) describes Helen as having a scar on her chin, "which Paris called *Cos amoris*, the Whetstone of love."[4] On one hand, the blemish may be the place where the imperfect lover can find sameness in the supposedly perfect beloved. On the other hand, the lover's exuberance allows him to ignore the flaw and focus more intently on the beloved's beautiful elements. The flaw throws into relief the desirable qualities; it re-ignites the engine of fantasy to overcome the gap between expectation and encounter. Lyly explains that "in all perfecte shapes, a blemmish bringeth rather a liking every waye to the eyes, than a loathing any waye to the mind."[5] Within the calculus of Lyly's formulation, we can interpret a performance in which Helen is portrayed as a corpse or demon, as a signal not of Faustus' foolishness but of his effectiveness as a desiring subject. Disappointment in Helen as a desirable object lies not only in the possibility that her appearance has flaws but also in the inevitability that her appearance will change over time. Golding's 1567 translation of Ovid's *Metamorphoses* has her weeping "when shee saw her aged wrincles in / A glasse."[6] She herself is saddened by the gap between the present encounter with the reflection in the mirror and the memory of being lovelier in the past. Ovid has her "musing in herself what men had seene," which leaves her lamenting not only the gap between memory and sensory reality but also the promise of more disappointment to come as she ages. Fitting within the overall focus on transition that dominates Ovid's epic, Helen's changeability functions at more than one level. Her personal appearance has changed, along with her claims to beauty, and the degree of desire among those who once sought her is imagined to change. Faustus seems to already sense that an encounter with Helen is an encounter with something to be treasured and something that will fade when he describes her as "spoils" that Paris brings to Troy (5.1.22).[7]

Disappointment in the encounter with the desirable Other calls upon the force of fantasy to overcome the shortcomings of appearance, and such operations tie closely to the functions of memory. Disappointment links directly to memory in the sense that we have a collision between our expectations—a type of future-oriented memory of a thing, how we hope to remember an experience—and the real-time generation of the memory itself. During the encounter, the lover realizes that she or he will be remembering the experience in a way that differs from how she or he fantasized during the expectation phase. The initial encounter with the beloved also propels us into the realm of memory because the new experience always involves a return to the past, to old patterns, to previous experiences that constitute the negative against which we construct the vision of positive experiences. Memories of earlier encounters, after all, allow the subject to imagine how good a new experience might be. In Faustus' hesitation at the sight of his conjured paramour, we see perhaps an expression of what Lauren Berlant describes as "cruel optimism," where the object of desire, that ultimately constitutes "a cluster of promises we want someone or something to make to us and make possible for us," is associated with "dread" or knowledge that the engagement with the object involves "the surrender to the return to the scene where the object hovers in its potentialities."[8] Helen offers a particularly potent example of the process by which memory-making is jarred by erotic experience, as ancient authors linked her desirability to the force of forgetting. In Book 3 of *The Iliad* (760–710 BC), for example, "men of good counsel" sit outside the gates of Troy alongside Priam and complain that Helen should be returned to the Greeks. Upon seeing her, though, they briefly forget their stance and announce, "surely there is no blame on Trojans and strong-greaved Achaians / if for long time they suffer hardship for a woman like this."[9] In the *Lysistrata* (411 BC), Aristophanes depicts Menelaus about to kill Helen after the fall of Troy, but then the king forgets his vengeful intent once he sees her breasts.[10] The actual encounter is never what we expect, and this jars the process of memory formation.

Marlowe seems to seize upon the ancient coupling of forgetting and desire when Faustus likens the encounter between him and Helen to that between Zeus and Semele. Hera discovers her husband's affair with Semele when the human woman later becomes pregnant. The *Metamorphoses* describes the goddess appearing in the guise of Semele's nurse, Beroë, and in an attempt to befuddle Semele straight out of *Gaslight* (Dir. Cukor, 1944), Hera urges Semele to second-guess the veracity of her memory:

> I wish with all my heart that Jove bee cause to thee of this.
> But daughter deare I dreade the worst, I feare it be amisse.
> For manie Varlets under name of Gods to serve their lust,
> Have into undefiled beddes themselves full often thrust.[11]

The encounter with the divine lover undermines the certainty of personal memory and, in Semele's case, leads to oblivion as she is incinerated when she demands certainty that the lover who impregnated her was Zeus.

In Faustus' attraction to the classical world and to its exemplar of beauty, we see glimpses of the Marlowe whom Stephen Orgel characterizes as an "erotic classicist."[12] Both the playwright and his character plumb the literature of classical antiquity to revivify ancient pleasures. In Faustus' subsequent surprise that this "paragon of excellence," as one of Faustus' scholar-colleagues describes her, does not match expectations, we glimpse the Marlowe of the later works whom Robert Darcy aptly describes as a writer "who understood love with pastoral simplicity and wisdom" (5.1.31).[13] Marlowe's Faustus naively discovers that when he confronts the beloved he also confronts the inevitable disenchantment at the heart of the erotic encounter. Yet Faustus overcomes this disenchantment by foregoing a solely romantic encounter for an entry-point into the shared memory of the classical age of heroes.

Faustus' demand of Helen, "make me immortal with a kiss," links physical touch with the stuff out of which Renaissance humanists build their dreams. Shifting his object of desire from the single woman to the rich history that centers around her, Faustus inserts himself into the pages of *The Iliad* and then transfers the events of the Trojan War to his own time period:

> I will be Paris, and for love of thee,
> Instead of Troy, shall Wittenberg be sack'd;
> And I will combat with weak Menelaus,
> And wear thy colours on my plumed crest;
> Yea, I will wound Achilles in the heel,
> And then return to Helen for a kiss. (5.1.97–102)

My reading of these lines seeks to extend and also re-direct Garrett Sullivan's claim that "the kissing of the succubus Helen marks the culmination of Faustus' self-forgetting."[14] Faustus may indeed experience the ego-destroying properties of desire here, but he makes an intriguing move to dissolve personal memory and instead re-constitute himself in the narrative of history. Faustus' vision—that with a single kiss he can penetrate an entire fictional world—adds new dimension to what Michael Warner has described in his exploration of the phenomenology of the anonymous sexual encounter. Warner helps us see how erotic engagement is "an experience of world making. It's an experience of being connected not just to this person but to potentially limitless numbers of people, and that is why it's important that it be with a stranger."[15] Upon realizing that he does not know and in fact cannot know this Helen, Faustus forgets any desire for personal intimacy and instead writes himself into cultural memory as an attempt to enter the larger realm of *kleos*. He links to the erotic experience of others, including Paris, Menelaus, and Achilles, and enters into the shared world of stories told and retold in commemoration of the age of heroes. Michael Keefer reads the encounter between Faustus and Helen as an instance of "sexual commerce between corporeal and disembodied beings."[16] I suggest an alternate reading where both entities are simultaneously corporeal (as physical actors seen on stage) and disembodied (as Faustus inserts himself into the past events from which Helen has sprung). While the play leaves ambiguous whether or not Faustus and his Helen have sex, we can understand his penetration into literary history as a rich and complex erotic act.[17]

Faustus derives pleasure from play with memory because he, like the speaker in Barthes' *A Lover's Discourse*, remembers "pathetically, punctually, and not philosophically, discursively; I remember to be unhappy/happy—not in order to understand."[18] Even as early as the second act, Faustus refuses to repent and focuses instead on how "sweet pleasure conquered deep despair" because he "made blind Homer sing to me" (2.3.25–26). The eroticism of the memory here anticipates the personal encounter with Helen's body and looks back upon his engagement with the received literature of antiquity. Both anticipatory memory and recollective memory bring pleasure in the present. The distinction between the two forms of memory-infected eros is pinpointed nicely by Foucault's response to Casanova's notion that "the best moment of love is when one is climbing the stairs." Rather, Foucault argues, "the best moment of love is likely to be when the lover leaves in the taxi."[19] The comment suggests that our best moments of erotic experience lie in recollection, when the power of fantasy begins to assert its narrative over the raw material provided by memory.

Faustus productively complicates the distinction between Casanova's focus on expectation and Foucault's focus on recollection. He envisions his future romantic experience in terms of what has already taken place, not as a repetition of his own past experience but as rehearsing for his own self-pleasure those experiences imagined by Homer. This is the *anamnesis* that Barthes associates with the memory of love, where "the amorous scene, like the first ravishment, consists only of *after-the-fact* manipulations."[20] Erotic recollection operates by recovering "a fragrance without support, a texture of memory."[21] Faustus' placement of himself and his Wittenberg into the history of the Trojan War enters this Renaissance humanist into the practice of what Elizabeth Freeman has termed "erotohistoriography," a practice she describes as

> distinct from the desire for a fully present past, a restoration of bygone times. Erotohistoriography does not write the lost object into the present so much as encounter it already in the present, by treating the present itself as a hybrid.[22]

Freeman's formulation helps us see how Marlowe's Helen might function as an empty vessel into which Faustus can project a range of desires: to experience visceral pleasure from a kiss, to participate in an already-scripted literary history, to author new history himself, and to ensure immortality (like Achilles and other ancient figures into whose erotic experiences he inserts themselves) in the stories told by others.

The erotics of Marlowe's Helen seem closely tied to her ability to generate fantasies about engaging with the stuff of history, rather than linked to material erotics of connecting with her body. M.L. Stapleton has argued that Faustus' plea for a kiss "emphasizes [...] his lack of normal interaction with women and his ignorance of matters generally associated with the female sex. His Helen is unreal, delusory."[23] The notion of Helen as an illusion or as an engine for generating illusions, rather than a fully realized person, seizes upon the *eidolon* tradition in classical literature. In Herodotus' *Histories* (450–420 BC) and in Euripides' *Helen* (412 BC), Helen does not accompany Paris to Troy. Instead, she patiently and chastely awaits Menelaus' return while what goes along with the Trojans is a simulacrum of Helen created by Hera. Staying in Egypt, Euripides' Helen laments, "oh! that Hellas had forgotten the evil fate that now I bear, and were now remembering my career of honour as surely as they do my deeds of shame."[24] Marlowe taps into the *eidolon* tradition by suggesting that separating or replicating the self enables the production of multiple narratives, multiple histories. Euripides' Helen, like Marlowe's Faustus, wishes to rewrite history, to change the relationship between history and the erotic encounter, to recast the encounter in recollection. George Peele's depiction of Helen reinforces such a reading. In "The Tale of Troy" (a long poem published in the same year as Marlowe's play), she seems to double herself when

> her heart was from her body hent,
> To Troy this Helen with her lover went,
> Thinking, perdy, a part contrary kind,
> Her heart so raught herself to stay behind.[25]

The desiring heart is seized upon, or "hent," in the moment and leaves the hesitant body behind, thus creating a double of the self. Part of Helen stays behind to lament her place in history while a phantasmatic, desiring self goes with Paris. There's even an echo of this notion in that big budget disaster movie, I mean historical epic, *Troy* (Dir. Petersen, 2004), when Helen tells Paris, "before you came to Sparta I was a ghost. I walked and I ate and I swam in the sea, but I was a ghost."

While Faustus will eventually be destroyed by his encounter with the supernatural, just as Semele is destroyed when she sees the full face of her beloved, his fantasy is that he will live on in history. Faustus never realizes his fantasy of being the new Paris in a Renaissance *Iliad*. Marlowe forecloses this possibility by leaving such an epic unwritten and only imagined. The playwright also forecloses another possible way in which Faustus might write himself into future history by denying him access to sexual reproduction. Marlowe's source text, the German *Faustbook* (first published in English in 1588), describes how Helen "in the end brought [Faustus] a man childe, whome Faustus named Iustus Faustus."[26] The child is linked to Faustus' extension into the future not only as an offspring but also because "this childe tolde Doctor Faustus many things that were to come."[27] Goethe takes up this detail from the Faustus legend and, by naming the child "Euphorion," the later playwright interpolates Faustus into history in a way that tracks to the fantasy that Marlowe's Faustus expresses in conjunction with kissing Helen. This miraculous child can fly, recalling Helen's mother's impregnation by Zeus in the form of a swan and also recalling heroes of antiquity such as the winged crewmembers of the Argos: Zetes and Calais. The child's name echoes that of the son of Achilles and Helen as described in mythographic history, thus further realizing Faustus' fantasy that he can dip into history and take the place of a legendary hero by way of—in this case, procreative—sex.

Let me close by noting that, while this brief exploration of the erotics of recollection in *Doctor Faustus* does not necessarily help us answer questions about Marlowe's own degree of sexual desire, I think it does help us answer the question that appears as the subtitle of a 2000 *GLQ* article by Stephen Orgel, "Tobacco and Boys: How Queer was Marlowe?" In that essay, Orgel shows how Faustus' desire for Helen is *anything but heterosexual,* noting that because Mephistopheles promises to bring courtesans "chaste as Penelope and wise as Sheba, but beautiful as Lucifer: the moral and intellectual ideals are female, but the ideal of beauty is male."[28] My argument here takes a different tack, looking at how the erotics in Marlowe's text suggest that he thinks like a queer theorist. Marlowe positions the tantalizing promise of new erotic experience as capable of collapsing and intersecting diverse categories of expectation, memory, sensual pleasure, literary history, dread, and disappointment. Marlowe's Helen, seemingly an archetypal object of heterosexual male attraction, is a fruitful object for queer study because she appears as a shadow out of time, summoned by erotic desire, foreclosing the possibility of procreative sex but promising a mode of erotic engagement with literary history.

Just as Mephistopheles troubles our sense of place when he declares of Faustus' study, "why, this is hell, nor am I out of it," Faustus approaches his state of uncertainty to feel either this is Helen or he will insert himself into the broader history of Hellenism (1.3.75–78).[29] Garrett Sullivan frames the union with Helen as "Faustus's attempt to forget the state of his sin," while Ewan Fernie argues that the kiss exchanged between Faustus and Helen signifies the Reformation breakthrough, "to participate in and affirm one's own abandonment to sin and negation," which in turn "leads us into the cloaca."[30] Fernie chooses a term here that means both an ancient sewer and an opening from which things go out and go in, an orifice for expulsion and for ingestion. I suggest that we can reconcile two such readings by interpreting Helen as a site where Faustus can forget his initial disappointment with the beloved and his looming dread of the cost of his sin, even briefly, by memorializing himself in a recollected antiquity. That antiquity, we find, is driven by an erotic fantasy that stands simultaneously within and outside history.

Notes

1. Quotations from the play are drawn from Christopher Marlowe, *The Tragical History of Doctor Faustus*, in *English Renaissance Drama: A Norton Anthology*, eds. David Bevington, Lars Engle, Katharine Eisaman Maus, and Eric Rasmussen (New York and London: W.W. Norton & Company, 2002), 250–85.
2. Laurie Maguire, "Helen of Troy: Representing Absolute Beauty in Language," *Sederi* 16 (2006): 34.
3. For an intriguing discussion of a series of choices in portraying Helen by the Royal Shakespeare Company since the 1960s, see Laura Grace Godwin, "'There is nothin' like a Dame': Christopher Marlowe's Helen of Troy at the Royal Shakespeare Company," *Shakespeare Bulletin* 27.1 (Spring 2009): 69–79. For a useful history of arguments regarding whether or not Faustus sins by kissing a demonic Helen and a discussion of whether we should place this Helen in the literary tradition of depicting the succubus, see Nicolas Kiessling, "Faustus and the Sin of Demoniality," *Studies in English Literature 1500–1900* 15.2 (Spring 1975): 205–11.
4. John Lyly, *The Descent of Euphues: Three Elizabethan Romance Stories*, ed. James Winny (Cambridge: Cambridge University Press, 2015), 1.
5. Ibid.
6. Arthur Golding, *The xv bookes of P. Ovidius Naso, entytled Metamorphosis, translated oute of Latin into English meeter* (London: William Seres, 1567), 15.188–89.
7. The *OED* notes that several definitions of the noun, "spoils," circulated in the fifteenth and sixteenth centuries. In addition to our more familiar usage of the term as "goods, esp. such as are valuable, taken from an enemy or captured city in time of war," a now-rare usage indicated "damage, harm, impairment, or injury, esp. of a serious or complete kind."
8. Lauren Berlant, *Cruel Optimism* (Durham, NC: Duke University Press, 2011), 1.
9. Homer, *The Iliad*, trans. Richard Lattimore (Chicago and London: University of Chicago Press, 1961), 3.156–57.
10. Aristophanes, *Lysistrata and Other Plays*, trans. Alan M. Sommerstein (New York and London: Penguin, 2002), 146.
11. Ovid, *Metamorphoses*, 3.292–95.
12. Stephen Orgel, "Tobacco and Boys: How Queer Was Marlowe?" *GLQ: A Journal of Gay and Lesbian Studies* 6.4: 564.
13. Darcy's essay nicely traces how reading Marlowe's work in its sequence of appearance in print informs a perception of the author as gradually softening and becoming gentler in his depictions of love. Robert Darcy, "Marlowe and Marston's Cursus," in *Christopher Marlowe the Craftsman: Lives, Stage, and Page* (Farnham, Surrey, England and Burlington, VT: Ashgate, 2010), 149.
14. Garrett A. Sullivan, *Memory and Forgetting in English Renaissance Drama: Shakespeare, Marlowe, Webster* (Cambridge: Cambridge University Press, 2005), 77.
15. Michael Warner, *The Trouble with Normal: Sex, Politics, and the Ethics of Queer Life* (Boston: Harvard University Press, 2000).
16. Michael, Keefer, "Fairer than the Evening Air: Marlowe's Gnostic Helen of Troy and the Tropes of Belatedness of Historical Mediation," in *Fantasies of Troy: Classical Tales and the Social Imaginary in Medieval and Early Modern Europe*,

128 John S. Garrison

eds. Alan Shepard and Stephen D. Powell (Toronto: Centre for Reformation and Renaissance Studies, 2004), 48.

17. Christine Varnado does a wonderful job of reminding us that the audience is often asked to imagine sex acts off-stage in Renaissance plays but that we should hesitate before imaging what exact sex acts might or might be taking place. Christine Varnado, "'Invisible Sex!' What Looks Like the Act in Early Modern Drama?," in *Sex before Sex: Figuring the Act in Early Modern England*, eds. James M. Bromley and Will Stockton (Minneapolis and London: University of Minnesota Press, 2013): 25–52.
18. Roland Barthes, *A Lover's Discourse: Fragments*, trans. Richard Howard (New York: Hill and Wang, 2001), 217.
19. Michel Foucault, "Sexual Choice, Sexual Act." *Foucault Live: Collected Interviews, 1961–1984*, ed. Sylvère Lotringer (New York: Semiotext(e), 1996), 330.
20. Barthes, *A Lover's Discourse: Fragments*, 216.
21. Ibid.
22. Just as Warner sees contact with the partner's body as entry into the larger world of sex, Freeman sees the body as the means by which erotics gain access to the larger world of history-making. Eroto-historiography "uses the body as a tool to effect, figure, or perform that encounter" with the past in the present. Elizabeth Freeman, *Time Binds: Queer Temporalities, Queer Histories* (Durham, NC: Duke University Press, 2010), 95.
23. M.L. Stapleton, *Marlowe's Ovid: The Elegies in the Marlowe Canon* (Surrey and London: Ashgate, 2014), 191.
24. Euripides, *Helen*, in *The Bacchae and Other Plays*, trans. E. P. Coleridge. (New York: Digireads Publishing, 2012), 59.
25. George Peele, *The Works of George Peele: Collected and Edited with Some Account of his Life and Writing, by the Rev. Alexander Dyce* (London: William Pickering, 1829), 179.
26. Jones, John Henry, *The English Faustus Book* (Cambridge: Cambridge University Press, 1994), chapter 55.
27. Ibid.
28. Orgel, "Tobacco and Boys," 571.
29. This play's Helen is embedded with all the audience's (and Faustus') memory of previous Helens. As Will West reminds us, "each performance unfolds already scored by previous performances, which are recalled in part by props, scripts, recordings, and other mediations, but foremost the memories of the producers of theater, the actors, and spectators." William N. West, "Replaying Early Modern Performances," in *New Directions in Renaissance Drama and Performance Studies*, ed. Sarah Werner (Houndmills, UK, and New York: Palgrave Macmillan, 2010), 35.
30. Sullivan, 78, and Ewan Fernie, *The Demonic: Literature and Experience* (New York and London: Routledge, 2012), 48–49.

10 Strange Love
Funerary Erotics in *Romeo and Juliet*

Mark Dahlquist

I shall never be satisfied / With Romeo till I behold him—Dead

Facing Lady Capulet, who is enraged by the killing of Tybalt, Juliet cleverly equivocates, concealing her marriage and her true feelings, as her mother expresses a mortal rage against the banished Romeo. When Lady Capulet announces her plan to have Romeo murdered, and asks whether this will assuage Juliet's grief, Juliet replies:

> Indeed, I shall never be satisfied
> With Romeo 'till I behold him—Dead
> Is my poor heart, so for a Kinsman vext:[1]

Here I quote an emendation to the text adopted by Nicholas Rowe in his 1709 edition (one that is often adopted by modernized editions). By substituting a dash for the end-stop that precedes "Dead" in the folio and 1599 quarto editions, Rowe sought to preserve for readers the startling effect of these lines when delivered on stage.[2] For Juliet must pause only briefly before the word "Dead," if she is to mislead her mother, and the audience therefore must also hear Juliet describe her wish to behold her husband dead.

However, audiences cannot have been *too* surprised. Throughout the play, the act of proleptically remembering the living as deceased is a constant theme. Only moments before her conversation with her mother, Juliet and Romeo exchange their last goodbyes, Juliet telling Romeo, as he descends from her balcony into the morning gloom: "Methinks I see thee now, thou art so low, / As one dead in the bottom of a tomb." (3.5.55–56). We too, as readers or audience members may have found special poignancy in the story of these two lovers since being told of their "death-marked love" in the play's chorus.

The play's *carpe diem* erotics necessitate these morbid contemplations, in which the beloved is imagined as an object in order to be regarded as a desirable human person. However, in *Romeo and Juliet*, the remembering of the dead also has an explicitly social dimension, evident in the decision of the Montague and Capulet families to commemorate Juliet and her Romeo with a pair of gorgeous statues, to be displayed side by side, following the discovery of the dead couple.

The plan to erect these commemorative statues may recall for readers the first meeting of the two lovers, which is famously described in a sonnet inscribed in Act 1. This sonnet (1.5.94–107) blazons this crucial moment of love-making through a conceit that describes a pilgrim approaching, touching, and kissing a devotional statue, even though such objects of pilgrimage (usually near a tomb or a relic of a saint) had long since been removed from Shakespeare's England. During the course of the play readers and audience members observe as Juliet and Romeo are inexorably replaced in the world by the kind of memorial sculpture that the two young lovers had imagined together at the moment of their first kiss. For, as I will argue, many Elizabethans viewed devotional and funerary images as similar in kind. Shakespeare's addition of these key memorial statues to his version of this oft-told story signals both the play's well-known interest in the relationship between love and death, and also its less familiar concern with the relationship between erotic desire and memory.

Attending closely to post-Reformation discussions of memorial and devotional statues, I will argue, reveals that the play's sculpted monuments to the dead cannot be adequately understood as expressions of nostalgia for Catholic forms of worship or as sentimental reminders of the power of art; rather, the Reformation-era anxieties surrounding such images demonstrate that the funeral erotics of *Romeo and Juliet* can be read as more transgressive, dangerous, and strange than has usually been acknowledged.

Monuments to the Dead and the Book of Wisdom

Shakespeare's primary source text, Arthur Brooke's *Romeus and Juliet* (1562), mentions no sculpted saint when its protagonists first kiss. Moreover, in Brooke's *Romeus*, the couple is buried, together, in a rich tomb, but not one linked to figurative statuary:

> And lest that length of time might from our minds remove,
> The memory of so perfect, sound, and so approved love:
> The bodies dead removed from vault where they did die,
> In stately tomb, on pillars great, of marble raise they high.
> On every side above, were set and eke beneath,
> Great store of cunning Epitaphs, in honor of their death.
> And even at this day the tomb is to be seen.
> So that among the monument that in Verona been,
> There is no monument more worthy of the sight:
> Than is the tomb of Juliet, and Romeus her knight.[3]

This valedictory conclusion, describing a celebratory public memorial, seems to have disquieted the severely pious Brooke, who added to his translation a letter to his readers, in which he underscored the difference between his own perspective as a devout Protestant and the feelings of the mourning citizenry of Verona whose funeral monument celebrated the "perfect, sound, and approved" love of Romeo and Juliet.[4]

In this letter, the devout Brooke describes the subjects of his story disapprovingly. Brooke, who immediately after the publication of his translation would join a military expedition to rescue French Protestants from their Catholic oppressors,[5] explains that *Romeus and Juliet* illustrates, "the shameful and wretched ends of such as have yielded their liberty thrall to foul desires teach men to withhold themselves from the headlong fall of loose dishonesty."[6] Brooke elaborates, describing his reasons for writing about these unchaste lovers, and the immoral Catholic world they inhabit:

> [T]his tragical matter [is] written to describe unto thee a couple of unfortunate lovers, thralling themselves to unhonest desire, neglecting the authority and advice of Parents and friends, conferring their principle consuls with drunken gypsies, and superstitious Friars (the fit instruments of unchastity) attempting all adventures of peril, for the attaining of their wished lust, using auricular confession (the key of whoredom, and treason) [...] hastening to most unhappy death.[7]

Describing the fall of these lovers from the company and counsel of "parents and friends" into congress with gypsies, Friars, and the suspect secrecy of the confessional, Brooke explains that in order to teach, poets must describe both the virtuous and the reprobate: "those we esteem profitable in use and pleasure, and also those which we accompt noisome and loathsome,"[8] Brooke thus presents to his readers the story of two unprofitable and noisesome lovers and the Friars, the "instruments of unchastity," who abet them.

Shakespeare's *Romeo and Juliet* is the first retelling of the Verona love story to replace the stately tomb, marble pillars, and carved epitaphs described by Brooke and Boaistuau with a pair of splendid golden statues. As his play draws to a conclusion, Shakespeare writes:

MONTAGUE: [...] I will raise her statue in pure gold,
    That whiles Verona by that name is known,
    There shall be no figure at such rate be set
    At that of true faithful Juliet.
CAPULET: As rich shall Romeo's by his lady's lie
    Poor sacrifices of our enmity. (5.3.299–304)

Shakespeare's addition of these figurative public statues, as graven golden memorial images, would probably have concerned the Protestant Boaistuau[9] and would certainly have vexed the goodly Arthur Brooke, who had already taken such pains to disavow the voice of the monument with which his poem concludes.

132 *Mark Dahlquist*

Yet the studied artificiality of the commemorated lovers seems to have given pause to other early modern readers, including some whom we may find surprising. The antiquarian John Weever, for example, would later celebrate and preserve in print many English tombs and epitaphs in his 1631 *Ancient Fvnerall Monvments*. Nevertheless, in 1599 he expressed doubts about the concluding memorial gesture of *Romeo and Juliet*. In that year, Weever published his *Epigrammes in the Oldest Cut*, which includes a sonnet that offers some of the earliest surviving remarks about William Shakespeare. "Ad Gulielmum Shakespeare" is an ambiguous and perhaps ambivalent sonnet, which begins by praising Shakespeare's narrative poems. In its first two quatrains, it praises characters from Shakespeare's poems: Lucrece, Tarquin, Venus, and Adonis. However, the sonnet's final quatrain and couplet seem to contrast the instructive characters of Shakespeare's narrative poems with the seductive characters of his plays. In his sonnet's final six lines, Weever warns that the "power attractive beauty" of Shakespeare's publically staged characters makes them into something like erotic Saints, capable of kindling or "heting" uncouth sexual desires among audience members. Weever introduces this odd comparison of stage-persona and saint through the characters of Romeo—or, rather, Romea —and Richard:

> Romea Richard; more whose names I know not,
> Their sugred tongues, and power attractive beuty
> Say they are Saints although that Sts they show not
> For thousands vowes to them subjective dutie:
> They burn in loue thy childrē Shakespear het thē
> Go, wo thy Muse more Nymphish brood beget them.

William Jones suggests that the sonnet's final couplet invites Shakespeare to beget with his muse a purer ("more Nymphish") brood of plays and poems.[10] By implication, Shakespeare's audience, "het" into idolatrous love by the "sugared tongues and power attractive beauty" of characters such as Romeo and Richard, needs now to be cooled by exposure to characters with less power to ignite inappropriate desire. Citing Romeo and Richard as examples of erotic faux-saints, Weever draws an unexpected connection between Romeo and Richard Gloucester,[11] a villain who not only conspicuously presents himself to his subjects in the image of a saint, but whose death drive, frictive verbal inventiveness, and impersonal amatory intensity parody the conventions of Petrarchan love—"Let the soul forth that adoreth thee, / I lay it naked to the deadly stroke," says the supplicating Richard to Lady Anne Neville.

Moreover, the phrase "Romea Richard" invites scrutiny. Why no comma between the terms? Why Rome*a*? Perhaps mere sloppiness at the printshop, or an illegible manuscript passed on to the printers by Weever. Or, perhaps this phrase is meant not merely to compare, but to conjoin these two figures to whom Weever attributes such erotic power, feminizing Romeo's name in a way that links him to other androgynous figures such as Shakespeare's Adonis and the youth of *A Lover's Complaint*. By using a metaphor of sainthood to link Shakespeare's best-known historical character to the protagonist of Shakespeare's most famously erotic play, Weever plays upon two familiar antitheatricalist sentiments: that play acting involves "the confounding, interchanging, transforming these two sexes," and that stage-plays encourage "transforming even men themselves" into pagan "devil idols," as William Prynne put it in 1633.[12]

In 1563, a fear of presenting such perverse images prompted Brooke to offer an explanation as to why a godly poet would translate a poem that tells the story of an illicit sexual pairing. Brooke avers that, far from presenting gilded idols to "het" his readers into sexual desire, his translation does the opposite. He is instead presenting intentionally deformed monsters, in the manner of the ancient Spartans:

> This precedent, good Reader, shall be to thee, as the slaves of Lacedemon, oppressed with excess to drink, deformed and altered from likeness of men both in mind and use of body, were to the free-born children, so shewed to them by their parents, to th' intent to raise in them an hateful loathing of so filthy beastliness. Hereunto, if you apply it, ye shall deliver my doing from offence and profit yourselves. (xlvi)

When Brooke explains that this understanding of his poem will "deliver my doing from offence," he does not suggest that seeing the poem in this way will prevent readers from feeling insulted, but rather that by seeing Romeus and Juliet as "altered from the likeness of men," readers will be protected from idolatry—from the dangers of offense or scandal, in the theological sense.[13] Thus Brooke and Weever engage in analogous deformations: Weever connects Romeo and Richard (even hinting at an agglomeration of the two), and Brooke similarly marks as deformed the scandalous images his translation might otherwise appear to celebrate. Thus Weever and Brooke both notice and work to defeat the potential of *Romeo and Juliet* to present memorial images that are dangerously seductive.

The Normative Image

By 1870, the Puritan suspicion of images had long ago given way to the Victorian enthusiasm for monuments, decoration, and high church ceremony. In that year, Ernest Dowden offered a reading of *Romeo and Juliet*'s memorial statues as heroically redemptive:

> Juliet and Romeo [...] have accomplished their lives. They loved perfectly. Romeo had attained to manhood. Juliet had suddenly blossomed into heroic womanhood. Through her, and through anguish and joy, her lover had emerged from the life of dream into the waking life of

truth. Juliet had saved his soul; she had rescued him from abandonment to spurious feeling, from abandonment to morbid self-consciousness, and the enervating luxury of emotion for emotion's sake. What more was needed? And as secondary to all this, the enmity of the houses is appeased? Montague will raise in pure gold the statue of true and faithful Juliet; Capulet will place Romeo by her side. Their lives are accomplished.[14]

If Dowden's rapture was exceptional in its intensity, it was nevertheless such sentimental enthusiasm, rather than Puritan iconophobia, that underwrote much of the literary discussion of *Romeo and Juliet* in the twentieth century.

In an influential essay, Jonathan Goldberg rejects the lingering sentimentalism Dowden represents. Goldberg's immediate target, though, is editor of the Arden Romeo and Juliet (1980) Michael Gibbons, whose introduction he cites as an example of lingering sentimentalism with regard to *Romeo and Juliet*. Goldberg begins his argument by quoting *Romeo and Juliet*'s description of the golden statues and by citing Gibbons's explanation that the statues of Romeo and Juliet represent, "the artifice of eternity" and that their creation represents, "the alchemical transmutation of worldly wealth into property, earth, into the spiritual riches of the heart and imagination."[15] Finding this explanation not merely sentimental, but "formalist," and moreover, consistent with "the conservative nature of most high school curricula," Goldberg, writes: "[t]he idealization of the lovers, to be brief, serves an ideological function. The marriage of the corpses in the eternal monuments of 'pure gold' attempts to perform what marriage normally aims at in comedy: to provide the bedrock of the social order. Or, to speak somewhat more exactly, the heterosexual order" (219). Thus, while Brooke and Weever worried that *Romeo and Juliet* might present idols that encourage unlicensed or perverse sexual practices, Goldberg views the golden statues with which the play concludes as far removed from any such threat; rather, for him the golden statues with which the play concludes project the triumphal voice of Verona's two heteronormative patriarchs, who are given the play's last word.

Goldberg's reading of *Romeo and Juliet* contests the sentimental, formalist, and heteronormative reading of the play implicitly endorsed by readers such as Dowden and Gibbons. Attending especially to the play's use of metaphor to articulate a queer erotics of seriality, Goldberg builds upon the arguments of Joseph Porter's *Shakespeare's Mercutio* to argue that "the sexual field in which desire operates in the play is the forbidden desire named sodomy" (228). Yet Goldberg's reading does not profess to redeem *all* of the play from the sentimental obfuscations of patriarchal heteronormativity. Goldberg's wariness toward the golden statues persists throughout his essay; indeed, as it approaches its conclusion, Goldberg's essay takes an interesting rhetorical turn, declining to criticize Gibbons or others for misreading these shining funeral monuments, and looking instead towards the monuments themselves as sources of ideological error:

> [I]t is only by seeing the energies in the plays that are not dictated by a compulsory heterosexuality and gender binarism that one can begin to mark their productive energies. In the case of *Romeo and Juliet*, as I have been suggesting, this means to put pressure on the heterosexualizing idealization of the play and on the magical solution it arrives at over the corpses of the young lovers.

Goldberg sees these statues as enforcing a normative conclusion upon the subversive action of the play. Similarly, Carla Freccero underscores the inherent heteronormativity of the statues, while also reminding us that these golden monuments have particular purchase on collective memory. For Freccero, the placement of these statues at the story's end is, again, an oppressively sentimental gesture: "In the place of living flesh and blood, two golden statues; in the place of obstinate waste and refusal, valuable and perduring memorials. Isn't this what 'politics,' by which here we understand a certain social order, wants?"[16] In an essay that, like Goldberg's, reads *Romeo and Juliet* as challenging social norms, especially sexual ones, Freccero adopts a wary attitude toward the play's celebratory monuments, describing them as offering "elegiac recuperation" for sacrificed freedom: "[a]lthough the play does not stress that recuperation at its end, its futurities arouse my suspicion."[17] For Freccero, like Goldberg, these objects invite a mistaken devotion.

It is perhaps less an irony than a consequence of the concept of idolatry's lingering influence on critical thought that Brooke, Weever, Goldberg, and Freccero have regarded the sanctified statues of Romeo and Juliet through similarly narrowed eyes, warning against the dangers presented by this couple, publically glorified in death. Whereas John Weever and Arthur Brooke worried that the idealized representation of these lovers might present an inducement to "filthy beastliness," Goldberg and Freccero consider an analogous but opposite temptation, viewing the golden statues envisioned at the end of Shakespeare's play as promoting and naturalizing a raft of sexually and politically conservative ideological norms. However, I would argue that taking notice of the connections drawn by Shakespeare's contemporaries between memorial sculpture and the scandalous idols condemned by the English Church may be useful in recognizing the subversive potential of *Romeo and Juliet*'s golden statues and in considering how this potential underwrites the action of the play itself.

The Book of Wisdom and Monuments to the Dead

It is not always acknowledged that memorial statues would have been read as potentially idolatrous by at least some members of Shakespeare's audience. Discussing funerary sculpture, Allison Shell writes, for example: "the same English Protestants who deplored religious images in churches had no problem erecting lifelike and elaborately gilded funeral monuments there."[18] However, during the period in which *Romeo and Juliet* was likely written, the relationship between saint and sculpture, and between memory and perversity, was under careful and anxious consideration among English Protestants. In 1594, perhaps a year or so before Shakespeare wrote *Romeo and Juliet*, Richard Hooker published the first four books of his *Laws of Ecclesiastical Polity*. In the first book of this series, Hooker approaches the subject of sculptures to the dead, quoting and paraphrasing from chapter 14 of the apocryphal Book of Wisdom (known also as *The Wisdom of Solomon*). He explains the connection of memorial statues to the practice of idolatry:

> When a father mourned grievously for his son that was taken away suddenly, he made an image for him that was once dead, whom now he worshippeth as a god, ordaining to his servants ceremonies and sacrifices. Thus by process of time this wicked custom prevailed, and was kept as a law; the authority of rulers, the ambition of craftsmen, and such like means thrusting forward the ignorant, and increasing their superstition. (1.8.235)

Here, in his magisterial synthesis of the Church of England's reformed belief, Hooker explains how the creation of a memorial statue can lead to idolatry. In so doing, he supplies his own translation from the Greek of the Book of Wisdom and, significantly, quotes only half the sentence as it appears in the more dangerous version of this passage and had been printed in the Bishop's Bible of 1568:

> For when a father mourned heavily for his son suddenly taken away from him, he made him an image of him which was but a dead man, he now began to worship as a god, and ordained for his servants ceremonies and sacrifices. Thus by process of time this ungracious custom being waxen strong was kept as a law and enforced by commandment of tyrants. (14:15–16)

Hooker was taking up the question of memorial images and idols in an effort to curb the antiauthoritarian implications of the Book of Wisdom. Hooker omits the word "tyrants" from his quotation of Wisdom 14:16 because of the dangerous political implication of linking tyranny and idolatry; he makes other changes that tend to diminish the importance of this apocryphal incident. For example, by beginning his selection with "when," rather than "for," Hooker conceals that, in the Book of Wisdom, this story of a father who raises a statue to the memory of his beloved son is not only the source of one reprovable instance of idolatry but is the story of the *first* idolatry. Not just the first idolatry, for the birth of idols was, "the beginning of spiritual fornication, and the invention of them the corruption of life" (14:12).

Indeed, according to the Book of Wisdom, the consequences of the entry of idolatry into the world through this memorial statue have been terrible beyond reckoning, and have included both political and sexual disorder:

> So that there reigned in all men without exception blood, manslaughter, theft, dissimulation, corruption, unfaithfulness, perjury, disquieting of good men, forgetfulness of good turns, defiling of souls, changing of kind, disorders in marriages, adultery, and shameless uncleanness. For the worshipping of idols not to be named is the beginning, the cause, and the end of all evil. (14:25–27)

In discussing the connection made by the Book of Wisdom between memorial images and birth of idolatry, Hooker feels no need to introduce or explain his reference to this relatively obscure apocryphal book. On the contrary, Hooker assumes that his readers are just as familiar with its line of argument as Shakespeare would have been, whether or not the playwright indeed picked up a copy Hooker's 1594 *Lawes*.

The Book of Wisdom, with its alternative genealogy of evil, was a key text often cited by committed iconoclasts, despite the suspicions sometimes cast upon it as a result of its status as apocrypha and its unusual teachings on the origins of idolatry. John Calvin, for example, approached it cautiously: "In regard to the origin of idols, the statement contained in the Book of Wisdom has been received with almost universal consent," he writes; yet he remains skeptical: "I do not admit, however, that it was the first origin of the practice [...] the human mind is a perpetual forger of idols" (*Institutes* 1.1.96). In England, the teachings of the Book of Wisdom had been systematically promulgated, following the publication in 1562 of the second *Book of Homilies*, which was produced at Elizabeth's command to be used as an instrument of promoting Protestant uniformity in the realm she inherited from her Catholic sister. The Elizabethan *Book of Homilies* was a required purchase for all English Churches, to be used throughout the year with the *Book of Common Prayer* and the scriptures themselves.

Of all the homilies of the second book, the most remarkable and passionately anti-Catholic is the *Homily against Idolatry*, distinguished both by the tenor of its invective and by its sheer length. By far the longest sermon in the *Second Book of Homilies*, it is by itself about two-thirds the length of the entire *First Book of Homilies*. It relies heavily upon the Book of Wisdom's account of the origins and nature of idolatry, citing it on at least 10 occasions—more that it cites any canonical book of scripture. For example:

> For if the origin of Images, and worshipping of them, as it is recorded in the eight Chapter of the book of Wisdom, began of a blind love of a fond father, framing for his comfort an Image of his son, being dead, and so at the last men fell to the worshipping of the Image of

him whom they did know to bee dead: How much more will men and women fall to the worshipping of the Images of GOD, our Savior Christ, and his Saints, if they bee suffered to stand in Churches and Temples publically?

Likely written by Hooker's friend and mentor, John Jewel, the *Homily against Idolatry* condemns idolatry in vitriolic terms, arguing that images themselves were prohibited, not merely their misuse. The homily insists: "Idolatry cannot possibly be separated from imagery any long time, but that as an inseparable accident, or as a shadow follows a body when the sun shineth" (242). Moreover, according to the *Homily*, the consequences of permitting images to exist in churches would be severe and inevitable:[19]

> [P]reaching cannot possibly stay idolatry, if images be set up publicly in temples. And true is it, that no other remedy, as writing against idolatry, councils assembled, devices made against it, severe laws likewise, and proclamations of princes and emperors, neither extreme punishments and penalties, nor any other remedy could or can be possibly devised for the avoiding of idolatry, if images be publicly set up and suffered. (275)

By 1594, a generation of English women and men had grown to maturity having listened to the words of the *Homily* echoing from the pulpit on many occasions.

For the audiences who watched Shakespeare's *Romeo and Juliet*, the notions that memorial sculptures were sources of political sexual disorder and that they were the ancestors of the idols of paganism and the Catholic Church were familiar, even if the iconoclastic edicts issued by Henry, Edward, and Elizabeth had all taken care to specifically prohibit the destruction or removal of funeral monuments.

Strange Love

As Hooker strove in his *Laws of Ecclesiastical Polity* to temper the strident iconophobia of the Elizabethan *Homily on Idolatry*, William Shakespeare wrote his most famous love story. Among Shakespeare's most deliberate and significant additions to Brooke's *Romeus and Juliet* were the descriptions of memorial sculptures that, in his play, bookend the story of his doomed lovers, one appearing at the play's conclusion and the other appearing at the moment when Romeo and Juliet kiss for the first time.

The sonnet that presents the young couple's fateful first kiss has attracted a great deal of critical attention. When examined in religious terms, it has sometimes been regarded as evidence of Shakespeare's nostalgia for Catholic forms of devotion. Stephen Greenblatt explains that the sonnet's "beautiful, playful lines" express "the sly blend of displacement and appropriation, the refashioning of traditional religious materials into secular performance, and the confounding of the sacred and the profane[...] characteristic of virtually the whole of Shakespeare's achievement as dramatist and poet" (112). Greenblatt here ties Shakespeare's theatrical practice to a nostalgia for a vanished Catholic England.

Yet this emphasis on nostalgia is potentially misleading. Reading this sonnet, and the play as a whole, as also in conversation with the discourse of Protestant iconophobia as expressed in the *Homily Against Idolatry*, the apocryphal Book of Wisdom, and Richard Hooker's establishmentarian *Laws* reveals a sonnet (and a play) that is not simply nostalgic for a Catholic past, but also interested in the notion of images as dangerous and strange. Indeed, in *Romeo and Juliet*, the image imagined by the young lovers at the moment of their first kiss is nothing if not dangerous:

ROMEO: If I profane with my unworthiest hand
    This holy shrine, the gentle fine is this:
    My lips, two blushing pilgrims, ready stand
    To smooth that rough touch with a tender kiss.
JULIET: Good pilgrim, you do wrong your hand too much,
    Which mannerly devotion shows in this;
    For saints have hands that pilgrims' hands do touch,
    And palm to palm is holy palmers' kiss.
ROMEO: Have not saints lips, and holy palmers too?
JULIET: Ay, pilgrim, lips that they must use in prayer.
ROMEO: O, then, dear saint, let lips do what hands do;
    They pray, grant thou, lest faith turn to despair.
JULIET: Saints do not move, though grant for prayers' sake.
ROMEO: Then move not, while my prayer's effect I take.
    [kisses her] (1.5.94–107)

This sonnet today brings the archaic language of Catholic pilgrimage and material devotion to the attention of audience members who have little idea what a "holy palmer" might be. In *Romeo and Juliet*, it also marks the beginning of a process that is surprising and unsettling. Readers and audience members observe as Romeo and Juliet come to be replaced by images similar to the one they imagined together as they kissed for the first time. In this sense, Shakespeare's *Romeo and Juliet* tells the story of the erection of an idol or of the birth of a tomb.

The memorial statues, which mark the commencement and conclusion of the relationship at the center of the play, are also linked to the idea of strangeness. This aspect of idolatry is more fully explored in another pair of images—these still more explicitly sexualized—that Shakespeare also adds to Brooke's story. The first of these idolatrous images is invoked by Mercutio. Following the Capulet party, Mercutio seeks to summon the hidden Romeo—and Romeo's manhood—by describing fragments of Rosaline:

her "bright eyes," "scarlet lip," "quivering thigh," and "the demesnes that adjacent lie" (2.1.17–20). When Benvolio warns that Mercutio's shouted conjuration may only anger Romeo, Mercutio answers,

> This cannot anger him. 'Twould anger him
> To raise a spirit in his mistresses' circle
> Of some strange nature, letting it there stand
> Till she had laid it and conjured it down. (2.1.23–6)

As Mercutio tries to arouse or summon Romeo, his racy metaphor casts Romeo's penis (or the erection of a rival) as a kind of conjured demon, to be summoned from a darkness akin to the darkness where Romeo listens, hiding. Importantly, Mercutio here uses the word "strange" in its Biblical signification, relating to the idolatrous worship of "strange gods," and their idols, as for example in God's warning in Jeremiah, "Like as you have forsaken me, and served strange gods in your land, so shall you serve strangers in a land that is not yours" (KJV 5:19). As Moshe Halbertal and Avishai Margalit have observed in their study of Biblical representations of idolatry, the notion of the strange is drawn in its original significance from the concept of idol-worship: "The rabbinic term *avodah zarah*, which is generally translated as 'idolatry,' 'idol worship' or 'false worship,' literally means 'strange worship'" (3). Mercutio has this sense of the word in mind as he concocts a metaphor of sexual arousal as the summoning of demons or idols.

If the iconophobic discourse of the 1590s links funerary statues and the devotional sculptures venerated by pilgrims, *Romeo and Juliet* draws the idol into close proximity to erotic physicality, rendering the sexual connotations of the forbidden image into explicitly bodily terms. Mercutio's attempt to summon a penis of "strange nature" is followed in Act Three by a parallel conjuration, made by Juliet as she, like Mercutio, contemplates the emergence from the darkness of her forbidden lover:

> [...] Come, civil night,
> Thou sober-suited matron, all in black,
> And learn me how to lose a winning match,
> Played for a pair of stainless maidenhoods.
> Hood my unmanned blood, baiting in my cheeks,
> With thy black mantle til strange love grow bold[.] (3.2.10–15)

Juliet implores the night to help her learn to loose her "maidenhoods" and to conceal her beating blood, as she waits for Romeo and for his "strange love" to "grow bold." Her words here incorporate references to hawking[20] but convey more fundamentally Juliet's sexual anticipation of Romeo's arrival and the imminent loss of her virginity. Introducing metaphors of maidenhead and rushing, blushing, blood, Juliet asks that the black mantle of night conceal her excitement. Juliet's soliloquy continues in sexual terms, five times incanting and imploring night and Romeo to "come," before exclaiming finally,

> Give me my Romeo, and when I shall die
> Take him and cut him out in little stars,
> And he will make the face of heaven so fine
> That all the world will be in love with night
> And pay no worship to the garish sun. (3.2.21–25)

Thomas Bowder's assiduously desexualized *Family Shakespeare* of 1807 adopted the fourth quarto (1622) revision of line 21, printing "when he shall die," instead of Juliet's dangerously sexual "when I shall die," which as Mary Bly has observed was not only "both a ceasing to be and an erotic ecstasy" but an obvious pun ("in the case of a pun as ordinary as this," Bly notes, "a Renaissance audience would definitely grasp its double meaning").[21] However, this bawdy reference is more than a pun; it is of course also the climax of a prayer to the night, occasioned by the appearance of Romeo's "strange love" grown bold, and continued through a course of growing excitement Juliet images in the wake of her orgasmic death, which concludes not with the Ovidian translation of Romeo into the heavens, but with a risky devotional inversion, by which the day, the normative recipient of pious devotion, is suddenly replaced by night.

Structurally, this pair of strange summonings, one performed by Mercutio, and one by Juliet, is itself contained within the paired images of memorial statues that mark first the young couple's initial kiss and, finally, their burial together. These two strange prayers of arousal call to mind the sexually transgressive potential of the image, as it had been imagined by Protestant iconoclasts of the 1590s, for whom idols had the power to subvert "the glorious triumphs of the continent man" (the triumphs that Arthur Brooke preferred to praise) and to frustrate the efforts of churchmen to shape creatures who are "profitable in use."[22] Memorials, as public acts of remembrance, represented efforts at social control, but such objects were always subject to being re-read, made strange, or queered, for the notion of the strange is in some ways antecedent to the idea of the queer.

As it concludes, *Romeo and Juliet* stages a return to the kind of image that, in its first act, was employed by the play's young protagonists to mark their love with death, from the moment it is born. This return emphasizes that such memorial sculptures are, like the empty signs of language (the name "Romeo" for example), always subject to redescription or misprision. Furthermore, by using funerary images as symbols of desire, *Romeo and Juliet* embraces an erotic sensibility disassociated from sexual reproduction (indeed, Juliet rejects Paris just after the nurse remarks cheerfully that "women grow bigger by men" (1.4.95), and Romeo, although he mentions Rosaline's obligation to procreate (1.1214–219) never courts Juliet with such language. Instead, Romeo and Juliet seduce and celebrate one another through images of tombs, sacred statues, and funerary sculpture. The golden statues constructed at the play's conclusion therefore do not illustrate the triumph of Verona's patriarchs in their efforts to champion normative economic and sexual productivity. Rather, their appearance suggests that the scandalous eroticism of the figurative object—which is to say idolatry—will continue to exert its strange and illicit influence in Verona, long after the burial of Romeo and Juliet.

Notes

1. Nicolas Rowe, *The Works of Mr. William Shakespear*, vol. 5 (London: Jacob Tonson, 1709; New York: AMS Press, 1967), 2128.
2. Perhaps Rowe's revision was inspired by the 1597 "bad" quarto, in which Juliet declares, "For while he lives, my heart shall nere be light / Till I behold him, dead is my poor heart."
3. Brooke here dutifully translates the conclusion of Pierre Boaistuau's 1559 *Tragique Histories*, which like other earlier versions does not describe memorial statues of Romeo or Juliet. Masuccio's *Novelle* of 1474 mentions neither monument nor epitaph, while Porto's 1535 version explains simply that the grieving families "ordered a handsome monument, on which in a few days was engraved the cause of their death." Bandello's 1554 "Romeo e Giulietta" concludes with a sonnet summarizing the story of the young lovers, which the author explains was engraved upon their tomb. Epitaphs, not statues, also serve as memorials in Bernard Garter's *Tragicall and True Historie* (1563) and in William Painter's retelling of the story in *The Palace of Pleasure* (1567). Arthur Brooke, *Romeus and Juliet*, ed. J.J. Munro (New York: Chatto and Windus, 1908), 3011–20.
4. On Brooke's attitude toward the Friar, see Rene Weis's introduction to the Arden *Romeo and Juliet* (New York: Bloomsbury, 2012) 45–47. Unless otherwise noted, my citations of Romeo and Juliet refer to this edition.
5. Brooke's expedition to fight in the French Wars of Religion would end in nautical disaster, his ship wrecked off Sussex coast and Brooke drowned just outside safe harbor. Moreover, by March of 1563 the Huguenots whom the English forces sought to aid had already entered into a formal league with their fellow Catholic citizens. Brooke's death on March 19 occurred on the day after the Edict of Amboise was signed, granting French Protestants a degree of political toleration. English forces withdrew from LeHavre by the end of July.
6. Brooke, lxv.
7. Brooke, lxvi.
8. Brooke, lxv.
9. Stephen Bamforth has recently made a widely accepted case that Boaistuau, who at times dedicated works to both Catholic and Protestant patrons was, at least by the time of his visit to England in 1559, a self-identified Protestant. See *Histoires prodigieuses*, by Pierre Boaistuau, edited by Stephen Bamforth, annotated by Jean Céard (Geneva: Droz, 2010). On Huguenot burial practices in the seventeenth and also the later sixteenth centuries, see, Keith P. Luria, "Separated by Death? Burials, Cemeteries, and Confessional Boundaries in Seventeenth-Century France" *French Historical Studies*, Volume 24, Number 2, Spring 2001, pp.185–222.

10. William R. Jones, "Say They Are Saints Although That Saints They Show Not" *Huntington Library Quarterly*, Vol. 73, No. 1 (March 2010), 83–98.
11. The comparison could also have been to Richard II; however, the popularity of *Richard III*, which was printed in six quarto editions before 1623, makes a reference to Gloucester more likely.
12. William Prynne, *Histrio-mastix* (London, 1633), 89; 207.
13. Brooke follows his letter to the reader with a prefatory poem, which describes his translation using a conceit that seems again intended to distance his work from charges of idolatry. Brooke describes himself as a mother mountain bear, licking her cubs into shape. Brooke's poems are like cubs, he explains, to be shaped into patterns such as a courageous fighting bear, or the bear of Ursa Major, which provides sailors guidance by pointing out the pole-star, or the bear on the crest of the noble (and Protestant) Dudley family. Brooke represents his envisioned poems as lively, active, and roughly formed, describing them in terms intended to distance them from seductively beautiful memorial or contemplative objects.
14. Ernest Dowden, *Shakespeare: His Mind and Art* (1875), 97. See also Dowden's introduction to his edition of *Romeo and Juliet*: "And thus the dead lovers have become immortal victors" (London: Methuen, 1900), xxxiv.
15. Qtd. in Jonathan Goldberg, "Romeo and Juliet's Open Rs," in Jonathan Goldberg (ed.), *Queering the Renaissance* (Durham: Duke University Press, 1994) 219.
16. Carla Freccero, "Romeo and Juliet Love Death" in *Shakesqueer: A Queer Companion to the Complete Works of Shakespeare*, ed. Madhavi Menon (Raleigh, NC: Duke University Press, 2011), 306.
17. Freccero, 306.
18. Alison Shell, *Shakespeare and Religion* (New York and London: Arden, 2010) 64.
19. That the homily prohibited images and included tomb statuary within the category of images would not go unnoticed. In the 1640s some puritans, such as Edmund Gurnay, used the homily to argue for the removal of all sculpted images from churches.
20. Rene Weis ed., *Romeo and Juliet* (New York and London: Bloomsbury, 2012), 248.
21. Mary Bly, "Bawdy Puns and Lustful Virgins: The Legacy of Juliet's Desire in Comedies of the Early 1600" in Wells, Stanley, ed. *Shakespeare Survey*, Vol. 49 (Cambridge: Cambridge UP, 1996), 98.
22. Arthur Brooke, *Romeus and Juliet*, ed J.J. Munro (New York: Chatto and Windus, 1908), xlv.

11 "The monument woos me"
Necrophilia as Commemoration in Thomas Middleton's *The Lady's Tragedy*

Heather Wicks

I

From Hamlet's leap into Ophelia's grave to Juliet's searching kiss of Romeo's dead lips to *The Revenger's Tragedy's* poisoned kiss between the Duke and Gloriana's skull, the molestation and fondling of corpses constitute a conventional trope in early modern tragedy. In part, these necrophilic scenes participate in the traditional western association of sex with death, which as Jonathan Dollimore points out, "found its most extreme statement in the Renaissance."[1] However, while many critical projects have addressed the intersection of death and eroticism, few have considered this conventional association in context of memory studies. This paper argues for the import of memory to studies of the sex/death nexus, as well as the unique purchase of necrophilia on the subject of memory. While scholars such as Thomas Rist have demonstrated early modern drama's preoccupation with remembrances of the dead, even terming it the "drama of commemoration,"[2] this paper shows how integral the erotic is to acts of commemoration on the English stage. I argue that instances of dramatized implied or performed necrophilia, the phenomenological intersection between sex and death, show that the erotics of memory shape the ways characters remember the dead, contend with loss, and revenge their loved ones in early modern drama.

Certainly, the female body is central to this conventional portrayal of desire and death, and early modern dramatists used it often as a site to explore cultural anxieties. Portrayals of necrophilia particularly engage not only with death and desire, but also with issues about sexual agency and consent quite literally "over her dead body," to borrow Elisabeth Bronfen's phrase.[3] Although there are a few exceptions, such as Juliet's kiss mentioned above, most instances of necrophilia on the early modern stage involve a male agent eroticizing and engaging with a female corpse. Ultimately, the same patriarchal constructs of female sexuality that inform the period's construction of rape inform representations of necrophilia. Both representations derive from the same misogynistic ideas regarding female sexual purity and agency.[4] My reading of necrophilia as a form of erotic memory suggests that what is at stake in these performances is a woman's sexual agency and subjectivity. In this context, I examine Thomas Middleton's *The Lady's Tragedy* (1611),[5] arguably the most grotesque example of dramatized necrophilia, as my case study. Here, as in other plays, necrophilia functions as a type of perverse commemoration that pursues complete possession of the female body and her legacy and seeks to alleviate grief through erotic release.

Middleton's play demonstrates how the issue of consent intersects quite clearly with modes of erotic remembrances of the dead. In the play, the character known simply as "Lady" kills herself to avoid the Tyrant's attempted rape. After her death, the character known simply as "Tyrant" breaks into her tomb, steals her body, and brings it back to court. In memory of her, he commits unnamed acts to her corpse, costumes it, and demands that his attendants make obeisance to her. The Lady's spirit, fearful for her body, commands Govianus (the Tyrant's supposed foil, the rightful king, and the Lady's lover) to rescue her body and "restore" her "rest" (4.4.78). The Tyrant unwittingly hires Govianus, disguised as an artist, to fix the Lady's decomposing body and is killed by kissing the Lady's lips poisoned by Govianus. After the Tyrant dies, Govianus is restored as king and exalts the Lady by crowning her corpse his queen. The Lady's spirit enters a final time to ensure that her body is finally put to rest. This essay broadens the definition of necrophilia to include Lisa Downing's formulation of it as an aesthetic practice and builds upon her work to show how necrophilia can be used as a tool for articulating the intersection of desire and memory.[6] After setting this theoretical framework, the essay will proceed to examine the increasing conflation of men's grief and erotic impulses as the play progresses. Specifically, I argue that the male characters appropriate the Lady's body and manipulate her image and the memory of her, illustrating the ways that issues of memory, the erotic, and sexual agency intersect. Finally, I trace how the Lady's ghost resists the appropriation, suggesting Middleton disrupts and satirizes the fantasy of complete submission.

II

Pathologically speaking, necrophilia is one of the least studied conditions, in part due to its imprecise definition—forensic and psychological professionals disagree on its exact classification as it manifests in diverse behaviors from sexual interest in the dead to fantasies of unresisting partners to actual intercourse with a corpse and extends to other deviant behaviors like cannibalism.[7] The *Diagnostic and Statistical Manual of Mental Disorders* categorizes necrophilia as a general paraphilic disorder without assigning it a specific classification.[8] Recent forensic scholars and literary critics have argued to broaden the definition of necrophilia and challenge the rarity of the necrophilic fantasy even while the act of intercourse remains uncommon. Doing so, as Dany Nobus has proposed, can advance our understanding of "informed consent and the social taboo on the dead."[9] Ultimately, necrophilic behaviors and fantasies do not necessarily imply sadism or lead to an actual crime but rather indicate a fantasy for a compliant partner. Obviously, a corpse cannot consent or refuse, and often that is the allure for a necrophile—"the simple fact that the dead cannot refuse, reject, or resist; they also do not tell tales or talk back."[10] Moreover, the ways a society chooses to criminalize this act highlights the issue of consent central to representations of necrophilia and my reading of Middleton's play: what counts as consent? To what extent should the dead be considered to have agency? To what extent should necrophilia be considered an attack on a person if that person is dead? What does it mean when the dead do talk back? The legal history of necrophilia exemplifies these very issues by struggling to characterize the crime as theft from the bereaved, desecration of a body, or rape of a person.[11] Thus, studying necrophilia asks questions about a society's understandings of the corpse, consent, materiality, and, as this essay suggests, memory. Particularly, in Middleton's play, the Tyrant's and Goviannus' interest in her corpse elides not only the Lady's consent and her agency but also the memory of her.

The literary scholarship that contends with necrophilia usually interprets it in terms of nostalgic longing and recovery—recovery of a historical past or a lost love—or take it, like Downing's project does, as evidence of the psychoanalytical death drive, a manifestation of a culture's destructive urges that in turn function as the source of desire.[12] Early modern scholars have attended to necrophilia and its materiality in context of the period's scientific advancements, conceptions of the body, and the Reformation.[13] Joseph Roach, in discussing Samuel Pepys's necrophilia with Queen Katherine's corpse, argues that the erotic always informs memory, especially our cultural memory.[14] While these projects attend to the import of desire and materiality to our subjectivity, they often, and Downing does so deliberately, elide the issues of consent central to these representations.[15] While I turn away from Downing's psychoanalytical conclusions, I take up her argument "that necrophilia is as much an aesthetic, a mode of representation"[16] and when examined has cultural implications for the ways a society conceives of desire and death. In much early modern drama, the necrophilic aesthetic demonstrates not only the connection between sex and death, but, it reveals, with unresisting women's bodies at the center, a cultural fantasy of submission and appropriation. Moreover, if desire is integral to cultural memory, then it is also vital to acts of remembrance.

Although Middleton and his contemporaries were not concerned with pathologizing, they certainly used this mode of representation to think about the nature of loss and the living's complicated relationship with the dead that characterized the period.[17] Early modern society did consider necrophilia a perverse crime, although there was no term for it. Moreover, Protestant reformers worked to minimize the body's material importance by stressing the putrefaction process. However, the corpse itself was not necessarily a source of major taboo. The material realities of early modern existence—plague, famine, population growth, funerary practices—meant the dead were quite literally everywhere; also, the frequency of corpse medicine and anatomy theaters suggests a significant amount of curiosity about and assigned value to the dead.[18] Thus, the fact of the corpse in drama is not as remarkable as its presence that marks "the early modern love-affair with death."[19]

Many literary critics like, Graham Holderness, resist labeling desire in moments like Hamlet's exchange with Yorrick's skull or leap into Ophelia's grave necrophilia; instead, they argue that they demonstrate "a deeper rapprochement of loss and desire," not exactly an attraction to the dead, but "desire generated by loss."[20] However, considering these moments in the context of necrophilia articulates more obviously the intersection of desire and memory as it relates to erotic commemoration and appropriation of female bodies. While Yorrick's skull may merely rouse Hamlet to recollect and pontificate on loss, Ophelia's dead body inspires a material act, a fight literally in her grave over her dead body and her legacy. For Hamlet, the act is not about reconciling the loss of Ophelia but rather staging ownership of her body and love. He wants to humiliate Laertes and challenge Laertes' demonstration of erotic grief while performing his own: "Dost [thou] come here to whine? / To outface me with leaping in her grave?"[21] He uses desire in that moment to stage commemoration, one that rewrites his past actions and pursues possession of Ophelia. Because, dead, Ophelia and Middleton's Lady can no longer contradict or refuse, the male characters use the women's deaths to pursue their own desires. Ultimately, necrophilia functions as an erotic fantasy of grief that renders a woman's dead body as neatly compliant—a fantasy that for Middleton's Lady, at least, enacts a second destruction.

In *Lady's*, through their necrophilia, the men misappropriate the Lady's material self-representation and steal her intent of signification: first she gives up her life to avoid the Tyrant's sexual intentions, and then she loses agency in her death and legacy, which have been made void by the Tyrant's persistent advances to her body and demonstrated by the Lady's affected spirit. They act on the Lady's body regardless of her consent or desire and then inscribe it with meanings according to their own commemorative and erotic designs, which are often one in the same. Historically, analyses of necrophilic pathology emphasize this fantasy of possession and destruction. Magnus Hirschfeld argues that "to possess and destroy her beyond death" motivates the male necrophilic desire toward women.[22] Similarly, in performance, the erotic potential of the corpse, which is almost always female, is located in its "vacancy," that "it is supremely acquiescent."[23] Early modern drama contextualizes this particular fantasy in terms of the lover's grief. As Leo Bersani notes, death is "the happy condition for a total possession"; in death, the lover becomes an image to be consumed.[24] Moreover, the same absence that makes her dead body erotic also "renders it infinitely susceptible to imaginative inscription."[25] By the end of *Lady's*, the male characters quite literally imprint their desires on the Lady's compliant flesh, as they paint, position, and use her corpse according to their will. However, the Lady's ghost, by talking back, disrupts this fantasy somewhat and resists complete possession, or at the very least indicts it. Middleton's play uses necrophilia as a meta-theatrical illustration of this "imaginative inscription" onto female bodies, demonstrating the ways men appropriate women's bodies and deaths through acts of erotic commemoration.

III

Male characters and dramatists, including Middleton, often employ the dead female body as an erotic emblem to explore social ills; women's corpses serve as symbols for men's depravity, sexual politics, society's degradation, or the inability for revenge to satisfy the bereaved and betrayed. Many readings of the Lady's corpse point out the ways in which she is merely an object that passes between men, a site to manage patriarchal anxieties, and a body on which to displace male aggression. Her body is a stand-in for the kingdom, for the proper man's right to rule, and for the ultimate feminine ideal: the passive, silent mistress.[26] However, although standard early modern patriarchal values and assumptions about women's virtues—predicated on their sexual purity—shape much of *Lady's* action and the ways the men conceive of the Lady as honorable, rarely do scholars see the way Middleton's play satirizes these tropes, and the necrophilic fantasy integral to them, with his irreverent handling of the Lady's suicide, her rotting corpse, and indignant ghost.

Middleton's play is unique in that the Lady's death does not do the typical work of female suicide. It does not serve as the impetus for revenge nor does it stop the play's corruption, initiate political change, or solidify her emblematic status as a virtuous Lady. Provoked by the ghost to regain her body, Govianus seeks revenge only after he learns that her corpse has been "snatched away" (4.4.84). Moreover, it is the Tyrant's necrophilia, not his attempted rape or her death, that brings about his own downfall. More exactly, it is the "mere idolatry" of making obeisance to her corpse that disturbs his attendants more than the abuse committed or threatened to her body (5.2.20). Middleton disinvests the Lady's suicide with political and spiritual meaning and satirizes the depiction of female suicide as a positive outcome to men's power struggles and gender politics. *Lady's* uses the Tyrant's necrophilia to question the virtue of the Lady's suicide and the status of her honor, as her soul changes according to modifications on her material body. While this does not necessarily convey Middleton's feminist sympathies, it suggests the ways *Lady's* plays with theatrical convention and is representative of his characteristic cynicism.[27] Although the Lady's body is an erotic object misused by the men around her, the play at once participates in the eroticization and mocks those who do. In a very material way through necrophilia, Middleton's *Lady's* is preoccupied with how desire and the fantasy of submission is implicated in memorializing female bodies.

The Lady commits suicide because she believes it will prevent the Tyrant, or anyone else, from gaining control over her body or her legacy. She views it as a way to be "remembered" (3.1. 108) correctly, as honorable, faithful, and devout. From the beginning, she insists that she is "not to be altered" (1.1.123) by anyone's desires but her own. However, the Tyrant's impending sexual force threatens to alter her regardless of her will. To avoid a rape she sees as her physical and spiritual destruction, she seizes control the only way she is able: through suicide. Although it is problematic that patriarchal ideals of feminine virtue construct her agency, in the context of the play, she sees her death as a way to defeat the Tyrant and stay unaltered. However, the male characters consistently disregard her intent by positioning their contest of power on her body—both alive and dead. The Tyrant usurps the throne to win the Lady and because Govianus "dared to be [his] rival" for her love (1.1.13). The Tyrant situates his success in "her affection," and when she rejects him, he becomes "less than nothing," "banished" from his "kingdom" (42–46). Govianus too locates his victory in the Lady's body: upon realizing that the Lady has remained faithful, Govianus holds the lady and exclaims, "Here's liberty in my arms" (209). After her death, her body becomes the focus of their grief also, but now they can possess her according to their will: Govianus feels "comfort" that she can no longer be taken, and "joy" that she will remain forever his (3.1.231–33), while the Tyrant enjoys her unresisting body. They appropriate her corpse and in doing so undercut the intent of signification she sought in her suicide. The Lady's figurative status becomes literal; she becomes the Tyrant's painted lustful object, a literal weapon, and finally an emblem for chastity, crowned as Govianus' silent queen.

The Tyrant conceives his necrophilia as a compulsion from his grief. He makes his grief into an erotic act, a substitute for what she denied him in life. When the Tyrant discovers her suicide, he becomes consumed with obtaining the "sight" of her "in spite of death" (4.2.34) and devises a plan to steal her corpse. When he approaches her tomb, he sees a monument, probably in her likeness, and proclaims, "The monument woos me; I must run and kiss it" (4.3.9). The material representation of her death becomes an erotic representation of her absent self, and his grief compels him to kiss the memorial. Moreover, he hopes his actions will prove his grief and devotion, a kind of performance of erotic mourning. However, he is unable to weep and becomes frustrated at his inability to perform sorrow correctly. When he cannot find satisfaction in the Lady's monument, the Tyrant forces his way to her corpse. Here, the play imagines the theft of her body as a kind of rape. The soldiers accompanying the Tyrant feel uncomfortable with "the batt'ring of a lady's tomb" (41), and when the tomb resists, the Tyrant exclaims, "No, wilt not yield? / Art thou so loath to part from her?" (25–44). When he finally sees her body, his first words are not only that of an idolater,[28] but they also make her wholly into an object for his possession: "O, blest object! / I never shall be weary to behold thee. I could eternally stand thus and see thee" (61–63). His language neatly avoids recognizing the Lady's former resisting self; as an object, he can "take up her body" as he pleases (70). He even acknowledges the dissonance: "if she were alive," the soldiers "should not come near to touch her" (71–72). In fact, until his own death, the Tyrant wavers between lamenting the Lady's death and finding her conveniently dead.

The Tyrant's necrophilia ultimately serves as a commemorative act that seeks complete possession of the Lady's body and memory. When he disinters the Lady, at first, the Tyrant rationalizes his actions by fixating on the Lady's lifeless beauty, a commonplace treatment of dead women.[29] However, by the end, he finds her death itself beautiful. To the Tyrant, "Life is not more illustrious" (65) and this moment engages the fantasy of the trope: she appears alive and remains beautiful but is also lifeless and unresisting. Despite the fact that she feels cold to his touch, a fact continually pointed out, he kisses her, believing his desire can be generative.[30] When she stubbornly remains dead, he insists that her physical body will be able to satisfy him: "Since thy life has left me, / I'll clasp the body for the spirit that dwelt in't, / And love the house still for the mistress' sake" (112–14). Her body becomes a literal monument, a substitute for her "spirit" that the Tyrant will love for the "sake" and in memory of his mistress. His necrophilia is more than about his sexual pleasure; he wants ownership of her body that he could not achieve in life: "Thou art mine now, 'spite of destruction / And Govianus; and I will possess thee" (115–16). The Tyrant makes the Lady's body into an erotic monument; it acts as a representation of her memory, and of herself, that he can fashion according to his desire.

Unlike other beautiful, lifeless women on stage, such as Juliet or Ophelia, Middleton's Lady rots. Her decay symbolizes the spiritual decay caused by the Tyrant's lust and the conventional association of women's bodies with pollution and disease.[31] More than that, however, the play also indicts the fantasy of possession—both of her body and memory of her—integral to the Tyrant's necrophilia. Her insistent decomposition mocks the Tyrant's desire for the body's compliancy and control of the narrative the Lady's body tells in death. The Lady's decaying beauty works against both. The Tyrant is distressed by her putrefaction, even while he tries to ignore it for his own pleasure. Where he sees "beauty that's so much adored," he also sees how "One night of death makes it look pale and horrid; / The dainty preserv'd flesh, how soon it moulders" (5.2. 14–17). After costuming her in such a way to draw attention to her beautiful paleness, he worries that she looks too dead:

> How pleasing art thou to us even in death!
> I love thee yet, above all women living,
> And shall do sev'n year hence.
> I can see nothing to be mended in thee
> But the too constant paleness of thy cheek.
> I'd give a kingdom but to purchase there
> The breadth of a red rose in natural colour,
> ... And I must only rest content with art,
> An that I'll have in spite on't. (5.2.24–34)

Unlike the fantasy of Juliet that displays the allure of embodying both death and life, the Lady's decay emphasizes the gross reality of the literary conceit. The Tyrant's unequivocal "But" and Middleton's insistence on her rot satirizes the eroticization of the dead female body. Alive she has too much individual will, but dead she is too constantly dead, and despite the Tyrant's erotic designs, he cannot conjure life. In the end, the natural process of decay is too much, and the Lady's body in this way betrays him, so he purchases the representation of life. He turns her into a piece of art to satisfy himself, which takes her further from her previous self; she becomes a memory of herself shaped according to his will.

Death's persistence on the Lady's body also demonstrates the limits of the Tyrant's erotic memory. As her body continually sags and slips further and further from representing the Lady that used to dwell in it, the erotic experience ultimately fails to satisfy him and his memory of her. In the end, the Tyrant's necrophilia works a second destruction upon the Lady. Not only does he abuse her body for his own perverse desires, but he also continues to molest it and her memory by physically shaping her into the mistress he wanted her to be. As the material realities of death impress upon his erotic commemorative designs, the Tyrant decides to keep her "in spite" of her moldering body by hiring an artist to paint her (5.2.34). His designs shift from loving her corpse "for the mistress' sake" to using it "to give [his] eye delight" (5.2.83). The Tyrant's perverse commemorative designs end up causing his downfall. Govianus, disguised as the artist, paints the Lady's lips with poison, and when the Tyrant kisses her in hopes that his "arms and lips shall labour life into her" (5.2.118–19), he ingests the poison. When the Lady's spirit enters to watch his death, she further indicts the Tyrant's commorative purposes. Her ghost, unlike her corpse or Ophelia's, is able to talk back and disrupt his necrophilic fantasy.

Theoretically, as a dead body, the Lady should have no agency, and although perverse, the Tyrant's actions should not affect her soul or her afterlife. At first, prioritizing her eternal memory, she believes death will preserve her legacy as well as her soul and will release her from the cares of material existence (3.1.144–45). When her spirit visits Govianus to tell him of the Tyrant's wrongs, he even wonders how her soul could be disturbed: "They cannot reach thee now. What dares offend thee? / No life … can now wrong my mistress!" (4.4.55–58). However, she insists that the Tyrant's "sinful kiss" disturbs her rest and that she is affected by his desire to "dissemble life" on her body to "please his lustful eye" (76–77)—both his necrophilia and his alterations to her body distress her. Her spirit's insistence on returning her body to the tomb and its fear that the desecration of her corpse disrupts her afterlife complicate her body's lack of agency. The Lady's ghost is affected to such an extent that when the ghost enters a second time, she is "in the same form as the Lady is dressed in the chair."[32] The Tyrant's use of her corpse has actually altered her spirit, and the Lady bears the mark of the Tyrant's erotic fantasies and acts. Her revenant spirit appears to resist the fantasy somewhat, and her persistent presence abiding over her rotting corpse accuses those who have disregarded her consent. She tries to assert her agency and does somewhat in that she is revenged, but the fact that her altered spirit reflects her altered body also demonstrates that the female body is always implicated in sin, even when dead.

For the men in the play, women have more value and stability as dead bodies. Govianus' commemorative acts demonstrate that the focus of his necrophilic fantasy is that she become a stable signifier of chastity. After the Tyrant's soldiers leave empty handed, Govianus finds "comfort ... to see 'em gone without her"; though "her life was so sweet" to him, he finds "joy" in "her everlasting sleep" (3.1.231–34). As the Lady predicted, he no longer will have to worry about her faithfulness or sexual purity. In death, she will become permanently his, which is really what he fears most, as evidenced by his anxiety at the beginning. She even allows for death's possession in her appeal to Govianus to kill her: "His lust may part thee from me, but death, never. / Thou canst lose me there, for dying thine" (3.1.144–45). Although Govianus is supposed to be the Tyrant's foil, his actions troublingly mirror the Tyrant's: Govianus appropriates her body for revenge and then makes her into his own "blest object." When Govianus takes the throne again, he crowns the disturbed corpse "in memory of her admired mistress" (5.2.188–89). The men on stage bow in reverence to her corpse, which parallels the Tyrant's earlier actions of obeisance. The Lady's ghost reappears, apparently concerned, as Govianus tells her, "Thou need'st not mistrust me" (5.2.199). Govianus tries to distinguish his treatment of her corpse by framing his final act as one of "honor" (5.3.190) not of worship or erotic desire like the Tyrant's actions. However, although he does not have intercourse with her corpse, in crowning the body "our queen," even "the first and last that ever we make ours" (202), he implicates his erotic designs by performing a kind of marriage ceremony. His last words locate his focus: "I would those ladies that fill honour's rooms / Might all be borne so honest to their tombs" (213–14).

In his essay on the Tyrant's necrophilia Kevin Crawford argues that in the context of the play's gender politics, the Tyrant's "repeated unmanning by his desire for the Lady has essentially forced him to this," inadvertently exhibiting the language of rape culture at work in the play.[33] The Lady, her beauty, and her refusal "force" the Tyrant to steal her body just as it would have "forced" him to rape her had she not killed herself. While the dead should have no agency or sexual identity according to Protestant and early modern conceptions of death, the Lady's ghost and her concern for her material body complicate her supposed absence, which should render her consent irrelevant. Middleton's play in particular uses necrophilia as a meta-theatrical exploration of the conceit of the beautiful dead woman: this love is about possession.

Necrophilia articulates the unique intersection between desire and memory, suggesting that the erotic is implicated in the ways people grieve and commemorate. Middleton's play is just one example of a number of early modern texts that demonstrates how the necrophilic fantasy is about appropriation of female bodies and their memories. The male characters' necrophilia functions as an erotic commemorative act that seeks complete possession over the Lady's body and its signification. Necrophilia is more than a discomfiting taboo: it denies a dead woman the agency to say no. Despite her ghost's assertion of her agency, the troubling conclusion of *Lady's* is that the actions of the male characters do affect the Lady's afterlife, and the audience is left wondering to what extent she has been altered. Although Govianus asserts that "They cannot reach thee now," the Lady's ghost and the play seem certain that they can.

Notes

1. Jonathan Dollimore, *Death, Desire, and Loss in Western Culture* (New York: Routledge, 1998), xi. Many necrophilic moments literalize the commonplace connection between sex and death. It is a conventional metaphor that acting on carnal desires leads to a spiritual death, a conceit that drives many revenge plots. Karin Coddon in "'For Show or Useless Property': Necrophilia and *The Revenger's Tragedy*" argues that the "intersection between death and the erotic throughout Elizabethan and Jacobean tragedy is a virtual commonplace of the genre" (71) *ELH* 1 (1994): 71–88. Also, see Michelle O'Callaghan, *Thomas Middleton, Renaissance Dramatist* (Edinburgh, Scotland: Edinburgh University Press, 2009); Susan Zimmerman, *The Early Modern Corpse and Shakespeare's Theatre* (Edinburgh: Edinburgh University Press, 2005); for destruction as accessed through women's bodies, see Eileen Allman, *Jacobean Revenge Tragedy and the Politics of Virtue* (Cranbury, NJ: Associated University Press, 1999); and Valerie Traub, *Desire and Anxiety Circulations of Sexuality in Shakespearean Drama* (London: Routledge, 1992).
2. Thomas Rist, *Revenge Tragedy and the Drama of Commemoration in Reforming England* (Burlington: Ashgate, 2008).
3. Elisabeth Bronfen, *Over Her Dead Body: Death, Femininity and the Aesthetic* (New York: Routledge, 1992), 13.
4. Karen Bamford in *Sexual Violence on the Jacobean Stage* (New York: St. Martin's Press, 2000), points out that, for the rape victim, "Because her beauty 'provokes' the attack, the heroine implicitly shares responsibility for the aggression" (7). For further discussion on how women and their beauty are often implicated in their rapes see Barbara J. Baines, *Representing Rape in the English Early Modern Period* (New York: The Edwin Mellen Press, 2003) and Jocelyn Catty, *Writing Rape, Writing Women* (New York: St. Martin's Press, 1999).
5. Previously called *The Second Maiden's Tragedy* and now commonly attributed to Middleton. Thomas Middleton, *The Lady's Tragedy* in *Middleton: The Collected Works*, ed. Gary Taylor and John Lavagnino (Oxford: Clarendon Press, 2007), 839–905.
6. Lisa Downing, *Desiring the Dead: Necrophilia and Nineteenth-Century French Literature* (Oxford: Legenda, European Humanities Research Centre, University of Oxford, 2003).
7. Necrophilia's legal and pathological histories show how the field has had difficulty establishing a concrete definition and trouble discerning its prevalence.

See Anil Aggrawal, *Necrophilia Forensic and Medico-legal Aspects* (Hoboken: CRC Press, 2010); John Troyer, "Abuse of a Corpse: A Brief History and Re-theorization of Necrophilia Laws in the USA," *Mortality* (2008): 132–52; for a critical history see, B.R. Burg, "The Sick and the Dead: The Development of Psychological Theory on Necrophilia from Krafft-Ebing to the Present," *Journal of the History of the Behavioral Sciences* (1982): 242–54; for earlier history, Magnus Hirschfeld, *Sexual Anomalies* [Rev. Ed.] (New York, Emerson Books, 1948).

8. American Psychiatric Association, *Diagnostic and Statistical Manual of Mental Disorders*, 5th edition (Washington, D.C.: American Psychiatric Publishing, 2013), 685. Necrophilia has no unique diagnostic code and is grouped with other uncommon paraphilic disorders.
9. Dany Nobus, "Over My Dead Body: On the Histories and Cultures of Necrophilia," in *Inappropriate Relationships: The Unconventional, the Disapproved, and the Forbidden*, ed. Robin Goodwin and Duncan Cramer (Mahwah: Lawrence Erlbaum Associates, Inc., 2009), 173–92; 185.
10. Aggrawal, *Necrophilia*, 4.
11. Most studies of necrophilia, legal and pathological, address the issue of consent and agency of the dead, and the ways the questions reveal interesting assumptions about a society's view on the dead. In particular see Nobus, "Over My Dead Body" and Troyer, "Abuse of a Corpse."
12. Joseph Roach, "History, Memory, Necrophilia," *The Ends of Performance*, ed. Peggy Phelan and Jill Lane (New York: New York University Press, 1998), 23–30; and Scott Dudley, "Conferring with the Dead: Necrophilia and Nostalgia in the Seventeenth Century," *ELH* 2 (1999): 277–94.
13. See Coddon "Necrophilia and *The Revenger's Tragedy*"; Sheetal Lodhia "'The House is Hers, the Soul is but a Tenant': Material Self-Fashioning and Revenge Tragedy" *Early Theatre* 12.2 (2009): 135–61; Susan Zimmerman, *The Early Modern Corpse and Shakespeare's Theatre* (Edinburgh: Edinburgh University Press, 2005).
14. Roach, "History," argues Pepys's necrophilia "seeks to preserve a sense of the relationship with the past by making physical contact with the dead" (29).
15. Downing's project responds to modern society's urge to categorize sexuality, suggesting that necrophilia has larger cultural implications for how we conceive of desire for both men and women. While she understands the objections to her argument, she also asserts that insisting on the misogyny of necrophilia instead of seeing at as a genderless unconscious deathly desire means that "women may have no choice but to identify erotically with the readily available representations of themselves as victims" (126). She wants to break this pattern. Also, while Zimmerman and Lodhia address the misogyny of the play and Coddon the scientific treatment of the female corpse, these are not the focus of their readings.
16. Downing, *Desiring the Dead*, 4.
17. The Reformation instituted a new, more secular commemorative model and altered the landscape of the afterlife and the grieving process. Throughout the period medical advancements, anatomy theaters, and the material realities of the dead, made crucial by plague years, population surges, and food shortages, caused early modern society to rethink their relationship to the deceased, spiritually, physically, and scientifically. While critics debate to what extent these

"*The monument woos me*" 155

changes demystified the body or shook foundational belief systems, these shifts contributed to a sense of uncertainty regarding the place of the dead. For an introduction to these issues, see Clare Gittings, *Death, Burial, and the Individual in Early Modern England* (London: Croom Helm, 1984); Peter Marshall, *Beliefs and the Dead in Reformation England* (Oxford: Oxford University Press, 2002); and Michael Neill, *Issues of Death: Mortality and Identity in English Renaissance Tragedy* (Oxford: Clarendon Press, 1997).

18. For an in depth discussion of death's material realities for early modern people, see Vanessa Harding, *The Dead and the Living in Paris and London, 1500–1670* (Cambridge: Cambridge University Press, 2002). For more on corpse medicine and the complicated nature of taboo regarding the corpse, see Richard Sugg's *Mummies, Cannibals, and Vampires: The History of Corpse Medicine from the Renaissance to the Victorians* (New York: Routledge, 2011); and Hillary Nunn, *Staging Anatomies: Dissection and Spectacle in Early Stuart Tragedy* (Burlington: Ashgate, 2005).
19. Graham Holderness, "'I Covet Your Skull': Death and Desire in Hamlet," *Shakespeare Survey* 60 Theatres for Shakespeare (2007): 223–36, 224.
20. Holderness, "'I Covet Your Skull,'" 232–33.
21. William Shakespeare, *The Tragedy of Hamlet* in *The Riverside Shakespeare*, 2nd ed., eds. Herschel Baker, Anne Barton, and Frank Kermode (New York: Houghton, 1997), 1189–1245. V. i. 276–77.
22. Hirschfeld, *Sexual Anomalies*, 424.
23. Howard Barker, "Afterword: The Corpse and Its Sexuality" in *Eroticism and Death in Theatre and Performance*, ed. Karoline Gritzner (Hertfordshire: University of Hertfordshire Press, 2010), 242–45, 243. Also, see Gritzner's introduction for a critical and philosophical overview of the relationship between eroticism and death and the ways this encounter is "intrinsically theatrical or performative" (10).
24. Leo Bersani, *A Future for Astyanax: Character and Desire in Literature* (Boston: Little, Brown and Company, 1976), 286–87.
25. Barker, "The Corpse," 244.
26. For example, Lisa Hopkins argues that the Lady's body "exposes the rigidities of the society it portrays and the difficulties which visibly beset the attempt to maintain those rigidities" in *The Female Hero in English Renaissance Tragedy* (Houndmills, Basingstoke, Hampshire: Palgrave Macmillan, 2002), 7. Sara Eaton argues that the main action of "the play and the fate of the kingdom evolve out of the two men's struggle to physically possess her" (69). In the end, the Lady is complicit in her "iconic idealization" of herself as a silent, passive queen (73). "'Content with Art'?: Seeing the Emblematic Woman in *The Second Maiden's Tragedy* and *The Winter's Tale*," in *Shakespeare Power and Punishment, a Volume of Essays*, ed. Gillian Murray Kendall (Cranbury: Associated University Press, Inc., 1998), 59–86.
27. Middleton's version of the Lucrece myth works a similar satirical critique; it is both a complaint poem, in that it wholly focuses on Lucrece's horror and pain, and a satire in that it lightly mocks Shakespeare's version and the complaint genre's typical obsession with female virtue. In the end, Lucrece is dragged to hell with Tarquin for being pagan, typical of Middleton's cynicism. Her body does not initiate political change, and it completely bears the mark of the personal atrocities Tarquin committed. "The Ghost of Lucrece," *Middleton: The Collected Works*,

1985–1998. For a further discussion on Middleton's "monstrous humour" and that of Jacobean tragedy, see O'Callaghan, *Thomas Middleton*, 123–24.
28. A common reading of the Tyrant's necrophilia. Susan Zimmerman reads the play in context of Reformation attitudes toward idolatry, arguing that that the play is anti-Catholic and the Tyrant's necrophilia is a hyperbolic form of idolatry. She asserts that his character "underscores the iconoclastic connection between overvaluation of the self and overvaluation of the material body," *Corpse*, 98.
29. Robert Watson suggests that this pattern "allowed men to isolate the condition of annihilation in women." Watson argues that "The behavioral traits that Renaissance manuals repeatedly suggest were prized in wives—silence, coldness, containment, and passivity—bear a striking resemblance to the traits of the dead as conceived by annihilationism," The Rest is Silence: Death as Annihilation in the English Renaissance (Los Angeles: University of California Press, 1994), 31. Or as Bronfen suggests, a beautiful dead woman masks "the inevitability of human decomposition" and demonstrates the "conjunction of femininity, death and aesthetisation." *Over Her Dead Body*, 62, 72.
30. Zimmerman argues, by the end, the Tyrant "has hypostatised materiality itself as antecedent to spirit and his own erotic energy as a life giving force" *Corpse*, 101.
31. For more analysis on how women's bodies were associated with pollution, see Gail Kern Paster, *Body Embarrassed* and *Humoring the Body: Emotions and the Shakespeare Stage* (Chicago: University of Chicago Press, 2004); Jennifer Vaught's introduction to *Rhetorics of Bodily Disease and Health in Medieval and Early Modern England* (Burlington: Ashgate, 2010); Zimmerman, *Corpse*.
32. 5.2.153, stage direction.
33. Kevin Crawford, "'All His Intents Are Contrary to Man': Softened Masculinity and Staging in Middleton's *The Lady's Tragedy*," *Medieval and Renaissance Drama in England: An Annual Gathering of Research, Criticism and Reviews* 16 (2003): 101–29, 105.

Part III
Intimate Refusals

12 Well-Divided Dispositions
Distraction, Dying, and the Eroticism of Forgetting in *Antony and Cleopatra*

Jonathan Baldo

A play that spends a significant portion of its time on the water, *Antony and Cleopatra* appropriately has choppiness as one of its salient characteristics. A mirror for our distracted times, it shifts locale more often than any other play by Shakespeare. Among critics who value unity above all other aesthetic values, the play has had its detractors. The French romantic editor, translator, and critic Jean-Baptiste Joseph Émile Montégut characterized *Antony and Cleopatra* as Shakespeare's least unified play. With its numerous episodes that disperse rather than concentrate the audience's attention and that are insufficiently connected to the play's main subject, it lacks "unité morale."[1] It will be the argument of this essay that far from pursuing unity, the play celebrates what the early modern period knew as "distraction," the momentary division of the self and the consequent forgetting to which this play especially grants an erotic dimension.[2] After exploring extreme forms of distraction like *Hamlet* and *King Lear*, in *Antony and Cleopatra* Shakespeare posed questions in a tragicomic vein about the aesthetic and ethical advantages of a distracted self or "well-divided disposition," as Cleopatra says of Antony. Exhibiting a well-divided disposition itself, the play sports a hero and heroine who embody the capacity for distraction as a virtue as well as a flaw. Set against them, the seemingly indivisible or indistractable Octavius Caesar resists his author's tendency to pull his audiences in two or more directions at once. Like a poor spectator of the play, Octavius resists the well-divided dispositions that its two eponymous heroes share with their audiences.

Shakespeare's Cleopatra is known primarily for her eroticism, particularly her skill in "dying," jokingly referred to early in the play by Enobarbus, and her powers of distraction, which are far more significant to Shakespeare's conception than her power of attraction. In what follows I hope to show how these two defining aspects of Cleopatra are related by attending to a momentary memory lapse common to both. A figure of mnemonic disfiguration like Falstaff, Cleopatra evinces a trend already apparent in Shakespeare's history plays: namely, a widespread rethinking, in the related contexts of the rise of nationalism, the rise of printing, and the Protestant Reformation, of the values attending remembering and forgetting.[3] Cleopatra's "celerity in dying" and her skill in the art of distraction point to her larger significance as a figure for the disruption of memory that audiences associated with sexual and theatrical pleasure alike. In *Antony and Cleopatra*, Shakespeare was inclined to show that such disruptions have both a moral and an aesthetic value.

Slings and Eros

During Antony's absence in Rome, Cleopatra recalls placing her "tires and mantles" on a drunken, wavering Antony (first laughed "out of patience" and then "into patience"), while she donned "his sword Philippan" (2.5.19–20, 23).[4] The play as a whole, one might say, similarly and provocatively dresses the genre of tragedy in feminine attire. The structure of *Antony and Cleopatra* imitates female sexual experience. Unlike *Hamlet*, with its massive dying off at the end, *Antony and Cleopatra* has several distinct, consecutive climaxes: the multiple defeats of Antony, Antony's botched suicide, his reunion with Cleopatra, his ultimate death, Octavius Caesar's conquest of Cleopatra, Cleopatra's conquest of herself and suicide, and Octavius Caesar's eulogy mimic the prolific sexuality of the queen.

Buried beneath the serial deaths in the final two acts of the play—those of Enobarbus, Eros, Antony, Cleopatra, and Charmian—one may hear an unmistakable note of eroticism, like the music of hautboys from beneath the stage that signal Antony's abandonment by his gods.[5] Enobarbus plants the seed of the familiar Elizabethan wordplay on sexual climax as akin to "death" early in the play, so that it may grow throughout. After hearing of his wife Fulvia's death, Antony vows to return to Rome in language that strangely suggests his somehow joining his recently deceased wife ("a great spirit gone," 1.2.119): "I must be gone" (1.2.133), as if his going from Egypt is itself a dying and implicitly a sexualized act. The identification of going and staying is further reinforced by the bawdy use of the word "go" earlier in the same scene, as in Charmian's imploring the soothsayer to give Alexas a cursed fortune: "O, let him marry a woman that cannot go, sweet Isis, I beseech thee, and let her die too, and give him a worse, and let worse follow worse till the worst of all follow him, laughing to his grave, fiftyfold a cuckold!" (1.2.58–61). Antony's use of the same word for Fulvia's death and his determination to depart Egypt—namely, "gone"—suggests the inescapability of Cleopatra's sexuality and of her great skill in "dying." Enobarbus' subsequent wordplay reinforces the sense that going or staying will have similar effects: a massive dying off of Egyptian women if Antony departs and an orgy of pleasurable "dying" if he and his soldiers remain. If we leave, Enobarbus, maintains, "Why, then, we kill all our women. We see how mortal an unkindness is to them; if they suffer our departure, death's the word" (1.2.130–32).

After Antony's curt response, his vow to be gone, Enobarbus delivers one of a series of "light answers" (1.2.169) that trouble Antony:

> Under a compelling occasion, let women die. It were pity to cast them away for nothing, though between them and a great cause they

should be esteemed nothing. Cleopatra, catching but the least noise of this, dies instantly; I have seen her die twenty times upon far poorer moment. I do think there is mettle in death, which commits some loving act upon her, she has such a celerity in dying. (1.2.134–40)

The refrain of "die," "dies," "die," "death," and "dying" comically mimics the multiple deaths (or petites morts) of which Cleopatra is presumably capable, as well as auguring like a coarse version of the soothsayer the multiple deaths and climaxes of Acts IV and V. Playing on a slang term for the female genitalia ("nothing"), Enobarbus decries the folly of throwing away the female "for nothing." In so doing, he curiously suggests what Antony already hinted at in his meditation on Fulvia's death: namely, that satisfying the female "nothing" and abandoning it senselessly ("for nothing") are somehow equivalent. The oscillating movement toward and away from Egypt and Cleopatra resembles the to-and-fro rhythm of sexuality, which in turn mirrors the rhythm that characterizes the psychology of attraction and repulsion. In spite of his impatience with Enobarbus' play on "dying," Antony himself cannot avoid the erotic implications that swirl about all discourse in Egypt. Indeed, in the eastern half of the playworld, discourse is a species of intercourse. Even Antony's reflection on his reactions to Fulvia's death bears an unmistakably erotic element, as if it were as inescapable as death itself:

> There's a great spirit gone! Thus did I desire it.
> What our contempts doth often hurl from us,
> We wish it ours again. The present pleasure,
> By revolution lowering, does become
> The opposite of itself. She's good, being gone;
> The hand could pluck her back that shoved her on.
> I must from this enchanting queen break off. (1.2.119–25)

Antony's meditation on his strange desire for Fulvia after her death reveals not only why he will never leave Cleopatra (long before Enobarbus assures Maecenas that he will not leave her, 2.2.244); it also hints at a sexual dimension to the mind's back-and-forth movement between desire and revulsion.[6] In a sense Antony symbolically dons Cleopatra's "tires" in this speech, suggesting why he—and indeed every human being—is a fickle Cleopatra, lurching "by revolution" back and forth between inclination and aversion. To play with desire is to be a divided self. The only means to avoid such division is to avoid desire itself, like the chaste Octavia, described by Enobarbus as "of a holy, cold, and still conversation" (2.6.120).

In the chaste and decidedly un-erotic Rome of the play, by contrast, the rhythmical to-and-fro of desire and contempt is regarded with patrician scorn. From the Roman perspective the "varying tide" of our affections, the affective "to and back" that Antony remarks in his reaction to his own wife's death, is a mark of susceptibility to outside influences, a lack of control that

Octavius associates with the plebeian hordes. Soon after Antony meditates on his strange affection for Fulvia, Octavius delivers the same thought in a Roman key, in reference to the sudden affection the Roman people ("this common body") show toward Sextus Pompeius:

> It hath been taught us from the primal state
> That he which is was wished until he were;
> And the ebbed man, ne'er loved till ne'er worth love,
> Comes deared by being lacked. This common body,
> Like to a vagabond flag upon the stream,
> Goes to and back, lackeying the varying tide
> To rot itself with motion. (1.4.41–7)

Like a reed or rush upon the stream, the affections of the common people drift to and fro in an idle, passive motion washed of any hint of eroticism. Octavius gives Antony's thought, whose subject was private affection, a public and collective dimension. Whereas Antony universalizes his oscillating private feelings of attraction and repulsion, the putative "universal landlord" Octavius first generalizes ("It hath been taught us from the primal state") but then seeks to limit the implications of distracted selves by localizing the claim, interpreting it as a failing of Rome's common people.

As deaths pile up, it is probably no accident that the word and syllable "come" sounds repeatedly in our ears. As Philip J. Traci observes, the proliferation of the word "come" toward the end of the play bears a bawdy association that links dramatic climax with sexual climax.[7] Antony pronounces the word "come" six times within 30 lines toward the end of Act IV, most tellingly in his command, "Come, Eros, Eros!" (4.14.54). It continues to echo in the remainder of the scene (4.14.101, 126, 131, 135, 142). In the next scene, Charmian's "Be comforted, dear madam" enfolds the word of climax in the arms of a word, "comfort," that suggests the opposite of strenuous "coming." Cleopatra, with her commitment to climaxes of all kinds, rejects the kindly gesture: "No, I will not. / All strange and terrible events are welcome, / But comforts we despise" (4.15.2–4). Strange and terrible events, those theatrical "comings" or climaxes, are "welcome," but not "comfort." "Come" continues to pepper this scene, used by Cleopatra in a rapid-fire exchange with Antony six times within nine lines (4.15.30–38), leading into a repeated and perhaps bawdy "welcome, welcome!" as her lover is heaved aloft to her (4.15.39). So prolific does the word become that it may be hard to resist a linkage between the highly theatrical Cleopatra and those other practitioners in the art of the climax, the "quick comedians" whose future power over her she seems to fear more than that of Octavius Caesar himself:

> The quick comedians
> Extemporally will stage us, and present
> Our Alexandrian revels; Antony

Shall be brought drunken forth, and I shall see
Some squeaking Cleopatra boy my greatness
I'th'posture of a whore. (5.2.215–20)

Like whores, the "quick comedians" are masters of simulated climaxes or "comings," and Cleopatra is loath to see her most "becoming" sexuality travestied. Her lines express resentment that in death her formidable sexuality, her commitment to "coming," will be coopted by the "quick," a word that condenses so many properties the play projects onto Egypt. Ironically, Egyptian values will live on in Rome but only in the marginalized and contained spaces of theater. "Quick" suggests "living" (the quick will represent the dead) as well as "quick witted," "quick acting," and "alive with possibilities."[8] It also revives or makes quick the creative and procreative abundance of Egypt, since "quick" could also mean pregnant.[9] Cleopatra is threatened with becoming Rome's Mistress Quickly. In a remarkably condensed form, "quick" expresses the way in which Cleopatra's world of "comings" (or "dyings") and "becoming" will endure in a world of simulation or "comedy."

Cleopatra's association with the verb "to come" evokes her highly charged eroticism. A related Egyptian word, "becoming," places her sexual nature, her talent for "coming" and "going," in the broader context of a transvaluation of values, an elevation of process over stasis. Indeed the two words "come" and "become" were even more closely connected in Shakespeare's day than they are now. C. T. Onions lists "to become" as the primary meaning of the verb "to come" in his *Shakespeare Glossary*.[10] When Antony delightedly and admiringly chides, "Fie, wrangling queen, / Whom everything becomes, to chide, to laugh, / To weep, to make itself, in thee, fair and admired!" (1.1.50–53), the twin meanings of "becomes"—to adorn and to be transformed into—align Cleopatra and Egypt with an aesthetic of becoming. In Egypt all is in the process of "becoming": "the present pleasure, / By revolution lowering, does become / The opposite of itself." It is the Egyptian embrace of becoming that makes it, in most spectators' eyes, becoming: "for vilest things / Become themselves in her, that the holy priests / Bless her when she is riggish" (Enobarbus, 2.2.248–50). Judging by its chaste female representative Octavia, Rome is as averse to coming as to becoming, valuing instead the virtues of steadfastness and stillness that are perpetually in short supply in Egypt. The Roman attitude toward Egyptian coming (or eroticism) and becoming (the wavering, distracted state that helps give Egypt an air of receptiveness and unprecedented freedom) is encapsulated in Octavius' complaint against "this common body," the first syllable of "common" driving home the point that Rome is averse to "coming" in all its diverse forms.[11]

Cleopatra's eroticism and the theater have a deeper connection that goes beyond her outrageous theatricality: a theatricality that makes her fear of having "Some squeaking Cleopatra boy my greatness / I'th'posture of a whore" (5.2.219–20) an even more daring theatrical gesture. They are linked by the prospect of a temporary forgetting, an eclipse of memory, a *petite mort* of awareness that enemies of the theater found distressing. Garrett Sullivan has explored the strand of early modern antitheatrical discourse that accuse it of fomenting forgetfulness: "the antitheatricalist conception of theatre as generative of both forgetting and forgetful bodies."[12] A similar theme appears in early modern discourse on sexual experience, which was associated with the suspension of memory, as Elizabeth Harvey demonstrates in the course of a reading of Spenser's *Fairie Queene*. Citing the influential anatomical treatise of King James's court physician Helkiah Crooke, *Mikrokosmographia* (1615), Harvey shows that the "linkage between procreative pleasure and amnesia and between birth and forgetting is a reiterated topos in early modern culture."[13] According to Crooke, the sexual act produces a temporary forgetfulness, transporting us "for a time out of ourselves" in an erotic madness that, in Harvey's words, "makes women willing to endure pregnancy, arduous childbirth, and the 'disquiet' of child-rearing, and it makes men able to bear the degradation that Crooke associates with sexual coupling."[14] Given this linkage of eroticism with forgetfulness, when Cleopatra "dies" within her monument, she paradoxically enshrines an eclipse of memory, associated with the sexual form of dying, at the very heart of a visual embodiment of enduring memory. It is as if she were reminding us that in "the deep heart's core" (Yeats, "The Lake Isle of Innisfree") of our public remembrances, of the monuments we build to remind us of our own forgetfulness, lies a throb or spasm of forgetting that helps shape those memories, causing them to live.

The play reminds us repeatedly of the close partnership of remembering and forgetting. Maecenas indicates as much while trying to broker a peace between Octavius and Antony: "If it might please you to enforce no further / The griefs between ye; to forget them quite / Were to remember that the present need / Speaks to atone you" (2.2.106–109). Recalling the present need to unite their forces against Pompey requires an act of willed forgetting of past grievances. Maecenas tries to establish bonds not only between Antony and Octavius, but also between remembering and forgetting. In Egypt, by contrast, they are inextricably bound by strife, as forgetting, connected with the sexual superfluity of Egypt, threatens to overflow its banks and overwhelm memory. Memory is challenged by Cleopatra's powers to "distract" in several senses of the word, as I will argue in the next section of this paper. Furthermore, Egypt's eroticism threatens the construction of identity on the basis of orderly patrimonial succession. In answer to the Soothsayer's dark prophecy that "You have seen and proved a fairer former fortune than that which is to approach," Cleopatra's attendant Charmian responds, "Then belike my children shall have no names," followed by a joking prophesy of the prodigious number of children she should have: "If every of your wishes had a womb, / And fertile every wish, a million" (1.2.32–34, 36–37). Charmian evokes a superabundant sexuality that exposes the fragility of the patrilineal order, which is perilously and precariously dependent on the word of the mother, by imagining legions of children that "shall have no names": that is, no names that derive from the father. Reproductive excess, rather than stabilizing memory in Old Testament fashion, threatens to obliterate by disrupting the passage of names and identities from fathers. Cleopatra's sexuality represents the most vigorous challenge to the patrilineal order as the foundation of memory and identity, even though her name in Greek means "she who comes from glorious father" or "the glory of the father." The mistress of Julius Caesar who produced a son Caesarion or Ptolemy Caesar nine months after their initial meeting, while Caesar was married to Calpurnia, Cleopatra tried without success to have Caesar acknowledge their son as his heir. Instead he was passed over in favor of Caesar's grandnephew Octavius. In the play, although he never appears on stage, Caesarion plays a role as a pawn whose future security and power Cleopatra tries to secure in negotiations with Octavius. An ambassador delivers to Octavius her desire to have "the circle [crown] of the Ptolemies for her heirs" (3.12.18). Octavius in turn scornfully refers to her abundant sexuality and procreativity to Maecenas and Agrippa by recalling when she and Antony were enthroned in Alexandria's marketplace, and "at the feet sat / Caesarion, whom they call my father's son, / And all the unlawful issue that their lust / Since then hath made between them" (3.6.5–8). If she has indeed been coldhearted toward Antony, she says, may "the memory of my womb" (3.13.167) dissolve, "Together with my brave Egyptians all, / By the discandying of this pelleted storm, / Lie graveless, till the flies and gnats of Nile / Have buried them for prey!" (3.13.168–71). The "memory of my womb" represents the threat of a counter-memory, a matrilineal alternative to the patrilineal order, one that is tangible, palpable, and embodied. It is contained within a speech in which Cleopatra imagines all memory dissolving and disappearing, as Egypt is envisioned as becoming a country without monuments, without graves and the obligation to remember that they manifest. Cleopatra deploys the language of the constant lover, vowing the obliteration of all Egyptian memory if she has been inconstant, even though her singularity and her coherence (if indeed she may be said to possess a unitary self at all) depends on the manifold attractions of forgetting and the fluid possibilities and freedom of Egypt's "well-divided dispositions."

An Elegant Way of Barging in

Enobarbus' description of Cleopatra, derived almost verbatim from Sir Thomas North's translation of Plutarch's *Parallel Lives*, is often cited as evidence that even a quintessential Roman soldier is not entirely immune to Cleopatra's eroticism and to the attractions of Egypt generally. His account of Cleopatra on her barge represents the queen in a particularly Roman way—that is, according to the play's idea of what is Roman—by emphasizing Cleopatra's power to attract, a word that derives from the Latin *attrahere*, to draw or pull. It conceives Cleopatra in terms of power, a particularly Roman and masculine attribute in this play. Attributing power to Cleopatra does not threaten a masculine order so much as it secures it by leaving power in place as an ultimate value. Octavia, the Roman narrative would have it, cannot compete with the attractions of Cleopatra and therefore makes a less powerful female figure. But Enobarbus essentially misreads Cleopatra and Egypt, projecting Roman values onto a figure that resists them. Enobarbus sees in Cleopatra a power to draw even the air "which, but for vacancy, / Had gone to gaze on Cleopatra too, / And made a gap in nature" (2.2.226–28). Shakespeare's Egypt, however, is a place not of powerful attractions but rather more powerful "distractions." The English word derives from the Latin *distrahere*, to divide, scatter, forcibly separate or draw asunder, tear in pieces, or draw in different directions. In the early modern period, "distraction" bore the diverse but related senses of "The drawing away (of the mind or thoughts) from one point or course to another; diversion of the mind or attention. Usually in adverse sense; less commonly = diversion, relaxation (as in French)" (*OED*, 2A); "A drawing or being drawn asunder; pulling asunder, forcible disruption, division, or severance" (*OED*, 1a); "The fact or condition of being drawn or pulled (physically or mentally) in different directions by conflicting forces or emotions" (*OED*, 3a), which sounds very much like a description of the very basis of Shakespeare's stagecraft, or an extreme disorder of the mind so as to constitute madness (*OED*, 4), often of a temporary nature (*OED*, 5). In the early modern period the adjectival form "distracted" or "distract" meant "mentally drawn to different objects; perplexed or confused by conflicting interests; torn or disordered by dissension or the like" (*OED*, 3).

It may seem a lot to ask of a word to designate a range of meanings from entertainment to insanity, the temporary diverting of one's attention to outright madness, but considering the extent to which milder forms of distraction lie at the heart of Shakespeare's stagecraft, and especially of a play like *Antony and Cleopatra*, sheds light on why Shakespeare's plays seem fascinated by the more extreme form of distraction, madness. Carol Thomas Neely observes in her marvelous study of the relation between gender and madness in Shakespeare, *Distracted Subjects*, distracted "is an adjective denoting not permanent attributes, but temporary behaviors."[15] Distraction was a form of forgetfulness, one that caused a dispersion and disintegration of the self. One could be restored to wholeness through remembrance: as Neely writes, "Thomas More exemplifies the period's view when he says of one who recovered from distraction that he 'gathered hys remembraunce to hym and beganne to come agayne to hym selfe.'"[16]

Our first glimpse of Alexandria establishes it as a site of distraction, as Antony lays out a program of diversion to Cleopatra: "No messenger but thine, and all alone / Tonight we'll wander through the streets and note / The qualities of people" (1.1.52–54). Throughout this scene Cleopatra plays the role of a chiding or carping memory, repeatedly reminding Antony to hear the messengers of Rome and to remember his wife Fulvia and the vows of love he surely made to her. Fulvia's name nearly becomes a comic signature of memory itself (1.1.19f., 42f.). By contrast with the more historically minded Rome, Egypt is a place of pleasurable oblivion, of epicurean excess linked to forgetfulness,[17] where the dissolving of so great a monument to the human spirit as Rome itself in the solvent of present pleasure, a kiss or an embrace ('thus'), brings forth not a whisper of regret:

> Let Rome in Tiber melt and the wide arch
> Of the ranged empire fall! Here is my space.
> Kingdoms are clay; our dungy earth alike
> Feeds beast as man. The nobleness of life
> Is to do thus, when such a mutual pair
> And such a twain can do't—in which I bind,
> On pain of punishment, the world to weet
> We stand up peerless. (1.1.35–42)

Minutes become couches of pleasure, and hours, female servants attending Venus, not opportunities to be seized for heroic exploits of enduring memory (1.1.45–49). A residual Roman personality remains with Antony even in Egypt, as we hear a touch of Roman monumentalizing in his vow that the world will know "We stand up peerless": as if the lovers will replace in the popular memory the whole of the Roman Republic. One might even see his attitude toward the past in stoic Roman terms: "Things that are past are done, with me," he assures a messenger from Rome, urging him to speak the truth. (1.2.93). Antony is not inclined to manipulate the past, like Shakespeare's English kings, whom we often see doing battle with history and historical memory.

Our second glimpse of Alexandria reinforces its association with distractions of all kinds, planting the suspicion that Egypt may be a mirror of the theater itself. Charmian, Iras, and Alexas seek distraction from their present indolence by having their futures told by a soothsayer. Antony's line about finding out "new heaven, new earth" had already established Egypt as a place that pays homage to the present as a seat of pleasure and to the future as a place of imaginative play and possibility, but decidedly not to the past and to its reminders of ongoing responsibility. As we watch the soothsayer predict their futures, we share the Egyptians' sense of distraction, not only because we inhabit a theater, but also because in this second scene we have been temporarily diverted from the main characters' passionate love story by what seems like a deflection or redirection.

Rome, by contrast with Egypt, tends to think backwards. Honor for Romans exists only in the past tense, as Antony bitterly observes: "Our slippery people, / Whose love is never linked to the deserver / Till his deserts are past" (1.2.178–80). As if in keeping with the Roman tendency to bestow honors only on the past, Antony's departure transforms Egypt itself from a place of "Lethe'd dullness" (2.1.27) to a site of memory. Antony's "remembrance lay / In Egypt with his joy," Cleopatra asserts (1.5.60–61). She will not "forget to send to Antony" (1.5.67). Cleopatra appears to become no longer the agent but the object and victim of forgetfulness: "O, my oblivion is a very Antony, / And I am all forgotten" (1.3.91–92). Nevertheless, in Antony's absence, she calls upon a series of distractions in quick succession—music, billiards, angling—which rather than having the desired effect of helping her to forget Antony, leads eventually to recollection of an occasion when "I drunk him to his bed; / Then put my tires and mantles on him, whilst / I wore his sword Philippan" (2.5.21–23). The lines recall Octavius' bitter accusation that the reveling Antony "is not more manlike / Than Cleopatra, nor the queen of Ptolemy / More womanly than he" (1.4.5–7). Cleopatra's is a quintessentially Egyptian memory, one of identities put under erasure: a memory, therefore, that is the offspring of a complicated partnership (as complicated as Antony and Cleopatra's own) between remembering and forgetting.

Cleopatra's reminiscence and Octavius' accusation together point up one of the more intriguing aspects of the play: it is divided as to the very nature of division itself. The divided or distracted self, "drawn or pulled (physically or mentally) in different directions by conflicting forces or emotions" (*OED*), is a sign of breadth or enlargement in Egypt and of an incoherent and unstable identity lacking integrity in Rome. This play that is scenically distracted to an exaggerated degree may be said to divide us, causing us to be of two minds about division or distraction itself. The forms of division proliferate in Egypt. Antony is torn between pleasure and responsibility to the Roman Republic and its allies and to the other members of the Second Triumvirate. His is a composite self, divided between male and female, as both his admirer Cleopatra and detractor Octavius acknowledge, although the shared acknowledgment does not unite but rather further serves to divide Egypt from Rome. Antony himself discovers the widest sense in which we are all distracted selves when he muses, "What our contempts doth often hurl from us, / We wish it ours again" (1.2.120–21). Antony is an unusually distracted self: "He was disposed to mirth, but on the sudden / A Roman thought hath struck him" (1.2.77–78). Nevertheless, relating to Cleopatra the civil wars in Italy and his need to return to Rome, Antony fails to acknowledge the full extent of his own inner faction: "The strong necessity of time commands / Our services awhile, but my full heart / Remains in use with you. Our Italy / Shines o'er with civil swords; Sextus Pompeius / Makes his approaches to the port of Rome; / Equality of two domestic powers / Breed scrupulous faction" (1.3.42–48). Although the play has an infinite variety of ways of making us divided in our thoughts about division itself, division or distraction generally comes across as a sign of strength if not perfection in Egypt and a flaw in Rome. In answer to an anxious Cleopatra's question as to whether Antony in Rome was "sad or merry," Alexas reports, "Like to the time o'th'year between the extremes / Of hot and cold, he was nor sad nor merry" (1.5.53–55). Cleopatra then praises Antony's "well-divided disposition," its "heavenly mingle" of moods (1.5.56, 62). In Egypt a well-divided disposition adds scope and breadth, flexibility and variety, complexity and completion.

In Rome, unlike Egypt, distraction in the sense of "being drawn or pulled (physically or mentally) in different directions by conflicting forces or emotions" is usually exposed as a debilitating condition or a defect. A distracted self, like a distracted nation, is a weakened one in the Roman view. Thus, forced to drink by the other two world rulers, Lepidus "cries out, 'No more,' reconciles them to his entreaty, and himself to th' drink," raising "the greater war between him and his discretion": a war that, like all the battles he must fight, he is bound to lose (2.7.5–9). The weak triumvir Lepidus is "divided" in his love for and allegiance to Octavius and Antony (3.2.7f.). In the same scene as well as subsequent ones, Octavia appears similarly divided between love for her brother and her husband. Her imminent departure from her brother results in a kind of internal division and paralysis, making her unable to speak: "Her tongue will not obey her heart, nor can / Her heart inform her tongue—the swansdown feather / That stands upon the swell at the full of tide, / And neither way inclines" (3.2.47–50). In Rome an internally distracted self is a feminine or feminized self, attenuated by virtue of being pulled by conflicting forces or emotions. In Egypt, by contrast, it may seem a source of strength, a sign of a sturdier selfhood that is able to withstand division, bearing the buffeting by the violence of extremes. In an apostrophe to Antony, Cleopatra avows, "Be'st thou sad or merry, / The violence of either thee becomes, / So does it no man else" (1.5.62–64). A tragicomedy that itself exhibits the violence of extremes that Cleopatra attributes to Antony, *Antony and Cleopatra* advances an implicit argument for the moral claims of a theater of distraction.

Octavius defeats Antony in the end by distracting him: that is, by repeating the action of which he complained in Cleopatra. Mirroring Antony's perpetual distraction at the hands of Cleopatra, Maecenas urges Octavius Caesar to "make boot of [Antony's] distraction" (4.1.9). Enobarbus advises Antony not to engage the enemy by sea at Actium, for "you therein ... Distract your army" (3.7.41, 43).[18] A few lines later, however, we learn that Octavius Caesar's cunning has caused him to divide his own army, thereby distracting his enemy's scouts: "While he was yet in Rome / His power went out in such distractions / As beguiled all spies" (3.7.75–77). Octavius triumphs in part by distracting an already highly distracted opponent, hence, the apparent ease of his military victory. Although Octavius wins the battle, he loses the audience's sympathies by virtue of his very indistractibility. The eminently distractible Antony seems more like ourselves, the distracted spectators that Shakespeare's dramaturgy has trained us to be. It is appropriate that the empire's leadership becomes undistracted or whole, at least in leadership, a triumvirate yielding to the first Roman emperor, through the defeat of its eminently distractible member.

Unlike the stolid Roman identity that privileges remembering over forgetting, a distracted self is one in which remembering and forgetting work in constant, oscillating partnership. Octavius Caesar's final words ostensibly lay that partnership to rest, concealing it within the language of monumental history:

> No grave upon the earth shall clip in it
> A pair so famous. High events as these
> Strike those that make them; and their story is
> No less in pity than his glory which
> Brought them to be lamented. Our army shall
> In solemn show attend this funeral,
> And then to Rome. Come, Dolabella, see
> High order in this great solemnity. (5.2.353–60)

Forgotten in Octavius' eulogy is the way in which monumental history like this is erected on the shifting Egyptian sands of forgetting. Buried in his lines is the recollection of his taunt against the common people's fickle memory, which he now imitates. The vagaries of "this common body" for whom "the ebbed man, ne'er loved till ne'er worth love, / Comes deared by being lacked" (1.4.43–44) now becomes the slippery foundation of public, monumental memory, for at the end of the play, Antony and Cleopatra come deared by being lacked. The Egyptian word "come" haunts the edges of Octavius' eulogy.[19] It suggests that within the apparently fixed and monumental memory of the becoming lovers and lovers of becoming, audiences' memories of the pair will be more akin to the shifting sands of the Egyptian desert than to the marble of Rome. If lack or loss causes a thing to become dear, as both Antony and Octavius have claimed, and if memory is predicated on absence or loss, then recollection is necessarily bound up with desire, including all the vagaries and shifts of desire. The experience of loss makes Egyptians of us all. The play as a whole suggests that a fixed, monumental memory is the least probable myth in this mythogenic play.

An Early Modernity Thesis

According to the German-Jewish cultural critics Siegfried Kracauer and Walter Benjamin, modern urban life is characterized by an unprecedented sensory overload and intensification that leaves no room for contemplation. The environment of the modern city, with its excess of visual stimuli and intensification of sensory experience, offers unprecedented opportunities for distraction, and these new conditions of living are reflected in the popular entertainment that have emerged from this environment in the twentieth century: namely, the cinema. Benjamin states in his influential essay "The Work of Art in the Age of Mechanical Reproduction," "The film corresponds to profound changes in the apperceptive apparatus—changes that are experienced on an individual scale by the man in the street in big-city traffic, on a historical scale by every present-day citizen."[20] The arts in the modern era, especially film, reflect the distractedness of urban life: "Reception in a state of distraction, which is increasing noticeably in all fields of art and is symptomatic of profound changes in apperception, finds in the film its true means of exercise."[21] Film historians Charles Keil and David Bordwell have dubbed Benjamin and Kracauer's claim the "modernity thesis."[22]

A novel whose composition was contemporaneous with early cinema and one that bears many formal resemblances to the fledgling art form offers substantial support for the so-called modernity thesis. In the Scylla and Charybdis episode of Joyce's *Ulysses*, the Quaker librarian Mr. Best refers to Mallarmé's description of a French provincial performance of *Hamlet* with the quaint title of "*HAMLET ou LE DISTRAIT*" (9:118–20): *Hamlet, or the Distracted One*.[23] Stephen Dedalus translates the French as "The absentminded beggar," borrowing the title of a Kipling poem. His sardonic title proves apt in ways that he cannot imagine. It captures a defining quality of his as yet unknown spiritual father, Leopold Bloom, as well as a signal aspect of *Ulysses* itself beginning with episode 7, "Aeolus": namely, the ways in which a series of wildly fluctuating and intrusive styles might prove distracting. For the novel's readers do not merely live the distractions of the modern city at second remove, through Leopold Bloom; rather, they are subjected to torrents of distractions in Joyce's ever-changing prose styles. *Ulysses*, Franco Moretti contends, is a watershed in the history of distraction. Described as "perhaps the most absentminded character in world literature,"[24] Leopold Bloom roaming the new cosmopolis, with its notorious sensory overload, represents a change of function for absentmindedness or distraction: "Instead of being a lack, an absence, it has become an active tool: a kind of switchboard, simultaneously activating a plurality of mental circuits, and allowing Bloom to pick up as many stimuli as possible."[25]

Although early modern London may seem light years away from the cities of the early twentieth century, recent scholarship has emphasized that the metropolis in which Shakespeare's plays were staged was a rapidly transforming and burgeoning one with a mobile population.[26] Furthermore, the picture of the city that emerges from recent scholarship on actual lived conditions in early modern London does not differ greatly from the early modern idea of the city, which as Gail Kern Paster has argued, was something of a paradox, expressing "two opposing attitudes": "the city as a visionary embodiment of ideal community (either on earth or in heaven) or the city as a predatory trap, founded in fratricide and shadowed by conflict."[27] Early modern London arguably knew the powers of an urban environment to distract, as Christopher D'Addario has recently shown with respect to John Donne, whom he characterizes as "wonderfully and ruefully attuned to the inevitable power of the external world to distract us from our own thoughts."[28] He cites Donne's complaint in a sermon of 1626: "I throw my selfe downe in my Chamber, and I call in, and invite God, and his Angels thither, and when they are there, I neglect God and his Angels, for the noise of a Flie, for the ratling of a Coach, for the whining of a doore."[29] Reading Donne's lyrics in relation to the physical spaces of early modern London and "the exchanges and distractions attendant upon living amidst the press of people in the metropolis," D'Addario persuasively demonstrates how both the satires, highly distracted poems with rapidly shifting attention that generally take us through the streets of London, and love lyrics, ostensibly more private poems written from sequestered spaces, "engaged with the movements and flux of the metropolis and not merely from a purely antagonistic position."[30] The satires of Marston and Donne, D'Addario argues, reflect the lived conditions of the rapidly changing early modern metropolis "in their speed, in their digressive energies," but not only to satirize those conditions with their "quick associations and illogical movements": their satires contain moments in which "their speakers are happily immersed in the flow of information and people that characterizes the London streets," exploring and even embracing "the swift movements and interactions that characterized urban life."[31] In a turn that curiously resembles Benjamin's argument about the ways in which the modern art form of the cinema reflects the distracted conditions of modern urban life, D'Addario maintains that "the layering of experience in Donne's satires and elegies, the multiple and swift connections that are the basis of Donne's wit, can be seen as an attempt to recreate the richness with which significances and meanings arise and dissipate from the complexity of the London everyday."[32]

The brisk pace of a theatrical performance in early modern London would align it more with the urban spaces of Donne's satires than with the love lyrics that seek quiet away from the "variegated soundscape of the city, the aural minutiae that draw the mind away from the spiritual and toward the sensual and sensory."[33] Furthermore, in Shakespeare's *Antony and Cleopatra*, the distracted nature of life in the early modern metropolis is reflected in the distracted construction of the play as well as in the frequently deliberate distractedness of its hero and heroine. Like Joyce's distracted hero Leopold Bloom, Shakespeare's early modern figure of distraction, Antony, bears a sexual ambiguity, a "well-divided disposition" in terms of gender identity, and a mental circuitry that easily switches from passive to active and back again. Shakespeare's tragicomedy is his *Ulysses* in the sense that it proposes a revaluation of the very idea of distraction, harnessing it to all that Cleopatra represents, including her eroticism and a fluid, on again, off again relationship between remembering and forgetting (not unlike that between Antony and Cleopatra), in contradistinction to that quintessential Roman, the severe and indistractable Octavius Caesar. It is also the Shakespearean play that has most frequently been described as "cinematic."[34] Because of its lightning-quick shifts of locale and action, Benjamin might very well have been writing about this play when describing the film spectator's perpetual state of distraction. For Benjamin, the distracting element of film is "primarily tactile, being based on changes of place and focus which periodically assail the spectator."[35] Unlike a painting, which "invites the spectator to contemplation" and allows one to become absorbed by it, to "abandon himself to his associations," "before the movie frame he cannot do so. No sooner has his eye grasped a scene than it has already changed. It cannot be arrested."[36] Echoing Kracauer and Benjamin, I propose a limited "early modernity thesis": exhibiting the theater's own formidable powers of distraction as embodied in its highly theatrical heroine, Shakespeare's *Antony and Cleopatra* reflects the distracted living conditions in an increasingly crowded and changing metropolis, but also advances an implicit argument for the advantages of distracted and therefore more flexible and receptive minds like Antony's and Cleopatra's. Through her virtual personification of swift change and the temporary forgetting that goes by the name of distraction, Cleopatra teaches us to see the allure and perhaps even the beauty of the theaters that a significant number of Shakespeare's contemporaries deplored as sites of distraction from more somber pursuits like devotion and work.

The play does not necessarily ask us to embrace distraction, for it too seems to be divided on the subject and produce division in its spectators. Perhaps it takes an apparently unified self like Octavius Caesar to unify an empire; at least that is one of the implications of the play's ending and its ultimate prophesy, not of the future erotic exploits of Iras, Charmian, and Alexas but of the "time of universal peace" (4.6.5), the *pax romana*. It is crucial, however, to note the play's asymmetry in this regard. If it is designed to make us distracted—"perplexed or confused by conflicting interests; torn or disordered by dissension or the like" (*OED*, 3)—about distraction itself, then perhaps we must be left with the feeling that the overweening sensibility of the play is Egyptian rather than Roman. The play molds us into distracted Egyptians, divided about the very value of distraction. If, in other words, *Antony and Cleopatra* causes us to suspend our judgments between Egypt and Rome, Antony and Octavius, the highly distracted and the indistractable, then it at least poses if not answers the question about both the aesthetic and the moral advantages of distraction, leaving us with a powerful if evanescent monument to those selves who practice the play of remembering and forgetting with formidable passion.[37]

Notes

1. Quoted in Michael Steppat, *The Critical Reception of Shakespeare's Antony and Cleopatra from 1607 to 1905* (Amsterdam: Verlag B. R. Grüner, 1980), 308.
2. On the association of eroticism and forgetting in the play, see Garrett Sullivan, Jr.'s fine reading in *Memory and Forgetting in English Renaissance Drama: Shakespeare, Marlowe, Webster* (Cambridge: Cambridge University Press, 2005), 88–108.
3. I make this argument in *Memory in Shakespeare's Histories: Stages of Forgetting in Early Modern England* (New York and London: Routledge, 2012). This essay also builds upon a broader argument about distraction as a fundamental value

of Shakespeare's stagecraft, in "Shakespeare's Poetics of Distraction," *Shakespeare: The Journal of the British Shakespeare Association*, v. 10, no. 2 (2014).
4. All quotations from *Antony and Cleopatra* refer to the New Cambridge Shakespeare edition of the play, ed. David Bevington (Cambridge: Cambridge University Press, 1990).
5. Philip J. Traci provocatively sees the whole play as structured like the sexual act, with foreplay followed by pre-sexual feasting and drinking and finally by the sexual act itself, signaled by the appearance of Antony's loyal armorer Eros and playfully approximated by all the references to 'dying' that occur toward the end of the play. See *The Love Play of Antony and Cleopatra* (The Hague: Mouton, 1970). Even a sympathetic reader of Traci like L. T. Fitz demures from endorsing all of his findings. According to Fitz, "Traci's theory may be a little far-fetched, but it brings a whole new world of meaning to passages like 'What poor an instrument may do a noble deed,' 'The soldier's pole is fallen,' and 'Husband, I come.'" "Egyptian Queens and Male Reviewers: Sexist Attitudes in *Antony and Cleopatra* Criticism," *Shakespeare Quarterly* 28 (1977): 302. I would not only endorse Traci's insight about the proliferation of the word 'come' at the climax of the play, but also link it to an Egyptian aesthetic and ethics of 'becoming' (as opposed to the stasis or stillness of "being" valued by the Romans) and even of those other dealers in climaxes, the "quick comedians" whose future power Cleopatra fears as much as that of Octavius (5.2.217).
6. The connection between eroticism and the mind's vacillations, the body's pleasures and the mind's torments, may be further suggested by the play's use of two opposite verbs of motion, 'come' and 'go,' for sexual activity. For 'come,' see below. In I.2, Charmian says to Iras of Alexas, "O, let him marry a woman that cannot go": i.e., have sexual intercourse.
7. Traci, *The Love Play of Antony and Cleopatra* 156. Although the OED gives the first instance of the verb 'to come' in the sense of "to experience sexual orgasm" as "a1650" (II.17), the sense surely has an earlier date. Eric Partridge cites an exchange between Margaret and Benedick in *Much Ado about Nothing* to illustrate the sense of 'to come' as "To experience a sexual emission," and further suggests that the sense may be implied in a response by Malvolio to Olivia. *Shakespeare's Bawdy: A Literary and Psychological Essay and a Comprehensive Glossary*, rev. ed. (New York: E. P. Dutton, 1955), 89. See also the entries for 'come' and 'come over' in Gordon Williams' more recent *Shakespeare's Sexual Language: A Glossary* (1997; rpt. London and New York: Continuum, 2006), 75–76.
8. David Crystal and Ben Crystal, *Shakespeare's Words: A Glossary and Language Companion* (London and New York: Penguin Books, 2002), 358.
9. "She's quick," Costard says to Armado of Jaquenetta in *Love's Labour's Lost*.
10. C. T. Onions, *A Shakespeare Glossary* (Oxford: The Clarendon Press, 1963), 40.
11. The word 'common' is uttered three times in the play, and only by Romans: once by Demetrius and twice by Octavius.
12. Sullivan, *Memory and Forgetting in English Renaissance Drama*.
13. Elizabeth D. Harvey, "Pleasure's Oblivion: Displacements of Generation in Spenser's *Faerie Queene*," in Christopher Ivic and Grant Williams, eds., *Forgetting in Early Modern English Literature and Culture: Lethe's Legacies*, Routledge Studies in Renaissance Literature and Culture (London and New York: Routledge, 2004), 53.

14. Harvey, "Pleasure's Oblivion," 53.
15. Carol Thomas Neely, *Distracted Subjects: Madness and Gender in Shakespeare and Early Modern Culture* (Ithaca: Cornell University Press, 2004), 3.
16. Ibid.
17. See Sullivan, 90, for a discussion of intoxication and "shallow memories" in the play.
18. Montaigne also discusses diversion as a military tactic (N.d., 748).
19. Antony and Cleopatra utter the word 'come(s)' 29 times each, as opposed to Octavius Caesar's eight.
20. Walter Benjamin, "The Work of Art in the Age of Mechanical Reproduction," in *Illuminations*, ed. Hannah Arendt, trans. Harry Zohn (New York: Schocken Books, 1969), 250 n.19. See also Siegfried Kracauer, "Cult of Distraction," in *The Mass Ornament: Weimar Essays*, ed. and trans. Thomas Y. Levin (Cambridge, MA: Harvard University Press, 1995).
21. Benjamin, "The Work of Art," 240.
22. See Charlie Keil, "'To Here from Modernity': Style, Historiography, and Transitional Cinema," in *American Cinema's Transitional Era: Audiences, Institutions, Practices*, ed. Charlie Keil and Shelley Stamp (Berkeley: University of California Press, 2004), 51–65. For a cogent defense of the modernity thesis, see Ben Singer, *Melodrama and Modernity: Early Sensational Cinema and Its Contexts* (New York: Columbia University Press, 2001). For a recent criticism of the thesis, see Malcolm Turvey, "Film, Distraction, and Modernity," in *The Filming of Modern Life: European Avant-Garde Film of the 1920s* Cambridge, MA: The MIT Press, 2011), 163–81.
23. Mallarmé's note as first published in *La revue blanche*, 15 July 1896 under the title "Hamlet et Fortinbras," contrasting the characters of Hamlet and Fortinbras in a French provincial performance of the play. Citations of *Ulysses* refer to the Hans Walter Gabler edition (New York: Vintage Books, 1986).
24. Franco Moretti, *Modern Epic: The World System from Goethe to García Márquez* (London: Verso, 1996), 137.
25. Moretti, *Modern Epic*, 137–38.
26. See, for example, Jean Howard, *Theater of a City* (Philadelphia: University of Pennsylvania Press, 2007); *The Places and Spaces of Early Modern London*, ed. Deborah Harkness and Jean E. Howard, special issue of *Huntington Library Quarterly* 71 (2008); Lena Cowen Orlin, *Locating Privacy in Tudor London* (Oxford: Oxford University Press, 2007); Karen Newman, *Cultural Capitals: Early Modern London and Paris* (Princeton: Princeton University Press, 2009); Lena Cowen Orlin, ed., *Material London, ca. 1600* (Philadelphia: University of Pennsylvania Press, 2000); and Lawrence Manley, *Literature and Culture in Early Modern London* (Cambridge: Cambridge University Press, 2005).
27. Gail Kern Paster, *The Idea of the City in the Age of Shakespeare* (Athens, GA: The University of Georgia Press, 1985), 3.
28. Christopher D'Addario, "Stillness and Noise: The Ambiences of John Donne's Lyrics," *Philological Quarterly* 91 (2012): 419.
29. Evelyn Simpson and George R. Potter, eds., *The Sermons of John Donne*, 10 vols. (Berkeley: University of California Press, 1954), 7:264.
30. D'Addario, "Stillness and Noise," 437, 434.
31. D'Addario, "Stillness and Noise," 428, 425–26.
32. D'Addario, "Stillness and Noise," 429.

33. D'Addario, "Stillness and Noise," 419.
34. In a recent review of *Antony and Cleopatra* in criticism and in performance, Sara Munson Deats notes the following irony: "Despite its much-touted cinematic qualities, *Antony and Cleopatra* has been filmed only four times for television and once for the cinema." "Shakespeare's Anamorphic Drama: A Survey of *Antony and Cleopatra* in Criticism, on Stage, and on Screen," in *Antony and Cleopatra: New Critical Essays*, ed. Sara Munson Deats (New York and London: Routledge, 2005), 74.
35. Benjamin, "The Work of Art," 238.
36. Benjamin, "The Work of Art," 238.
37. Compare Joel Altman's claim that Elizabethan plays "did not merely raise questions, in the general sense, but literally were questions—or rather fictional realizations of questions." *The Tudor Play of Mind: Rhetorical Inquiry and the Development of Elizabethan Drama* (Berkeley: University of California Press, 1978), 2–3. Altman provocatively links the drama to scholastic training in arguing both sides of a question.

13 Desiring Memory in Spenser's *Amoretti* and *The Faerie Queene* or "Is there Sex in the Library of Memory?"

Kyle Pivetti

A number of readers would surely raise an eyebrow at Camille Paglia's description of *The Faerie Queene*. It is, she writes, "a catalog of perversions," including but not limited to bestiality, incest, and bondage.[1] Paglia continues, "Some of the poetically strongest and most fully realized material in *The Faerie Queene* is pornographic."[2] Her endorsement seems a far cry from the famous dismissals of readers such as David Hume, who quips that "the pencil of the English poet was employed in drawing the affectation, and conceits, and fopperies of chivalry" to the point that it "render[s] *The Fairy Queen* peculiarly tiresome."[3] So "Spencer maintains his place in the shelves among our English classics: But he is seldom seen on the table."[4] Those two summaries point to a basic tension in the poem itself. How best to categorize Spenser's allegory—as a sober exploration of virtue, temperance, and chastity, or as an indulgent imagining of highly charged sexual acts? As M. L. Stapleton puts it, "Edmund Spenser struggles to reconcile the sacred with the erotic throughout his career as a writer."[5] Indeed, the terms of reconciliation, struggle, and resistance pervade the writing on Spenser's erotic material. This poet, it seems, could not commit to either side—to the indulgent perversion or the virtuous education.

For many, answers to the dilemmas of Spenser's erotics come in the form of negotiation and refusal. Lauren Silberman, for instance, argues, "Spenser's transformation of traditional erotic discourses, represented by the concluding figure of the Hermaphrodite, becomes a way of positing creativity and the growth of knowledge as the ideal model of engagement with the outside world."[6] The poem is never a static object, never a final statement of value, and what Stapleton calls the "struggle to reconcile the sacred with the erotic" is an opportunity as much as a failure in Silberman's account. Because the hermaphrodite combines and transforms gender, limits are overcome and convention refuted. This essay asks, though, what happens when we examine how those erotic transformations operate on other categories like nationhood, monarchy, and—most pressingly—memory. If *The Faerie Queene* can at any point ascend into pornography, then could the same erotic potential run through the historical and political aims of the poem? In other words, sexual desire determines Spenser's strategies of recollection in *The Faerie Queene*. Memory, depends upon the conflicts of lust, shame, and struggle—the same conflicts underlying the sacred values of this Christian allegory and the representation of the poem's primary figure, Queen Elizabeth.

Alone in the Library

This essay, then, will take us back into the chamber of memory that launches the other studies of Spenser in this volume. At this moment, Guyon and Arthur complete their tour of the House of Alma. In this far removed chamber, they discover Eumnestes—the allegorical figure for "remembering well"—sifting through what are essentially history books. Spenser writes that

> His chamber all was hangd about with rolls,
> And old records from auncient times deriud,
> Some made in books, some in long parchment scrolls,
> That were all worm-eaten, and full of canker holes.[7]

Within those rotting volumes, Guyon and Arthur find two historical tomes that will make up the next cantos of Spenser's own poem: "*Briton moniments*" and "*Antiquitee* of *Faery* lond." Given the setting, it is no wonder that scholars such as Jennifer Summit read the episode in terms of the early modern library, a comparison that allows her to address the English Reformation, censorship, and national identity.[8] Such an approach echoes the dominant conversation on Eumnestes and his chamber of memory. When Guyon and Arthur sit down with volumes explicitly covering English and Faerie history alike, they prompt critical readings of history and nationalism, centered on the figure of Queen Elizabeth.[9] While these works grapple with the writing of history and the value of memory in Spenser's socio-political projects, they have not asked one important question: is there sex in the library?

I ask because the description of Eumnestes ends with a well-known point of contradiction. Guyon is the knight of temperance, meaning that throughout the book he learns to control passions, to balance the physical world with the spiritual, and so on. However, as Guyon and Arthur grab their history books, they both seem overly eager. Spenser writes:

> Whereat they burning both with feruent fire,
> Their countreys aunestry to vnderstond,
> Crau'd leaue of Alma, and that aged sire,
> To read those books; who gladly graunted their desire. (2.9.60)

The bower of bliss attracts attention for Guyon's violent outburst, but so too does this moment appear out of character. The language points to the themes of chastity and lust that dominate so much of Book II and Book III. When Spenser rhymes the "feruent fire" with the "desire" to know national pasts, he suggests that remembering is a distinctly erotic experience.

An earlier episode, when Belphoebe first confronts the giant Braggadochio, makes those connotations clear. In his letter to Raleigh, Spenser explains that Belphoebe figures Queen Elizabeth, yet it is not necessarily the monarch he has in mind. He tells Raleigh that Elizabeth "beareth two persons, the one of a most royall Queene or Empresse, the other of a most

Desiring Memory in Spenser's Amoretti and The Faerie Queene

vertuous and beautifull Lady."[10] The Faerie Queene comes to represent the royal queen, and Belphoebe, then, signals her private person, the virtuous model of chastity. That latter value becomes the subject of an extended Petrarchan description in an early episode of Book II, in which we learn of cheeks "like roses in a bed of lillies" (2.3.22) and her "faire eyes" in which "two liuing lamps did flame" (2.3.23). Spenser develops that image of flames in the next lines:

> In them the blinded god his lustfull fyre
> To kindle oft assayd, but had no might;
> For with dredd Maiestie, and awfull yre,
> She broke his wanton darts, and quenched base desyre. (2.3.23)

The "blinded god" in this moment is Cupid, who finds himself stymied by Belphoebe's chastity. The rhyme, however, is telling. Cupid attempts to inspire both "lustfull fyre" and "base deyre," both associated with the corruption of Belphoebe's virtues. Those same terms define both Guyon's and Arthur's reactions to the volumes of history that they find in the Chamber of memory. They too are driven by a "feruent fire"—an impulse here associated with the lust of the poem's villains. In other words, like a pair of overly enthusiastic history students, Guyon and Arthur have found particularly captivating library books.

This pattern continues throughout the sections on temperance. In his description of Belphoebe, Spenser cannot help but draw his figure of chastity into the provocations of lust. Her eyes, beautiful yet simultaneously chaste, contrast with those of Acrasia, who inspires one of the filthiest passages late in Book II. In the Bower of Bliss, Acrasia looms over the hapless knight Verdant, and Spenser dwells on her naked body: "Her snowy brest was bare to ready spoyle / Of hungry eies, which n'ote threweith be fild" (2.12.78). The image of the bare chest only provokes more stares, more indulgence, to the degree that even our narrator takes care to mention the drops of sweat "that like pure Orient perles adowne it trild" (2.12.78).[11] The lustful blazon continues with "her faire eyes sweet smyling in delight" which "thrild / Fraile harts, yet quenched not" (2.12.78). These eyes, as A. C. Hamilton implies, do not turn away the enraptured male attention; they invite intemperate, disordered lust.[12] And their "delight" once again recalls the charms of memory's library. When Guyon and Arthur finish their reading, Alma discovers them particularly entranced with the material, rendered as helpless as Verdant underneath the enrapturing Acrasia. Spenser writes:

> Beguyld thus with delight of nouelties,
> And naturall desire of countries state,
> So long they red in those antiquities,
> That how the time was fled, they quite forgate[.] (2.10.77)

The desire remains, an echo of the lust fostered in a figure like Braggadochio. So too remains the "delight of nouelties," echoing the "delight" Acrasia uses to capture her male victims. In fact, the very next canto features an attack on the House of Alma by the enemies of temperance, those bodily senses that seek to undo reason's good governance. The faculty of tactile touch—here figured by a "troupe" of enemies—sieges the castle last, and their erotic potential is clear: "Crueely they assayed that fift Fort, / Armed with dartes of sensuall delight / With stinges of carnal lust" (2.11.13). The "delight" constantly threatens, even in the chamber of memory. In that faculty far removed from the physical realities of the body, erotic desire assays, intruding upon the pasts of the English queen.

So why do the valences of erotic desire continue to intrude upon the chamber of memory? For Spenser, recollection is neither a passive nor an innocent activity. Instead, it requires constant activity; thus Eumnestes is buttressed by the librarian's assistant flitting about the chamber of memory. The old man, we learn, is accompanied by Anamnestes, a small child who can retrieve that which Eumnestes cannot. "Oft when things were lost, or laid amis," writes Spenser, "That boy them sought, and unto him did lend" (2.9.58). Without that moving force of Anamnestes, the books remain on the selves, unavailable to Guyon, Arthur, and Spenser's reader alike. The reminder proves an essential component of memory, one in line with a theory of memory that Goran Stanivukovic in this collection reveals in the work of Spenser—the ancient memory arts.

Critics have in the past discovered the memory arts running throughout early modern literature in general, and in *The Faerie Queene* more specifically.[13] Yet they have not read with attention to the poem's sexualized mnemonic appeals. In short, the process requires that a speaker imagine a series of figurative cues spread across an architectural space. Through representative images—for instance, an anchor if one is addressing naval matters—able speakers could memorize long passages and recite them on cue.[14] Maurice Evans finds that process running throughout Spenser's epic: "The art of memory gave Spenser both methods and material which he exploited more comprehensively than any other Renaissance poet."[15] Evans, though, carefully distinguishes between the memorization of verse and the memorization of the poem's descriptive content. In other words, a reader leaves *The Faerie Queene* not with lines of verse in mind, but with a series of vivid images implanted in the mind—images like "Guyon carrying the bloody handed child" or "Amoret with her heart transfixed with a knife and borne before her in a silver basin."[16] Yet absent from his list are those scenes provoking "fire" and "desire" alike. That is, the erotic images prove in *The Faerie Queene* just as memorable as the violent images, whether the descriptions offer Acrasia's sweaty chest or Belphoebe's delightful eyes.

The tradition in which Spenser worked, after all, depended upon certain imaginative effects to accomplish its goals. Yates even suggests that the insistence of mnemotechnicians on the strange and memorable prompted the "medieval love of the grotesque, the idiosyncratic."[17] Violence is not, though, the only source for a provocative image. Paolo Rossi gives the example of the famed memory artist Pietro da Ravenna, who published an essay on his memorization techniques in Venice in 1491. Reprinted by the Englishman Robert Copland in 1548 under the title *The Art of Memory, that Otherwise Is Called the Phoenix*, this text in Rossi's estimation "exercised a significant influence on all subsequent mnemotechnic works."[18] Ravenna presents his strategies as if he were confessing, alternately embarrassed by his methods while simultaneously impressed by their efficacy:

> I usually fill my memory-places with the images of beautiful women, which excite my memory ... and believe me: when I use beautiful women as memory images, I find it much easier to arrange and repeat the notions which I have entrusted to those places. You now have a most useful secret of artificial memory, a secret which I have (through modesty) long remained silent about: if you wish to remember quickly, dispose the images of the most beautiful virgins into memory places; the memory is marvelously excited by images of women ... I hope chaste and religious men will pardon me: I cannot pass over in silence a rule which has earned me much praise and honour on account of my abilities in the art, because I wish, with all my heart, to leave excellent successors behind me.[19]

The "beautiful women" undeniably assist Ravenna, to the point that he exclaims both memory's marvelous excitement over the visions and the ease with which he recalls anything associated with "the most beautiful virgins." Ravenna, however, hesitates to reveal the secret he has "through modesty" kept from public knowledge, even when displaying his feats of memorization before powerful audiences. The shame is apparent. "Praise and honour" come from his memory, yet the secret will offend some. Ravenna notes specifically that he hopes "chaste and religious men will pardon me." Although Spenser may not have known Ravenna's work directly, the struggles between the sacred and the profane—or the chaste and the erotic—resonate. In imagining the "most beautiful virgins," Ravenna offends the "chaste and religious men." To remember, in a sense, violates the very virginity that prompts the memory. So too will Spenser find himself in the quandary—how to remember Elizabeth's pasts without offending the "chaste and religious." He may separate his monarch into two dominate figures, the Faerie Queene and Belphoebe, but when he recalls one's national and royal pasts, he also eroticizes the other, dragging one back into the negotiations of sexual desires.

To speak of the author's longings of Elizabeth I, though, suggests his longings for another Elizabeth, and in a poetic form more erotically charged than the allegorical epic of Christian virtue. I describe, of course Spenser's sonnet sequence, in which his desires for political pasts collide with the physical appetites of the body. Those appetites, I suggest, cannot be separated from the processes of memory.

Sex Trophies

Certainly, Elizabeth I was surrounded by a number of representations, many of which competed against one another in the struggle to define this monarch.[20] Spenser's competitions are more personal, between the queen and his object of affection in the *Amoretti* and *Epithalamion*, Elizabeth Boyle, whom Spenser married in the summer of 1594 after the first three volumes of his epic were published.[21] Throughout the sequence, Spenser admits that he neglects the conclusion of *The Faerie Queene* by writing a sonnet sequence dedicated to a more immediate love interest, but the conflict emerges most prominently in Sonnet 33, when Spenser admits,

> Great wrong I doe, I can it not deny,
> To that most sacred Empresse my dear dred,
> Not finishing her Queene of faery,
> That mote enlarge her living prayses dead:[22]

The poet, it appears, is distracted.[23] He cannot complete the national epic "without another wit" as "this one is tost with troublous fit, of a proud love" (11–12). The competition between female objects of affection, in fact, invokes the matter of future remembrance. *The Faerie Queene* will "enlarge" Elizabeth I's "living prayses" after she is long dead; the sonnets, however, preserve the other woman in Spenser's life. As the poet proclaims late in the sequence, "My verse your vertues rare shall eternize, / And in the hevens wryte your glorious name" (75.11–12). That promise echoes in a number of sonnet sequences of the period, but the legacy in this case threatens the political ambitions of the epic. In the most basic sense, the pursuit of one Elizabeth disrupts the glorification of the other. Both motivate the sonnets; both are the objects of Spenser's desire; and both require his commemoration.

While the sonnet sequence and its concluding poem are renowned for their movement toward consummation, the poet often struggles to achieve those successes. Marriage, the *Epithalamion* insists, elevates the courtship to one of Christian virtue, heavenly grace, and divine fulfillment. In this way, the sequence as whole becomes in Prescott's hesitant terms "loosely Neo-Platonic," for "Elizabeth lifts her lover above the mundane."[24] Such a reading treats the sexual relationship as the means to spiritual triumph, or as William C. Johnson phrases it, "an education in loving much like being educated in faith and for redemption."[25] M. L. Stapleton, though, finds the baser desire throughout. "Sex," he argues, "still appears to be an important motivation in the sonnet sequence, perhaps the one and only—despite [Spenser's] protestations to the contrary within."[26] In the sequence's initial moments, the struggle is apparent. The body continually weighs down the subject, and memory serves only insomuch as it confines one to the physical.

We find in Sonnet 13, for instance, that the lady's beauty reflects heaven's, in the most neo-Platonic of ways. Yet at the same time, her eyes cast downward in memory of fleshy limits:

> In that proud port, which her so goodly graceth,
> Whiles her faire face she reares up to the skie:
> And to the ground her eie-lids low embaseth,
> Most goodly temperature ye may descry,
> Myld humblesse mixt with awfull majesty,
> For looking on the earth whence she was borne,
> Her minde remembreth her mortalitie,
> What so is fairest shall to earth returne. (13.1–8)

Initially, the upturned face reflects the "graceth" of heaven, made "faire" just as the Faerie Queene who attracts so much attention. The glance downward, though, checks the lady's pride; simultaneously, it serves as memory. In looking to the earth, she remembers the flesh, acknowledging that it prevents the premature ascension to grace. The recollection, that is, "hinders heavenly thought with drossy slime" (13.12). And that same "slime" that circles the castle of Alma also happens to house the male poet. He pleads, "Yet lowly still vouchsafe to looke on me" (13.13), as if her memory of flesh also brings her to the "drossy slime" of Spenser himself. It is worth noting that the *OED* defines "slime" as "A viscous substance or fluid of animal or vegetable origin; mucus, semen, etc." and as a term "applied to what is morally filthy or otherwise disgusting."[27] It is, then, an alternately repugnant and sexual reference. In this conflict between high and low spirituality—and social status—Daniel Juan Gil finds the beginnings of erotic relationships, what he sees as romantic love "before intimacy." Of the *Amoretti*, he writes, "The dirty secret that poetry is a belabored effort to renegotiate the terms of a class system that excludes lowborn authors ... is foregrounded here, where it becomes the basis of an eroticism of endless, unsuccessful self-refinement."[28] In other words, the erotic experience emerges in the vacillation between earth and sky, between high and low. For Spenser, that also invokes the powers of memory to recall the "drossy slime" and keep things on earth—and apparently in the bed.

That pattern persists across the *Amoretti*. In a similar manner, Sonnet 27 rebukes any overestimation of beauty. "Faire proud now tell me," Spenser asks, "why should faire be proud, / Sith all worlds glories is but drosse uncleane?" (27.1) The flesh, once again, contaminates, and death will check the powers of fairness. At that point, "That goodly Idoll, now so gay beseene, / shall doffe her fleshes borrowd fayre attire: / and be forgot as it had never beene" (27.5–7). Oblivion comes to free one from the body and from its "uncleane" desires. The "protestation" and "struggles" reveal themselves—the sequence longs to free the love from earthly memory, seeking forgetfulness from the memorials of the body.

The turn comes when the Petrarchan sequence describes the speaker's victory over his love interest. As Reed Way Dasenbrock observes, "[Spenser] replaces Petrarch's passionate but unconsummated love by marriage, presenting that union as the sacred harbor of stability. And, in so doing, he rejects Tasso's Platonic conception of love that would have the lover rise above the realm of the physical."[29] In consummating love, then, Spenser keeps his eye on the physical, just as the lady looks both to heaven and the ground. So when the relationship moves toward consummation in the *Amoretti*, we find ourselves once again in the chamber of memory. By Sonnet 69, Spenser has given a series of laments and complaints typical of the sonneteer, but as the courtship of Boyle makes its turn toward success, Spenser turns to martial imagery. The battle has been won; the question now is one remembrance:

> The famous warriors of the anticke world,
> Vsed Trophees to erect in stately wize:
> in which they would the records hauve enrold,
> of theyr great deeds and valorous emprise.
> What trophee then shall I most fit deuize,
> in which I may record the memory
> of my loues conquest, peerelesse beauties prise,
> adorn'd with honour, loue, and chastity. (69.1–8)

Like an epic hero, the poet must commemorate his victory; he must discover the trophy that will "record the memory / of my loues conquest." The language should be familiar to anyone who has spent time with Eumnestes. Spenser rhymes "memory" with "chastity," suggesting that the past intertwines with the questions of sex, here made a distinct reality by the promise of the forthcoming marriage to Boyle. The "trophee" so upheld by "famous warriors" acts as a monument, cueing further remembrance. As the *OED* suggests, the "trophy" is alternatively a prize of victory and a "monument; a memorial; a memento."[30] Moreover, the "records" in which the victories of heroes such as Achilles are "enrold" could easily slip among the volumes of British history in Eumnestes' library. Before Spenser narrates *Briton moniments* in *The Faerie Queene*, he remarks to his "soueraine Queene" that her male ancestors' "noble deeds aboue the Northern starre / Immortal fame for euer hath enrold; / As in that old mans booke they were in order told" (2.10.4). The victory over Elizabeth Boyle is also "enrold" in its own volume, and how could it not be? The experience of desire translates to the experience of memory, just as Ravenna knew.

In the second half of the sonnet, Spenser strengthens those connections and turns the sonnet itself into a trophy commemorating the erotic victory.

The parallels to Eumnestes here grow even stronger than in the preceding lines:

> Euen this verse vowd to eternity,
> shall be thereof immortall monient:
> and tell her prayse to all posterity,
> that may admire such worlds rare wonderment.
> The happy purchase of my glorious spoile,
> gotten at last with labour and long toyle. (69.9–14)

Both Fred Blick and Maurice Hunt note the sophisticated puns on Elizabeth Boyle's name ("my glorious spoile" elides to "Glorious Boyle" in pronunciation), and the somewhat conventional claim of poetry as the means to immortality.[31] What stands out in this moment, though, is the resonance with Eumnestes. Spenser consumes himself with the "immortall moniment" just as the old man sweats over his "immortall scrine" and the volumes of "*Briton moniments.*" The poet's "labour and long toyle" in the sonnets transform in *The Faerie Queene* to "A labor huge" (2.10.2)—the transcription of British histories. That these memories in the *Amoretti* pertain to the conquest of love and to the inevitable sexual fulfillment of that love is of no coincidence. The sonnets record and remember the experience of desire; just as desire comes to define the practice of remembrance. The body and memory and inextricably bound in these poems, so when Spenser crafts his own national memories, he will invoke the body alongside its sexual urges.

The sonnet sequence itself, finally, transforms one to the other, the past to sex and sex to the past. If writers desire to have memories, indeed to make memories, they will find that memory too desires its objects of sexual attraction, and Pietro da Ravenna indicates why. Spenser himself invokes those urges of the memory arts when he compares Elizabeth Boyle to a saintly icon in Sonnet 22:

> Her temple fayre is built within my mind,
> In which her glorious ymage placéd is,
> On which my thoughts doo day and night attend
> Lyke sacred priests that never think amisse. (22.5–8)

While the metaphor images the religious dedication, its invocation of the memory space and its images cannot be ignored. The imagined structures work in concert with the "glorious ymage," to fix the mind's activity. The object of affection becomes, then, the reminder, an erotic cue to recollection the memory artist could exploit. Spenser continues,

> There I to her as th'author of my blisse,
> While build an altar to appease her yre:
> And on the same my hart will sacrifise,

> Burning in flames of pure and chast desire:
> The which vouchsafe O goddesse to accept,
> Amongst they deerest relicks to be kept.

In this conclusion, Spenser develops the image of the temple, proclaiming his affections of "pure and chast desire." His appetites join the memory palace. He may proclaim "desire" as the force of pure chastity, yet sexual longings remain, described already as memory. Thus, the poet's heart becomes a relic, a memorial or trophy to be preserved in the temple alongside the images of beauty.

That "ymage," then, illuminates the political ambitions of *The Faerie Queene*. In his epic, Spenser declares his desires to preserve Elizabeth I's memory. The *Amoretti* suggest that doing so requires he render her another memory image—a vision of beauty that cues memory through its sexual appeal.

Memory "Ymages"

Spenser's memorial dilemmas manifest in the opening statements of Book II of *The Faerie Queene*. The poem, our narrator tells us, is a "famous antique history" and a "matter of just memory" (2.proem.1). More specifically, it recites to the monarch her own past:

> And thou, O fairest Princesse vnder sky,
> In this fayre mirrhour maist behold thy face,
> And thine owne realms in lond of Faery,
> And in this antique ymage thy great auncestry. (2.proem.4)

The numerous puns indicate the degree to which pasts overlap for Spenser. The "fairie queene" puns on "the fairest Princesse," the lond of "Faery," and the "fayre mirrhour." Elizabeth can discover her national pasts in this poem just as she can behold herself and the geography of Britain. For a proficient mnemotechnician like Spenser, the "ymage" does not communicate virtue alone; it communicates the memories upon which England will be built. In the very next stanza, Spenser asks for forgiveness "to enfold in couert vele and wrap in shadows light" (2.proem.5) his monarch. He must use such figuration, he remarks, so "that feeble eyes your glory may behold" (2.proem.5). The "vele," though, will also make the past available. It will reveal "auncestry" in ways that "feeble eyes" can comprehend. So too will it invite eroticization.

In the long description of Belphoebe, the metaphor of the mirror returns. As we have seen, this character invites simultaneous lust and chastity, her virtue marked by the potential dangers of sexual impulse. Braggadochio, upon seeing her, is "fild with delight / Of her sweete words" and "with her wondrous beauty rauisht quite" (2.3.41), reacting in ways strikingly similar to Guyon and Arthur upon finding the works of British history. Dragging hero and villain together, Spenser remarks that Braggadochio begins to "burne in filthy lust" (2.3.41), overcome by perverse and violent impulses. Those reactions cannot be separated from the narrator's own praise of virtuous beauty, given in the metaphor of that fair mirror:

> So glorious mirrhour of celestial grace,
> And sovereign moniment of mortal vowes,
> How shall frayle pen descriue her heauenly face,
> For feare through want of skill her beauty to deface? (2.3.25)

The reflection promises to show chaste virtue, envisioned in the beauty of "celestial grace" and Elizabeth herself. The face is "heauenly" in the grandest sense, but this description includes the term that also marks Guyon's volume of history—"Britons moniments." This "mirrhour" too serves as a "moniment," an indication that the past too is revealed in her 'beauty.'[32] In another pun, Spenser insists that he fears "defacing" that beauty, but the circumstances show why the poem inevitably disfigures its very subject. The first to see Belphoebe, the first to note her beauty, is Braggadochio. His lust is the reader's and the narrator's. If a "moniment" appears in this mirror, it is noteworthy only by the "filthy lust" it inspires.

One other mirror tends to dominate discussions of *The Faerie Queene*. In Book III, Britomart recounts the beginnings of her own quest by describing the mysterious object that is Merlin's glass. This bizarre "looking glasse" (3.2.18), well noted for its ability to show "What euer thing was in the world contaynd, / Betwixt the lowest earth and heuens hight" (3.2.19), prompts readings of magic and prophecy. Its reflections warn monarchs of impending dangers, and critics have been careful to distinguish its virtuous abilities in opposition to the deceptive dangers of Duessa or Imago.[33] This is 'white magic,' to be trusted for its virtuous images—just like the mirror that is the poem as a whole. To Britomart, however, Merlin shows her Arthegall, and while she does not immediately burn in "filthy lust," the image certainly delights. Cupid, if he did not find success with Belphoebe, accomplishes his work here: "the false Archer, which that arrow shot / So slyly, that she did not feele the wound, / Did smyle full smoothly at her weeless wofull stound" (3.2.26). Without knowing, Britomart falls in love. When she seeks explanation from Merlin, she hears a prophecy of her marriage to this figure in the mirror, a prophecy that ironically serves as the history for Elizabeth herself.

As evidenced by Howard Dobin's work on prophecy, the episode clearly invokes prognostication.[34] Before Spenser gives that prophecy, though, he gives another invocation of the muses to echo that in Book II. Here, the valences of lust—however much denied—make themselves apparent. Love is a "Most sacred fyre, that burnest mightily / In liuing brests" (3.3.1), that which Spenser specifically says is not "that same, which doth base affection moue / In brutish minds, and filthy lust inflame" (3.3.1). The flame burns either way. In the effort to avoid defamation, Spenser yet again blurs

188 Kyle Pivetti

his categories, suggesting that this love could indeed be mistaken for lust, for sexual desire. Spenser goes on to praise this love, noting that "Well did Antiquity a God thee deeme" (3.3.2), but the invocation shifts abruptly at the fourth stanza. Turning to another deity, Spenser writes:

> Begin then, O my dearest Dame,
> Daughter of Phoebus and of Memorye,
> That does ennoble with immortal name
> The warlike Worthies, from antiquitye,
> In thy great volume of Eternitye. (3.3.4)

The muse's "great volume" could substitute for the rolls, parchments, and tomes of Eumnestes in the chamber of memory. The desires prompted by love, then, give way to work of memory. The episode is not so much about prophecy as it is about the past, and it is sexual desire that provokes the retelling. The mirror, then, does not simply show what is to come. Because it stirs desire, it also stirs the memory. Spenser stares in the mirror and sees his own objects of affection—British history and his own queen.

Desiring Memory

The poem, I am arguing, does not simply make the erotic memorable. It is not just that the "pornographic" images fix themselves in readers' minds. Instead, the memorable *is* erotic. The desire to record, recall, or recollect inevitably succumbs to the "filthy" lusts of Braggadochio, who is just as swept up by Elizabethan pasts as Arthur, Guyon, and the poet are.

In the end, is there sex in Eumnestes' library? The poem's language insists upon yes, for the act of remembering itself intimates the act of sex. Memory, in Spenser's poem, does not simply "happen." Instead, Spenser works within a tradition that treated memory itself as a rhetorical object, constructed and manipulated to serve purpose. If allegory depends upon the entertaining images "which for the most part men delight to read," then we should not be surprised if that "delight" arises in the images that Pietro da Ravenna found so pleasing.[35] The poet must transform even national history, which means that he will be risking the erotic, the invocations of desires at odds with the stated projects of "vertuous and gentle discipline."[36] When Camille Paglia describes *The Faerie Queene* as a "catalog of perversions," she knows that the poet himself would most likely disagree. "Most criticism assumes that what Spenser says is what he means," Paglia writes. "But a poet is not always master of his own poem, for imagination can overwhelm moral intention."[37] Elsewhere, she continues this thought, "*The Faerie Queene* is didactic but also self-pleasuring. In the midst of dissipation and atrocity, we hear a voice saying 'Ain't it awful.'"[38] The awful, of course, proves most memorable.

I did leave out one line in Pietro da Ravenna's advice to would-be mnemotechnicians. He admits that images of beautiful women will most easily cue the memory, but he goes on to warn that "This precept is useless to those who dislike women and they will find it very difficult to gather the fruits of this art."[39] The images of Arthegall, Belphoebe, Acrasia, and even Silberman's hermaphrodites demonstrate the range of Spenser's memory art. All are subject to memory, and all may transform into objects of desire, whether male, female, or both. And in Ravenna's claim of using "forty beautiful virgins" for memory, we can witness the transformation at work in the depiction of chaste Elizabeth. Chastity, in the ends, proves memorable for the very reason that it invites desire. Ravenna remembers 40 beautiful virgins, but not because they are models of Christian or national virtue. He remembers them because they are the objects of his "base desire." That is his shameful secret, and perhaps Spenser's too.

Notes

1. Camille Paglia, "sex," in *The Spenser Encyclopedia*, ed. A.C. Hamilton (Toronto: University of Toronto Press, 1992), 640. See also Paglia, *Sexual Personae: Art and Decadence from Neferiti to Emily Dickinson* (Cumberland: Yale University Press, 1990), esp. 170–93.
2. Paglia, "sex," 641.
3. David Hume, *The History of England*, Volume 4, Appendix III (Indianapolis: Liberty Fund, 1983), 386.
4. Ibid.
5. M. L. Stapleton, "Devoid of Guilty Shame: Ovidian Tendencies in Spenser's Erotic Poetry," *Modern Philology*, 105.2 (2007): 271–99, 271.
6. Lauren Silberman, *Transforming Desire: Erotic Knowledge in Books III and IV of The Faerie Queene* (Berkeley: University of California Press, 1995), 5.
7. Edmund Spenser, *The Faerie Queene*, revised second edition, ed. A.C. Hamilton (Harlow: Pearson/Education Limited, 2007), 2.9.57. All subsequent references to this edition will be cited within the text.
8. See Jennifer Summit, *Memory's Library: Medieval Books in Early Modern England* (Chicago: University of Chicago Press, 2008).
9. For a range of examples that analyze history writing and nationalism, see Jacqueline T. Miller, "The Status of Faeryland: Spenser's 'Vniust Possession'" *Spenser Studies* 5 (1985): 31–44; David Lee Miller, *The Poem's Two Bodies: The Poetics of the 1590 Faerie Queene* (Princeton: Princeton University Press, 1988); Andrew King, *The Faerie Queene and Middle English Romance: The Matter of Just Memory* (Oxford: Clarendon Press, 2000); Andrew Escobedo, *Nationalism and Historical Loss in Renaissance England* (Ithaca: Cornell University Press, 2004); and Matthew Woodcock, *Fairy in The Faerie Queene: Renaissance Elf-Fashioning and Elizabethan Myth-Making* (Aldershot: Ashgate, 2004).
10. Edmund Spenser, "Letter to Raleigh," in *The Faerie Queene*, 716.
11. Stephen Guy Bray, in "Spenser's Filthy Matter," *Explicator* 62.4 (2004): 194–95, compares the description of Acrasia to both Book I's Duessa and to Tasso's Armida from *Gerusalemme Liberata*. In contrast to Duessa, Acrasia does not actively disguise herself with the appearance of beauty. Spenser implies that "Acrasia really is *that* beautiful" and that Guyon must "use his particular virtue of temperance to control his response to the beauty he (and we) cannot help but perceive" (195).

12. See *The Faerie Queene*, ed. A.C. Hamilton, note to 2.12.78.
13. Scholars have traced the implications of the memory arts in categories that include epistemological philosophy, visual arts, and even real architectural spaces. For examples, see Mary Carruthers, *The Book of Memory: A Study of Memory in Medieval Culture* (Cambridge: Cambridge University Press, 1990); Lina Bolzoni, *The Gallery of Memory* (Toronto: University of Toronto Press, 2001) as well as *The Web of Images* (Aldershot: Ashgate, 2004); and Paolo Rossi, *Logic and the Art of Memory*, trans. Stephen Clucas (London: The Athlone Press, 2000). In these accounts, memory does not merely record autobiography through natural processes; it is a rhetorical skill developed through concentrated effort and artificial manipulation. Some scholars have questioned the extent to which the memory arts dominated early modern thought. For instance, Lina Perkins Wilder, in *Shakespeare's Memory Theater* (Cambridge: Cambridge University Press, 2010), "responds to what [she sees] as an overemphasis on prescriptive order of the memory arts in studies of early modern memory" (13). Their study, however, shows no signs of slowing, for the memory arts do reveal the cultural anxieties and appetites thought to generate recollection most effectively.
14. Frances A. Yates, in *The Art of Memory* (Chicago: University of Chicago Press, 1966), provides the foundational study of the medieval memory arts in literary criticism. See especially pp. 1–2 for a succinct account of the practice.
15. Maurice Evans, "memory," in *The Spenser Encyclopedia*, 468. See also Evans, *Spenser's Anatomy of Heroism: A Commentary on* The Faerie Queene (Cambridge: Cambridge University Press, 1970). Michael Murrin advances similar claims in *The Veil of Allegory: Some Notes Toward a Theory of Allegorical Rhetoric in the English Renaissance* (Chicago: University of Chicago Press, 1969).
16. Evans, "memory," 467.
17. Yates, *The Art of Memory*, 104.
18. Rossi, *Logic and the Art of Memory*, 22. For textual history, see n. 47, p. 254–55.
19. Qtd. in Rossi, *Logic and the Art of Memory*, 22.
20. See for example Louis Montrose, *The Subject of Elizabeth: Authority, Gender, and Representation* (Chicago: University of Chicago Press, 2006) and Ilona Bell, *Elizabeth I: The Voice of a Monarch* (New York: Palgrave Macmillan, 2010).
21. See Anne Lake Prescott, "Spenser's Shorter Poetry," in *The Cambridge Companion to Spenser*, ed. Andrew Hadfield (Cambridge: Cambridge University Press, 2001), 152.
22. Edmund Spenser, "Sonnet 33," *Amoretti* and *Epithalamion*, in *Edmund Spenser's Poetry*, 3rd edition, ed. Hugh Maclean and Anne Lake Prescott (New York: W.W. Norton & Company, 1993), lines 1–4. All subsequent references to the Amoretti will refer to this edition and will be cited within the text.
23. As Prescott observes, the sonnets often "glance at the epic Spenser has interrupted" ("Spenser's Shorter Poetry," 152).
24. Ibid.
25. William C. Jonson, *Spenser's* Amoretti: *Analogies of Love* (Lewisburg: Bucknell University Press, 1990), 20.
26. Stapleton, "Devoid of Guilty Shame," 285.
27. See "slime," *Oxford English Dictionary*, www.oed.com, accessed 1 May 2015. See especially definition 2a. and 3b.
28. Daniel Juan Gil, *Before Intimacy: Asocial Sexuality in Early Modern England* (Minneapolis: University of Minnesota Press, 2006), 47.

29. Reed Way Dasenbrock, "The Petrarchan Context of Spenser's Amoretti," *PMLA* 100.1 (1985): 38–50, 47.
30. "trophy," *Oxford English Dictionary*, www.oed.com, accessed 5 January 2015. See especially definition 4a, which notes Spenser as a primary example of this usage.
31. See Fred Blick, "Spenser's *Amoretti* and Elizabeth Boyle: Her Name Immortalized," *Spenser Studies* 23 (2008): 309–35 and Maurice Hunt, "Hellish Work in *The Faerie Queene*," *Studies in English Literature, 1500–1900* 41.1 (2001): 91–108.
32. In the definition of Bart Van Es, the term "moniments" refers to history marked by physical evidence. The face, too, may offer physical evidence, but the blazon blends that physical reminder into Christian virtue and the "antique ymage" of British pasts. See *Spenser's Forms of History* (Oxford: Oxford University Press, 2002), 24.
33. See, for instance, Frances Yates, *The Occult Philosophy in the Elizabethan Age* (New York and London: Routledge, 1979, rpt. 2001), especially 127. Kenneth Borris, in "Platonism and Spenser's Poetic: Idealized Imitation, Merlin's Mirror, and the Florimells," *Spenser Studies* 24 (2009): 209–68, argues that Merlin's glass helps Spenser to subvert Plato's rejection of the poets by operating as 'good poetry.'
34. See Howard Dobin, *Merlin's Disciples: Prophecy, Poetry, and Power in Renaissance England* (Stanford: Stanford University Press, 1990). Dobin writes, "Despite the Faerie Queene's effort to employ Merlin to legitimate and glorify Elizabeth's reign, the prophetic impulse ultimately destabilizes rather than consolidate the machinery of power by presenting political change and disruption" (6). The same destabilization works in reverse. The telling of the past has just as much power for disruption, as indicated by the ties to lust, Braggadochio, and intemperance.
35. Spenser, "Letter to Raleigh," 715.
36. Ibid., 714.
37. Paglia, "sex," 641.
38. Paglia, *Sexual Personae*, 190.
39. See Rossi, *Logic and the Art of Memory* 22.

14 Spenser's Erotic Refusals
Su Fang Ng

The Proem to Book II of *The Faerie Queene* voices Spenser's fears that his poem will be judged "painted forgery, / Rather then matter of just memory" (II.Proem.1).[1] Contrasting true history with false show, it paradoxically insists on the historicity of the "happy land of Faery" (II.Proem.2), which like the late discovered Indies are true even if yet "In couert vele and wrap in shadowes light" (II.Proem.5). Spenser hints at the erotic pleasures of fantasy, but does eroticism, a subset of the passions, help or hinder memory? Renaissance works on the arts of memory emphasize the passions' role in recollection. Influenced by Aristotle, Renaissance thinkers understood memory as corporeal in nature. Since passions are physiological responses, memory is imagined as embodied. Spenser himself locates memory in an allegory of the body, the House of Alma, and figures memory as an old man, Eumnestes, "of infinite remembraunce" (II.ix.56). But erotic passions in *The Faerie Queene* are falsely induced by the wrong character. Memory's fragility often cannot compete with the immediacy of erotic presence. Duessa, for example, is exposed in Book I, which seems to de-eroticize her, but she reappears in Book IV, her past seemingly forgotten. The memory of the image of her true ugliness is forgotten in the face of her present erotic seductions. Memory loses out to fancy when fancy is stimulated by an erotic image, causing a forgetting that leads to poor ethical judgments.

The problem of evaluating erotic images, exacerbated by memory's failures, becomes far more acute in the 1596 *Faerie Queene*. While in the 1590 poem, the revelation of evil happens at the narrative's pace so the reader discovers it with the narrator, in the 1596 poem, the narrator evinces a palpable frustration as characters remain oblivious to evil. Book IV even begins by noting memory's importance. The Proem invites readers to "looke backe to former ages, / And call to count the things that then were donne" (IV.Proem.3), an exhortation mostly disregarded by characters who wander in an apparent state of amnesia. Book II's allegory of the body shows how memory is supposed to work. Together with Phantastes—the personification of fancy or imagination—and the unnamed function of judgment, Eumnestes resides in the head of the body; as theorized by classical and Renaissance arts of memory, he occupies the backmost room. In the 1596 poem, Eumnestes' ancient but solid room in the house of Alma—"The chamber seemed ruinous and old / ... / Yet were the wals, that did the same vphold / Right firme and strong" (II.ix.55)—is replaced by Ate's dark and ruinous dwelling, a place of vile memory associated with Duessa: "And all within the riuen walls were hung / With ragged monuments of times forepast, / All which the sad effects of discord sung" (IV.i.21). Ate's house contains memories of things broken—"rent robes, and broken scepters plast, / Altars defyl'd, and holy things defast" (IV.i.21)—of friendship severed, and of acts of tyranny and violence, including the acts of Nimrod and of Alexander the Great.

Examining Spenser's engagement with the poetics of memory, Rebeca Helfer points to his pervasive use of the *topos* of ruin as a site for cultural renewal; however, in his late works, including the last three books of *The Faerie Queene*, the meditation on ruin and recollection, and especially Ireland as their *locus*, is complicated by an ironic perspective on empire, as ruin turns into a site of imperial tyranny.[2] Rather than engaging directly with empire, I focus on the more intimate failures of memory in Book IV. *The Faerie Queene*'s second half is concerned with private conflict; private quarrels turn into "broken bandes," "girlonds rent," and "bowres despoyled," and such as "The moniments whereof there byding beene, / As plaine as at the first, when they were fresh and greene" (IV.i.24). In Book IV, and to an extent Book VI, failure of memory is linked to sexual cupidity, enemy to the book's virtue of friendship. Public acts of reformation of the state in the 1590 *Faerie Queene* cannot be sustained in the 1596's second half—the Blatant Beast is only barely muzzled, and Artegall returns to court only to be greeted with slander and backbiting—finding their corollary in broken friendships and broken social relations, due to failures of memory. Finally in Book VI, even courtesy is under threat at court with memory's weakness in need of aid.

I examine two objects, both articles of clothing, that function as *aide-mémoire*.[3] The first is Florimell's girdle that does not allow itself to be worn by the unchaste False Florimell. The girdle becomes a repository of memory, able to recognize its true owner, when other characters cannot remember her. A tactile memory inhering in the material object thus enacts a performance of proper erotic refusal. This proper memory is in contradistinction to the other characters' forgetfulness and immoderate desires. The second mnemonic object is Brianna's mantle of hair in Book VI. In both cases, the object's owner is a desiring female whose beloved initially rejects her advances. Crudor's refusal of love is turned into an eroticized garment, a mantle memorializing both Briana's love for Crudor and his rejection of her. Like the girdle, the mantle enacts erotic refusal or frustration, though an improper one. Spenser links the two by categorizing each as a *waif*, a legal term meaning an ownerless property. I argue that Spenser underlines the precariousness of memory and the dangers of forgetting—especially the danger of unlawful eroticism that must be contained by memory—the right assignment of ownership and finally marriage.

When Spenser worries about whether his poetry will be read as "painted forgery" or "matter of just memory"—a concern played out in miniature in the episodes of mnemonic clothing—he uses terms set by works on the arts of memory. These works argue that striking images, whether ugly or beautiful, create lasting memories by arousing the passions. A classical rhetoric popular in the Renaissance, the *Rhetorica ad Herennium*, attributed to Cicero, notes the importance of passions as a component of memory:

> When we see in every day life things that are petty, ordinary, and banal, we generally fail to remember them, because the mind is not being stirred by anything novel or marvellous. But if we see or hear something exceptionally base, dishonourable, unusual, great, unbelievable, or ridiculous, that we are likely to remember for a long time. ... Thus nature shows that she is not aroused by the common ordinary event, but is moved by a new or striking occurrence.[4]

Calling attention to the passage, Frances Yates points out that the treatise suggests "helping memory by arousing emotional affects through these striking and unusual images, beautiful or hideous, comic or obscene."[5] Thus, *The Faerie Queene*'s scenes of grotesque ugliness are striking images that impress the memory through affect. Mary Carruthers outlines medieval understanding of the physiological workings of memory: "The nature of the memorial phantasm as *passio* or *affectio animi* ... makes possible, the virtue of prudence or moral judgment," for "memory is the faculty that presents (or re-presents) experience, the basis upon which moral judgments must be made," and moreover, as we respond to it, is "bound up with the physiology of emotion."[6] The close link of emotions, imagination, and memory is illustrated by Spenser's Eumnestes who, in concert with Phantastes, creates judgment or prudence. The exercise of memory is an ethical act, intended to lead to virtue. The corollary is that memory's failure leads to vice.

Early modern authors on the arts of memory, however, find erotic passion ambiguous. In his *Mnemonica, or The Art of Memory* (pub. in Latin, 1618, English translation, 1661), John Willis warns against erotic (and other) passions as harmful to memory: detrimental emotions include those of "VI. *Venus*, i. if it be immoderate ... XI. Filthy desires, as avarice, envy, thirst of revenge, lust, love of harlots, and the ardent Passion, *Love*."[7] While erotic emotions are only harmful if immoderate, love is nonetheless grouped among other uncontrolled, negative passions. Cambridge radical Puritan William Perkins goes further to argue against the arts of memory precisely for their arousal of the passions:

> Artificial memorie, which standeth upon places and images, will very easilie without labour teach how to commit sermons to the memorie: but it is not to be approved. 1. The animation of the image, which is the key of memorie, is impious, because it requireth absurd, insolent

and prodigious cogitations, and those especially, which set an edge upon and kindle the most corrupt affections of the flesh.[8]

Perkins supposes that exciting the imagination has deleterious effects on the body. In rejecting "absurd, insolent and prodigious cogitations," he objects precisely to the striking images that rhetorical handbooks advocate for training memory.

The danger lies in how women's bodies may kindle corrupting passions. Not only women's bodies, but also their clothing, have the power to stimulate (and over-stimulate) memory. The Renaissance theater poses an acute instance of this problem, as male actors donned women's garments to play female parts. A contemporary critic, John Rainolds, citing authorities like the Bishop of Paris and Aquinas, argues against male actors' wearing of women's clothes: "For the apparell of wemen … is a great provocation of men to lust and leacherie: because a womans garment beeing put on a man doeth vehemently touch and moue him with the remembrance & imagination of a woman; and the imagination of a thing desirable doth stirr vp the desire."[9] Lina Perkins Wilder argues that Rainolds's description shows how the workings of memory depended on a "complementary cycle of remembering and desire," making "the absent object [the female body] a source of danger but also of theatrical elaboration."[10] In Spenser, this cycle of remembering and desire is interrupted by false images.

The story of Florimell spans several books, but in Book IV, the ownerless girdle, bitterly fought over, is a presence signaling her absence. I suggest that the dynamic of absence/presence in the sequence corresponds to memory's relation to eroticism. From the start, Florimell embodies erotic desire. When she first appears in Book III, she is fleeing the Foster; by the end, the god Proteus has her imprisoned in his dungeon, as he tries to coerce her into marriage. In Book IV, the assignment of ownership, whether of the girdle or Florimell herself, can be read as a process of memory's workings to reach judgment. In this process, erotic passion can be both help and hindrance.

The girdle's origin, as a memorial of marriage, makes it a mnemonic device from the start. Fashioned by Vulcan for his wife, it functions as livery, marking her belonging to him, but she loses the girdle in her affair with Mars. Left behind on the Acidalian mount, it is given to Florimell by the Graces who fostered her. Vulcan's purpose is to restrain erotic passions let loose by sexual relations: "Therewish to bind lasciuious desire, / And loose affections streightly to restraine; / Which vertue it for euer after did retaine" (IV.v.4). It is thus an instrument to moderate erotic passions. Venus's forgetting of married chastity is an improper de-coupling, a detachment, from her proper "owner." Consequently, the girdle passes on to a new owner. The transfer of the girdle from owner to new owner shows a similar pattern of forgetfulness. Florimell loses it when she is separated from Marinell and only regains it at marriage. Pursued by the hyena-like Monster sent by the witch, she escapes by leaping into the sea (to fall instead into the clutches of the Fisher), and when the Monster devours her palfrey, her girdle, left ownerless, is found by Satyrane (III.vii.20–36). While Thomas Roche sees it as a loss of virginity, Pamela Benson suggests that it figures the loss of social support.[11] In grave sexual danger, Florimell is soon threatened by Proteus, the most powerful of her suitors/rapists. Their restraint of her calls into question the girdle's power to curb female sexuality. Whether in the face of female desire (Venus) or male (Proteus and others), despite its virtues, the girdle can neither restrain desire nor protect the chaste virgin. The girdle's loss signals the threat of forgetting in another way. While Florimell is steadfast in her love for Marinell, her act of erotic refusal leads to her imprisonment, rendering her forgotten. When Satyrane shows up with the girdle, it is only a reminder of how "she her selfe was lost and gone" (IV.ii.26).

Lost by Florimell in Book III, the girdle is fought over in Book IV. Objecting to Satyrane's possession of the girdle, the knights agree that "of them all she that is fayrest found / Shall haue that golden girdle for reward, / And of those Knights who is most stout on ground, / Shall to that fairest Ladie be prefard" (IV.ii.27). Two competitions are put in motion. First, the knights compete in a tournament to win the right to claim their lady is the fairest, a competition that Britomart wins by beating Artegall, who earlier defeated the other knights (IV.iv.44). Next, the ladies strive to be judged the most beautiful. A series of women is brought before an audience who finds each successive one even more beautiful than the last, until Britomart displays Amoret. In response, Blandamour, believing he has Florimell, reveals the sight of the False or Snowy Florimell, the dark creation of the witch to please her love-sick son. Initially outshining the others, False Florimell fails to achieve absolute victory: "Yet all were glad there *Florimell* to see; / Yet thought that *Florimell* was not so faire as shee [Amoret]" (IV.v.14). Still, she is declared the victor: "that golden belt by doome of all / Graunted to her, as to the fayrest Dame" (IV.v.16). At this point, the girdle acquires a life of its own:

> Which being brought, about her middle small
> They thought to gird, as best it her became;
> But by no meanes they could it thereto frame.
> For euer as they fastned it, it loos'd
> And fell away, as feeling secret blame.
> Full oft about her wast she it enclos'd;
> And it as oft was from about her wast disclos'd. (IV.v.16)

Having tactile memory of its true possessor—or of virtue, since Satyrane is able to wear it—the girdle resists unchastity. Importantly, the girdle's memory is activated by emotion as it feels "secret blame." (Later I show how Spenser links erotic assent, and thus also erotic refusal, to memory.) Like the workings of memory described by rhetorical manuals, the emotions called up by memory depend on a striking image. But as a realistic forgery False Florimell is an ambiguous image. The girdle, however, readily detects her true nature.

Yet rhetorical handbooks say that memory is not dependent on the nature of the image. To aid memory, *Rhetorica Ad Herennium* advises coming up with striking images:

> We ought, then, to set up images of a kind that can adhere longest in the memory. And we shall do so if we establish likenesses as striking as possible; if we set up images that are not many or vague, but doing something; if we assign to them exceptional beauty or singular ugliness; ... or if we somehow disfigure them, as by introducing one stained with blood or soiled with mud or smeared with red paint, so that its form is more striking, or by assigning certain comic effects to our images, ... The things we easily remember when they are real we likewise remember without difficulty when they are figments, if they have been carefully delineated.[12]

Striking images can be at either end of the spectrum, either exceptionally beautiful or singularly ugly. The kinds of disfigurements described here recall some of Spenser's own images, such as Ruddymane, the babe with the bloody hands (II.ii-iii), or the striking image of the stripping of Duessa—Spenser spends three stanzas describing the singular ugliness of her "misshapen parts" (I.viii.46). Elsewhere, he uses comic effects to mock foolishness, as with Braggadochio, chosen by the False Florimell (IV.v.23–27). But while rhetorical handbooks may not distinguish between the two kinds of images, Spenser gives them moral valence. The problem is with detecting whether they are strikingly beautiful or strikingly ugly. The girdle can distinguish between the two, its tactile memory superior to the merely visual memory of the knights.

Indeed, Spenser's characters have singularly poor memories, often failing to tell true and false apart. False Florimell's failure to wear the girdle is a comic scene, inducing laughter. Upon observing the girdle's continual untying, the Squire of Dames "lowly gan to laugh, and thus to iest" (IV.v.18). However, this comedy does not lead to the correct judgment that she is a false idol. The failure of judgment (and soon of memory) occurs even when the characters are clearly presented with a striking image: "all men wondred at the vncouth sight" (IV.v.17). This comic striking image is multiplied as "many other Ladies likewise tride, / About their tender loynes to knit the same; / But it would not on none of them abide, / But when they thought it fast, eftsoones it was vntide" (IV.v.17). The Squire of Dames's laughter leads him not to identify falsehood but to dismiss the image, blaming the maker of the belt: "Fie on the man, that did it first inuent, / To shame vs all with this, *Vngirt vnblest*" (IV.v.18). Failures of judgment persist even when Amoret proves the girdle's power by succeeding in wearing it: "And hauing it about her middle set, / Did find it fit, withouten breach or let" (IV.v.19). Snatching the girdle from her, False Florimell tries again in vain. The crowd simply responds with envy, refusing to budge from their prior judgment: "Yet natheelesse to her [False Florimell], as her dew right, / It yeelded was by them, that iudged it" (IV.v.20). Unable, or unwilling, to use the girdle as mnemonic device, they misappraise the women, forgetting both the true Florimell and sexual virtue itself.

The ambiguity of the striking image's effects is emphasized by the response to Florimell. The difficulty the knights have in recognizing true Florimell highlights memory's frailty. Braggadochio's response to Florimell's thanks for defeating the knights at the wedding tournament (though it was Marinell who did so, using Braggadochio's shield) is to proclaim boastfully that he did it for the sake of False Florimell, whom he unveils before the people:

> Whom when discouered they had throughly eide,
> With great amazement they were stupefide;
> And said, that surely *Florimell* it was,
> Or if it were not *Florimell* so tride,
> That *Florimell* her selfe she then did pas.
> So feeble skill of perfect things the vulgar has. (V.iii.17)

So poor is their memory that they cannot recognize true Florimell even when she stands before them. Despite the narrator's dismissal of the vulgar, so typical of Spenser, Marinell has the same difficulty, astounded by the image: "with fast fixed eies / He gazed still vpon that snowy mayd; / Whom euer as he did the more auize, / The more to be true *Florimell* he did surmize" (V.iii.18). Compared to rival suns, the two Florimells present a "strange prodigious sight," causing Marinell to be "rapt with wonder" (V.iii.19). Marinell needs Artegall to break the spell by setting the two right beside each other "Like the true saint beside the image set":

> Streight way so soone as both together met,
> Th'enchaunted Damzell vanisht into nought:
> Her snowy substance melted as with heat,
> Ne of that goodly hew remayned ought
> But th'emptie girdle, which about her wast was wrought. (V.iii.24)

Both Florimells are striking images that make an impression upon memory. Placed side-by-side, the true erases the false, but it requires a prudential intervention. The passage presents a textual crux: the strange sight of False Florimell apparently wearing the girdle belies the properties earlier ascribed to it. If the girdle refuses any unchaste bearer, why is it located where False Florimell stood? Rebecca Yearling suggests that by Book V False Florimell has earned the girdle, proving herself faithful to Braggadochio, and so is "both chaste and unchaste at the same time, able to assume the girdle in its most limited sense, that of simple fidelity, but unfit to stand beside the image of true chastity."[13] This perhaps gives the false image too much credit. Another way to read the crux is in the context of the scene's portrayal of uncertain memory. We do not actually see False Florimell wearing the girdle but see only the empty girdle as a signifier of an absence. The characters' response to the girdle proves their judgments subject to the vagaries of memory, for even Marinell fails to recognize his own true love. In the contest over Florimell's girdle, the garment's mere sight provokes sexual lust and conflict for its possession. The audience does not even miss the true Florimell, the authentic sign of virtue. The girdle is an uncertain mnemonic device for the true Florimell, but the absent body of the False Florimell leaves behind a memorial trace in the empty space within the girdle's ring. False Florimell's hollow emptiness is aptly emblematized by the girdle's cipher, but the memory of erotic presence seems troublingly stronger than that of virtue.

Book VI's episode of Briana's love for Crudor, featuring another mnemonic piece of clothing, the mantle of hair, memory is again inextricably linked to erotic passion. The proud Crudor demands from Briana a mantle of hair before he would return her love: "Refused hath to yeeld her loue againe, / Vntill a Mantle she for him doe fynd, / With beards of Knights and locks of Ladies lynd" (VI.i.15). To fulfill his request, Briana's seneschal Maleffort challenges passing knights to exact a hair toll: the lewd custom of the castle is that "they that Ladies lockes doe shaue away, / And that knights berd for toll, which they for passage pay" (IV.i.13). The mantle's completion is always future tense, making this work-in-progress Briana's on-going memorialization of Crudor's rejection. His erotic refusal is turned into an eroticized garment as hairs, especially beards, signify sexual maturity—Maleffort mocks Calidore's youthfulness, saying, "Wilt giue thy beard, though it but little bee? (IV.i.19)—and the mingled hairs of knights and ladies suggest sexual coupling. Ironically, the mantle enacts the sexual consummation refused by Crudor, even as the memory coat inflicts pain and suffering. In both episodes, a disdainful knight rejects the desiring female's love: Crudor and Marinell's erotic refusals become acts of tyranny. Erotic refusal is the other side of tyrannous seduction that Melissa Sanchez says is difficult to resist in *The Faerie Queene*'s last books.[14] Arguably, erotic refusal makes tyrannous seduction possible. Florimell and Marinell is the mirror image of Amoret and Scudamour.

These tyrannical acts, however, are private ones, while earlier medieval analogues of the hair toll Spenser probably borrowed have public, even national, significance. With a prior literary history, the mantle of hair is a mnemonic device that asks readers to recall prior nationalist Arthurian history. *The Faerie Queene* turns that collective history into private quarrels. A similar Castle of Beards episode appears in the medieval French prose romance *Perceval le Gallois*, or *Perlesvaus*, but other analogues appear in Geoffrey of Monmouth's *History of the Kings of Britain* and in English in Thomas Malory's *Morte Darthur*. Whether or not Spenser knew *Perlesvaus*, he would have known Geoffrey.[15] At the end of Geoffrey, Arthur wages a war against Rome after rejecting their demands for tribute. Enroute to Rome, the Britons stop in Barfleur where a giant is terrorizing the land. After killing the giant, Arthur compares him to another he had killed, Retho, who "mad made himself a fur cloak from the beards of the kings whom he had slain," and who demanded Arthur's beard, promising "in his honor to sew his beard higher up the cloak than the others"; defeating Retho, Arthur "took the giant's beard and the trophy too."[16] The cloak in Geoffrey's embedded narrative is both a display of masculine prowess and a sign of tyranny. As the beards are royal, the hair toll is a claim of sovereignty, analogous to Rome's demand for tribute. As with Calidore, Arthur defeats the challenger to reassert British imperial sovereignty, and given the story's placement within Arthur's Roman wars, her independence from Rome. Malory's *Le Morte Darthur* renders it into two separate but similar episodes, both also involving the struggle for sovereignty. In one, the tyrant is king Royns of North Wales, Ireland, and the Islands, who demands Arthur's beard to complete his complement of beards of eleven kings he subdued: "For kynge Royns had purfilde a mantell with kynges berdis, and there lacked one place of the mantell," threatening to make war and have "the hede and the bearde bothe" if Arthur does not comply.[17] Arthur refuses, angering Royns, but the episode stops there. The second closely follows Geoffrey with Arthur fighting a giant in Barfflete (Barfleur), who fashions "a coote full of precious stonys, and the bordoures thereof is the berdis of fyftene kynges, and they were of the grettyst blood that dured on erthe."[18] Both incidents in Malory, like Geoffrey, are about Arthur's assertion of British sovereignty against Roman imperialism.

Malory is silent about the fate of the unusual coats, as is Spenser in Book VI. Geoffrey, however, tells us that Arthur takes as his prize both the fur cloak and the giant's beard. By imitating his defeated challenger, Arthur ironically resembles the monster, an act symbolizing the political danger of tyranny.[19] Is this potential tyranny in Arthur present in his descendant Gloriana or Queen Elizabeth, Spenser's prime addressee? There is no hint of a connection between Briana and Elizabeth, but the 1596 *Faerie Queene*'s general pessimism raises the possibility of a covert critique. By having Arthur take possession of the cloak of hair, Geoffrey's rendition raises questions of property and ownership important to both the Florimell and Briana episodes in Spenser. Just as Florimell's girdle is livery, the giant's mantle of beards marks the owner's territorial possession—what else, after all, is sovereignty? In *The Faerie Queene*, despite apparent focus on private loves and private relations, the two articles of clothing are characterized as *waif*, which fall under the monarch's purview.

Florimell's status as *waif* is first defined by Marinell's mother Cymoent. Appealing to Neptune for Florimell's release—so her son may be cured of his love-sickness—Cymoent contends that Neptune has a royal claim:

> For that a waift, the which by fortune came
> Vpon your seas, he [Proteus] clam'd as propertie:
> And yet not his, nor his in equitie,
> But yours the waift by high prerogatiue. (IV.xii.31)

Citing Nicholas Knight, A. C. Hamilton notes *waif*'s obsolete sense of "'wafted,' carried over water; but chiefly in the legal sense, property left ownerless, as Hellenore at III x 36.3. If left at sea, it reverts to the crown, here Neptune, to be granted at his pleasure."[20] Andrew Zurcher suggests that Florimel is "a kind of moveable property, or chattel," consonant with women's lack of legal identity in Tudor common law; he quotes the definition of the word from John Rastell's 1579 edition of legal terms, *An exposition of certaine difficult and obscure words*:

> Wayfe is when a theefe hath feloniously stolne goods: & beinge neerely followed, wyth hue, and crye, or els ouercharged wyth the burden or trouble of the goodes: for hys ease sake and more speedy trauaylinge, without hue & crye, flyeth away, and leaueth the goodes or any part of them behynd him &c. Then the Queens officer, or the Reeue, or Bailife to the Lorde of the manneur (wythin whose Iurisdictyon or circuit they wer eleft) that by prescryptyon, or graunt from the Queene hath the fraunchyse of wayfe: may seyse the goods so wayued to their Lordes vse, whoe may keepe them as his owne proper goods.[21]

Zurcher too argues the word links Florimell to False Florimell and to Hellenore. False Florimell is a waif because she is stolen goods: Sir Ferraugh "from Braggadocchio whilome reft / The snowy *Florimell*, whose beautie bright / Made him seeme happie for so glorious theft; / Yet was it in due triall but a wandring weft" (IV.ii.4). The sense is of something not only purloined but also worthless. Zurcher notes Spenser's preference for the spelling *weft* "for its morphological links with *waft*, suggesting a piece of lost property at the mercy of the winds and waves" and that only in the case of Cymoent's legal plea to Neptune does he use the vowel *a*.[22] But if Florimell and False Florimell can both be considered *waif/weft*, so can the stolen girdle, which is subject to hollow, windy characters like Braggadochio. *Waif*'s close association to another legal term, *waive*, points to the term's dimension of memory. Zurcher notes that "waive" is defined by Rastell as "a woman that is vtlawed, & shee is called wayue, as left out or forsaken of the law: & not an vtlawe as a man is: ... for that cause they cannot be said out of the lawe in so much as they neuer were within it."[23] While it is true, as Zurcher states, that

Florimell is not proscribed, yet lying in Proteus' dungeon she is forsaken and forgotten. As a purloined good, Florimell is both *waif* and *waive*. Memory of her rightful belonging is forgotten by the community, requiring memory instead to inhere in an object like the girdle.

What has not been noted, however, is that Spenser also uses the term *waif* to describe the hair taken by Maleffort. The description of what happens to the hair in Calidore's confrontation with Maleffort interestingly parallels Rastell's definition of *waif* in his handbook of legal terms. Calidore left the squire

> For to pursue that villaine, which had reft
> That piteous spoile by so iniurious theft.
> Whom ouertaking, loude to him he cryde;
> Leaue faytor quickely that misgotten weft
> To him, that hath it better iustifyde. (VI.i.18)

The hair is "misgotten weft" because it is stolen, and Calidore pursues Maleffort in an attempt to make him abandon the *waif/weft*. While in Florimell's case, the proper owner is the sovereign, Neptune, who can reassign the property, here the proper owner is the Squire, a private person. Calidore displays his courtesy by not demanding a fee for his part in the stolen hair's return or in getting Crudor to love Briana: refusing Briana's offer of sovereignty of the castle, he "would not retaine / Nor land nor fee, for hyre of his good deede" (VI.i.47) in restoring the lady to the Squire. Calidore behaves better than Geoffrey's Arthur, graciously declining compensation. As with Florimell, restoration of the stolen goods to their rightful owners leads to the proper outcome for erotic passions: marriage. Crudor has to be converted from a thief of stolen goods (though at a remove from the violent act, he is the originator of the mantle) into a lover.

Briana and Crudor's relation thus parallels that of Florimell and Marinell. Marinell is not only disdainful of love, he is also the keeper of ownerless property, guarding the strand onto which his grandfather the god Nereus throws up treasures lost at sea: Nereus

> his heaped waues he did commaund,
> Out of their hollow bosome forth to throw
> All the huge threasure, which the sea below
> Had in his greedy gulfe deuoured deepe,
> And him enriched through the ouerthrow
> And wreckes of many wretches, which did weep,
> And often wayle their wealth, which he from them did keep. (III.iv.22)

A kind of thief, Marinell keeps lost property, wafted by the waves, from their original owners. While Spenser would only come to use the term in the 1596 *Faerie Queene*, the treasure Marinell guards are also *waft/weft*, though the true owners are not forgotten as they clamor for the return of their property. In another kind of forgetting, the *waft/weft* prevents Marinell from engaging his affections. His dangerous erotic refusal leads to his wounding by Britomart. Incidentally, the story of Florimell and Marinell is itself a *waft/weft* as it is dispersed through a number of cantos of several books. Both Marinell and Crudor are like the giant of Geoffrey's story, but eventually reformed.

Spenser underlines memory's importance for binding social relations in Book IV by showing its opposite: memory's part in undoing social bonds. At the start of Book IV Duessa appears accompanied by Ate, the enemy of friendship and the "mother of debate" (IV.i.19). Discord's close association with the workings of memory is allegorized in the description of Ate's house. If the House of Alma contains histories of Britain and Faeryland, eagerly poured over by Arthur and Redcrosse, the house of Ate, as mentioned, is also filled with memories, with "ragged monuments of times forepast" (IV.i.21). Blandamour and Paridell's fight over False Florimell is based on memory: "she [Ate] prickt him [Paridell] forth, / Now with remembrance of those spightfull speaches, / Now with opinion of his owne more worth, / Now with recounting of like former breaches / Made in their friendship" (IV.ii.12). The parisons underline how memory spurs emotion to goad Paridell into challenging Blandamour. Rhetorical handbooks teach that striking images raise passions to creating lasting memories; Ate uses memories to raise passions that lead to action. In a reversal of the girdle, Ate, using memories, loosens passions to unbind friendship.

If both of Spenser's episodes feature ownerless objects, in which memory sometimes inheres and sometimes not, the problem of memory may have to do with absent bodies. The absent female body in the contest over Florimell's girdle points to the acute problems of memory and of judgment caused by over-stimulated passions. In Book V, the presence of beards marks the absent male body. Absent male (and female) bodies in turn signal an over-excess of memory and passion. The problem of the absent male body extends later into Book V, when Artegall goes missing in action, imprisoned by Radigund.

Yet, the absent body can point to alternate means of accessing memory to bring about proper erotic passion. From the start, Spenser is suspicious of the image. If in the arts of memory, the striking image can be either beautiful or ugly, Spenser shows through several characters, such as Duessa, how beauty and ugliness are closely allied or even the same thing. In the story of Florimell and Marinell, Spenser tries to do away with the image. Despite the visual nature of the girdle as a mnemonic device, it is not the girdle that leads Marinell finally to love Florimell. Time and again characters ignore the girdle's visual sign. Rather, Marinell is finally guided to Florimell by her voice lamenting her "grieffe" (IV.xii.5), her separation from Marinell.[24] Hearing this voice leads him to pity and from pity to love: "His stubborne hart, that neuer felt misfare / Was toucht with soft remorse and pitty rare" (IV.xii.12).

Florimell's voice, not her image, excites his memory. Returning home, Marinell remembers the voice: "He gan record the lamentable stowre, / In which his wretched loue lay day and night, / ... / The thought whereof empierst his hart so deepe" (IV.xii.19). Marinell's resulting disease comes from the affliction of memory created by erotic passion: "he did languish of some inward thought, / The which afflicted his engrieued mind" (IV.xii.25). However, the impetus for the passion and memory is not the striking image but the voice. Tellingly, in this section, Marinell's visit to Proteus' hall for the marriage of the Thames and the Medway, Spenser turns to a different poetic mode. He leaves off, at least temporarily, creating striking images, moving instead to the catalogue of rivers. He begins the catalogue by invoking Clio, the muse of history, "thou sacred imp of *Ioue* / The nourpling of Dame *Memorie* his deare" (IV.xi.10). This is not just a reaffirmation of the power of the poetic voice; the turn to naming offers a sober, even banal, account of the past.

In the 1596 *Faerie Queene*, Spenser's fears of being forgotten as a poet become far more acute. Memory is pictured as ruined monuments; Spenser inserts a long digression on Chaucer, continuing the unfinished *Squire's Tale* as an attempt at poetic restoration (IV.ii). While the 1590 *Faerie Queene* is an ambitious national epic undergirded by historical memory, the 1596 *Faerie Queene* focuses on private memories as questions of sovereignty in earlier texts like Geoffrey become issues of private ownership. The 1596 *Faerie Queene* and later poems evince a much less sanguine view of the possibilities for national renewal and a far more deep-seated disillusionment with court. Richard Helgerson identifies in Books V and VI the loss of a heroic age and therefore heroic poetry, while David Miller sees a withdrawal that reveals Spenser's loss of faith in poetry; Mihoko Suzuki sees in Radigund's "subversion of Britomart" Spenser's "disillusionment with the Elizabethan order," while others like Christopher Highley notes Spenser's disagreement with Elizabeth's Irish policies.[25] The 1596 *Colin Clouts Come Home Againe* uses the shepherd's persona to critique Elizabeth's court. In *Faerie Queene* VI, Colin appears in Canto x, where his pastoral song calling up the Graces' dance represents nostalgia for an idealized past. Notably, Calidore blunders into the scene, causing the vision of the Graces, along with Colin's love, to vanish into thin air, leaving an empty open green, reminiscent of the girdle's cipher (VI.x.18), to suggest the fragility also of private memory.

The last books all have their virtues reinstated, but they are fragile. Book IV ends with Marinell reunited with Florimell, but not yet espoused. Spenser defers their marriage to the middle of Book V, leaving Marinell close to death: "his limbs could not his bodie beare" (IV.xii.35). His earlier refusal of erotic love having taken a heavy toll, he is so frail he almost becomes another one of Spenser's absent bodies. Books V and VI end just as inconclusively. Forced to return after only partially reforming Ireland, Artegall is beset at court by two hags, Envie and Detraction, who accuse him of cruelty and tyranny. They set on him the Blatant Beast that "At him began aloud to barke and bay, / With bitter rage and fell contention" (V.xii.41). In the Legend of Justice, communal bonds are broken. By the end of Book VI, Calidore, the Knight of Courtesy, is only able to subdue the Blatant Beast temporarily. After Calidore, the Beast "broke his yron chaine, / And got into the world at liberty againe" (VI.xii.38), never again to be mastered: "Ne euer could by any more be brought / Into like bands, ne maystred any more: / ... / Yet none of them could euer bring him into band" (VI.xii.39). The fragility of Florimell's girdle yet has the power of tactile memory to enact erotic refusal, but no band can be found to control the negative emotions released by the Blatant Beast.

The problem of judgment due to faulty memory and misdirected erotic passion in the two episodes of mnemonic and erotic garments—Florimell's girdle and Briana's mantle of hair—is repeated on a larger scale in the last three books' major episodes. Memory's fragility stems from the difficulty of managing the passions. While the arts of memory suggest the use of the striking image for arousing passions to fix memory, Spenser's examination of the process suggests the myriad ways both memory and erotic passions can be misused, especially when they depend on the striking image.

Notes

1. Edmund Spenser, *The Faerie Queene*, ed. A. C. Hamilton, rev. Hiroshi Yamashita and Toshiyuki Suzuki, rev. 2nd ed. (Harlow and London: Pearson Longman, 2001, 2007). All citations to *The Faerie Queene* are from this edition and given parenthetically.
2. Rebeca Helfer, *Spenser's Ruins and the Art of Recollection* (Toronto: University of Toronto Press, 2012).
3. For clothing as forms of memory, see Ann Rosalind Jones and Peter Stallybrass, *Renaissance Clothing and the Materials of Memory* (Cambridge: Cambridge University Press, 2000). For memory in early modern literature, see Andrew Hiscock, *Reading Memory in Early Modern Literature* (Cambridge: Cambridge University Press, 2011).
4. [Cicero], *Rhetorica Ad Herennium*, trans. Harry Caplan, Loeb Classical Library (Cambridge: Harvard University Press, 1968), III.xxii.35, 219.
5. Frances A. Yates, *The Art of Memory* (Chicago: University of Chicago Press, 1966), 10.
6. Mary Carruthers, *The Book of Memory: A Study of Memory in Medieval Culture*, 2nd ed. (Cambridge: Cambridge University Press, 1990, 2008), 85.
7. John Willis, *Mnemonica, or The Art of Memory Drained out of the Pure Foundations of Art & Nature Digested into Three Books. Also a Physical Treatise of Cherishing Natural Memory; Diligently Collected out of Divers Learned Mens Writings* (1661), 140–41.
8. William Perkins, *The Arte of Prophecying: or A Treatise Concerning the Sacred and Onely True Manner and Methode of Preaching* (London, 1607), 130, sig. I6v.
9. John Rainolds, *Th'overthrow of Stage-Playes* (London, 1599), 97, sig. N3.
10. Lina Perkins Wilder, *Shakespeare's Memory Theatre: Recollection, Properties, and Character* (Cambridge: Cambridge University Press 2010), 3.
11. Thomas P. Roche, Jr., *'The Kindly Flame': A Study of the Third and Fourth Books of Spenser's 'Faerie Queene'* (Princeton: Princeton University Press,

206   Su Fang Ng

1964); Pamela J. Benson, "Florimell at Sea: The Action of Grace in *Faerie Queene*, Book III," *Spenser Studies* 6 (1986): 83–94.
12. *Rhetorica Ad Herennium*, III.xxii.37, 221.
13. Rebecca Yearling, "Florimell's Girdle: Reconfiguring Chastity in *The Faerie Queene*," *Spenser Studies* 20 (2005): 137–44 [140].
14. Melissa E. Sanchez, *Erotic Subjects: The Sexuality of Politics in Early Modern English Literature* (Oxford: Oxford University Press, 2011), 57–85.
15. For Spenser's borrowing from Old French, see Edgar A. Hall, "Spenser and Two Old French Grail Romances," *PMLA* 28.4 (1913): 539–54.
16. Geoffrey of Monmouth, *The History of the Kings of Britain*, trans. Lewis Thorpe (London: Penguin, 1966), 240.
17. *The Works of Sir Thomas Malory*, ed. Eugène Vinaver, 2nd ed., 3 vols (Oxford: Clarendon Press, 1967), 1:54.
18. Malory, *Works*, 1: 201.
19. Geraldine Heng notes that beardless Latins were remarked upon in the Levant while in "Europe, the beard also circulated as a symbol of racial-religious difference," and thus Arthur defends Christian civilization from Muslim (*The Empire of Magic: Medieval Romance and the Politics of Cultural Fantasy* [New York: Columbia University Press, 2003], 38).
20. *Faerie Queene*, ed. Hamilton, 506 n. IV.xii.31; Nicholas W. Knight, "The Narrative Unity of Book V of *The Faerie Queene*: 'That Part of Justice which is Equity,'" *Review of English Studies* 21 (1970): 267–94.
21. John Rastell, *An Exposition of Certaine Difficult and Obscure Words, and Termes of the Lawes of this Realme, Newly Set Foorth and Augmented, both in French and English, for the Helpe of such Younge Students as Are Desirous to Attaine the Knowledge of the Same* (London, 1579), f. 195r-195v; quoted in Andrew Zurcher, *Spenser's Legal Language: Law and Poetry in Early Modern England* (Cambridge: D. S. Brewer, 2007), 103.
22. Zurcher, *Spenser's Legal Language*, 103.
23. Rastell, f. 196r-196v; cited in Zurcher, 103 n.34.
24. For Spenser's relation to Neoplatonic debates about whether hearing or sight is the superior sense in apprehending beauty, see David Frantz, "The Union of Florimell and Marinell: The Triumph of Hearing," *Spenser Studies* 6 (1985): 115–27.
25. Richard Helgerson, *Self-Crowned Laureates: Spenser, Jonson, Milton and the Literary System* (Berkeley: University of California Press, 1983), 91; David L. Miller, "Spenser's Vocation, Spenser's Career," *ELH* 50 (1983): 215–16; Mihoko Suzuki, *Metamorphoses of Helen: Authority, Difference, and the Epic* (Ithaca: Cornell University Press, 1989), 178; Christopher Highley, *Shakespeare, Spenser, and the Crisis in Ireland* (Cambridge: Cambridge University Press, 1997), 13–39.

15 "Despisèd straight"
Shakespeare's Observation of Semantic Memory Bias

Ian F. MacInnes

The number of early modern works devoted to memorization and mnemonics suggests how important the topic of memory was at the time. These works tend to foreground the epistemology of memory (its accuracy, lack of bias, and thus its ability to lead to a justified true belief) because they are interested in memory as a deliberate process of storage and recollection: what were called the "memory arts." To some extent, modern scholarship on Shakespeare's *Sonnets* has naturally tended to replicate the early modern focus on the epistemology of commemoration. Scholars interested in memory have concentrated on the poems devoted to the young man, which explicitly invoke memory, and on the metaphorical models that suggest the adequacy or inadequacy of memory. Few focus on the process of recollection itself, and fewer still on the ways that emotions such as erotic desire shape remembrance. Further, the sonnets devoted to the dark lady, which do not explicitly invoke memory, have been largely disregarded by those writing on these issues. Modern psychology, however, offers a way of approaching issues of remembrance in the dark lady sonnets by distinguishing between the episodic or autobiographical memory so common in the poems to the young man and the more subtle and pervasive semantic memory that underlies basic elements of knowledge, and most crucially, judgment. In the course of the *Sonnets*, the speaker moves from an obsession with the adequacy of memory as a record of the beloved toward a recognition of memory as a deeply biased form of knowledge affected by and contingent upon erotic desire.

The popularity of books on memory in the latter part of the sixteenth century demonstrates how fascinated early moderns were with the topic. By the time of Shakespeare's death there were at least five major works available, including a few in Latin and some translations of European works.[1] Without exception these works explain memory in simple Aristotelian terms. As Gratarolo puts it in the *Castel of Memorie* (English 1562):

> Memorye is a retayning of the Images or symilitudes first perceyued of the soule, the which neuertheless is vnprofitable except it both retayne all, and also restore theym in the same order wherein it conveyued theym. And it belongeth not to present thinges nor thinges to come, but onlye to thynges past, as Aristotle saith.[2]

Aristotle's much-repeated insistence that memory applies only to the past might seem odd (who would claim to remember the future?), but it serves to distinguish memory from other similar mental agencies, such as the imagination. It also characterizes memory as the usually deliberate recollection of past experience inscribed on the brain: it "traces in something like an outline of the thing perceived, in the same way people mark designs into things with rings."[3] Perhaps because this version of memory is so clearly a conscious act, early modern works are primarily concerned with the memory "arts," or ways of improving deliberate recollection, including mnemonics. Their results were as astonishing then as now, and their work still fuels the somewhat arcane modern hobby of memory competitions. But this approach focuses on the faithfulness of the memory to the item to be remembered and the availability of that memory. As we shall see in the discussion of the dark lady, below, it tends to disregard implicit and unconscious forms of memory on the one hand and the potential for desire to destabilize and bias memory on the other.

Early modern memory texts are also concerned primarily with verbal or visual memory. In part this emphasis derives from Aristotle, who held that it is not possible to think without an image.[4] The huge popularity of emblems (and emblem books) in the sixteenth-century may also play a role. Scholars like William Engel have pointed out "the fundamentally mnemonic quality of emblems,"[5] but his formula works equally well in reverse: if emblems are mnemonic then memory is emblematic. Because visual images were often considered to be sources of emotion in early modern materialist psychology, emotion was likewise recognized to have an important role in memory. In *The Passions of the Minde in Generall*, for example, Thomas Wright echoes claims that crop up throughout Shakespeare's *Sonnets* when he says that passions can be provoked both by sense and memory:

> To our imagination commeth by sense or memory, some object to be known, convenient or disconvenient to Nature, the which being known (for Ignoti nulla cupido) in the imagination which resideth in the former part of the braine, (as we prove) when we imagine any thing, presently the pure spirit, flocke from the brayne, by certain secret channels to the heart.[6]

For the Renaissance memory arts, however, emotions were primarily represented as catalysts or fixatives in the conscious process. Readers were encouraged to create mnemonics using images associated with strong emotion, usually erotic desire.[7] For example, Peter of Ravenna (1448–1508) advised using images of beautiful women, although some of his readers worried about such libidinous objects. But the overall thrust of the memory arts is against embodiment: they are designed to take memory away from "the dirt added to thoughts by the body."[8] The few writers who persistently connected emotion to memory were, like Thomas Wright, interested primarily in the passions rather than in memory itself. Overall, therefore, memory as a subject in the early modern period is dominated by an Aristotelian conscious commemoration.

Modern scholarship on memory in Shakespeare's *Sonnets* has tended to reflect early modern texts' preoccupation with commemoration, particularly by focusing exclusively on the sonnets directed to the young man (1–126). The theme of conscious memory is certainly ubiquitous in these poems. Memory is clearly the key to smaller units within the collection, such as the procreation sonnets, and it underpins some of the most famous and powerful expressions of the *Sonnets*, from "the living record of your memory" (55.8) to "remembrance of things past" (30.2), so easily and famously called upon when Moncrieff reached for a title for the first English translation of Proust's *À la Recherche du Temps Perdu*.[9] No introduction to an edition is complete without a reference to memory in the young man sonnets, and it is an important topic for any comprehensive collection on the *Sonnets*. In Schoenbaum's fine *Companion to Shakespeare's Sonnets*, both essays in the memory section, by Amanda Watson and Garret Sullivan, focus on the sonnets to the young man. As Watson explains, these poems are concerned primarily with commemoration, whether visual or poetic.[10] The object of commemoration is either the young man himself or the feelings the young man generates in the poet. Both Watson and Sullivan call attention to the number of different ways that the poems describe memory. For Watson these are "commemorative strategies," or "competing models for the way we retain and collect ideas."[11] The models are frequently metaphorical; memory is likened to perfume (Sonnets 5 and 6), a law court (30), home maintenance (13), gardening (15), a pilgrimage (27), dreaming (43), etc.

Many of these models are explicitly epistemological: the poet is concerned with the quality and durability of memories of the young man, hence their ability to ground true beliefs about him. The memory-as-perfume model, for example, foregrounds a contrast between appearance and essence.[12] Overall, "the sonnets seem more concerned with the way in which any memorial must capture the beloved approximately rather than fully."[13] Because these poems emphasize the memorial process itself, the opposite of remembering is not mis-remembering, but simply forgetting. The poet acknowledges that memory might be approximate, but the real battle is to maintain memory in the face of forgetfulness and the erasures of time. This is why Sullivan argues that "self-forgetting" in the procreation sonnets is the young man's counter to the work of the poet, a paradoxical alternate form of selfhood.[14] All of this focus on the memorializing process and on the recollection of a particular object fits perfectly into the dominant discourse on memory in the early modern period. Like the formal memory arts, the young man sonnets and the scholarship they have generated focus on memory as the deliberate record of personal experience.

There appear to be good reasons why the dark lady poems (Sonnets 127–52) are absent from virtually all discussions of memory in the *Sonnets*.

In a footnote, Sullivan says, "It should be noted that memory is a much greater preoccupation for the young man sonnets than it is of those devoted to the dark lady."[15] This is an understatement, at least in terms of explicit references. The word "memory" never occurs in the poems to the dark lady. Nor does "remembrance," "remember," or "recall." These sonnets, though, should be ideal ground for an interest in memory. Memory is a greater preoccupation for the young man sonnets only if you're looking for a particular kind of memory. If we look for a different sort, we can find it in the erotic discourse. Lina Bolzoni, for example, argues that as lovesickness was treated as the result of an image becoming literally stuck in the brain, erotic love closely relates to memory for the early moderns. She notes that medicines for love and for memory were similar.[16] Bolzoni also shows that the process can be reversed by authors who recommend including beautiful women or sexual images in systems designed to improve memory.[17] The speaker's love for the dark lady is certainly erotic and repeatedly described in terms familiar from treatises of lovesickness. For instance, the speaker of Sonnet 147 even calls his love "a feaver longing still, / For that which longer nurseth the disease" (ll. 1–2). On balance, the dark lady sonnets are far more explicitly erotic than those devoted to the young man. The dark lady sonnets are equally concerned with epistemological questions: what constitutes a justified true belief where the dark lady is concerned? What can the poet truly know about their relationship? All of this suggests that memory ought to be an issue in these poems.

If we approach memory slightly differently, however, we can find an explanation for this apparent silence on the question of memory. Since the work of Tulving and Donaldson in the early 1970s, modern cognitive psychology has separated conscious memory into two different categories. The first is episodic memory (sometimes called autobiographical). Episodic memory consists of the memory of times, places, people, and emotions we have personally experienced. It is the kind of memory that we still most commonly imagine when we speak of "remembering," and it is the kind of memory the sonnets to the young man most frequently depict. In Sonnet 30, for example, when the poet summons "to the sessions of sweet silent thought / ... remembrance of things past," those 'things' are "old woes," "precious friends," "greevances," and "vannisht sight[s]." All of these are autobiographical, items the speaker has personally experienced and stored away to be summoned and reconsidered. Episodic memory is not always individual or purely subjective. When we share our memories with a larger group, they become what Maurice Halbwachs called "collective memory," but this kind of memory is still episodic.

The second kind of memory is semantic (sometimes called generic). Our semantic memory involves meanings, understandings, and concepts. Remembering that 7 x 8 is 56 (semantic) is not the same as remembering learning one's multiplication tables from Miss Chumakov (episodic). These two forms of recall also *feel* different. In daily life neither we nor the early moderns often use the word "memory" to describe semantic recollection because we tend to reserve the word for events in our past (our episodic memory). We don't think of ourselves as "remembering" that sugar is sweet even if we experienced an event that made that fact known to us; we just "know" it is. Sometimes episodic and semantic memory can be juxtaposed to humorous or narrative effect. The third Indiana Jones movie, for example, includes a scene in which the hero realizes whom he is facing. "Nazis!" he says "I hate these guys!" The line gets its effect from the fact that the vast majority of the audience despises Nazis from semantic memory (we no longer need to actually remember their despicable deeds in order to "know" they are bad), but the character hates them from episodic memory, because he faced them personally in the first movie of the series. The war has not occurred, the incipient Holocaust is not yet known, and yet our sterling hero manages to find himself on the right side. Semantic memory is both subtle and pervasive, as it determines our attitudes toward things irrespective of our personal autobiographical memory, just as it does for the speaker of Shakespeare's *Sonnets* when he considers the dark lady.

Tulving suggested that we ought to consider semantic memory as a separate category not just because the information contained in it is qualitatively different but because it is cognitively different. To begin with, semantic memories seem to be stored in a different area of the brain. A number of studies of people suffering from different forms of amnesia have supported this idea. In one famous case described by Daniel Schacter, a man, "Gene," survived a motorcycle accident that damaged some of his frontal lobe. Gene cannot recall any specific *event* from his past, even when provided with detailed cues, yet at the same time he recalls many facts of his past, including for example the names of his coworkers, his place of employment, etc. Schacter argues that it is as though Gene has the kind of knowledge about himself that we have about other people's lives, and he recalls his life as if it were lived by another, without all the personal experience. His semantic memories are intact, but his episodic memories are gone.[18] Tulving also argues that semantic and episodic memory operate on different principles and are thus part of two distinct "memory systems."[19] He uses the word "semantic" to describe factual and conceptual memory because he believes the system relies on logical connections between memory "nodes," which are arranged hierarchically in a network that minimizes redundancy. Calling upon a particular memory node activates logically connected nodes, thus creating whole concepts and explaining the existence of stored knowledge. As we will see in the discussion of the dark lady sonnets below, the interconnected quality of semantic memory means that any bias in such memory can profoundly trouble our most basic assessment of other people.

Much work in cognitive psychology over the years has focused on the actual nature of the semantic network, and psychologists who seek to explain the way we connect and store conceptual knowledge have proposed a variety of models that are less simplistic and hierarchical than Tulving's nodes. The concept of mental "schema," for example, offers a way of explaining how general knowledge about the world combines with factual knowledge about specific items or events to create larger categories of knowing. Schemata are large packets of simultaneously activated memory items that together represent everything from basic concepts through complex situations and actions. Schemata also explain semantic memory as an ongoing process rather than a set of stored items. In a standard textbook account that curiously echoes the thought process of Shakespeare's speaker in the dark lady sonnets, schemata "are not simply called up from memory and passively processed. Instead, people are thought to be constantly assessing and evaluating the fit between their current situation and a number of relevant schemata and subschemata."[20] Finally, although we create schemata by progressively reinforcing memories, we experience them simply as knowledge, a defining feature of semantic memory in general. This feature of semantic memory, that it feels more like "knowing" than "remembering," helps explain how it can sometimes pass unnoticed.

Yet when we lay down conceptual knowledge, we often clearly understand this process as a memorial act, and so did the early moderns. Early modern texts describing the memory arts aimed more often at the recall of factual or conceptual knowledge than the recall of autobiographical details.[21] When early modern writers refer to issues related to semantic memory, however, they tend to use terms like "judgment" rather than memory. Technically, judgment was usually represented as a separate mental category but in fact was strongly associated with memory. Mary Carruthers points out that Aristotle believed memory to be crucial in creating moral judgment through a series of repeated memories.[22] She also traces how Thomas Aquinas and others connected the concept of prudence (a form of judgment), with the memory:

> Memoria was also an integral part of the virtue of prudence, that which makes moral judgment possible. Training the memory was much more than a matter of providing oneself with the means to compose and converse intelligently when books were not readily to hand, for it was in trained memory that one built character, judgment, citizenship, and piety.[23]

Strictly speaking, Aristotle, Aquinas, and others are not describing what we would call "semantic memory," although the effects are similar. For these thinkers, what we call semantic memory was the result of accumulated episodic memories.

Occasionally, the broad topic of judgment appears in Shakespeare's sonnets to the young man, although the focus remains firmly on episodic, and explicitly erotic, memory. A poem about absence such as Sonnet 113, for example, takes the traditional Petrarchan trope in which the lover perceives his absent love object imprinted on the landscape around him and turns it into an examination of truth:

> that which governes me to goe about
> Doth part his function and is partly blind,
> ...
> For if it see the rud'st or gentlest sight,
> The most sweet-favour or deformedst creature,
> The mountain, or the sea, the day, or night:
> The Croe, or Dove, it shapes them to your feature. (ll. 2–8)

The problem, the speaker says, is that he is "Incapable of more, replete with you." The inward memory of the young man has filled up and thus exhausted his ability to consider new images of new things. This is certainly a way of describing erotic obsession as a memory issue. But it appears to be at least partly an issue of semantic judgment, too. It's not just that he cannot create new images. He cannot separate things that ought by judgment be separated: the rude and the gentle, the sweetly favored and the deformed, the crow and the dove. The mental error described is one covered by Wright in his chapter entitled "Passions Blinde the Judgment":

> Hee that once apprehendeth the pleasure of the passion, ordinarily followeth it, and the passion increaseth the imagination thereof, and the stronge imagination rendreth the passion more vehement ... whereupon ensueth, that false imagination corrupteth the understanding, making it believe that thinges are better than they are in very deed ... . The false representation breedeth a false conceit in the minde ... Men, in great paine, or exceeeding pleasure, can scarce speake, see, heare, or think of anything, which concerneth not their passion.[24]

Ultimately, however, this poem is characteristic of the young man poems in its level of comfort with errors in judgment. Because the error concerns the world rather than the young man, the poet sees it mostly as a confirmation of his ability to commemorate his beloved. The memories at issue are themselves entirely episodic. It is direct memory of the young man himself that prevents him from forming a new memory of a mountain or a dove, for example. The final line achieves its effect by redefining truth: "My most true mind thus maketh mine [eye] untrue." His eye is "untrue" because it is inaccurate; his mind is "true" because it is faithful to his beloved. True minds, in the young man sequence, trump everything. As in Sonnet 116, they admit no "impediment." The poem thus rests contentedly on the superiority of erotic passion to judgment.

In the sonnets to the dark lady, on the other hand, the triumph of erotic passion over judgment becomes not a source of comfort but a huge anxiety. The topic dominates these poems as much as episodic memory dominates the poems to the young man. There are signs throughout these poems that judgment specifically contrasts semantic memory with episodic or autobiographical memory.[25] The sense of epistemological crisis is consistent, but the speaker is no longer simply questioning the power of love or poetry to commemorate the beloved. Instead he questions his own ability to understand truth itself as it concerns the beloved. In the three sonnets beginning with 130, for example, he skips from aggressively asserting the truth of his judgment to doubting his judgment completely. Sonnet 130 spends most of its energy delineating the difference between the dark lady and the Petrarchan ideal that the poet had previously assigned, usually not ironically, to the young man. The tone throughout is one of honesty, truth, and clear judgment: separating the real from the ideal. Yet all the statements are negative or conditional: "nothing like," "I never saw," "If haires be wiers," etc. The final couplet, "And yet by heaven I think my love as rare / As any she beli'd with false compare," looks entirely secure in its attack on Petrarchan poetry. Yet the phrase "I think" hovers insecurely in the penultimate line, filling out the meter but also suggesting that his judgment is still ultimately subjective and thus perhaps not really judgment at all. In 131, he takes on subjectivity more explicitly.

> And to be sure that is not false I sweare
> A thousand grones, but thinking on thy face,
> One on anothers necke, do witnesse beare
> Thy blacke is fairest in my judgements place.
> In nothing art thou blacke save in thy deeds,
> And thence this slaunder, as I thinke, proceeds. (ll. 9–14)

The legal language so common in the *Sonnets* here intensifies the potential conflict. The poem does not simply assert the subjective nature of erotic desire. The sarcastic weight of the last line tends to overshadow something that has actually been rendered problematic all along. The object of the instrumental "to be sure" is unclear. Is he reassuring himself? And the alteration of word order that places "sweare" at the end of the line makes it lean forward (ungrammatically) as though the thousand groans are part of his swearing rather than evidence supporting it. "Thinking on thy face" clearly refers to episodic memory, but it is immediately paired with the impossibility of "thy blacke is fairest in my judgements place." If this statement were about traditionally subjective love, one might expect "heart" rather than "judgment." A judgment that says black is fair is not really judgment at all, and the fact that the poet knows the dark lady is both black in complexion and black in deed suggests that his judgment is at least contradictory. The phrase "in my judgement's place" makes a more profound suggestion. "Place" finishes the meter of the line, but it also means that the oxymoronic "black is fairest" has taken the place of his judgment rather than simply being an error. These kinds of inconsistencies pervade the dark lady poems.

By Sonnet 132 he is swearing with equal contradiction that "beauty her selfe is blacke" (l. 13).

If the poet's judgment had simply been corrupted or altered by the recollected image of the dark lady, the poems might argue for a simple and permanent imbalance in which knowledge derived from episodic memory (e.g., "thinking on thy face" in Sonnet 131) trumps knowledge derived from semantic memory (beauty is not black). But the conflict between these two forms of knowledge remains alive throughout the sequence. Sonnet 148 makes the speaker's conflict clear:

> O me! what eyes hath love put in my head,
> Which have no correspondence with true sight;
> Or, if they have, where is my judgment fled,
> That censures falsely what they see aright?
> If that be faire whereon my false eyes dote,
> What meanes the world to say it is not so?
> If it be not, then love doth well denote
> Loves eye is not so true as all mens: no. (ll. 1–8)

The poem appears to explain the influence of erotic passion on the poet's assessment of the dark lady, but the explanation remains a series of questions in which the poet both knows and does not know that the dark lady is not "fair." The poem begins by casting doubt on the phantasm of autobiographical memory (the poem is retrospective, not addressed to a present love object) that has "no correspondence with true sight." But the "Or" in the third line introduces immediate doubt. Perhaps his eyes *have* laid down a correct image, and it is his judgment itself that is false ("censures" in line 4 almost certainly is being used neutrally [*OED* 3]). This possibility leads the speaker into a hypothesis that collapses almost immediately. "If that be faire" posits that he is seeing truly, but he finishes the line by calling his eyes "false" and using "dote," both of which imply that his vision has been flawed. The only solution is to call upon "the world," which in line 6 agrees with the idea that his eyes are false, but the whole hypothesis is phrased as an unanswered question. The world and his overall assessment agree because both rely on conceptual knowledge of beauty. Both conform to the semantic memory of beauty. That judgment, though, contrasts with the speaker's episodic memory. In the grip of a memory contaminated by erotic passion, he is no longer sure whether semantic knowledge is true.

The culprit behind the poet's epistemological crisis in the dark lady sonnets, of course, is erotic love, the very thing so frequently connected with memory by early modern memory arts in general. The sonnet among those to the dark lady that is most directly concerned with the relationship between memory and erotic desire is Sonnet 129. This poem stands apart from all the others, even the highly philosophical 144, in its rigorous avoidance of personal detail. Instead, the poet appears to be working toward a stable semantic memory that would explain his difficulties. Helen Vendler's brief analysis of this poem in her critical edition of the *Sonnets* explains beautifully how the poem ultimately depicts a "change of heart."[26] It certainly begins with impartial authority: "The expence of Spirit in a waste of shame / Is lust in action." Both judgment and censure are clear. Only the highly charged words suggest subjectivity. It is certainly possible that the poet's personal experiences have led him to this claim (the surrounding poems certainly suggest as much), but he is trying to speak from a more general perspective. The words "in action," however, lead the poet to make a series of less and less coherent judgments because they require him to explain lust as a temporal process (with a before, during, and after) and one that is subject to retrospective acts of memory.

> TH'expence of Spirit in a waste of shame
> Is lust in action, and till action, lust
> Is perjurd, murdrous, blouddy full of blame,
> Sauage, extreame, rude, cruell, not to trust,
> Injoyd no sooner but dispised straight,
> Past reason hunted, and no sooner had
> Past reason hated as a swollowed bayt,
> On purpose layd to make the taker mad.
> Made In pursut and in possession so,
> Had, having, and in quest, to have extreame,
> A blisse in proofe and provd [a] very wo,
> Before a ioy proposd behind a dreame,
> All this the world well knowes yet none knowes well,
> To shun the heaven that leads men to this hell. (129)

The process of retrospection seems initially to underline the initial claim. What is a "shame" and "expense" in action is equally bad leading up to that action: "perjurd, murdrous, blouddy, full of blame, / Savage, extreame, rude, cruell, not to trust." But the next line starts to undercut what Vendler calls the poem's "axis of similarity": lust is "Injoyed no sooner but dispised straight." At first, this looks very much like the process Wright describes in his chapter on the relationship between passion and judgment:

> I never knew any man troubled with a vehement passion of hatred, ire, or love, who would not bring many reasons, to confirme his purpose, although after he had performed his pleasure, and the tempestuous passion was past, he condemned himself, and thought his fact vitious, and his reasons frivolous.[27]

In Wright's view, judgment effectively returns once a passion has passed, and man's self-condemnation is valid. Sonnet 129, however, casts doubt on the very possibility of a clear judgment. The word "injoyed," which by itself could be fairly neutral, becomes entirely positive when contrasted with "dispised" and suggests that all judgment of lust might depend on one's perspective. Is it to be enjoyed or despised? The speaker scrambles to give an objective evaluation that will take both into account and tries to reconcile the attitudes surrounding the enjoyment: "Past reason hunted; and no sooner had, / Past reason hated, as a swallowed bayt, / On purpose layd to make the taker mad." Rather than clarifying matters, this evaluation casts all in doubt, because the poet himself is not separate from the process he is evaluating. If attitudes toward remembered lust are "past reason," then all of the poet's judgments are flawed, including the censure that begins the poem. Because the evaluation of lust is a matter of semantic memory, this discovery is not just true of the speaker. The poem's first claim "Th'expence of spirit in a waste of shame / Is lust in action" is so conventional that it could easily be imagined as the motto for a Renaissance emblem. By suggesting that this claim is itself clouded by passion, Shakespeare is undermining the status of semantic memory itself. He is suggesting that the emotions surrounding the experience of erotic love are so powerful that they permanently bias any attempt at a rational explanation, and *any* semantic memory about the status of lust is fundamentally untrustworthy.

The final quatrain merely operates as a kind of conceptual cage in which the poet offers more problematic assessments:

> Made In pursut and in possession so,
> Had, having, and in quest, to have extreme,
> A blisse in proofe and provd and very woe;
> Before, a joy proposd behind a dreame.

Calling all aspects of lust "extreame" is the most dispassionate assessment, and it is clearly a kind of turning point for the poem. Vendler says the word "enables the second part of the poem to reverse the morning-after model of the octave."[28] The language that follows ("blisse," "wo," "joy") is certainly far more neutral, but "extreame" also reminds the reader that there is no vantage point from which a stable semantic memory can be constructed because any experience of lust renders all semantic judgments suspect. The best the poet can do is to call it a "dream." The final couplet, which so many have seen as ironic, actually reflects an accurate universal assessment of the impossibility of a meaningful escape from semantic memory bias: "All this the world well knows; yet none knows well / To shun the heaven that leads men to this hell." This knowledge is conceptual, not collective. The world, which elsewhere in the dark lady poems is the arbiter of semantic memory (as it is for modern psychologists), knows everything revealed by the poet, including his knowledge about the presence of bias, but that knowledge is not enough because no position is outside of experience. This fundamental bias in semantic memory informs the rest of Shakespeare's dark lady sonnets; it is part of the way they portray subjectivity itself. If we understand how the anxieties of the dark lady poems hinge on the relationship between erotic desire and semantic memory, we can explain how they are connected to the issues of memory in the young man sonnets, and ultimately we have another way of understanding the unity of the *Sonnets*.

Notes

1. Alexander Dickson, *Alexandri Dicsoni Arelii de Vmbra Rationis & Iudicij Siue de Memoriae Virtute Prosopopoeia* (London, 1583); G. P. Cantabrigiensis, *Libellus de Memoria* (London, 1584); Guglielmo Gratarolo, *The Castel of Memorie* (London, 1562); Ravennas Petrus, *The Art of Memory* (London, 1545); Thomas Watson, *Compendium Memoriae Localis. Autore Thoma Watsono Londinensi, I.V. Studioso* (London, 1585).
2. Guglielmo Gratarolo, *The Castel of Memorie* (London, 1562).
3. Aristotle, *Aristotle's On the Soul ; And, On Memory and Recollection* (Santa Fe, NM: Green Lion Press, 2001), 170.
4. Richard Sorabji, *Aristotle on Memory* (Chicago: University of Chicago Press, 2004).
5. William E. Engel, *Mapping Mortality: The Persistence of Memory and Melancholy in Early Modern England* (Amherst: University of Massachusetts Press, 1996), 1.
6. Thomas Wright, *The Passions of the Minde in General* (London, 1630), 45.
7. Mary J Carruthers, *The Book of Memory: A Study of Memory in Medieval Culture* (New York: Cambridge University Press, 2008), 59–60.
8. Sutton Qtd. in Lina Perkins Wilder, *Shakespeare's Memory Theatre: Recollection, Properties, and Character* (New York: Cambridge University Press, 2014), 58.
9. References to Shakespeare's *Sonnets* are to the 1609 edition and will be noted by sonnet and line number.
10. Amanda Watson, "'Full Character'd': Competing Forms of Memory in Shakespeare's Sonnets," in *A Companion to Shakespeare's Sonnets*, ed. Michael Schoenfeldt (Oxford: Blackwell, 2007), 348.
11. Watson, "'Full Character'd,'" 343–44.
12. See also Holly Dugan, *The Ephemeral History of Perfume: Scent and Sense in Early Modern England* (Baltimore: Johns Hopkins University Press, 2011).
13. Watson, "'Full Character'd,'" 349–50.
14. Garrett Sullivan, "Voicing the Young Man: Memory, Forgetting, and Subjectivity in the Procreation Sonnets," in *A Companion to Shakespeare's Sonnets*, ed. Michael Schoenfeldt (Oxford: Blackwell, 2007), 340.
15. Sullivan, "Voicing the Young Man," 340.
16. Lina Bolzoni, *The Gallery of Memory Literary and Iconographic Models in the Age of the Printing Press* (Toronto: University of Toronto Press, 2001), 145.
17. Bolzoni, *The Gallery of Memory*, 147.
18. Daniel L. Schacter, *Searching for Memory: The Brain, The Mind, And The Past*, Reprint edition (Basic Books, 2008), 149–50.
19. Endel Tulving, "Episodic and Semantic Memory," in *Organization of Memory*, ed. Wayne Donaldson and Endel Tulving (New York: Academic Press, 1972), 392.
20. Kathleen M. Galotti, *Cognitive Psychology In and Out of the Laboratory* (New York: Cengage Learning, 2008), 257.
21. Bolzoni, *The Gallery of Memory*, xvi.

22. Mary J. Carruthers, *The Book of Memory: A Study of Memory in Medieval Culture* (New York: Cambridge University Press, 2008), 85.
23. Carruthers, *The Book of Memory*, 9.
24. Wright, *Passions of the Minde*, 52.
25. One broad sign that the poet works diligently to assert the possibility of a stable semantic memory in the dark lady sonnets is the slight uptick in the number of similes in the dark lady sonnets compared with those devoted to the young man. Similes depend entirely upon semantic memory for their effect, since they deliberately link their tenor with a vehicle that is conceptually rather than autobiographically remembered. When the speaker in Sonnet 140 compares himself to "testie sick-men, [who] when their deaths be neer, / No newes but health from their Phisitions know," he does not assume that only readers who have personally experienced such a testy fellow will understand him.
26. Helen Vendler, *The Art of Shakespeare's Sonnets* (Cambridge: Belknap Press, 1999), 551.
27. Wright, *Passions of the Minde*, 48.
28. Vendler, *The Art of Shakespeare's Sonnets*, 552.

16 *Hamlet* without Sex
The Politics of Regenerate Loss

Amanda Bailey

> There are more things in heaven *and* earth, Horatio,
> Than are dreamt of in our philosophy.[1]

Retrograde Futurism

The notion that the time is out of joint disturbs Hamlet and continues to intrigue readers of Shakespeare's play. For Hamlet, his father's death and ghostly return is untimely, his uncle's assumption of the throne preemptive, and his mother's remarriage premature. For us, Hamlet's move from contemplation to action occurs too late, even as the play itself is seen as ahead of its time. Richard Halpern describes *Hamlet* as a kind of irruption, "a startlingly prophetic meditation on the nature of modernity."[2] Margreta de Grazia reviews the canon of critics who ascribe to the character Hamlet "a strange futurity," which has come to be associated with modernity itself.[3] Gilles Deleuze understands the phrase "the time is out of joint" as elegantly conveying a distinctively postmodern awareness of the disorienting "unhinging" of past, present, and future.[4] Indeed, something is amiss when, in contradistinction to Gertrude's bromide, "'tis common—that all lives must die, / Passing through nature to eternity" (1.2.70–74), some lives recursively pass through *eternity*, signaling "a strange eruption" in nature (1.1.68). At once a metaphysical breach and terrestrial upset, Hamlet Senior's visitations disrupt the kingdom's biosymbolic order, whereby cycles of birth, life, and death among the elite dictate Elsinore's political rhythms.[5] As Horatio explains, the state itself is "disjoint and out of frame" (1.2.20), and he associates these ghostly appearances with the portents that signaled the demise of the Roman Republic. He describes the cosmic disturbances marking the eve of Caesar's assassination: "graves stood tenantless, and the sheeted dead / Did squeak and gibber in the Roman streets / At stars with trains of fire, and dews of blood, / Disasters in the sun; and the moist star, / Upon whose influence Neptune's empire stands, / Was sick almost to doomsday with eclipse." ([Q2] 1.1.106.8–106.13). In accordance with Horatio's analogical thinking, Denmark's political order will not be brought back into balance until temporal and natural processes are rehinged.[6]

This rehinging is precisely what a patrilinear monarchy ensured as the production of an heir conjoined temporal and natural processes. Both on and off the early modern stage, prosperity was predicated on generation; the creation of heirs was the primary means of honoring the past and guaranteeing the future.[7] As Linda Charnes emphasizes, the perpetual entail laws ratified in England over the course of the sixteenth century designated that the "father's place, position, property, and name is expected to flow in the same direction as his semen" (56). The heir proves central to Lee Edelman's analysis of *Hamlet*, which he demonstrates is deeply invested in the ideology of reproductive futurism. Edelman elucidates ways the play "anticipates modernity's ideology of cultural survival" by holding up the heir as "the promise of secular temporal closure intended to restore an imaginary past in a future endlessly deferred."[8] Edelman's insights into *Hamlet*'s commitment to reproductive futurism are crucial but even as futurity depends upon generation, the play forecloses heteronormativity. It elaborates Hamlet's attempts to imagine the interdependency of paternal and political legacies beyond the realm of human sexuality.

Hamlet, as I will argue, constructs a fantasy of primogeniture protected from the complications of sexual reproduction. This fantasy is reflected in Hamlet's seemingly inexplicable interest in worms. Here Shakespeare introduces us to creatures whose clone-like activities proclaim that nothing could be more natural than perpetuity. Throughout the medieval period, the word "regenerate" appeared in sermons and religious tracts to describe the spiritually reborn, and the term was linked to the reincarnation of Christ (*OED*). By the mid-sixteenth century, however, "regenerate" also appeared with regularity as a medical term for the process by which flesh restored itself after injury (*OED*). In late-sixteenth-century medical treatises, for instance, "regenerate" served as an alternative term for reproduction when the writer referenced generation that occurred spontaneously within the natural world (*OED*). Spontaneous generation, a concept with theological overtones grounded in naturalist and medical discourses, informs *Hamlet*'s perspective on sovereignty. In the play, worm activity functions as an allegory for political perpetuity as a form of scissipation, such that one creature may perpetuate itself through self-division that bypasses the act of copulation altogether.

While for the Romantics Hamlet's worm references signaled his sensitivity to the processes of decay, in our current moment, they are cited as evidence of the character's pre-Enlightenment ecological perspective.[9] Emphasizing the early modern zoological categories of generation and corruption, recent eco-critical readings of *Hamlet* point out that the play's conflation of conception and decay is by no means particular to Shakespeare but representative of a fundamental late-sixteenth-century biological principle.[10] Worms, importantly, were not considered the sign of disease, an invasive element that came from without, but were understood as endemic to organic and non-organic matter. Well into the eighteenth century, natural scientists regarded man as "one mass of worms, a walking corpse continually feeding these myriads of insects that gradually destroy him."[11] All matter was enwormed, and early moderns versed in the findings of the ancients accepted that all matter putrefies and is therefore productive of worms. Aristotle's extensive writings on generation in *History of Animals* and *On the Generation of Animals* held wide sway throughout the period. Theorizing the incidence of spontaneous generation among plants and animals, he notes that worms typically breed from dew, mud, dung, timber, hair, flesh, and excrement.[12] According to early modern natural philosophers, worms originated in snow, humidity, foul water, slime of wells, vinegar, wine, old wax, dried sweat of animals and humans, fire, paper, dust, books, and even stones.[13] Undoing the dichotomy between destruction and creation, worms also blurred the distinctions among human, animal, vegetable, and mineral. Worm activities demonstrated that putrefaction was associated not with mortality so much as with materiality.

In what follows, I offer a less sanguine account of the role of worms than my ecologically minded colleagues, as I seek to demonstrate that Hamlet enlists worms in support of a position resonant with a conservative strand of early modern political thought. This strand viewed patrilineal succession as natural and therefore as indefeasible.[14] Hamlet's retrograde agenda, which compels him to suppress maternal origins and herald the self-perpetuating nature of paternal will, comes into full view when we bring our focus back to the human investment in the processes of decomposition and breeding, references to which drive the metaphorical engine of the play. While Hamlet's preoccupation with corruption and generation, generally, may anticipate a "bio-centric perspective" as pointed out by Martin (38), this preoccupation is also squarely grounded in concerns marking the play's own historical moment. As recent discussions of the play have emphasized, *Hamlet* begins and ends with Norway's claims, and in the context of English anxieties about succession marking the final years of Elizabeth's reign, the precarity of the state would have registered as urgently as the vexed dynamics of the Hamlet family romance. Shakespeare takes pains to remind us that "the better wisdoms" of the Danish Council have prevailed (1.2.15), enabling Claudius to preempt Hamlet's succession, which results in a violation of the patrilineal system.[15] More pressingly, Gertrude's fecundity threatens to completely disenfranchise Hamlet. Faced with the possibility of new bloodlines and the new political affiliations they would entail, Hamlet confronts the problem of the relation between lineage and legitimacy, a question that, expressed in its most rudimentary form, could be phrased as: where do monarchs come from?

The most obvious answer to the question where do monarchs come from was, of course, women. This was an answer, however, that inspired political conflict as often as it guaranteed continuity. From the late sixteenth to the early seventeenth century, the problem of succession dominated English political life and inspired vehement debate about the right to rule, the authority of the monarch, and the conditions of resistance. Joseph Campana has recently argued that as much as sovereignty depended upon the production of heirs, childbirth had a potentially deleterious effect on sovereign perpetuity. As much was evidenced by "Henry VIII's complexly shifting allegiances and, more pointedly, his multiple wives, divorces, and children," which did not solidify his lineage but consistently challenged the notion of "the 'indivisibility' of sovereignty, not to mention the clarity of succession, which guaranteed the perpetuity of sovereignty."[16] Succession crises also marked Elizabeth's tenuous claim to the throne and continued throughout the reign of the childless queen and into the troubled transfer of rule from Elizabeth to James. Competing consanguineous claims to the throne opened the political system up to electoral ratification, which in *The Trew Law of Free Monarchies* (1598) James implicitly links to usurpation when he contrasts Scotland, which had a hereditary monarchy, to those "false states" that are illegitimately ruled by elective kings.[17] de Grazia emphasizes that warnings to prospective heirs about the dangers of their widowed mothers' second marriages were commonplace in the instructional literature of the period since conjugal union could legitimate rule, thus demonstrating the extent to which the integrity of patrimonic tradition was vulnerable to the erotic and political desires of women.[18] In *Hamlet*, paternal succession is threatened by election and usurpation alike—distinct political phenomena—which, like James I, Hamlet conflates. Human reproduction does not, however, hold out the prospect of restoration. The fantasy of the eternal twinning of worms, "the cellular dream of scissiparity—the purest form of parenthood in that it allows us at last to dispense with the other and go directly from one to the same" encourages Hamlet to revitalize the myth of uninterrupted lineal descent, as he attempts to hinge prosperity to natural cycles of generation that are spontaneous, impersonal, and continuous.[19]

Recycling Monarchs

T. S. Eliot's reading of *Hamlet* still exerts influence insofar as it has become second nature to interpret Hamlet's preoccupation with "things rank," a coded reference to his mother's sexuality (1.2.136), as inducing a general tenor of "disgust" that defines the affective atmosphere of the play.[20] The theory that Hamlet experiences revulsion at the thought of his mother's carnality has been explored further by Janet Adelman in her influential psychoanalytic reading, in which she locates the "fantasy of spoiling at the site of origin" as the "under-text of the play."[21] Hamlet's disgust toward his mother and Ophelia, Adelman argues, is engendered by his belief that female sexuality contaminates the patrilineal order by threatening to obliterate the distinction between fathers.[22] Adelman avers that female erotic appetite elicits within Hamlet a sense of disgust so strong that it overrides the moral revulsion that may be occasioned by his discovery that his father has been murdered (15).

While Hamlet spares little in outlining his imagination of Gertrude's sexuality, he never explicitly addresses her procreative potential. Yet in describing what he finds most repellent about her erotic tendencies he resorts to images associated with gestation. Importantly, circa 1600, there would be nothing about the process of conception per se that would have been seen as disgusting, especially as human gestation was regarded as the same in kind as "the sprouting of a plant from the decay of its seed, the breeding of a chick from the decay of its egg, the breeding of maggots in a dead dog from the decay of its flesh."[23] No one in Shakespeare's audience would have found it paradoxical that the human embryo emerged from putridness. As Samuel Purchas writes in *Microcosmus* or *The History of Man* (1619), in his section on "Generation," "what else is Generation, but from and to Corruption" (156). He goes on to note that the embryo remains for months sandwiched in the dark, dank recesses of the mother's womb, where the developing fetus is imprisoned "between the Mother's excrement" and makes its "Bed like a young Viper" (159). Understandings of generation were informed by the teachings of Aristotle who advanced the belief that "basically all generation of life has the same cause. Whether birth proceeds from the seed, the egg, or the womb, or spontaneously from putrid matter, it is really the same process, subject to local variations. ... All things are subject to corruption and decay, which are a necessary prelude to any new generation of existence."[24] In human procreation, the embryonic child was formed of a seed consisting of the seminal fluid of the father and the menstrual fluid of the mother. The seed, motionless in the womb for several days, would then begin to ferment, which is why, as Hankins notes "Aristotle compares the process [of gestation] to the curdling of milk" (510).

Once we consider that putrefaction was associated with the beginning stages of life, we can see that *Hamlet* is less concerned with galvanizing the audience's repulsion toward gestation as it is interested in the epistemological problem of denaturalizing human procreation. What Hamlet finds "weary, stale, flat, and unprofitable" about the world (1.2.135) is not what is to be discovered in nature, for instance purification and generation, but rather "all the *uses* of this world" (136). Contrary to modernizing narratives, which presume putrefaction was associated with disease and decay, in the late sixteenth century people recognized that organic life was engined by decomposition and fermentation. Hamlet strains to disaggregate these natural processes from artificial "uses" (136), that is those degenerate human behaviors that have brought the world to the hopeless state of "this" (138). The ambiguity of the word "this" may be resolved if we read Hamlet's disenfranchised state as its antecedent. The word "uses" refers generally to human activities but more specifically to those habits that entail the using up or consuming of matter such that matter becomes worn and deteriorates through use (*OED*). Also conveyed by the word "use" is one human's use of another for sexual purposes (*OED*). The rank seed possessing the garden is then an image of a normal fermenting womb. The curdling process of gestation may be productively contrasted to the luxuriant aspects of Gertrude's insatiable and indiscriminate erotic appetite. Described by a monstrous "increase" Gertrude's desire grows exponentially more hungry as it feeds (1.2.145), leading her to "batten on this moor" (3.4.67). His mother's generative potential is figured as an act of incessant devouring, which in this case leads to the gobbling up of the precious resources of patrimony: land, titles, and heirs. Importantly, there is nothing revolting about "the rank sweat of an enseamed [greasy] bed" (3.4.92), which offers the ideal conditions for germination. Rather, what Hamlet finds objectionable is the *use* to which this bed may be put, which can only result in the extinction of his line. Thus from Hamlet's perspective, Gertrude's greasy fermenting can lead only to sterility.

Hamlet turns to natural philosophy to forge a materialist vision of political resurrection that dovetails with the theologically inflected theory of the king's two bodies, reconceived as the theory of the king's one body. By imagining that the essence of sovereignty inheres in the natural body of the king, Hamlet endows the perpetuity of the office of kingship in monarchial matter, which by presumption exists only in those who are made of the same stuff. Matter, for Hamlet, is what enjoins and endows generations, ensuring that the firstborn son will naturally assume the place of the father in an undisturbed political order. If, as de Grazia emphasizes, "the generational shift constitutes the weak point in the genealogical chain" (85), then a conservative interpretation of the theory of the king's two bodies, which regarded the natural body of the king and the office of monarch as identical, potentially smoothed over this transition even as it laid the ground for a discourse of absolutism.[25] As early as 1560, common lawyers puzzled over the paradox inherent in the idea of the realm as a perpetual corporation, which depended upon conceiving of the state and the monarch as separate entities. The concept of the king's two bodies was an attempt to acknowledge that even though the king dies, the Crown survives. In writing about the reign of the childless Elizabeth, Marie Axton notes:

> [F]or the purposes of law it was found necessary by 1561 to endow the Queen with two bodies: a body natural and a body politic. (This body politic should not be confused with the old metaphor of the realm as a great body composed of many men with the king as head. The ideas are related but distinct.) The body politic was supposed to be contained within the natural body of the Queen. When lawyers spoke of this body politic they referred to a specific quality: the essence of corporate perpetuity. The Queen's natural body was subject to infancy, infirmity, error and old age; her body politic, created out of a combination of faith, ingenuity and practical expediency, was held to be unerring and immortal.[26]

In advancing the notion that the political order is tied to the natural body of the monarch, Hamlet does not, however, then go onto disassociate the mortal body of his father from the office of the monarchy. Rather than regard the sovereign as a disembodied sacred entity, he conceives of his father's body as a material memorial.

In *A Comparative Discourse of the Bodies Natural and Politique,* Edward Forset emphasizes the mnemonic function of the monarch as he explains that the person of "the Soveraigne is well stored with remembraces, nothing passeth from him, or setleth in him but by record" (20). Memory is essential to orderly political succession because "fore-attainted knowledges" protect against the intrusive demands of flatterers, malcontents, and traitors (20). Moreover, it is tantamount to treason to "corrupt" or "embezell" the Records because if "memories should be cleane taken from the mind," then the Sovereigne office cannot "endure" (20). For Forset, sovereignty "surmounteth the person it selfe," and thus the monarch should be as "Hercules ... being at not time abridged or enfeebled but to be supposed ever of a full strength, age, and power" (34). For this reason, the sovereign "admitteth no termes or titles of consanguinitie" (34). In his personal respects, "hee is as one man, single and individual, yet as in the right of Soveraignte, he sayeth the appellation and capacities of a corporation" (34). While the king is mortal, and he may die, "soveraignte never faileth" but persists "in a successive continuation" (34).

As *Hamlet* demonstrates, the theory of the king's two bodies does not necessarily lead to the preservation of political memory and when interpreted liberally, could open the door to the argument that subjects of the commonwealth (counselors in particular) and not the monarch alone should guide the decisions of the office of the monarch, an argument that buttressed constitutionalists. In order for the natural body of the king to serve as the site of memory it had to be protected from the intrusion of the unwanted heir. (As much is suggested by King Hamlet's command "remember me," which can be read as his attempt to establish himself as a political mnemonic and in this way foreclose the generation of new memory on the part of the queen). For Hamlet, the unwanted heir is the product of his mother's voracious sexual appetite. The gnawing of worms, which is juxtaposed with the wasteful consumption of humans, offers the fantasmic allegory of absorption and scissipation as commemorative and restorative. Hamlet's association of his mother's unrestrained feeding of her desires with political danger echoes Forset, who warns his readers "the more liberally we feed, the more dangerouslie wee doe offend" (42). Forset compares political ambition to appetite, which he then likens to the "Courtiers of the soule," who in "immoderately seeking to satisfie their own desires, giveth the soule no rest, till he bestow all his faculties of understanding, wit, and devise to accomplish their requests" (19).[27] Insatiable hunger for advancement is imagined as a revolutionary impetus, as Forset associates the act of eating with the appetitive behaviors of "begging and flattering petitioners, pleasing and applauding parasites, who using all cunning insinuating, are never without their varietie of sutes, to advance their owne good, howsoever their Soveraigne be thereby either impoverished or dishonored" (19).

The political dangers of the consuming multitudes, as Richard Halpern points out, are invoked in *Hamlet* by Guildenstern when he stresses to Hamlet, "Most holy and religious fear it is / To keep those many bodies safe / That live and feed upon your Majesty" (3.3.8–10; as in Halpern, 463). Here Shakespeare presents an image of the body politic that in theory perpetually nourishes the people becoming depleted and transformed by insatiable feeders. Scheming political dependents create an unnatural (and untenable) situation by using up what they take in. Halpern calls our attention to the language of feeding in the messenger's description of Laertes leading a popular mob to the palace doors, as the messenger warns Claudius, "Save yourself, my lord. / The ocean, overpeering his list, / Eats not the flats with more impetuous haste / Than the young Laertes, in a riotous head, / O'erbears your officers (4.5.98–108). "Antiquity forgot, custom not known," (4.5.104), political upheaval is indifferent to recorded memory, as members of this amorphous crowd have become "ratifiers and props of every word" (4.5.106) and enact as Halpern puts it "the consuming of a traditional order so as to produce a novel one" (464).

From Hamlet's perspective, the greatest threat to the office of the monarchy is the consumption of his prospects by the indiscriminate appetite of his mother. As in Forset, politically dangerous appetite is the province of women. Forset likens court rebels to women and then to serpents. Court flatterers are, in turn, described as appearing with the "hideous & snakie head of *Medusa*" (19). These Medusa-like flatterers "malcontents and forward cinicks" eat away at the office of the monarchy, as they "feed upon theire owne disliking conceits" (19). Hamlet's association of female sexuality with waste culminates in his exhortation to his mother to refrain from engaging in erotic rituals that erode the apparatus of consent, as "that monster custom, … all sense doth eat" ([Q2] 3.4.151.1). Hamlet's anxiety about consumption (and consummation) necessitates a rewriting of female fecundity. The imaginary solution seems to be a mode of sovereignty that preserves its indivisibility by, ironically, splintering off from itself, and in this respect by recycling its own raw materials.

Hamlet outlines a vision of preservative appetite in his response to Claudius' question about the whereabouts of Polonius' corpse. In this exchange, Hamlet explains that Polonius is now "where he is eaten" (4.3.20) by a "convocation of politic worms" (4.3.21). By emphasizing that "we fat all creatures else to fat us, and we fat ourselves for maggots," Hamlet then explains, "a man may fish with the worm that hath eat of a king. And eat of the fish that hath fed of that worm" (4.3.26–27). This is for Hamlet the king's proper "progress" that is through "the guts of a beggar" (4.3.30–31). On the face of it, these sardonic comments call attention to the worm as a metonym for the process of corruption associated with death and may serve to remind Claudius of the social leveling entailed by mortality. But more particularly,

Hamlet's observation highlights how worm and human consumption, digestion, and excretion mirror one another up to a point. Importantly, worms and humans occupy different temporal frames. Worm activities are not tied to any one individual lifecycle, and their continuation is predicated on the use they make of all terrestrial matter, including the rotting bodies of others and their own excrement. Hamlet's imagination of worms allows him to recast sovereign mortality as "a transitional stage of ongoing ecological interdependency rather than terminal physical closure."[28] Feeders and yet food themselves, worms nourish the fish that nourishes the king. By eating the worm that nourishes and consumes the monarch, living and dead kings alike contribute to the preservation of sovereignty. Here ingestion replaces copulation.

I'th' Sun

Ultimately, Hamlet finds a reassuring prospect seeking his "father in the dust" (1.2.71) and being guided by an entity engendered out of the "dead waste" of the night (1.2.198), which, like a worm, "works 'i'th earth so fast" (1.5.170). Contrary to Horatio's assessment, Hamlet Senior's visits do not signal an eruption, according to de Grazia, but initiate the realignment of temporal and natural orders insofar as his ghostly comings and goings are coordinated with "multiple time-telling intervals—planetary, mechanical, martial, diurnal" (74). Hamlet's own desire to embed himself in the earth, rather than escape from it, points to his orientation toward regeneration and not annihilation. The regenerative impulse is present in his wish that his flesh would "resolve itself into dew" (1.2.130). As the word "resolve" suggests, we can take Hamlet literally, that is as one who fantasizes that his flesh could immediately condense into liquid and, more specifically, that it like all matter could quickly undergo the disintegration inherent in the process of decomposition (*OED*). In hoping to undergo the transformation and restoration to which all matter is subject, Hamlet looks to dew, as did the natural philosophers of the period, as holding out the prospect of generativity. These writers signaled out the moistness of dew, water condensed by the heat of the sun, as that out of which worms bred and regenerated.[29]

Through such references Hamlet obliquely approaches the political problem of transmission, which in accordance with Hamlet's symbolic economy relies on the parthenogenic power of the sun. Aristotle laid the ground for early modern theories about the sun's generative powers when he argued that local variations in forms of matter were determined by the ecliptic, or the sun's path around the earth.[30] Sixteenth-century natural scientist Helmont claimed to have observed the spontaneous generation of scorpions when he:

> Scoop[ed] out a hole in a brick, put into it some sweet basil. Lay a second brick upon the first so that the hole may be imperfectly covered.

[He then] expose[d] the two bricks to the sun, and at the end of a few days the smell of the sweet basil, acting as a ferment ... change[d] the herb into a real scorpion.[31]

In Hamlet's warning to Polonius that he prevent Ophelia from "walk[ing] i'th'sun" lest she become impregnated (2.2.185–86), he alludes to the Aristotelian principle that "Man and the sun generate man."[32] This belief in the parthenogenic powers of the sun is echoed within the writings of Aquinas, the Greek Neo-Platonists, as well as Ficino, who states, "The universal virtue of the sun produces man only through the medium of another man as the particular and proper cause."[33] By envisioning the sun "breed[ing] maggots in a dead dog," Hamlet conjures the process of putrefaction, evidenced in this instance by the vital matter of the dead dog actively seeking contact with the generative energy of the sun. "Good kissing carrion" (2.2.182)—the dog is envisioned here as an animated, erotic entity.

In late sixteenth-century religious writings, maggots, a variation of worms, which were associated with death and the consumption of the corpse, served as part of the *vanitas mundi* tradition. If we are all meat for worms, religious writers emphasized, then during our time on earth we may be also be plagued by the worm of conscience, if not occasionally reminded that in the scheme of things we are but silly worms, small and insignificant compared to God.[34] Worms were simultaneously featured, however, in a secular tradition that began with the writings of the ancients and carried over into the early modern period. In accordance with a naturalist discourse, worms were recognized as extraordinary creatures that demonstrated the capacity for thrifty archiving, as well as spontaneous generation. In the act of consuming, worms preserved all matter that existed on the earth's surface. In his capacious *History of Serpents* (1608), Edward Topsell observes, centuries before Darwin, that worms hoard their excrement for which they find "commodious use":

> Those little heapes which are cast vp and lye shining and wrinkled before the mouth or edges of their holes, I take them to bee their miety excrements: for I could neuer as yet find other excrementitious substances drossy matter, or other feculency, but onely bare earth in them, whose alimentary Iuyce and moysture beeing cleane exhausted, they cast out the remaynder, as an vnprofitable burthen, nothing fit for nourishment. At the entrance of their doores, which yet steadeth them to some commodious vse, for stopping & damming vp theyr holes that the raine cannot so easily soke in, they are by these meanes safely defended from many annoyances and daungers, that otherwise might light vppon them.[35]

Topsell explores the "naturall" and "morall" aspects of serpents, broadly defined as "creeping thinges" (2), which include amphibians, a variety of snakes, the grubs of various insects, maggots, lice, caterpillars, and worms (title page). In the final section devoted to earthworms, Topsell emphasizes that worms, which dwell in slime, are "engendered ... indifferently, out of the dead bodies of good & euill men" alike (7). Most prodigious during rainy season, worms are born of anything moist, including dew, drops of blood and dung (7). Topsell goes on to note that, worms "breede of the slime of the earth, taking their first beeing from putrefaction, and of the fat moysture of the same earth they are againe fed and nourished, and into earth at last are resoulved" (306). As in the human world putrefaction marked the end of corruption and the beginning of generation, as during gestation when the seed was putrefied in the womb, worms did not distinguish themselves as a species that bred in putrefaction. However, they did offer a unique vehicle for imagining an ever renewable, naturally endowed collective, whose prosperity was immune to the fallibility of humanity, including female inconstancy or barrenness.

Spontaneous generation served as a metonym for memorialization itself. As Mary Carruthers, who has written on the divisional aspects of memory systems, notes "the fundamental principle [of memory] is to 'divide' the material to be remembered into pieces short enough to be recalled in single units."[36] Augustine's experiments with worms demonstrate the preservative aspects of their regenerative activities insofar as they serve as a biological example of the process by which dismemberment may index the relation of parts to whole. He reports of having one of his students "cut the worm in the middle, whereupon the two sections made by the stroke moved in opposite directions with as great speed and as firm tread as if they were two living animals of the same kind." Augustine marvels when he sees "that the living pieces were able to run upon a board in all directions." He then cuts the worms into smaller parts, discovering that "all moved about in such a way, that if we had not done the cutting, we would have thought that each of these parts had been created as a separate worm, and that each had lived its life distinct from the others."[37] Worms demonstrate that anatomization allows not simply for the orderly dissection of various pieces but the miraculous coincidence of preservation and generation. As Pierre de la Primaudaye writes in *The Third Volume of the French Academie*:

> [I]n all these generations, it is necessarie that something remaine, from which they are drawne in their first originall. When then any creature is engendred by another, if the forme perish, and any thing do remaine, it must (of necessitie) be the matter: which the corruption it selfe doth manifest, because that nothing can wholy perish so long as it corrupted. For the apple perisheth, and is conuerted into wormes. ...[38]

One of the most influential proponents of the memorializing benefits of spontaneous generation was the Aristotle of the English translation of *Master-Piece or the Secrets of Generation* (Eng., 1694). The translator cites the resurrection of Job to illustrate the Aristotelian belief in the "renewing of many inconsiderable Creatures and their returning to life after they seem dead" (41). The prime example and definitive proof of the archival function of spontaneous generation, according to this text, is the Arabian Phoenix, which after expiring on a funeral pyre, "out of her Ashes springs a worm, and from that worm another Phoenix" (42).

The Aristotelian premise that "hidden vnder euerie forme" is that which cannot "perish by corruption" (as in Pierre de La Primaudaye, 173), inflects Hamlet's musings in the Graveyard scene, where he identifies a skull as "my lady Worm's" (5.1.81). Here Hamlet ruminates on the "base uses" to which we return, and once again aims to disarticulate nature from use. Modern critics have interpreted the graveyard scene as a turning point in Hamlet's psychology and philosophical outlook. The political implications of his exchange with the gravedigger have gone unremarked but may be retrieved when we consider Hamlet's revisionist interpretation of the fall of Caesar. Revising Horatio's cosmic reading of that ancient crisis, Hamlet proffers a mechanistic version of the king's one body when he suggests that Caesar's death does not signal rupture but exemplifies continuity. Once he is dead, Hamlet explains, Caesar's corpse, like that of Alexander, turns to dust. It then returns to earth and at some later point is made into loam (Topsell's drossy matter) used to "stop a hole to keep the wind away" (5.1.196–97). Rather than provide insight into the meaninglessness of existence, or even his own mortality, here Hamlet constructs the fantasy of the monarch that never dies, even though he retains his material essence and overturns the principle of indivisibility.[39] Alexander the Great is a particularly important figure for Hamlet because, according to ancient myth, he was not of woman born but was spontaneously generated from an invertebrate. As Topsell writes:

> *Alexander* was thought to bee begotten of a Serpent, for it is said, that one a time there was found a great Serpent vppon his Mother *Olympia* as shee was sleeping; and some say (for the honour both of the Mother and the Sonne) that this Serpent was *Iupiter*, turned into the likenesse of a Serpent, as wee reade he changed himselfe into many other shapes. (5)

Hamlet suggests that while empires rise and fall—kings live and die—monarchical matter endures. Faced with having inherited nothing more than the patronymic, Hamlet has a stake in the recursive activities of worms that model undisturbed dominion and hinge natural processes to uninterrupted lineage. Through his subsequent reference to himself as a caught fish, near the play's end, Hamlet inserts himself into the imperial pantheon organized in accordance with the ecological cycle he outlined previously to Claudius after the death of Polonius. Before Osric's announcement of Laertes' challenge to a duel, Hamlet confesses to Horatio that Claudius had "thrown out his angle for [his] proper life" (5.2.67). By reiterating the angler, fish, worm economy that sustains monarchal matter, Hamlet is able to envision himself as a fish that has been caught by presumably having eaten the worm. In this formulation, begetter and begotten are one in the same, a conceit that resonates with the notion that the monarch, "like a Phoenix" is son to himself, his own father, and his own heir.[40] Now Hamlet can figure his impending demise as part of a natural process by which he will be preserved, recycled, and memorialized, perhaps as the loamy stuff worms rely on to stop their holes.

Conclusion

The asexual regenerative activities of worms offer the ground for a fantasy of generative potential that relieves Hamlet, and the political system more broadly, of the taint of female appetite. Transmission through parthenogenesis bypasses human sexuality and its potential complications. Toward the end of the play, Hamlet confesses to Horatio that Claudius "Pop't in between the election and [my] hopes" (5.2.65). In admitting his political ambitions, Hamlet reintroduces the centrality of paternity despite the play's acknowledgement that Denmark is an elective monarchy. By linking election and usurpation the play is able to juxtapose the regenerative cycles of worms as a corrective force operating through the natural world untouched by man-made institutions. Yet rather than idealize nature, Shakespeare exposes the limits of this fantasy. Drilling down into the "between" space—the chasm between electoral procedure, which relies upon the consent of a parliamentary body, on the one hand, and Hamlet's ecstatic ambitions, on the other hand—we find a dark, dank pit of nostalgia for a model of sovereignty affirmed by creaturely asexuality and sustained by spontaneous generation. The relationship of this fantasy to Fortinbras' assumption of the Danish throne at the play's end is ambiguous. Fortinbras takes over not like a conqueror but with the claim to something like heredity when he proclaims, "I have some rights of memory in this kingdom / which now [to] claim my vantage doth invite me" (5.2.394–95). Is this armor-clad, warrior king, reminiscent of Hamlet Senior, one of Augustine's wormy creatures cut off from the sovereign source and regenerated? Complicating matters further is the play's unresolved attitude toward electoral process. Hamlet gives Fortinbras his "dying voice" (5.2.298). Yet Horatio's summation of events introduces ambiguity. He announces either that in support of the ratifying authority of the Danish Council, Hamlet's voice "will draw on more" (5.2.336), or (as in Q2), he notes that from Hamlet's mouth his "voyce will drawe no more," suggesting that monarchical politics begins and ends with the body of the monarch, a prerogative Hamlet enjoyed briefly in the interval between the death of Claudius and entrance of Fortinbras.

Hamlet may be read as an argument for the biopolitics of kingship insofar as the laws of nature are determinative of *bio* and *polis*. But the generative potential that inheres in matter leads only to regressive statecraft. Here we have an alternative answer to the question posed at the onset of

Hamlet *without* Sex 233

this essay: where do monarchs come from? Flesh and dust, which may be dispersed and transformed but never destroyed. As Michael Roth notes, "in modernity memory is the key to personal and collective identity," yet the materialization of memory in *Hamlet* divorces memory from human identity and subjectivity so as to protect it from use—that is the wearing out or consuming of material artifacts and human bodies that serve as its repository.[41] This is a vision of collective memory as neither cathartic nor redemptive but as that which lies beyond the historical agent.[42] We might stretch the parameters of our philosophy to attend to "things in heaven," as evidenced by metaphysical and cosmological approaches to the play. But as I have suggested, when we take seriously the injunction to attend to things "in earth," we are confronted by a host of pressing questions about the relation of memory, mortality, embodiment, and political perpetuity within and beyond the world of the play.

Notes

1. William Shakespeare, *Hamlet*, *The Norton Shakespeare*, Second Edition, ed. Stephen Greenblatt et al., (Oxford: Oxford UP, 2008), emphasis mine, 1.5.168–69. All quotations are from this edition.
2. Richard Halpern, "Eclipse of Action: Hamlet and the Political Economy of Playing," *SQ* 59 (Winter 2008): 450 [450–82].
3. Margreta de Grazia, *Hamlet without Hamlet* (Cambridge: Cambridge UP, 2007), 22. De Grazia notes that Hamlet's "deep and complex inwardness was not perceived as the play's salient feature until around 1800," 1.
4. Gilles Deleuze, *Kant's Critical Philosophy*, trans. Hugh Tamlinson and Barbara Haberjam (Minneapolis: U of Minnesota Press, 1999), "Preface: On four poetic formulas which might summarize Kantian philosophy," vii. For Derrida, Hamlet's father's ghost signals the future as an uncanny iteration of an unfinished past that haunts the present, *Specters of Marx*, trans. Peggy Kamuf (New York: Routledge, 1994), 65.
5. The term is Linda Charnes's in *Hamlet's Heirs: Shakespeare and the Politics of a New Millennium* (New York: Routledge, 2006), 56.
6. A Schmittian reading would associate this disruption of the natural order with the sovereign decision on the exception embodied by Claudius. Arguably, the plays opens with Denmark in a state of emergency, a situation that heralds the separation of the sovereign from the rule of law and, hence, the decision from the juridical norm. Yet, as I will argue, in this play, the corporatist fiction of the king's two bodies, and Hamlet's one-body fantasy, function to smooth over the potential for political disruption caused by King Hamlet's death. In this sense, Hamlet's idea of monarchical authority is more in line with Jean Bodin than Schmitt (or Agamben). See Carl Schmitt, *Hamlet to Hecuba: The Intrusion of the Time into the Play*, trans. David Pan with Introduction by Julia Reinhard Lupton (New York: Telos Press, 2009).
7. Much scholarship on *Hamlet* focuses the mnemonic function of the theater and meta-theater. It has become a critical commonplace to review the various ways the play engages the task of memory, a task initiated by Hamlet's father's injunction to honor his memory by committing revenge. For recent examples, see

Zackariah C. Long, "*The Spanish Tragedy* and *Hamlet*: Infernal Memory in English Renaissance Revenge tradgy," *ELR* 44 (Spring 2014): 153–92; and Rhodri Lewis, "*Hamlet*, Metaphor, and Memory," *Studies in Philology* 109 (Fall 2012): 609–41. See also, Lina Perkins Wilder, *Shakespeare's Memory Theatre* (Cambridge: Cambridge UP, 2010), 107–39; Garrett Sullivan, *Memory and Forgetting in English Renaissance Drama: Shakespeare, Marlowe, Webster* (Cambridge: Cambridge UP, 2005); and Stephen Greenblatt, *Hamlet in Purgatory* (Princeton: Princeton UP, 2001).

8. Lee Edelman, "Against Survival: Queerness in a Time That's out of Joint," *SQ* 62 (Summer 2011): 148 [148–69].

9. Discussions of the agentic capacities of worms by Bruno Latour and Jane Bennett have inspired a recent spate of essays on the role of worms in *Hamlet*. See Bruno Latour, *Pandora's Hope: Essays on the Reality of Science Studies* (Cambridge, MA: Harvard UP, 1999), 24–80 and Jane Bennett, *Vibrant Matter: A Political Ecology of Things* (Durham: Duke UP, 2010), 95–100.

10. For Randall Martin, Hamlet obtains a "bio-centric perspective" over the course of the play, as his awareness of human mortality within larger cycles of organic nature reshapes his attitude toward revenge. Randall Martin, "Ecology, Evolution, and Hamlet," *Renaissance Shakespeare/Shakespeare Renaissances Proceedings of the Ninth World Shakespeare Conference* Vol 1 (Newark: University of Delaware Press, 2014): 38. For Ian MacInnes, Hamlet's references to worms are not simply metaphorical or symptomatic of Hamlet's psycho-social condition; the connections between humans and worms imply that humans and nonhumans share a domain and thus are metonymically related. Ian MacInnes, "The Politic Worm: Invertebrate Life in the Early Modern English Body," in *The Indistinct Human in Renaissance Literature*, ed., Jean Feerick and Vin Nardizzi (Palgrave, 2012), 254–55. [253–73].

11. G. De Gols, *A Theologico-Philosophical Dissertation concerning Worms* (London, 1727), 6 as in John Farely, "The Spontaneous Generation Controversy (1700–1860): The Origin of Parasitic Worms," *Journal of the History of Biology* 5 (Spring 1972): 101 [95–125].

12. Aristotle, *History of Animals*, trans. D. Arcy Wentworth Thompson, Book 5, part. 19, lines 16–20, as in MacInnes, "The Politic Worm," 255. Topsell writes that worms "may be found both in the secret Mines of stone, and some-times allso amongst Mettalls" (315), and he concurs, that as "*Aristotle* saith, that liuing creatures will breede also euen in those things that are not subiect to putrefaction, as for example, in the fire and snow, which of all things in the world, one would take neuer to be apt to putrefie, and yet in old snowe Wormes will be bred" (314). On stones breeding worms, see MacInnes, 258.

13. Eugene S. McCartney, "Spontaneous Generation and Kindred Notions in Antiquity," *Transactions and Proceedings of the American Philological Association* 51 (1920): 105 [101–15].

14. Both Catholic and Protestant writers called on this connection to support the claims of Mary Queen of Scots and later James, respectively. See Paul M. Shupack, "Natural Justice and *King Lear*," *Cardoza Studies in Law and Literature* 9.1 Boalt Hall Law and Literature Symposium Part 2 (Spring-Summer, 1997): 70 [67–105]. Lorna Hutson shows that by the 1540s, sermons, petitions, and dialogues calling for practical legislative remedies for social reform did not naturalize the commonwealth as the body of the monarch and that resistance

Hamlet *without* Sex   235

to this idea was developed further in Plowden's *Reports* of 1571 and the first 11 volumes of Sir Edward Coke's *Reports* of 1616. Hutson, "Imagining Justice: Kantorowicz and Shakespeare," *Representations* 106 (Spring 2009): 126 [118–42].

15. In Shakespeare's play, as Margreta de Grazia emphasizes, Gertrude's status as "th' imperial jointress" (1.2.9) is the crucial factor in Claudius' electability.
16. Joseph Campana, "The Child's Two Bodies: Shakespeare, Sovereignty, and the End of Succession," *ELH* 81 (Fall 2014): 813 [811–39].
17. As in Andrew Hadfield, "The Power and Rights of the Crown in *Hamlet* and *King Lear*: 'The King—the King's to Blame,'" *The Review of English Studies* 54 (No. 217) (Oxford: Oxford UP, 2003): 567 [566–86].
18. De Grazia, *Hamlet without Hamlet*, 106–107. Schmitt and Hadfield both identify the political problem of succession as the central issue of the play.
19. Jean Baudrillard as in Charnes, *Hamlet's Heirs*, 64.
20. Eliot as in R. Chris Hassel, Jr., "Hamlet's 'Too, Too Solid Flesh,'" *The Sixteenth Century Journal*, 25 (Autumn 1994): 609 [609–22].
21. Janet Adelman, *Suffocating Mothers: Fantasies of Maternal Origin in Shakespeare's Plays:* Hamlet *to* The Tempest (New York: Routledge, 1992), 23.
22. According to Adelman, Hamlet is unable to assume his father's identity because Hamlet Senior and Claudius tend to collapse into one another. The cause of this collapse is his mother's refusal to serve as a repository of his father's ideal image and her general inability to distinguish the two brothers (12–13). Hamlet is the only repository of his father's image, the only agent of differentiation in the court since Gertrude's "failure of memory—registered in her undiscriminating sexuality—in effect defines Hamlet's task in relation to his father as a task of memory," 13.
23. John E. Hankins, "'God Kissing Carrion:' A Theory of the Generation of Life," *PMLA* 64 (June 1949): 511 [507–16].
24. Aristotle, as in Hankins, 509.
25. A radical interpretation insisted on the importance of the distinction between the two bodies and argued that subjects of the commonwealth (counselors in particular) and not the monarch alone should guide the decisions of the office of the monarch. This idea underwrote the idea of constitutionalist monarchy. See Ernst Kantorowicz, *The King's Two Bodies: A Study in Medieval Political Theology* (Princeton: Princeton UP, 1957, reprint 1985). See also, Victoria Kahn, "Political Theology and Fiction in *The King's Two Bodies*," *Representations* 106 (Spring 2009): 77–101.
26. Marie Axton, *The Queen's Two Bodies: Drama and the Elizabethan Succession* (London: Royal Historical Society, 1977), 12. This perspective is in direct contrast with that of Doleman, the principal apologist for the Catholic position, who foregrounds the importance of the social contract when he claims that the legality of a succession claim is confirmed once the heir is elected by the people. Doleman, as in Paul M. Shupack, "Natural Justice and *King Lear*," *Cardoza Studies in Law and Literature* 9.1 Boalt Hall Law and Literature Symposium Part 2 (Spring-Summer, 1997): n11, 96 [67–105].
27. On the dysfunctional court of Elsinore, in which advice, counsel, and debate have degenerated into flattery and favoritism, see Andras Kisery, "'I Lack Advancement': Public Rhetoric, Private Prudence, and the Political Agent in *Hamlet*, 1561–1609," *ELH* 81 (Spring 2014): 29–60.

28. Randall Martin, 41.
29. As Ian MacInnes reminds us, early modern natural philosophers were influenced by classical theories that worms breed from dew (257).
30. *Of Generation and Corruption*, 2: 10, as in Hankins, 509.
31. As in J. E. Greaves, "some Interpretations of Life Phenomena and their Practical Significance," *The Monist* 33 (Jan. 1923): 2 [1–14].
32. *Physics*, Book 2, Chap. 2, as in Hankins, 511.
33. *De Immortalitate Animorum*, Book 15, Chap. 11, as in Hankins, 512.
34. With the exception of *Hamlet*, worms in Shakespeare's plays mostly evoke their religious and moral connotations: men die and worms eat them (AYL, 4.1.706); Gilded tombs do worms unfold (MV, 2.7.69); we are dust and food for worms (1 Hen. 4, 5.4.87); and beware the worm of conscience (Rich. 1, 1.3.222).
35. Edward Topsell, *History of Serpents* (London, 1608), 306–307.
36. Mary Carruthers, *The Book of Memory: A Study of Memory in Medieval Culture* (Cambridge: Cambridge UP), 7.
37. St. Augustine, as in Mary Emily Keenan, "St, Augustine and Biological Science," *Osiris* 7 (1939): 596 [588–608]. In "On Memory and Recollection," Aristotle also addresses the ways sequencing affects memory. He uses the alphabet for an example and describes the remembering subject going back and forth through a sequence of numbers.
38. Pierre de la Primaudaye, *The Third Volume of the French Academie*, trans. R. Dolman (London, 1601, 2nd ed.), 173.
39. On A. C. Bradley and the existential Hamlet, see de Grazia, Hamlet *without* Hamlet 130.
40. Kantorwicz 417, as in Stephen Greenblatt, "Introduction: Fifty Years of the King's Two Bodies," *Representations* 106 (Spring 2009): 64 [64–67].
41. As in Klein, 135.
42. Here I take Kerwin Lee Klein's point about the relatively recent theoretical turn to memory as a means to rework history's boundaries, especially in light of the relation between historical imagination and memorial consciousness. Yet, as he demonstrates, our "new memory is both very new and very old" in that it aligns current theoretical tenets with an older sense of memory as the "union of divine presence and material object" (129). In the early modern period, memory was associated with political theology as it was related to the divine authority and authenticity of the sovereign. The contemporary phrase 'collective memory' can thus easily reference the social rituals and material practices that bridged the physical and physic by creating collective mnemonic systems that perpetuated the continuity of the monarch (such as forms of writing, commemorative rituals, mementos, tombs, shrines, monuments, parades, progresses and public performances). If mnemonic traces have displayed the category of History, we have yet to explore fully the relation between memory and ideology in historical context. See Kerwin Lee Klein, "On the Emergence of Memory in Historical Discourse," *Representations* 69 Special Issue: Grounds for Remembering (Winter 2000): 127–50.

Afterword
"A Prescript Order of Life": Memory, Sexuality, Selfhood

Garrett A. Sullivan, Jr.

Sexuality and memory: for many early modern writers, the terms are antithetical. Memory treatises and psycho-physiological texts represent sexual desire as erosive of memory. John Willis includes among memory's nemeses "[f]ilthy desires, [such] as avarice, envy, thirst of revenge, lust, love of harlots, and the ardent Passion, *Love*."[1] Strong desire threatens to undermine memory, which, significantly, is commonly understood as being integral to self-regulation. Memory is "a joynt-worker in the operations of Reason," as Edward Reynoldes puts it[2]; it has a role to play not only in the cognitive operations of judgment, but also in the subjective business of rational self-management. If memory is, as faculty psychologists routinely contended, the "Gardian and Register of all the species or kindes and images, apprehended by the sense," or "a place of greatest trustines to keepe the same the most precious treasures of the soule," its capacity to retain and preserve information—to register and guard—exists in quasi-metonymic relation to the consolidation and maintenance of the fortified subject.[3] As Willis notes, a precondition for a strong memory is "a prescript order of life"—which is, by definition, a life not dominated by filthy desires and ardent passions.[4] A by-product (or perhaps even an objective) of the *ars memorativa*, then, is the construction of a selfhood as internally ordered and purpose oriented as the elaborate architectural mnemonics famously associated with the memory arts.

According to Renaissance literary critics, the memory-aided construction of the self is a primary function of literature. In *The Art of English Poesy* (1589), George Puttenham devotes a chapter to "historical poesy" that begins with a discussion of the place of memory in the exercise of judgment[5]:

> There is nothing in man of all the potential [potent] parts of his mind (reason and will except) more noble or more necessary to the active life than memory, because it maketh most to a sound judgment and perfect worldly wisdom, examining and comparing the time past with the present, and by them both considering the time to come, concludeth with a steadfast resolution what is the best course to be taken in all his actions and advices [deliberations] in this world.[6]

For Puttenham, the poetic example, defined as "the representation of old memories and like successes [i.e., events] happened in times past," is of paramount importance to the operation of rational judgment.[7] Drawing on memory, the wise subject compares past and present, considers the future, and "concludeth with a steadfast resolution what is the best course to be taken." More is at issue than a single act of judgment, however; recollection is integral to a broader process of self-formation. Memory not only assists judgment, it inaugurates "a steadfast resolution what is the best course to be taken" in all worldly affairs. That is, memory works to produce a steadfast subject, one who clings to "the best course to be taken" in the face of the vicissitudes of worldly existence—including, of course, sexual desire.

We find an example of such a subject in Sir Philip Sidney's adulatory account of Virgil's Aeneas[8]:

> Only let Aeneas be worn in the tablet of your memory, how he governeth himself in the ruin of his country; in the preserving his old father, and carrying away his religious ceremonies; in obeying the god's commandment to leave Dido, though not only all passionate kindness, but even the human consideration of virtuous gratefulness, would have craved other of him; ... lastly, how [he governs] in his inward self, and how in his outward government.[9]

Aeneas is worthy of being "worn in[to] the tablet of your memory" because of "how he governeth himself" in the face of calamity. Most importantly, he "obey[s] the god's commandment to leave Dido" when his desires direct him to do otherwise. This act of obedience is a triumph of reason over both "passionate kindness" and "virtuous gratefulness"; it represents the victory of judgment over both "inward self" and "outward government," a victory that, for Sidney, renders Aeneas worthy.

While Virgil's Aeneas is the greatest positive exemplar in the period, his behavior is not always exemplary. If, as Boccaccio wrote, Aeneas displays "strength of character in spurning and breaking the chains of an obstreperous passion," he also for a time succumbs to that passion.[10] Moreover, in the Ovidian tradition Aeneas appears as a selfish opportunist for abandoning Dido, and English writers such as Chaucer and Barnabe Rich advanced a negative view of Aeneas as one who betrayed his country as well as his amorous bond with Dido. Even granting the merits of Aeneas' abandonment of Dido, his behavior in Carthage speaks to a problem woven into the logic of exemplarity. As Timothy Hampton puts it,

> the life of the hero can easily be sliced into a multitude of discrete metonymically related segments or moments. Some of these may connote virtue, but some may suggest vice, and their interaction always produces conflict and moral dialectics, with the potential to turn back and subvert the pedagogical intention of the humanist who evoked the exemplar as a model for his student or reader in the first place.[11]

To maintain Aeneas' exemplarity, in other words, one must bracket his sexual intemperance, or frame it much as Sidney does, as "passionate kindness." Or, perhaps, one can read that intemperance as an act of (self-)forgetting, as when in Virgil Hermes upbraids Aeneas by exclaiming, "degenerate Man, / Thou Woman's Property, what mak'st thou here, / These foreign Walls and *Tyrian* Tow'rs to rear, / Forgetful of thy own?"[12]

If memory and sexual desire are uneasy bedfellows, forgetting and sexuality are seasoned canoodlers. Elizabeth Harvey has discussed the association of orgasm with oblivion in Helkiah Crooke and Edmund Spenser, while Jonathan Baldo, writing in this volume, traces the links among eroticism, forgetfulness (in the form of "distraction"), and the theater.[13] Crucially, Baldo demonstrates that, as with the relationship between memory and eroticism discussed above, selfhood is at stake: "Distraction was a form of forgetfulness, one that caused a dispersion and disintegration of the self."[14] Indeed, self-forgetting is a literary and cultural trope that describes various forms of divergence from the model of consolidated selfhood presumed by the memory arts tradition—forms to which sexuality is central.[15]

And yet, as Kyle Pivetti, Ian MacInnes, Goran Stanivukovic, and Su Fang Ng make plain in this volume, there is also a prominent place for sexual desire in the memory palace. Pietro da Ravenna advocated that the presumptively male and heterosexual practitioners of the *ars memorativa* fill memory *loci* with images of beautiful women to stimulate recollection. In this regard, sexual desire serves as the engine rather than the enemy of memory. Pivetti shows that this is the source of some anxiety for Ravenna, who, after revealing his mnemonic trick, states: "I hope chaste and religious men will pardon me: I cannot pass over in silence a rule which has earned me much praise and honour on account of my abilities in the art, because I wish, with all my heart, to leave excellent successors behind me."[16] To be remembered, Ravenna must own up to sexual desire's centrality to his memory system. His request for a pardon notwithstanding, Ravenna recognizes that sexual images not only sell, they also prove to be tenaciously memorable.

What do we make of Ravenna's salacious memory images? Do they give the lie to the model of rational subjectivity at least tacitly enshrined in early modern memory systems? Or do they speak to a sexuality aptly subordinated to reason and its "joynt-worker," memory? The answer, I suppose, is "both/and," but perhaps these are the wrong questions to ask. This book demonstrates how often the views of memory and reason-directed sexuality that I've been discussing are inadequate to early modern English literature. A number of essays in this volume show that, while literary texts don't invalidate normative conceptions of memory, sexuality, and selfhood, they expose the wishful thinking residing at their core: that memory is always an agent of purposeful decision-making; that desire is always regulable (if, in practice, seldom adequately regulated); and that the subject, when true to itself, is coherent, stable, and fortified, neither divided or distracted nor uncertain of its own will (as in Douglas Clark's analysis).

The essays in this volume repeatedly demonstrate that sexuality resides at the heart of many cultural categories to which memory is central, such as exemplarity (Andrew Fleck), commemoration (Dee Anna Phares, Mark Dahlquist, Heather Wicks), history (Joyce Green MacDonald, Su Fang Ng, John Garrison) and nationhood (Goran Stanivukovic, Kyle Pivetti). Moreover, early modern literature emerges in these analyses as a distinctive conduit for the transmission of affect from the past. As Kenneth Hodges puts it, "Eroticism ... is not simply the product of individual moments but of intertextual memory"; for him as well as many of his fellow contributors, literary meaning is generated "through a promiscuous series of intertextual entanglements."[17]

If an interest in promiscuous intertextuality informs this collection, so does the way in which memory and sexuality are implicated in relations of power. Several contributors (Phares, Fleck, Dahlquist, Wicks, and Amanda Bailey) underscore the fact that memory is a site of individual or cultural contestation; rather than offering a neutral recollection of the other, memory strives for mastery. As Stephen Guy-Bray provocatively puts it, "[E]rotic memory is essentially the memory of oneself, of one's own thoughts, feelings, and experiences. The other person is really just a prop." Guy-Bray also notes that "to remember something is inescapably to change it."[18] Rather than "*keep[ing] the same* the most precious treasures of the soule," memory is an agent of transformation. In this regard, memory and forgetting are implicated in one another. Indeed, many of the contributors to this volume show how memory and forgetting, in Baldo's apt phrase, "work in constant, oscillating partnership."[19]

Put another way, the essays in *Sexuality and Memory in Early Modern England* bring into focus three things that early modern theorists of memory tend to disavow or downplay: first, that memory at its core is interwoven with forgetting; second, that "[i]ts relation to the past is not that of truth but of desire"[20]; and third, that, like other cognitive processes, memory operates not only in the head, but throughout the body and, indeed, across body and environment.[21] (Robert Darcy's discussion of muscle memory demonstrates the fully somatic nature of recollection and the failure to recollect, as well as the relationship of each to sexual desire.) Recent criticism informed by what cognitive scientists term "the extended mind hypothesis" has underscored the extent to which memory functions as part of as "an extended [cognitive] system, a coupling of biological organism and external resources."[22] From this perspective, the model of cognitive and subjective order discussed at the outset of this essay—memory as "Gardian and Register," as a metonym for the consolidated self—comes into focus not as a given, but as, at best, an achievement that is always provisional, disrupted by somatic or environmental change, and in perpetual need of renewal. It's no wonder that so many of this volume's contributors take up Spenser's *The Faerie Queene*, a work both committed to self-fortification and keenly aware of the dynamic and reciprocal relationship between subjects and the cognitive and passionate ecologies into which they are embedded.[23] Indeed, Eumnestes' famous chamber of memory (which is discussed by Stanivukovic, Pivetti, and Ng) can be understood not merely as an allegorical depiction of the seat of memory in the brain, but also as a remembrance environment within which Guyon and Arthur consolidate their heroic identities through a textual encounter with national histories filled (in a way that Sidney would approve of) with "braue ensample[s], both of martiall, / And ciuill rule to kings and states imperiall."[24] What Spenser recognizes, though, is that such consolidation needs to be continually re-performed—only two cantos later, Guyon almost succumbs to the sexual temptations of Arcasia and the Bower of Bliss. As Ng astutely observes, in Spenser "[m]emory's fragility often cannot compete with the immediacy of erotic presence."[25] While sexuality is at the core of Spenserian memory, it poses a powerful challenge both to it and to the model of heroic selfhood that it underwrites.

We have seen memory depicted as both fragile (compared with the "immediacy of erotic presence") and strong (as the basis for the steadfast subject); and we have seen sexuality represented as both the nemesis and the agent of memory. Such apparent contradictions can be resolved in a range of ways—for instance, by differentiating temperate from intemperate sexuality or bidden from unbidden memories. It is less important to resolve them, however, than it is to recognize them for what they truly are: an indication of the conceptual richness and diversity of early modern ideas about memory and sexuality. Taken together, the essays in *Sexuality and Memory in Early Modern England* embark upon the important critical task of mapping that diversity. Not only do contributors offer a strong rebuttal to the rational judgment-centered conception of memory discussed above, almost all of them foreground something that readers of literature, early modern and otherwise, have long cherished in spite of the prescriptions of Sidney, Puttenham, and others: an understanding of erotic memory as powerfully transformative and beyond our control, a register and conduit of the pleasures derived not from the consolidation but the dissolution or shattering of the self.[26]

Notes

1. John Willis, *Mnemonica, or, The Art of Memory* (London, 1661), 140.
2. Edward Reynoldes, *A Treatise of the Passions and Faculties of the Soule of Man* (London, 1640), 13.
3. Pierre Charron, *Of Wisedome*, trans. Samson Lennard (London, 1608), 46; M. Andreas Laurentius, *A Discourse of the Preservation of the Sight*, trans. Richard Surphlet (London, 1599), 77.
4. Willis, *Mnemonica*, 145. Compare Douglas Clark's point that "perfect memory, moral temperance, and religious piety should shape the 'memorial of our immortality' of the last will and testament" (32).
5. "For as wee have neede of such a Judge as reason is, ... so is it requisite, that the conclusion and definitive sentence should be registred in *Memorie* ... that it may

alwaies be ready and found when neede requireth" (Pierre de la Primaudaye, *The Second Part of the French Academie* [London, 1605], 160).
6. George Puttenham, *The Art of English Poesy: A Critical Edition*, ed. Frank Whigham and Wayne A. Rebhorn (Ithaca and London: Cornell UP, 2007), 128.
7. Puttenham, *The Art of English Poesy*, 128.
8. For more on exemplarity in Sidney and Puttenham, see Fleck.
9. Sir Philip Sidney, *An Apology for Poetry, Or The Defence of Poesy*, 3rd ed., ed. Geoffrey Shepherd, rev. and expanded R.W. Maslen (Manchester and New York: Manchester UP, 2002), 99–100.
10. Boccaccio, *De Genealogia Deorum, Boccaccio on Poetry*, ed. and trans. Charles G. Osgood (Princeton: Princeton UP, 1930), 74–75. Quoted in Sidney, *An Apology for Poetry*, 193.
11. Timothy Hampton, *Writing from History: The Rhetoric of Exemplarity in Renaissance Literature* (Ithaca: Cornell UP, 1990), 26–27.
12. *Virgil's Aeneid* [1697] trans. John Dryden, ed. Frederick M. Keener (London: Penguin, 1997), 4.390–92.
13. Elizabeth D. Harvey, "Pleasure's Oblivion: Displacements of Generation in Spenser's *Faerie Queene*," *Forgetting in Early Modern English Literature and Culture: Lethe's Legacies*, eds. Christopher Ivic and Grant Williams (London and New York: Routledge, 2004), 53–64.
14. Baldo, 166.
15. Garrett A. Sullivan, Jr., *Memory and Forgetting in English Renaissance Drama: Shakespeare, Marlowe, Webster* (Cambridge: Cambridge UP, 2005). On the importance of unbidden memories and forgetting for the representation of dramatic character, see Lina Perkins Wilder, *Shakespeare's Memory Theatre: Recollection, Properties, and Character* (Cambridge: Cambridge UP, 2010).
16. Quoted in Pivetti, 181. See also Ng: "While the arts of memory suggest the use of the striking image for arousing passions to fix memory, Spenser's examination of the process suggests the myriad ways both memory and erotic passions can be misused, especially when they depend on the striking image" (205).
17. Hodges, 85, 92
18. Guy-Bray, 47. Guy-Bray ascribes the second point to Cedar Sigo. See also Ian MacInnes's point that Shakespeare's dark lady sonnets depict memory as "a deeply biased form of knowledge affected by and contingent upon erotic desire" (207).
19. Baldo, 170.
20. John Frow, *Time and Commodity Culture: Essays in Cultural Theory and Postmodernity* (Oxford: Clarendon Press, 1997), 229.
21. *Embodied Cognition and Shakespeare's Theatre: The Early Modern Body-Mind*, eds. Laurie Johnson, John Sutton and Evelyn Tribble (New York and London: Routledge, 2014).
22. Andy Clark and David J. Chalmers, "The Extended Mind" (1995) in Andy Clark, *Supersizing the Mind: Embodiment, Action, and Cognitive Extension* (Oxford and New York: Oxford UP, 2011), 220–32, esp. 232. See also John Sutton, "Spongy Brains and Material Memories," *Environment and Embodiment in Early Modern England*, eds. Mary Floyd-Wilson and Garrett A. Sullivan, Jr. (Basingstoke: Palgrave, 2007), 14–34; Gail Kern Paster, "Thinking with Skulls in Holbein, *Hamlet*, Vesalius, and Fuller," *The Shakespearean International Yearbook* 11 (2011): 41–60; and Evelyn Tribble, *Cognition in the Globe: Attention and Memory in Shakespeare's Theatre* (Basingstoke: Palgrave Macmillan,

2011). It should be stressed that this "extended system" is fluid and dynamic rather than static. It is made up of, in John Sutton's words, "webs of continuous reciprocal causation between insides and outsides, between self and culture, and between physiology and technology" (15); moreover, "cognitive order and stability were not natural to the isolated brain, but were integrative achievements often distributed over tools and other people as well as the unstable nervous system" (16).
23. Gail Kern Paster, "Becoming the Landscape: The Ecology of the Passions in the Legend of Temperance," *Environment and Embodiment*, 137–52.
24. Edmund Spenser, *The Faerie Queene*, ed. Thomas P. Roche, Jr. (Harmondsworth: Penguin Books, 1978), 2.10.74.8–9.
25. Ng, 192.
26. Cynthia Marshall, *The Shattering of the Self: Violence, Subjectivity, and Early Modern Texts* (Baltimore and London: Johns Hopkins UP, 2002).

Contributors

Amanda Bailey Associate Professor of English at the University of Maryland, is the author of *Of Bondage: Debt, Property, and Personhood in Early Modern England* (2013), *Masculinity and the Metropolis of Vice, 1550–1650*, (2010), co-edited with Roze Hentschell, and *Flaunting: Style and the Subversive Male Body in Renaissance England* (2007). Her essays have appeared in *Criticism, Renaissance Drama, English Literary Renaissance,* and *Shakespeare Quarterly*, as well as in several edited collections, including *A New Companion to Renaissance Drama* and *The Oxford Handbook of Embodiment*. She is currently completing an edited collection, with Mario DiGangi, *Affect Theory and Early Modern Texts*, and a single-authored monograph tentatively titled *A Natural History of Politics: Shakespeare, Sympathy, and the Stars*.

Jonathan Baldo is Professor of English at the Eastman School of Music, the University of Rochester. His most recent book, *Memory in Shakespeare's Histories: Stages of Forgetting in Early Modern England* (Routledge, 2012), concerns the contention between remembering and forgetting in early modern England, particularly in reference to the rise of nationalism and the disturbances wrought to historical memory by the Reformation. He is also the editor, with Isabel Karremann, of the forthcoming *Forms of Faith: Negotiating Confessional Conflict in Early Modern England* (Manchester University Press, 2015).

Douglas Iain Clark is a doctoral candidate at the University of Strathclyde. His research examines the conceptualization of the will in early modern English writing. He also publishes on the work of Emily Dickinson. His essays have appeared in two edited collections: *Transgression and Its Limits* (Cambridge Scholars Press, 2012) and *Reclaiming the Soul: Thinking Beyond the Body in Renaissance England* (Ashgate, 2013). He is currently completing a monograph entitled *Theorizing the Will in English Renaissance Literature*.

Mark Dahlquist is Assistant Professor of English at the University of Southern Mississippi, where he specializes in sixteenth and seventeenth century English literature. His recent work and current book project consider the relationship of the literature of the English Renaissance to Reformation-era iconoclastic controversy and explore the ways that sixteenth century secular and religious attitudes toward visual images helped give rise to the explosive power that iconoclastic political rhetoric acquired in the years preceding the British Civil Wars. His article, "Technological Iconoclasm in Robert Greene's *Friar Bacon and Friar Bungay*" recently appeared in *ELH*.

Robert Darcy is Associate Professor of English at the University of Nebraska at Omaha. He has published in JEMCS, *Renaissance Drama*, and in the book collections *Money in the Age of Shakespeare*, *Christopher Marlowe: The Craftsman*, and in *Shakespeare's World/World Shakespeares*, the selected proceedings of the 2012 World Shakespeare Congress. He has work forthcoming in *Sexuality and Memory in Early Modern England*, and also has manuscripts in progress on misanthropic representation in Renaissance literature and on formal verse satire from the sixteenth century.

Andrew Fleck is Associate Professor of English at the University of Texas at El Paso. His essays have appeared in *Modern Philology*, *Studies in English Literature*, and the *Journal of British Studies*.

John S. Garrison is Associate Professor of English at Carroll University. His essays have appeared in *Exemplaria*, *Literature Compass*, *Medievalia et Humanistica*, *Milton Quarterly*, and *Studies in Philology*. He is the author of *Friendship and Queer Theory in the Renaissance* (Routledge, 2014) and *Glass* (Bloomsbury, 2015). Dr. Garrison has held fellowships from the American Philosophical Society, the Medieval Academy of America, the Folger Shakespeare Library, and the National Endowment for the Humanities.

Stephen Guy-Bray is Professor and Chair of the department of English at the University of British Columbia. He is also a faculty associate in the Institute for Gender, Race, Sexuality and Social Justice. He is the author of *Against Reproduction: Where Renaissance Texts Come from* (University of Toronto Press, 2009), *Loving in Verse: Poetic Influence as Erotic* (University of Toronto Press, 2006), and *Homoerotic Space: The Poetics of Loss in Renaissance Literature* (University of Toronto Press, 2002). He has edited two collections of essays, as well as published more than 30 articles and chapters in books.

Kenneth Hodges is Professor of English at the University of Oklahoma. He is the author of *Forging Chivalric Communities in Malory's* Morte Darthur (Palgrave, 2005) and co-author of *Mapping Malory: Regional Identities and National Geographies in "Le Morte Darthur"* (Palgrave, 2014). His essays have appeared in *Arthuriana*, *Journal of English and Germanic Philology*, *Genre*, *PMLA*, *Studies in Philology*, and elsewhere. He is currently at work on the next book project (tentatively titled *Re-Arming the Renaissance*) that analyzes Spenser's cultural engagements with medieval material.

Joyce Green MacDonald is Associate Professor of English at the University of Kentucky, where she specializes in Shakespeare; Renaissance literary genres; and race and performance. She is the author of *Women and Race in Early Modern Texts* (Cambridge University Press, 2002), as well as articles in *Early American Literature, Studies in English Literature 1500–1800, Tulsa Studies in Women's Literature,* and *Early Modern Literary Studies.* She is currently at work on a monograph entitled *New World Shakespeares: Race, Nation, and Cultural Value.*

Ian F. MacInnes is Professor of English at Albion College, Michigan, where he teaches Elizabethan literature, Shakespeare, and Milton. His scholarship focuses on representations of animals and the environment in Renaissance literature, particularly in Shakespeare. He has published essays on topics such as horse breeding and geohumoralism in Henry V and on invertebrate bodies in Hamlet.

Su Fang Ng is Associate Professor of English at the University of Oklahoma. She is the author of *Literature and the Politics of Family in Seventeenth-Century England* (Cambridge University Press, 2007) and her second book project is *Reviving Alexander's Empire: Renaissance Classicism from Britain to Islamic Southeast Asia.* Her new project has been supported by year-long fellowships at the Radcliffe Institute and the National Humanities Center. She has also won short-term grants from the International Institute for Asian Studies in Leiden, Oklahoma, Humanities Council, the American Philosophical Society, the British Academy and others. Her work has appeared in *Modern Philology, Milton Studies, Comparative Literature, Studies in the Age of Chaucer, ELH, Studies in Philology, The Seventeenth Century, the Journal of Commonwealth Literature, Feminist Interpretations of Thomas Hobbes,* and elsewhere.

Dee Anna Phares is Assistant Professor of English at North Central College, where she specializes in Shakespeare and early modern culture. She has served as both Textual Editor and Associate Editor of *The Royal Shakespeare Company's Complete Works of William Shakespeare* (Random House, 2007–10). Her work has appeared in *The Upstart Crow: A Shakespeare Journal.*

Kyle Pivetti is Assistant Professor of English at Norwich University. His degrees are from University of California at Los Angeles (BA) and the University of California at Davis (PhD). His writing has appeared in *Modern Philology* and will appear in the forthcoming collection *Early Modern Women: Remapping Routes and Spaces* (Ashgate, 2014). He has recently completed a monograph entitled *The Busy Reminder: National Memory and Literary Form in Early Modern England.*

Goran V. Stanivukovic is Professor of English at Saint Mary's University, Canada, and author, most recently of *Prose Romance, Masculinity, and*

Eastern Mediterranean Trade in Early Modern England, 1565–1655. He has published widely on early modern drama and prose romance, especially on masculinity, queer early modern sexuality, Ovid, and the Mediterranean. He is currently at work on a book of Shakespeare's early styles of writing.

Garrett A. Sullivan, Jr. is Professor of English at Penn State University. He is the author of *The Drama of Landscape: Land, Property, and Social Relations on the Early Modern Stage* (Stanford University Press, 1998), *Memory and Forgetting in English Renaissance Drama: Shakespeare, Marlowe, Webster* (Cambridge University Press, 2005) and *Sleep, Romance and Human Embodiment: Vitality from Spenser to Milton* (Cambridge University Press, 2012).

Heather Wicks is a PhD candidate at Purdue University. She specializes in early modern drama, performance, and gender; her current research focuses on representations of female death on the early modern scaffold and stage. Her dissertation "Love Her After: Necrophilia, Consent, and Female Agency on the Early Modern Stage" shows how performance often made a dead woman alluring, even in the case of torture, execution, and murder, in order to demonstrate the deep cultural roots of our preoccupation with violence against female bodies, particularly female bodies on display.

Selected Bibliography

Adams, Joseph Quincy, ed. *The Ghost of Lucrece*. Thomas Middleton. New York: Charles Scribner's Sons, 1937.
Adelman, Janet. *Suffocating Mothers: Fantasies of Maternal Origin in Shakespeare's Plays: Hamlet to The Tempest*. New York: Routledge, 1992.
Aggrawal, Anil. *Necrophilia Forensic and Medico-legal Aspects*. Hoboken: CRC Press, 2010.
Ahmed, Sara. *The Cultural Politics of Emotion*. New York: Routledge, 2004.
Altman, Joel. *The Tudor Play of Mind: Rhetorical Inquiry and the Development of Elizabethan Drama*. Berkeley: University of California Press, 1978.
American Psychiatric Association. *Diagnostic and Statistical Manual of Mental Disorders*. 5th Edition. Washington D. C.: American Psychiatric Publishing, 2013.
Andrews, Meghan C. "Michael Drayton, Shakespeare's Shadow." *Shakespeare Quarterly* 65, (2014): 273–306.
Aristophanes. *Lysistrata and Other Plays*. Translated by Alan M. Sommerstein. New York and London: Penguin, 2002.
Aristotle. *Aristotle's On the Soul; and, On Memory and Recollection*. Santa Fe, NM: Green Lion Press, 2001.
Armstrong, Dorsey, and Kenneth Hodges. *Mapping Malory: Regional Identities and National Geographies*. New York: Palgrave, 2014.
Ascham, Roger. *The Scholemaster. The English Works of Roger Ascham*. Edited by William Aldis Wright. Cambridge, UK: Cambridge University Press, 1904.
Axton, Marie. *The Queen's Two Bodies: Drama and the Elizabethan Succession*. London: Royal Historical Society, 1977.
Baines, Barbara J. *Representing Rape in the English Early Modern Period*. New York: The Edwin Mellen Press, 2003.
Baldo, Jonathan. *Memory in Shakespeare's Histories: Stages of Forgetting in Early Modern England*. New York and London: Routledge, 2012.
———. "Shakespeare's Poetics of Distraction." *Shakespeare: The Journal of the British Shakespeare Association* 10, no. 2 (2014).
Bamford, Karen. *Sexual Violence on the Jacobean Stage*. New York: St. Martin's Press, 2000.
Barkan, Leonard. *Mute Poetry, Speaking Pictures*. Princeton and Oxford: Princeton University Press, 2013.
Barker, Howard. "Afterword: The Corpse and its Sexuality." In *Eroticism and Death in Theatre and Performance*. Edited by Karoline Gritzner. Hertfordshire: University of Herfordshire Press, 2010.
Barthes, Roland. *A Lover's Discourse: Fragments*. Translated by Richard Howard. New York: Hill and Wang, 2001.

Selected Bibliography

Battenhouse, Roy W. *Shakespearean Tragedy: Its Art and Its Christian Premises.* Bloomington: Indiana University Press, 1969.

Baxter, Nathaniel, and John Calvin. "Epistle Dedicatorye." *The Lectures of Daily Sermons, of that Reverend Diuine, D. Iohn Caluine, Pastor of the Church of God in Geneua, vpon the Prophet Ionas.* London: J. Charlewood for Edward White, 1578.

Bell, Ilona. *Elizabeth I: The Voice of a Monarch.* New York: Palgrave Macmillan, 2010.

Benbow, R. Mark. "The Araygnement of Paris." In *The Dramatic Works of George Peele.* Edited by C.T. Prouty. Vol. 3. New Haven: Yale University Press, 1970.

Bender, John B. *Spenser and Literary Pictorialism.* Princeton: Princeton University Press, 1972.

Benjamin, Walter. "The Work of Art in the Age of Mechanical Reproduction." *Illuminations.* Edited by Hannah Arendt. Translated by Harry Zohn. New York: Schocken Books, 1969.

Bennett, Jane. *Vibrant Matter: A Political Ecology of Things.* Durham, NC: Duke University Press, 2010.

Benson, Pamela J. "Florimell at Sea: The Action of Grace in *Faerie Queene*, Book III." *Spenser Studies* 6 (1986): 83–94.

Berger, Harry, Jr. *Revisionary Play: Studies in The Spenserian Dynamics.* Berkeley and London: University of California Press, 1988.

Berlant, Lauren. *Cruel Optimism.* Durham, NC: Duke University Press, 2011.

———. "Intimacy: A Special Issue." Introduction to *Critical Inquiry.* Chicago: University of Chicago Press, 2000.

———. *The Queen of America Goes to Washington City: Essays on Sex and Citizenship.* Durham: Duke University Press, 1997.

Berland, Lauren, and Lee Edelman. *Sex, Or The Unbearable.* Durham and London: Duke University Press, 2014.

Bersani, Leo. *A Future for Astyanax: Character and Desire in Literature.* Boston: Little, Brown and Company, 1976.

Bevington, David, ed. *Antony and Cleopatra.* Cambridge: Cambridge University Press, 1990.

Blake, Liza. "Dildos and Accessories: The Functions of Early Strap-Ons." *Ornamentalism: The Art of Renaissance Accessories.* Edited by Bella Mirabella. Ann Arbor: University of Michigan Press, 2011, 130–55.

Blick, Fred. "Spenser's *Amoretti* and Elizabeth Boyle: Her Name Immortalized." *Spenser Studies* 23 (2008): 309–35.

Bly, Mary. "Bawdy Puns and Lustful Virgins: The Legacy of Juliet's Desire in Comedies of the Early 1600." Edited by Stanley Wells. *Shakespeare Survey* 49, Cambridge: Cambridge University Press, 1996.

Boaistuau, Pierre. *Histoires prodigieuses.* Edited by Stephen Bamforth. Annotated by Jean Céard. Chicago, 2012.

Bocaccio. *De genealogia deorum, Boccaccio on Poetry.* Edited and Translated by Charles G. Osgood. Princeton: Princeton Univeristy Press, 1930.

Boehrer, Bruce. "Behn's 'Disappointment' and Nashe's 'Choise of Valentines': Pornographic Poetry and the Influence of Anxiety." *Essays in Literature* 16.2 (1989): 172–87.

———. "Ovid and the Dilemma of the Cuckold in English Renaissance Drama." *Ovid and the Renaissance Body.* Edited by Goran V. Stanivukovic. Toronto: University of Toronto Press, 2001, 171–90.

Bolzoni, Lina. *The Gallery of Memory: Literary and Iconographic Models in the Age of the Printing Press*. Toronto: University of Toronto Press, 2001.
——. *The Web of Images*. Aldershot: Ashgate, 2004.
Bronfen, Elisabeth. *Over Her Dead Body: Death, Femininity and the Aesthetic*. New York: Rutledge, 1992.
Borris, Kenneth. "Platonism and Spenser's Poetic: Idealized Imitation, Merlin's Mirror, and the Florimells." *Spenser Studies* 24 (2009): 209–68.
Bromley, James M., and Will Stockton. *Sex before Sex: Figuring the Act in Early Modern England*. Minneapolis: University of Minnesota Press, 2013.
Bromley, Laura G. "The Lost Lucrece: Middleton's *The Ghost of Lucrece*." *Papers on Language and Literature*, 21 (1985): 258–74.
——. "Lucrece's Re-creation. *Shakespeare Quarterly* 34, no. 2 (Summer 1983): 200–11.
Brooke, Arthur. *Romeus and Juliet*. Edited by J.J. Munro. New York: Chatto and Windus, 1908.
Brown, Georgia. *Redefining Elizabethan Literature*. Cambridge: Cambridge University Press, 2004.
——. *Thomas Nashe*. Edited by Georgia Brown. Surrey, UK: Ashgate, 2011, 29–88.
Burg, B. R. "The Sick and the Dead: The Development of Psychological Theory on Necrophilia from Krafft-Ebing to the Present." *Journal of the History of the Behavioral Sciences* (1982): 242–54.
Burton, Robert. *The Anatomy of Melancholy*. Edited by Holbrook Jackson. New York: New York Review of Book, 2001.
Butterfield, Andrew. "Monument and Memory in Early Renaissance Florence." In *Art, Memory, and Family in Renaissance Florence*. Edited by Giovanni Ciappelli and Patricia Lee Rubin. Cambridge: Cambridge University Press, 2000.
Cambrensis, Giraldus. Vol. 8, *Opera*. Edited by George F. Warner. Wiesbaden: Kraus Reprints, 1964.
Camino, Mercedes Maroto. *'The Stage Am I': Raping Lucrece in Early Modern England*. Lewiston, New York: Edwin Mellen Press, 1995.
Campana, Joseph. "The Child's Two Bodies: Shakespeare, Sovereignty, and the End of Succession." *ELH* 81, (Fall 2014): 811–39.
——. *The Pain of Reformation: Spenser, Vulnerability, and the Ethics of Masculinity*. New York: Fordham University Press, 2012.
Cantabrigiensis, G. P. *Libellus de Memoria*. London, 1584.
Carruthers, Mary. *The Book of Memory: A Study of Memory in Medieval Culture*. Cambridge: Cambridge University Press, 1990.
Carter, Sarah. *Ovidian Myth and Sexual Deviance in Early Modern English Literature*. Basingstoke, United Kingdom: Palgrave Macmillan, 2011.
Case, John. *Speculum Moralium Quaestionum*. Oxford: Barnes, 1585.
Catty, Jocelyn. *Writing Rape, Writing Women in Early Modern England*. Basingstoke, UK: Macmillan, 1999.
Cicero. *Rhetorica Ad Herennium*. Translated by Harry Caplan, Loeb Classical Library. Cambridge: Harvard University Press, 1968.
——. *Ad Herennium*. Edited by Harry Caplan. Cambridge, MA: Harvard University Press. London: William Heinemann, 1989.
Charnes, Linda. *Hamlet's Heirs: Shakespeare and the Politics of a New Millennium*. New York: Routledge, 2006.

Charron, Pierre. *Of Wisedome*. Translated by Samson Lennard. London, 1608.
Cheeke, Stephen. *The Aesthetics of Ekphrasis*. Manchester and New York: Manchester University Press, 2008.
Child, Francis James. *The English and Scottish Popular Ballads*, 5 vols. Boston: Houghton, Mifflin, and Company, 1884–1898. Reprint. New York: Dover, 1965.
Christianson, Sven-Ake. *The Handbook of Emotion and Memory: Research and Theory*. New York: Psychology Press, 1992.
Clark, Andy, and David J. Chalmers. "The Extended Mind." In *Supersizing the Mind: Embodiment, Action, and Cognitive Extension*. Oxford and New York: Oxford University Press, 2011.
Clark, Danielle. "Ovid's *Heroides*, Drayton and the Articulation of the Feminine in the English Renaissance." *Renaissance Studies* 22.3, (2008): 385–400.
———. "'Signifying, but not Sounding': Gender and Paratext in the Complaint Genre." *Renaissance Paratexts*. Edited by Helen Smith and Louise Wilson. Cambridge: Cambridge University Press, 2011.
Coddon, Karin. "For Show or Useless Property: Necrophilia and *The Revenger's Tragedy*." *ELH* 1 (1994): 71–88.
Collington, Philip David. *"O Word of Fear": Imaginary Cuckoldry in Shakespeare's Plays*. Toronto: University of Toronto, 1998.
Cooper, Helen. *The English Romance in Time: Transforming Motifs from Geoffrey of Monmouth to the Death of Shakespeare*. Oxford: Oxford University Press, 2004.
Crawford, Kevin. "All His Intents Are Contrary to Man: Softened Masculinity and Staging in Middleton's *The Lady's Tragedy*." *Medieval and Renaissance Drama in England: An Annual Gathering of Research, Criticism and Reviews* 16 (2003): 101–29.
D'Addario, Christopher. "Stillness and Noise: The Ambiences of John Donne's Lyrics." *Philological Quarterly* 91, (2012): 419–42.
Daniel, Samuel. *Poems and a Defence of Ryme*. Edited by Arthur Colby Sprague. Cambridge, MA: Harvard University Press, 1930.
Dante. *Inferno*. Translated by Robert Hollander and Jean Hollander. New York: Doubleday, 2000. Reprint. New York: Anchor Books, 2002.
Danziger, Kurt. *Marking the Mind: A History of Memory*. Cambridge: Cambridge University Press, 2008.
Darcy, Robert. "Marlowe and Marston's *Cursus*." *Christopher Marlowe the Craftsman: Lives, Stage, and Page*. Farnham, Surrey, England and Burlington, VT: Ashgate, 2010.
Dasenbrock, Reed Way. "The Petrarchan Context of Spenser's Amoretti." *PMLA* 100.1 (1985): 38–50.
de Grazia, Margreta. *Hamlet without* Hamlet. Cambridge: Cambridge University Press, 2007.
Deats, Sara Munson, ed. *Antony and Cleopatra: New Critical Essays*. New York and London: Routledge, 2005.
Deleuze, Gilles. *Kant's Critical Philosophy*. Translated by Hugh Tamlinson and Barbara Haberjam. Minneapolis: University of Minnesota Press, 1999.
Deleuze, Gilles, and Félix Guattari. *A Thousand Plateaus: Capitalism and Schizophrenia*. Translated by Brian Massumi. New York: Continuum, 2003.
Deloney, Thomas. *The Works of Thomas Deloney*. Edited by Francis Oscar Mann. Oxford: Clarendon, 1912.

Derrida, Jacques. *Specters of Marx*. Translated by Peggy Kamuf. New York and London: Routledge, 1994.

———. *Specters of Marx: The State of the Debt, the Work of Mourning, and the New International*. London: Routledge, 2006.

Dickson, Alexander. *Alexandri Dicsoni Arelii de Vmbra Rationis & Iudicij Siue de Memoriae Virtute Prosopopoeia*. London, 1583.

Dimmock, Matthew. *Mythologies of the Prophet Muhammad in Early Modern English Culture*. Cambridge: Cambridge University Press, 2013.

Dobin, Howard. *Merlin's Disciples: Prophecy, Poetry, and Power in Renaissance England*. Stanford: Stanford University Press, 1990.

Dollimore, Jonathan. *Death, Desire, and Loss in Western Culture*. New York: Routledge, 1998.

Doody, Margaret Anne. *The True Story of the Novel*. New Brunswick, NJ: Rutgers University Press, 1996.

Dowden, Ernest. *Shakespeare: His Mind and Art*. London: Henry S. King & Company, 1875.

Downing, Lisa. *Desiring the Dead: Necrophilia and Nineteenth-Century French Literature*. Oxford: Legenda, European Humanities Research Centre, University of Oxford, 2003.

Drayton, Michael. *Englands Heroicall Epistles*. London: Iames Roberts, 1597.

Drinkwater, Megan O. "Which Letter: Text and Subtext in Ovid's *Heroides*." *American Journal of Philology* 128, 3 (2007): 367–87.

Du Vair, Guillarme. *The True Way to Virtue and Happiness*. London, 1623.

Dudley, Scott. "Conferring with the Dead: Necrophilia and Nostalgia in the Seventeenth Century." *ELH* 2 (1999): 277–94.

Duffy, Eamon. *The Stripping of the Altars: Traditional Religion in England 1400–1580*. New Haven: Yale University Press, 1992.

Dugan, Holly. *The Ephemeral History of Perfume: Scent and Sense in Early Modern England*. Baltimore: Johns Hopkins University Press, 2011.

Duncan, Helga. "'Headdie Ryots' as Reformations: Marlowe's Libertine Poetics." *Early Modern Literary Studies* 12.2 (2006): 1–38.

Duncan-Jones, Katherine, ed. *Shakespeare's Sonnets*. Revised Edition. A & C Black, 2010.

Eaton, Sara. "'Content with Art?: Seeing the Emblematic Woman in *The Second Maiden's Tragedy* and *The Winter's Tale*." In *Shakespeare Power and Punishment, a Volume of Essays*. Edited by Gillian Murray Kendall. Cranbury: Associated University Press, Inc., 1998.

Edelman, Lee. "Against Survival: Queerness in a Time That's out of Joint," *Shakespeare Quarterly* 62, (Summer 2011): 148–69.

———. *No Future: Queer Theory and the Death Drive*. Durham: Duke University Press, 2004.

Engel, William. *Death and Drama in Renaissance England: Shades of Memory*. Oxford: Oxford University Press, 2002.

Engel, William E. *Mapping Mortality: The Persistence of Memory and Melancholy in Early Modern England*. Amherst: University of Massachusetts Press, 1996.

Escobedo, Andrew. *Nationalism and Historical Loss in Renaissance England*. Ithaca: Cornell University Press, 2004.

Euripides. "Helen." *The Bacchae and Other Plays*. Translated by E. P. Coleridge. New York: Digireads Publishing, 2012.

Evans, Maurice. "Memory." In *The Spenser Encyclopedia*. Edited by A.C. Hamilton. Toronto: University of Toronto Press, 1992.

———. *Spenser's Anatomy of Heroism: A Commentary of The Faerie Queene*. Cambridge: Cambridge University Press, 1970.

Ewell, Barbara C. "Unity and the Transformation of Drayton's Poetics in *Englands Heroicall Epistles*. From Mirrored Ideals to 'The Chaos of the Mind.'" *MLQ* 44, (1983): 231–50.

Farely, John. "The Spontaneous Generation Controversy (1700–1860): The Origin of Parasitic Worms." *Journal of the History of Biology* 5, (Spring 1972): 95–125.

Ferguson, Margaret W. "2015 Presidential Theme: Negotiating Sites of Memory," https://www.mla.org/2015_pres_theme (Retrieved June 8, 2015).

Fernie, Ewan. *The Demonic: Literature and Experience*. New York and London: Routledge, 2012

Finn, Kavita Mudan. *The Last Plantagenet Consorts: Gender, Genre, and Historiography 1440–1627*. New York: Palgrave, 2012.

Fisher, Will. "'Had It a Codpiece, 'Twere a Man Indeed': The Codpiece as Constitutive Accessory in Early Modern English Culture." *Ornamentalism: The Art of Renaissance Accessories*. Edited by Bella Mirabella. Ann Arbor: University of Michigan Press, 2011, 102–29.

Fitz, L. T. "Egyptian Queens and Male Reviewers: Sexist Attitudes in *Antony and Cleopatra* Criticism." *Shakespeare Quarterly* 28 (1977): 302.

Foucault, Michel. "Sexual Choice, Sexual Act." *Foucault Live: Collected Interviews, 1961–1984*. Edited by Sylvère Lotringer. New York: Semiotext(e), 1996.

Frantz, David O. "The Union of Florimell and Marinell: The Triumph of Hearing." *Spenser Studies* 6, (1985):115–87.

Freccero, Carla. *Queer/Early/Modern*. Durham: Duke University Press, 2006.

———. "Queer Times." *After Sex: On Writing Since Queer Theory*. Edited by Janet Halley and Andrew Parker. Durham: Duke University Press, 2011.

———. "Romeo and Juliet Love Death." *Shakesqueer: A Queer Companion to the Complete Works of Shakespeare*. Edited by Madhavi Menon. Raleigh, NC: Duke University Press, 2011.

Freeman, Elizabeth. *Time Binds: Queer Temporalities, Queer Histories*. Durham, NC: Duke University Press, 2010.

Friedman, Jeff. "Muscle Memory: Performing Embodied Knowledge." *Art and the Performance of Memory*. Edited by Richard Candída Smith. London: Routledge, 2002.

Frow, John. *Time and Commodity Culture: Essays in Cultural Theory and Postmodernity*. Oxford: Clarendon Press, 1997.

Fulkerson, Laurel. *The Ovidian Heroine as Author: Reading, Writing, and Community in the Heroides*. Cambridge: Cambridge University Press, 2005.

Galotti, Kathleen M. *Cognitive Psychology In and Out of the Laboratory*. New York: Cengage Learning, 2008.

Gil, Daniel Juan. *Before Intimacy: Asocial Sexuality in Early Modern England*. Minneapolis: University of Minnesota Press, 2006.

Girouard, Mark. *Elizabethan Architecture*. New Haven and London: Yale University Press for The Paul Mellon Centre for Studies in British Art, 2009.

Gittings, Clare. *Death, Burial, and the Individual in Early Modern England*. London: Croom Helm, 1984.

Godwin, Laura Grace. "'There is nothin' like a Dame': Christopher Marlowe's Helen of Troy at the Royal Shakespeare Company." *Shakespeare Bulletin* 27.1, (Spring 2009): 69–79.
Goldberg, Jonathan, ed. *Queering the Renaissance*. Durham: Duke, 1994.
Goldberg, Jonathan, and Madhavi Menon. "Queering History." *PMLA* 120.5 (2005): 1608–17.
Golding, Arthur. *The xv bookes of P. Ovidius Naso, entytled Metamorphosis, translated oute of Latin into English meeter.* London: William Seres, 1567.
Gouge, William. *Of Domesticall Duties*. London: 1622.
Grafton, Richard. *A Chronicle at large*. London: 1569.
Gratarolo, Guglielmo. *The Castel of Memorie*. London, 1562.
Greaves, J. E. "Some Interpretations of Life Phenomena and their Practical Significance." *The Monist* 33, (1923): 1–14.
Greenblatt, Stephen. *Hamlet in Purgatory*. Princeton: Princeton University Press, 2001.
———. *Renaissance Self-Fashioning: From More to Shakespeare*. Chicago and London: The University of Chicago Press, 1984.
Guthke, Karl S. *The Gender of Death: A Cultural History in Art and Literature*. New York: Cambridge University Press, 1999.
Guy-Bray, Stephen. *Homoerotic Space: The Poetics of Loss in Renaissance Literature*. Toronto: University of Toronto Press, 2002.
———. *Loving in Verse: Poetic Influence as Erotic*. Toronto and London: University of Toronto Press, 2006.
———. "Rosamond's Complaint: Daniel, Ovid, and the Purpose of Poetry." *Renaissance Studies* 22.3, (2008): 338–50.
———. Spenser's Filthy Matter," *Explicator* 62.4 (2004): 194.
Hadfield, Andrew. *Edmund Spenser: A Life*. Oxford: Oxford University Press, 2012.
———. "The Power and Rights of the Crown in *Hamlet* and *King Lear*: 'The King—the King's to Blame.'" *The Review of English Studies* 54, no. 217 (2003): 566–86.
Hall, Edgar A. "Spenser and Two Old French Grail Romances." *PMLA* 28.4 (1913): 539–54.
Hall, Michael. "Lewd but Familiar Eyes: The Narrative Tradition of Rape and Shakespeare's *The Rape of Lucrece*." In *Women, Violence, and the English Renaissance Stage: Essays Honoring Paul Jorgensen*, 51–72. Edited by Linda Woodbridge and Sharon Beehler. Tempe, AZ: Arizona Center for Medieval and Renaissance Studies, 2003.
Halpern, Richard. "Eclipse of Action: Hamlet and the Political Economy of Playing." *Shakespeare Quarterly* 59, (2008): 450–82.
Hamilton, A. C. et al., eds. "Marinell." *The Spenser Encyclopedia*. Toronto: University of Toronto Press, 1990.
Hampton, Timothy. *Writing from History: The Rhetoric of Exemplarity in Renaissance Literature*. Ithaca: Cornell University Press, 1990.
Hankins, John E. "'God Kissing Carrion:' A Theory of the Generation of Life." *PMLA* 64, (June 1949): 507–16.
Hardie, Philip R. *Ovid's Poetics of Illusion*. Cambridge: Cambridge University Press, 2002.
Harding, Vanessa. *The Dead and the Living in Paris and London, 1500–1670*. Cambridge: Cambridge University Press, 2002.
Harkness, Deborah, and Jean E. Howard, ed. *The Places and Spaces of Early Modern London*. Special issue of *Huntington Library Quarterly* 71 (2008).

Harris, Jonathan Gil. *Untimely Matter in the Age of Shakespeare*. Philadelphia: University of Pennsylvania Press, 2009.
Harvey, Elizabeth D. "Pleasure's Oblivion: Displacements of Generation in Spenser's *Faerie Queene*." *Forgetting in Early Modern English Literature and Culture: Lethe's Legacies*. Edited by Christopher Ivic and Grant Williams. London and New York: Routledge, 2004.
Hassel, R. Chris Jr. "Hamlet's 'Too, Too Solid Flesh.'" *The Sixteenth Century Journal*, 25 (Autumn 1994): 609–22.
Hebel, J. William, ed. "Englands Heroicall Epistles." Vol. 2, *Works of Michael Drayton*. Oxford: Blackwell, 1961.
Heffernan, James A. W. *Museum of Words: The Poetics of Ekphrasis from Homer to Ashbery*. Chicago and London: The University of Chicago Press, 2004.
Helfer, Rebeca. *Spenser's Ruins and the Art of Recollection*. Toronto: University of Toronto Press, 2012.
Helgerson, Richard. *Self-Crowned Laureates: Spenser, Jonson, Milton and the Literary System*. Berkeley: University of California Press, 1983.
Heltzel, Virgil B. *Fair Rosamond: A Study of the Development of a Literary Theme*. Evanston: Northwestern University Studies, 1947.
Henderson, Diana E. *Passion Made Public: Elizabethan Lyric, Gender, and Performance*. Urbana: University of Illinois Press, 1995.
Heng, Geraldine. *Empire of Magic: Medieval Romance and the Politics of Cultural Fantasy*. New York: Columbia University Press, 2003.
Herron, Haly. *A New Discourse of Moral Philosophy*. London: 1579.
Higden, Ranulf. *Polychronicon*. Translated by John of Trevisa. Westminster: Caxton, 1482.
Highley, Christopher. *Shakespeare, Spenser, and the Crisis in Ireland*. Cambridge: Cambridge University Press, 1997.
Hirschfeld, Magnus. *Sexual Anomalies*. New York: Emerson Books, 1948.
Hiscock, Andrew. *Reading Memory in Early Modern Literature*. Cambridge: Cambridge University Press, 2011.
Hodges, Kenneth. "Making Arthur Protestant: Translating Malory's Grail Quest into Spenser's Book of Holiness." *The Review of English Studies*, 62.254, (2011): 193–211.
———. "Reformed Dragons: *Bevis of Hampton*, Sir Thomas Malory's *Le Morte Darthur* and Spenser's *Faerie Queene*." *Texas Studies in Literature and Language*, 54.1, (2012): 110–31.
Holderness, Graham. "'I covet your skull': Death and Desire in Hamlet." *Shakespeare Survey 60 Theatres for Shakespeare* (2007): 223–36.
Holinshed, Raphael. *Chronicles* 3 (1587).
Holland, Peter. *Shakespeare, Memory, and Performance*. Cambridge, UK: Cambridge University Press, 2006.
Homer. *The Iliad*. Translated by Richard Lattimore. Chicago and London: University of Chicago Press, 1961.
Honigmann, E. A. J. "Shakespeare's Will and Testamentary Traditions." *Shakespeare and Cultural Traditions. The Selected Proceedings of the International Shakespeare Association, World Congress, Tokyo, 1991*. Eds. Tetsuo Kishi, Roger Pringle and Stanley Wells, 127–37. Newark, NJ: University of Delaware Press, 1994.
Honigmann, E. A. J. and Susan Brock. *Playhouse Wills 1558–1642: An Edition of Wills by Shakespeare and his Contemporaries in the London Theatre*. Manchester: Manchester University Press, 1993.

Hooker, Richard. *Of the Lawes of Ecclesiastical Politie.* London: 1604.
Hopkins, Lisa. *The Female Hero in English Renaissance Tragedy.* Houndmills, Basingstoke, Hampshire: Palgrave Macmillan, 2002.
Houlbrooke, Ralph. *Death, Religion, and the Family in England 1480–1750.* Oxford: Clarendon Press, 1998.
Howard, Jean. *Theater of a City.* Philadelphia: University of Pennsylvania Press, 2007.
Howell, Wilbur Samuel. *Logic and Rhetoric in England, 1500–1700.* Princeton: Princeton University Press, 1956.
Hume, David. *The History of England.* Vol 4. Indianapolis: Liberty Fund, 1983.
Hunt, Maurice. "Hellish Work in *The Faerie Queene*." *Studies in English Literature, 1500–1900* 41.1 (2001): 91–108.
Hutson, Lorna. "Imagining Justice: Kantorowicz and Shakespeare." *Representations* 106, (Spring 2009): 118–42.
Irigaray, Luce. "The Bodily Encounter with the Mother." In *The Irigaray Reader*, 34–46. Edited by Margaret Whitford. Oxford: Blackwell, 1991.
Ives, E. W. "The Genesis of the Statue of Uses." *The English Historical Review* 82.325 (Oct., 1967): 673–97.
Ivic, Christopher. "Spenser and Interpellative Memory." *Ars Reminiscendi: Mind and Memory in Renaissance Culture.* Edited by Donald Beecher and Grant Williams. Toronto: Centre for Reformation and Renaissance Studies, 2009.
Jellerson, Donald. *Ghost Complaint: Historiography, Gender, and the Return of the Dead in Elizabethan Literature.* Nashville: Vanderbilt University, 2009.
———. "Haunted History and the Birth of the Republic in Middleton's *Ghost of Lucrece*," *Criticism* 53, no. 1 (Winter 2011): 53–82.
Jewell, William. *The Golden Cabinet of True Treasure: Containing the Summe of Morall Philosophy.* London, 1612.
Johnson, Laurie, John Sutton, and Evelyn Tribble, eds. *Embodied Cognition and Shakespeare's Theatre: The Early Modern Body-Mind.* New York and London: Routledge, 2014.
Jones, Anne Rosalind, and Peter Stallybrass. *Renaissance Clothing in the Materials of Memory.* Cambridge: Cambridge University Press, 2000.
Jones, John Henry. *The English Faust Book.* Cambridge: Cambridge University Press, 1994.
Jones, Melissa. "Spectacular Impotence: Or, Things That Hardly Ever Happen in the Critical History of Pornography." *Sex before Sex: Figuring the Act in Early Modern England.* Edited by James M. Bromley and Will Stockton. Minneapolis: University of Minnesota Press, 2013, 89–110.
Jones, William R. "Say They Are Saints Although That Saints They Show Not." *Huntington Library Quarterly* 73, no. 1 (March 2010): 83–98.
Jonson, Ben. "Explorata: Or Discoveries." *The Complete Poems.* Edited by George Parfitt. Harmondsworth: Penguin Books, 1974.
———. *Volpone, or, The Fox.* Edited by Brian Parker and David Bevington. Manchester: Manchester University Press, 1999.
Jonson, William C. *Spenser's Amoretti: Analogies of Love.* Lewisburg: Bucknell University Press, 1990.
Joyce, James. *Ulysses.* Edited by Hans Walter Gabler. New York: Vintage Books, 1986.
Kahan, Jeffrey. "Violating Hippocrates: Dildoes and Female Desire in Thomas Nashe's 'The Choise of Valentines.'" *Paradoxa* 2.2 (1996): 204–16.

Kahn, Coppélia. "*Lucrece*: The Sexual Politics of Subjectivity." In *Rape and Representation*. Edited by Lynn A. Higgins and Brenda R. Silver. New York: Columbia University Press, 1991.

———. "Publishing Shame: *The Rape of Lucrece*." In *A Companion to Shakespeare's Works*. 4:259–74. Edited by Richard Dutton and Jean E. Howard. Oxford, Blackwell, 2003.

Kahn, Victoria. "Political Theology and Fiction in *The King's Two Bodies*." *Representations* 106, (Spring 2009): 77–101.

Kantorowicz, Ernst. *The King's Two Bodies: A Study in Medieval Political Theology*. Princeton: Princeton University Press, 1957. Reprint 1985.

Keefer, Michael. "Fairer Than the Evening Air: Marlowe's Gnostic Helen of Troy and the Tropes of Belatedness of Historical Mediation." *Fantasies of Troy: Classical Tales and the Social Imaginary in Medieval and Early Modern Europe*. Edited by Alan Shepard and Stephen D. Powell. Toronto: Centre for Reformation and Renaissance Studies, 2004.

Keenan, Mary Emily. "St. Augustine and Biological Science." *Osiris* 7, (1939): 588–608.

Keener, Fredrick M., ed. *Virgil's Aeneid* [1697]. Translated by John Dryden. London: Penguin, 1997.

Keil, Charlie. "'To Here from Modernity': Style, Historiography, and Transitional Cinema." *American Cinema's Transitional Era: Audiences, Institutions, Practices*. Edited by Charlie Keil and Shelley Stamp. Berkeley: University of California Press, 2004.

Kennedy, Duncan F. "Epistolarity: The *Heroides*." *The Cambridge Companion to Ovid*. Edited by Philip Hardie. Cambridge: Cambridge University Press, 2002.

Kerrigan, John, ed. *A Lover's Complaint and The Sonnets*. New York: Penguin Classics, 1986.

Kiessling, Nicolas. "Faustus and the Sin of Demoniality." *Studies in English Literature 1500–1900* 15.2, (Spring 1975): 205–11.

King, Andrew. The Faerie Queene *and Middle English Romance: The Matter of Just Memory*. Oxford and New York: Clarendon, 2000.

Kisery, Andras. "'I Lack Advancement': Public Rhetoric, Private Prudence, and the Political Agent in *Hamlet*, 1561–1609." *ELH* 81, (Spring 2014): 29–60.

Klein, Kerwin Lee. "On the Emergence of Memory in Historical Discourse." *Representations* 69, (Winter 2000): 127–50.

Knight, G. Wilson. "The Spenserian Fluidity." *Edmund Spenser*. Edited by Paul J. Alpers. Harmondsworth: Penguin, 1969.

Knight, Nicholas W. "The Narrative Unity of Book V of *The Faerie Queene*: 'That Part of Justice which is Equity.'" *Review of English Studies* 21 (1970): 267–94.

Korda, Natasha. "Dame Usury: Gender, Credit and (Ac)counting in the 'Sonnets' and 'The Merchant of Venice'." *Shakespeare Quarterly* 60.2 (Summer 2009): 129–53.

Kostić, Veselin. *Spenser's Sources of Italian Poetry: A Study in Comparative Literature*. Beograd: Filološki fakultet, 1969.

Kracauer, Siegfried. "Cult of Distraction." *The Mass Ornament: Weimar Essays*. Edited and Translated by Thomas Y. Levin. Cambridge, MA: Harvard University Press, 1995.

Krieger, Murray. *Ekphrasis: The Illusion of the Natural Sign*. Baltimore and London: The Johns Hopkins University Press, 1992.

La Primaudaye, Pierre de. *The Second Part of the French Academie*. London, 1605.

———. *The Third Volume of the French Academie*. 2nd ed. Translated by R. Dolman. London: Eliot's Court Press, 1601.

Lambert, Franz. *The Mind and Judgment of Master Frances Lambert of Avenna of The Wyll of Man*. London: 1548.

Lambert, Mark. "Malory, Thomas." *The Spenser Encylopaedia*. Edited by A.C. Hamilton et al. Florence: KY: Routledge, 1990.

Latour, Bruno. *Pandora's Hope: Essays on the Reality of Science Studies*. Cambridge, MA: Harvard University Press, 1999.

Laurentius, M. Andreas. *A Discourse of the Preservation of the Sight*. Translated by Richard Surphlet. London, 1599.

Lees-Jeffries, Hester. *Shakespeare and Memory*. Oxford: Oxford University Press, 2013.

Leslie, Michael. *"Fierce Warres and Faithfull Loves": Martial and Chivalric Symbolism in* The Faerie Queene. Cambridge, UK: D.S. Brewer, 1983.

Lesnick, Henry G. "The Structural Significance of Myth and Flattery in Peele's *Arraignment of Paris*." *SP* 65.2 (1968): 163–70.

Lewis, Rhodri. "*Hamlet*, Metaphor, and Memory." *Studies in Philology* 109, (Fall 2012): 609–41.

Lindheim, Sara. *Mail and Female: Epistolary Narrative and Desire in the Heroides*. Madison: University of Wisconsin Press, 2003.

———. "*Omina Vincit Amor*: Or, Why Oenone Should Have Known It Would Never Work Out (Eclogue 10 and *Heroides* 5)." *Materiali e discussioni per l'analisi dei testi classici* 44 (2000): 83–101.

Llewellyn, Nigel. *The Art of Death: Visual Culture in English Death Ritual c. 1500–c.1800*. London: Reaktion Books, 1991.

———. *Funeral Monuments in Post-Reformation England*. Cambridge: Cambridge University Press, 2000.

Lodhia, Sheetal. "'The house is hers, the soul is but a tenant': Material Self-Fashioning and Revenge Tragedy." *Early Theatre* 12.2 (2009): 135–61.

Long, Zackariah C. "*The Spanish Tragedy* and *Hamlet*: Infernal Memory in English Renaissance Revenge Tragedy." *English Literary Renaissance* 44, (Spring 2014): 153–92.

Luria, Keith P. "Separated by Death? Burials, Cemeteries, and Confessional Boundaries in Seventeenth-Century France" *French Historical Studies* 24, no. 2 (Spring 2001): 185–222.

Lyly, John. *The Descent of Euphues: Three Elizabethan Romance Stories*. Edited by James Winny. Cambridge: Cambridge University Press, 2015.

MacDonald, Joyce Green. "Speech, Silence, and History in *The Rape of Lucrece*." *Shakespeare Studies* 22 (1994): 77–103.

MacInnes, Ian. "The Politic Worm: Invertebrate Life in the Early Modern English Body." *The Indistinct Human in Renaissance Literature*. Edited by Jean Feerick and Vin Nardizzi (2012): 253–73.

MacKendrick, Karmen. *Counterpleasures*. Albany, NY: SUNY Press, 1999.

Maguire, Laurie. "Helen of Troy: Representing Absolute Beauty in Language." *Sederi* 16, (2006): 31–51.

Manley, Lawrence. *Literature and Culture in Early Modern London*. Cambridge: Cambridge University Press, 2005.

Marlowe, Christopher. *Doctor Faustus: The A-Text*. In *Doctor Faustus and Other Plays*, 138–83. Edited by David Bevington and Eric Rasmussen. Oxford: Oxford University Press, 1995.

260 Selected Bibliography

———. "The Tragical History of Doctor Faustus," in *English Renaissance Drama: A Norton Anthology*. Edited by David Bevington, Lars Engle, et al. New York and London: W.W. Norton & Company, 2002.

Marsh, Christopher. "Attitudes to Will-Making in Early Modern England." *When Death Do Us Part: Understanding and Interpreting the Probate Records of Early Modern England*. Edited by Tom Arkell, Nesta Evans, and Nigel Goose. Oxford: Leopard's Head Press, 2000.

Marshall, Cynthia. *The Shattering of the Self: Violence, Subjectivity, and Early Modern Texts*. Baltimore and London: Johns Hopkins University Press, 2002.

Marshall, Peter. *Beliefs and the Dead in Reformation England*. Oxford: Oxford University Press, 2002.

Martin, Randall. "Ecology, Evolution, and Hamlet." *Renaissance Shakespeare/Shakespeare Renaissances Proceedings of the Ninth World Shakespeare Conference* 1, (2014): 38–50.

Martz, Louis L., ed. *Hero and Leander by Christopher Marlowe: A Facsimile of the First Edition, London 1598*. Johnson Reprint: New York, 1972.

Masten, Jeffrey. *Textual Intercourse: Collaboration, Authorship, and Sexualities in Renaissance Drama*. Cambridge: Cambridge University Press, 1997.

McCartney, Eugene S. "Spontaneous Generation and Kindred Notions in Antiquity." *Transactions and Proceedings of the American Philological Association* 51, (1920): 101–15.

Middleton, Thomas. *The Ghost of Lucrece*, 1985–1998. Edited by G. B. Shand. In *The Complete Works of Thomas Middleton*. Edited by Gary Taylor and John Lavagnino. Oxford, Clarendon Press, 2010.

———. *The Lady's Tragedy*. In *Middleton: The Collected Works*. Edited by Gray Taylor and John Lavagnino. Oxford: Clarendon Press, 2007.

Miller, David L. "Spenser's Vocation, Spenser's Career." *ELH* 50 (1983): 215–16.

———. *The Poem's Two Bodies: The Poetics of the 1590 Faerie Queene*. Princeton: Princeton University Press, 1988.

Miller, David Lee. *The Poem's Two Bodies: The Poetics of the 1590 'Faerie Queene.'* Princeton: Princeton University Press, 1988.

Miller, Jacqueline T. "The Status of Faeryland: Spenser's 'Vniust Possession.'" *Spenser Studies* 5 (1985): 31–44.

Miller, Paul Allen. "The Parodic Sublime: Ovid's Reception of Virgil in *Heroides* 7." *Materiali e discussioni per l'analisi dei testi classici* 52 (2004): 57–72.

Monmouth, Geoffrey of. *The History of the Kings of Britain*. Translated by Lewis Thorpe. London: Penguin, 1966.

Montrose, Louis. *The Subject of Elizabeth: Authority, Gender, and Representation*. Chicago: University of Chicago Press, 2006.

Montrose, Louis Adrian. "Gifts and Reasons: The Contexts of Peele's *Araygnement of Paris*." *ELH* 47.3 (1980).

Moretti, Franco. *Modern Epic: The World System from Goethe to García Márquez*. London: Verso, 1996.

Mornay, Phillipe De. *The True Nature of Man's Owne Self. Written in French by Monsieur du Plessis, Lord of Plessie Marlay and Truly Translated by A.M.* London: 1602.

Moss, Daniel D. *The Ovidian Vogue: Literary Fashion and Imitative Practice in Late Elizabethan England*. Toronto: University of Toronto Press, 2014.

Moulton, Ian Frederick. *Before Pornography: Erotic Writing in Early Modern England*. Oxford, UK: Oxford University Press, 2000.

Muñoz, José Esteban. *Cruising Utopia: The Then and There of Queer Futurity*. New York: New York University Press, 2009.

Murrin, Michael. *The Veil of Allegory: Some Notes toward a Theory of Allegorical Rhetoric in the English Renaissance*. Chicago: University of Chicago Press, 1969.

Nashe, Thomas. *The Choise of Valentines: Or the Merie Ballad of Nash His Dildo*. Edited by John S. Farmer. London, 1899.

Neely, Carol Thomas. *Distracted Subjects: Madness and Gender in Shakespeare and Early Modern Culture*. Ithaca: Cornell University Press, 2004.

Neill, Michael. *Issues of Death: Mortality and Identity in English Renaissance Tragedy*. Oxford: Clarendon Press, 1997.

Newman, Karen. *Cultural Capitals: Early Modern London and Paris*. Princeton: Princeton University Press, 2009.

Newstok, Scott L. *Quoting Death in Early Modern England: The Poetics of Epitaphs beyond the Tomb*. New York: Palgrave Macmillan, 2009.

Nicholls, Andrew. "Venus and Adonis Frieze." *Shakesqueer: A Queer Companion to the Complete Works of Shakespeare*. Edited by Madhavi Menon. Durham and London: Duke University Press, 2011.

Nobus, Dany. "Over My Dead Body: On the Histories and Cultures of Necrophilia." In *Inappropriate Relationships: The Unconventional, the Disapproved, and the Forbidden*. Edited by Robin Goodwin and Duncan Cramer. Mahwah: Lawrence Erlbaum Associates, Inc., 2009.

Nohrnberg, James. *The Analogy of* The Faerie Queene. Princeton: Princeton University Press, 1976.

Nora, Pierre. "General Introduction: Between Memory and History." *Realms of Memory: Rethinking the French Past Volume 1*. Edited by Pierre Nora. Translated by Arthur Goldhammer. New York: Columbia University Press, 1996.

Norbrook, David. "Rhetoric, Ideology and The Elizabethan World Picture." *Renaissance Rhetoric*. Edited by Peter Mack. MacMillan Press: London, 1994.

Nunn, Hillary. *Staging Anatomies: Dissection and Spectacle in Early Stuart Tragedy*. Burlington: Ashgate, 2005.

O'Callaghan, Michelle. *Thomas Middleton, Renaissance Dramatist*. Edinburgh, Scotland: Edinburgh University Press, 2009.

Onions, C. T. *A Shakespeare Glossary*. Oxford: The Clarendon Press, 1963.

Orgel, Stephen. "Tobacco and Boys: How Queer Was Marlowe?" *GLQ: A Journal of Gay and Lesbian Studies* 6.4 (2000): 555–76.

Orlin, Lena Cowen. *Locating Privacy in Tudor London*. Oxford: Oxford University Press, 2007.

———. *Metamorphoses*. Translated by A.D. Melville. Oxford: Oxford University Press, 2009.

———. *Material London, ca. 1600*. Philadelphia: University of Pennsylvania Press, 2000.

Ovid. *Heroides and Amores*. Translated by Grant Showerman. Cambridge: Harvard University Press, 1914.

Paglia, Camille. "Sex." In *The Spenser Encyclopedia*. Edited by A.C. Hamilton. Toronto: University of Toronto Press, 1992.

———. *Sexual Personae: Art and Decadence from Neferiti to Emily Dickinson*. Cumberland: Yale University Press, 1990.

Parker, Patricia. *Literary Fat Ladies: Rhetoric, Gender, Property*. London: Methuen, 1987.

Partridge, Eric. *Shakespeare's Bawdy: A Literary and Psychological Essay and a Comprehensive Glossary*. rev. ed. New York: E. P. Dutton, 1955.

Paster, Gail Kern. "Becoming the Landscape: The Ecology of the Passions in the Legend of Temperance." *Environment and Embodiment*. Edited by Mary-Floyd Wilson and Garrett A. Sullivan, Jr. Basingstoke: Palgrave, 2007.

———. *The Body Embarrassed: Drama and the Disciplines of Shame in Early Modern England*. New York: Cornell University Press, 1993.

———. *The Idea of the City in the Age of Shakespeare*. Athens, GA: The University of Georgia Press, 1985.

———. "Thinking with Skulls in Holbein, *Hamlet*, Vesalius, and Fuller." *The Shakespearean International Yearbook* 11 (2011): 41–60.

Peele, George. *The Works of George Peele: Collected and Edited with Some Account of his Life and Writing, by the Rev. Alexander Dyce*. London: William Pickering, 1829.

Perkins, William. *A Treatise of Man's Imagination Shewing His Naturall Euill Thoughts: His Want of Good Thoughts: The Way to Reforme Them*. Cambridge, 1607.

———. *The Arte of Prophecying: or a Triste Concerning the Sacred and Onely True Manner and Methode of Preaching*. London, 1607.

Petrarch. *Canzoniere*. Edited by Marco Santagata. Milan: Arnoldo Mondadori, 1996.

Petrus, Ravennas. *The Art of Memory*. London, 1545.

Phayer, Thomas. *A Book of Presidents*. London: 1586.

Pikli, Natália "The Prince and the Hobby-Horse: Shakespeare and the Ambivalence of Early Modern Popular Culture." *Journal of Early Modern Studies* 2, (2013): 119-P40.

Plutarch, Thomas North, Jacques Amyot, Donato Acciaiuoli, and Simon Goulart. *The Lives of the Nobel Grecians and Romanes*. London: Thomas Vautroullier and Iohn Vight, 1579.

Porter, Joseph A. *Shakespeare's Mercutio: His History and Drama*. Chapel Hill: University of North Carolina Press, 1989.

Preedy, Chloe. "'I Am No Woman I': Gender, Sexuality, and Power in Elizabethan Erotic Verse." *E-Pisteme* 2.2 (2009): 46–57.

Prescott, Anne Lake. "Spenser's Shorter Poetry." *The Cambridge Companion to Spenser*. Edited by Andrew Hadfield. Cambridge: Cambridge University Press, 2001.

Prynne, William. *Histriomastix*. London: 1633.

Puttenham, George. *The Art of English Poesy: A Critical Edition*. Edited by Frank Whigham and Wayne A. Rebhorn. Ithaca and London: Cornell University Press, 2007.

Quiller-Couch, Arthur, ed. *Oxford Book of English Verse, 1250–1900*. Oxford: Clarendon Press, 1919.

Quintilian. *Institutio Oratoria*. Translated by H. E. Butler. Cambridge, MA and London: Harvard University Press, 1993.

Rainolds, John. *Th'overthrow of Stage-Playes*. London, 1607.

Reid, Lindsay Ann. *Ovidian Bibliofictions and the Tudor Book: Metamorphosing Classical Heroines in Late Medieval and Renaissance England*. Farnham: Ashgate, 2014.

Reynoldes, Edward. *A Treatise of the Passions and Faculties of the Soule of Man*. London, 1640.

Rich, Adrienne. *Poems: Selected and New, 1950–1974*. New York: W.W. Norton, 1975.

Riley, Henry T., ed. Vol. 2, *The Annals of Roger de Hovedon*. Translated by Henry T. Riley. New York: AMS Press, 1968.

Rimell, Victoria. *Ovid's Lovers: Desire, Difference, and the Poetic Imagination*. Cambridge: Cambridge University Press, 2006.

Rist, Thomas. *Revenge Tragedy and the Drama of Commemoration in Reforming England*. Ashgate: Burlington, 2008.

Ritscher, Lee A. *The Semiotics of Rape in Renaissance English Literature*. New York: Peter Lang, 2009.

Roach, Joseph. "History, Memory, Necrophilia." *The Ends of Performance*. Edited by Peggy Phelan and Jill Lane. New York: New York University Press, 1998.

Roche, Thomas P., Jr. *The Kindly Flame: A Study of the Third and Fourth Books of Spenser's* Faerie Queene. Princeton: Princeton University Press, 1964.

Rossi, Paolo. *Logic and the Art of Memory*. Translated by Stephen Clucas. London: The Athlone Press, 2000.

Rovang, Paul. *Refashioning 'Knights and Ladies Gentle Deeds': The Intertextuality of Spenser's* Faerie Queene *and Malory's* Morte Darthur. Madison, WI: Fairleigh Dickinson University Press, 1996.

Rowe, Nicolas. *The Works of Mr. William Shakespeare*. Vol. 5. London, 1709; New York: AMC Press, 1967.

Sanchez, Melissa. *Erotic Subjects: The Sexuality of Politics in Early Modern English Literature*. Oxford: Oxford University Press, 2011.

Schacter, Daniel L. *Searching For Memory: The Brain, The Mind, And The Past*. Reprint edition. Basic Books, 2008.

Schelling, Felix. "The Source of Peele's *Arraignment of Paris*." *MLN* 8.4 (1893): 103–104.

Schmitt, Carl. *Hamlet to Hecuba: The Intrusion of the Time into the Play*. Translated by David Pan with Introduction by Julia Reinhard Lupton. Telos Press, 2009.

Schwyzer, Philip. "Shakespeare's Arts of Reenactment: Henry at Blackfriars, Richard at Rougemont." *The Arts of Remembrance in Early Modern England: Memorial Cultures of the Post Reformation*. Edited by Andrew Gordon and Thomas Rist. Burlington: Ashgate, 2013.

Shakespeare, William. *Antony and Cleopatra*. Edited by David Bevington. Cambridge: Cambridge University Press, 1990.

———. *Hamlet, The Norton Shakespeare*, Second Edition. Edited by Stephen Greenblatt et al. Oxford: Oxford University Press, 2008.

———. *King Lear*. Edited by Walter Cohen, Stephen Greenblatt, J. E. Howard and K.nE. Maus. New York: W.W. Norton & Company, 1997.

———. *The Merchant of Venice*. Edited by Walter Cohen, Stephen Greenblatt, J. E. Howard and K. E. Maus. New York: W.W. Norton & Company, 1997.

———. *The Merry Wives of Windsor*. Edited by Walter Cohen, Stephen Greenblatt, J. E. Howard and K.. Maus. New York: W.W. Norton & Company, 1997.

———. *The Rape of Lucrece*. In *The Sonnets and Other Poems*. Edited by Jonathan Bate and Eric Rasmussen. New York: Modern Library, 2009.

———. *The Riverside Shakespeare*. Edited by G. Blakemore Evans et al. Boston: Houghton Mifflin, 1974.

———. *Shake-Speares Sonnets Never before Imprinted*. London, 1609.

———. *The Tragedy of Hamlet, Prince of Denmark*. Edited by Harold Jenkins. London: Thomson Learning, 2005.

264   Selected Bibliography

———. *The Tragedy of Julius Caesar*. Edited by David Daniell. London: Thomson Learning, 1998.

———. *Troilus and Cressida*. Edited by David Bevington. London: Arden, 1998.

Shell, Alison. *Shakespeare and Religion*. Arden, 2010.

Shepherd, Simon. *Spenser*. Atlantic Highlands, NJ: Humanities Press, 1989.

Sherlock, Peter. *Monuments and Memory in Early Modern England*. Aldershot: Ashgate, 2008.

Shichtman, Martin B. "Percival's Sister: Genealogy, Virginity, and Blood." Arthuriana 9, no.2 (1999): 11–20.

Shupack, Paul M. "Natural Justice and *King Lear*." *Cardoza Studies in Law and Literature* 9, no.1 (Spring-Summer, 1997): 67–105.

Sidney, Sir Philip. *An Apology for Poetry*. Edited by Geoffrey Shepherd. Manchester: Manchester University Press, 1973.

———. *An Apology for Poetry, Or The Defence of Poesy*. 3rd ed. Edited by Geoffrey Shepherd. Revised and Expanded by R. W. Maslen. Manchester and New York: Manchester University Press, 2002.

———. "The Defense of Poetry." *Miscellaneous Prose of Sir Philip Sidney*." Edited by Jan Van Dorsten and Katherine Duncan-Jones. Oxford: Clarendon, 1973.

Sigo, Cedar. "XXXV." *The Sonnets: Translating and Rewriting Shakespeare*. Edited by Sharmila Cohen and Paul Legault. Brooklyn: Telephone Books, 2013.

Silberman, Lauren. *Transforming Desire: Erotic Knowledge in Books III and IV of The Faerie Queene*. Berkeley: University of California Press, 1995.

Simpson, Evelyn, and George R. Potter, eds. *The Sermons of John Donne*. Vol. 10. Berkeley: University of California Press, 1954.

Singer, Ben. *Melodrama and Modernity: Early Sensational Cinema and Its Contexts*. New York: Columbia University Press, 2001.

Smith, Lucy Toulmin, ed. Vol. 1, *The Itinerary of John Leland*. Carbondale: Southern Illinois University Press, 1964, 328–29.

Solman, Joseph. *Aristotle's Master-piece: or The Secrets of Generation Displayed in all the Parts Thereof*. 1694. London: Garland, 1986.

Sorabji, Richard. *Aristotle on Memory*. University of Chicago Press, 2004.

Spenser, Edmund. "A Letter of the Authors ..." *The Faerie Queene*. 2nd ed. Edited by A.C. Hamilton et al. Harlow: Pearson, 2001.

———. "Letter to Raleigh." In *The Faerie Queene*. Edited by A.C. Hamilton et al. Harlow and London: Pearson Longman, 2001, 2007.

———. *The Faerie Queene*. Edited by A. C. Hamilton et al. Harlow and London: Pearson Longman, 2001, 2007.

———. *The Faerie Queene*. Edited by Thomas P. Roche, Jr. Harmondsworth. New York: Penguin Books, 1978.

———. *The Shepheardes Calender Conteyning Twelve Aeglogues Proportionable to the Twelve Monethes*. 1579.

———. "Sonnet 33." *Amoretti and Epithalamion*. In *Edmund Spenser's Poetry*. 3rd Edition. Edited by Hugh Maclean and Anne Lake Prescott. New York: W.W. Norton & Company, 1993.

Spentzou, Efrossini. *Readers and Writers in Ovid's Heroides: Transgressions of Genre and Gender*. Oxford: Oxford University Press, 2003.

Spivak, James W., and William Matthews, eds. *Caxton's Malory*. Berkley: University of California Press, 1983.

Sprague, Arther Colby, ed. "The Complaint of Rosamond." *Poems and a Defence of Ryme*. London: Routledge and Kegan Paul, 1950.

Stanivukovic, Goran. "Beyond Sodomy: What is Still Queer about Early Modern Queer Studies?" *Queer Renaissaince Historiography: Backward Gaze*. Edited by Will Stockton, Stephen Guy-Bray, and Vincent Nardizzi. Farnham: Ashgate, 2009.

Stapleton, M. L. "'Devoid of Guilty Shame: Ovidian Tendencies in Spenser's Erotic Poetry." *Modern Philology* 105.2 (2007): 271–99.

Stapleton, M. L. *Marlowe's Ovid: The Elegies in the Marlowe Canon*. Surrey and London: Ashgate, 2014.

Steppat, Michael. *The Critical Reception of Shakespeare's Antony and Cleopatra from 1607 to 1905*. Amsterdam: Verlag B. R. Grüner, 1980.

Stewart, Alan, and Garrett A. Sullivan, Jr. "'Worme-eaten, and Full of Canker Holes': Materializing Memory in *The Faerie Queene* and *Lingua*." *Spenser Studies* 17 (2003): 215–38.

Stockton, Kathryn Bond. *The Queer Child, or Growing Sideways in the Twentieth Century*. Durham: Duke University Press, 2009.

Stow, John. *Annales of England*. London: Ralfe Newbery, 1592.

Sugg, Richard. *Mummies, Cannibals, and Vampires: The History of Corpse Medicine from the Renaissance to the Victorians*. New York: Routledge, 2011.

Sullivan, Garrett. *Memory and Forgetting in English Renaissance Drama: Shakespeare, Marlowe, Webster*. Cambridge: Cambridge University Press, 2005.

———. "Voicing the Young Man: Memory, Forgetting, and Subjectivity in the Procreation Sonnets." In *A Companion to Shakespeare's Sonnets*. Edited by Michael Schoenfeldt. Oxford: Blackwell, 2007.

Summers, David. *Spenser's Arthur: The British Arthurian Tradition and* The Faerie Queene. Lanham, MD: University Press of America, 1997.

Summit, Jennifer. *Memory's Library: Medieval Books in Early Modern England*. Chicago: University of Chicago Press, 2008.

Surrey, Henry Howard, Earl of. *Poems*. Edited by Emrys Jones. Oxford: Clarendon, 1964.

Sutton, John. "Spongy Brains and Material Memories." *Environment and Embodiment in Early Modern England*. Edited by Mary Floyd-Wilson and Garrett A. Sullivan, Jr. Basingstoke: Palgrave, 2007.

Suzuki, Mihoko. *Metamorphoses of Helen: Authority, Difference, and the Epic*. Ithaca: Cornell University Press, 1989.

Swinburne, Henry. *A Briefe Treatise of Testaments and Last Wills*. London: 1590.

Taniguchi, Kyoko. "The Eroticism of the Maternal" So What If Everything Is about the Mother?" *Studies in Gender and Sexuality* 13 (2012):123–38.

Tassi, Marguerite A. *The Scandal of Images: Iconoclasm, Eroticism, and Painting in Early Modern English Drama*. New York: Susquehanna University Press, 2005.

Thompson, Joanna. *The Character of Britomart in Spenser's* Faerie Queene. Lewiston, NY: Edward Mellen Press, 2001.

Topsell, Edward. *History of Serpents*. London: William Jaggard, 1608.

Thorne, Alison. "'Large Complaints in Little Papers': Negotiating Ovidian genealogies of complaint in Drayton's *Englands Heroicall Epistles*." *Renaissance Studies* 22.3, (2008): 368–84.

Toulalan, Sarah. *Imagining Sex: Pornography and Bodies in Seventeenth-Century England*. Oxford, UK: Oxford University Press, 2007.

Tourneur, Cyril. *The Atheist's Tragedy, or, The Honest Man's Revenge*. Edited by Irving Ribner. London: Methuen & Co, 1964.

Traci, Philip J. *The Love Play of Antony and Cleopatra*. The Hague: Mouton, 1970.

Traub, Valerie. *Desire and Anxiety Circulations of Sexuality in Shakespearean Drama*. London: Routledge, 1992.

———. "The New Unhistoricism in Queer Studies." *PMLA* 128.1 (2013): 21–29.

———. *The Renaissance of Lesbianism in Early Modern England*. Cambridge: Cambridge University Press, 2002.

Tribble, Evelyn. *Cognition in the Globe: Attention and Memory in Shakespeare's Theatre*. Basingstoke: Palgrave Macmillan, 2011.

Troyer, John. "Abuse of a Corpse: A Brief History and Re-theorization of Necrophilia Laws in the USA." *Mortality* (2008): 132–52.

Tulving, Endel. "Episodic and Semantic Memory." In *Organization of Memory*. Edited by Wayne Donaldson and Endel Tulving. New York: Academic Press, 1972.

Turberville, George. *The Heroycall Epistles of Publius Ovidius Naso, in English Verse*. London, 1567.

Turner, Ralph V. *Eleanor of Aquitaine: Queen of France, Queen of England*. New Haven: Yale University Press, 2009.

Turvey, Malcolm. "Film, Distraction, and Modernity." *The Filming of Modern Life: European Avant-Garde Film of the 1920s*. Cambridge, MA: The MIT Press, 2011.

van Es, Bart. "Michael Drayton, Literary History, and Historians in Verse." *RES* 59, (2007).

———. *Spenser's Forms of History*. Oxford: Oxford University Press, 2002.

Varnado, Christine. "'Invisible Sex!' What Looks Like the Act in Early Modern Drama?" *Sex before Sex: Figuring the Act in Early Modern England*. Edited by James M. Bromley and Will Stockton. Minneapolis and London: University of Minnesota Press, 2013.

Vaught, Jennifer. *Rhetorics of Bodily Disease and Health in Medieval and Early Modern England*. Burlington: Ashgate, 2010.

Vendler, Helen. *The Art of Shakespeare's Sonnets*. Cambridge: Belknap Press, 1999.

Vickers, Brian. *In Defence of Rhetoric*. Oxford: Clarendon Press, 1988.

Viguers, Susan T. "Art and Reality in George Peele's *The Araygnement of Paris* and *David and Bethsabe*." *CLA Journal* 30.4 (1987).

Vinaver, Eugène, ed. *The Works of Sir Thomas Malory*. Vol 3. Oxford: Clarendon Press, 1967.

Virgil. *Opera*. Edited by R. A. B. Mynors. Oxford: Clarendon, 1969.

Von Hendy, Andrew. "The Triumph of Chastity: Form and Meaning in *The Arraignment of Paris*." *RenD* 1 (1968): 87–101.

Wall, Wendy. *The Imprint of Gender: Authorship and Publication in the English Renaissance*. Ithaca: Cornell University Press, 1993.

Warner, Michael. *The Trouble with Normal: Sex, Politics, and the Ethics of Queer Life*. Boston: Harvard University Press, 2000.

Warner, William. *Albions England: The Third time corrected and Augmented*. London: Thomas Orwin, 1592.

———. *The First and Second Parts of Albions England*. London: Thomas Orwin, 1589.

Watson, Robert N. *The Rest Is Silence: Death as Annihilation in the English Renaissance*. Berkeley: University of California Press, 1994.

Watson, Thomas. *Compendium Memoriae Localis*. London, 1585.

Webster, John. "The Duchess of Malfi." *Five Jacobean Tragedies*. Edited by Andrew Hadfield. Ware: Wordsworth Classics, 2001.

Weever, John. *Antient Funeral Monuments, of Great-Britain, Ireland, and the Islands Adjacent*. 1631. Edited by William Tooke. London, 1767.
Weis, Rene. "Introduction to Arden." *Romeo and Juliet*. Bloomsbury, 2012.
Wells, Stanley, and Gary Taylor, eds. *The Oxford Shakespeare: Complete Works*. Oxford: Clarendon Press, 2005.
West, William. *Symbolaeographia*. London: 1592.
West, William N. "Replaying Early Modern Performances." *New Directions in Renaissance Drama and Performance Studies*. Edited by Sarah Werner. Houndmills, UK, and New York: Palgrave Macmillan, 2010.
Whigham, Frank, and Wayne A. Rebhorn, eds. *The Art of English Poesy*. Ithaca: Cornell University Press, 2007.
Wilder, Lina Perkins. *Shakespeare's Memory Theatre: Recollection, Properties, and Character*. Cambridge: Cambridge University Press, 2010.
———. *Shakespeare's Memory Theatre: Recollection, Properties, and Character*. New York: Cambridge University Press, 2014.
Williams, Gordon. *Shakespeare's Sexual Language: A Glossary*. London and New York: Continuum, 2006.
Willis, John. *Mnemonica, or The Art of Memory Drained out of the Pure Foundations of Art & Nature Digested into Three Books. Also a Physical Treatise of Cherishing Natural Memory; Diligently Collected out of Divers Learned Mens Writings*. 1661.
———. *The Arte of Memory. So Far Forth as it Dependeth upon Places and Idea's*. London: W. Jones, 1621.
Wilson, Miranda. "Bastard Grafts, Crafter Fruits: Shakespeare's Planted Families." In *The Indistinct Human in Renaissance Literature*. Edited by Jean E. Feerick and Vin Nardizzi. New York: Palgrave Macmillan, 2012.
Wilson, Thomas. *The Art of Rhetoric*. Edited by G.H. Mair. Oxford: Benediction Classics, 2006.
Wilson-Okamura, David Scott. *Spenser's International Style*. Cambridge: Cambridge University Press, 2013.
Woodcock, Matthew. *Fairy in The Faerie Queene: Renaissance Elf-Fashioning and Elizabethan Myth-Making*. Aldershot: Ashgate, 2004.
Worden, Blair. "Historians and Poets." *Huntington Library Quarterly* 68, 1–2 (2005): 71–72.
Wright, Thomas. *The Passions of the Minde in General*. London: A.Mathews, 1621.
Wyatt, Sir Thomas. *Collected Poems of Sir Thomas Wyatt*. Edited by Kenneth Muir and Patricia Thomson. Liverpool: Liverpool University Press, 1969.
Yates, Frances A. *The Art of Memory*. Chicago: University of Chicago Press, 1966.
———. *The Occult Philosophy in the Elizabethan Age*. New York and London: Routledge, 1979.
Yearling, Rebecca. "Florimell's Girdle: Reconfiguring Chastity in *The Faerie Queene*." *Spenser Studies* 20 (2005): 137–44.
Young, W. T., ed. *An Anthology of the Poetry of the Age of Shakespeare*. Cambridge: Cambridge University Press, 1910.
Zimmerman, Susan. *The Early Modern Corpse and Shakespeare's Theatre*. Cranbury, NJ: Associated University Press, 1999.
Zurcher, Andrew. *Spenser's Legal Language: Law and Poetry in Early Modern England*. Cambridge: D.S. Brewer, 2007.

Index

actors 54, 55–6, 61, 128, 195
Ad Herennium, see *Rhetorica ad Herennium*
Adelman, Janet 223
Aeneid, see Virgil
Albions England 66, 70–71
amnesia 164, 192, 211
antitheatrical 133, 164
"An Apology for Poetry". See Sidney, Sir Philip
Aquinas, Thomas 195, 212, 229
Aristotle 107, 109, 192, 207–8, 212, 222, 224, 228, 230–1, 236
Arthurian 82–3, 92, 199
Art of Memory, The; see John Willis
art of memory. See Yates, Frances; memory arts
Arthur, King 81–7, 199–200
Ascham, Roger 82
audience 5, 36–7, 53–4, 56, 59, 129–130, 132, 153, 159–160, 169–170, 199, 211, 224
Augustine, St. 230, 232

Barthes, Roland 1–3, 9–10, 124
Benjamin, Walter 170–73
Berlant, Lauren 19, 122
Bersani, Leo 147
Bible 83, 136
Book of Common Prayer 31
brain 208, 210–11, 241
Bromley, James 3
Bromley, Laura 55
Brutus 35–37, 42

Carruthers, Mary 30, 62, 108, 194, 212, 230
catholic 83, 92, 130–1, 137–9
Cavafy, Constantin 9
Cicero 97, 109, 194 *See also* memory arts

Clio 103, 204
Coke, Edward 235
commonwealth 99, 105, 226, 234, 235
Cupid 101, 104–7, 179, 187

David, King 83–4
death 5, 12–13, 19, 27, 31–32, 35–37, 40–43, 49, 51, 58, 62–63, 66–69, 75–76, 78, 84–85, 92, 94,102, 117, 130–131, 135, 141–153, 155–156, 160–163, 183, 204, 207, 219–220, 227, 229, 231–233
Derrida, Jacques i, 119, 233
Doctor Faustus (Marlowe) 63, 120, 126–127
Donne, John 171–172, 175
Drayton, Michael ix, 6, 23, 66–67, 69–77, 79–80
Dudley, Scott 154
The Duchess of Malfi, See Webster, John

Edelman, Lee 13, 221, 234
Education 34, 177, 182, 189
ekphrasis 54, 99–107, 109–112
Eliot, T.S. 223, 235
Elizabeth I, Queen 41, 181–182, 186, 190
emblems 5, 208
emotion 7, 18, 20, 28–29, 43, 89, 104, 134, 156, 166, 168–169, 194, 196, 203, 205, 207–208, 210, 217
epitaphs 63, 130–132, 142
eros 3, 6, 124, 160, 162, 174

The Faerie Queene, see Spenser
Fisher, Will 119
forgetting ii, x, 5, 9–10, 12, 40, 42, 44–45, 47, 49–50, 64, 71, 80, 97, 99–100, 110, 122–123, 127, 159, 164–165, 168, 170, 172–174,

192–193, 195–196, 198, 203, 209, 218, 234, 239–240, 242
Foucault, Michel 78, 124, 128
Freccero, Carla 4, 12, 28, 135, 143
Freeman, Elizabeth 7, 13, 124, 128
funeral 61, 63, 130, 170

gender iii, 18, 21, 26, 28–29, 42, 64–65, 75, 77, 79, 113, 119, 135, 166, 175, 177, 190
Geoffrey of Monmouth 94, 200, 206
Gerald of Wales 67
Gil, Daniel Juan 183, 190
Goldberg, Jonathan 7, 13, 134–135, 143
Gratarolo, Guglielmo 218
Greenblatt, Stephen 111, 138–139, 233–234, 236
Guy-Bray, Stephen 2, 6, 11, 13, 28, 43, 79, 240, 242

Halbwachs, Maurice 210
Hamlet see Shakespeare
Harris, Jonathan Gil 13
Helen of Troy 51, 127
Henry VII, King 31, 82
Henry VIII, King 31, 68, 223
Hiscock, Andrew 5, 12, 108, 111, 205
historiography 5, 7, 13, 64, 77, 79, 109, 175; erotohistoriography 7, 124
history 7, 20–21, 45, 49, 60, 69, 123, 126, 170, 188, 204; monumental history 170
Holinshed, Raphael 66, 68–70
Homer 120, 124

identity 20, 34, 38–39, 82, 114, 152, 164–165, 170, 172, 201, 233
imagination 100, 108, 134, 188, 192, 194–195, 208, 213, 224, 228
inheritance 31, 33, 40, 89
intertextuality 240

Jonson, Ben 33, 103

Leland, John 68
Lethe 71–72, 168
letters 23, 67, 72–73
London 171–172

Marlowe, Christopher 2, 4, 8, 112–118, 120–126
marriage 57, 83, 88, 134, 137, 152, 182, 184, 202

Marvell, Andrew 88
memory arts 4–5, 102, 180, 185, 192, 194, 203, 205, 207–209, 212, 215, 237, 239 *See also* Cicero
Menon, Madhavi 7
Metamorphoses, see Ovid
mind, models of 207, 209, 212
Mirror for Magistrates 70
mnemotechnician. *See* memory arts
monuments 7, 72, 130, 133–135, 164–165, 204
mourning 131, 149
Muñoz, José Esteban 13
music 61, 168

nationalism 89, 104–106, 178, 199
necrophilia 144–158
Nora, Pierre 7
nostalgia 22, 130, 138–139, 204, 232

objects, *see* material objects
oblivion, *see* forgetting
Old Testament, *see* Bible
Ovid 1–6, 11, 22–27, 62, 67, 73–75, 102–104, 114, 117, 121, 141, 238

Paster, Gail Kern 37, 171
Peele, George *Arraignment of Paris* 17–29; "The Tale of Troy" 125
Pietro da Ravenna 181, 184–185, 188–189, 208, 239
Platonism 182–184, 206, 229
Proust, Marcel 209
Purchas, Samuel 224
Puritans 143
Puttenham, George 69–70, 89, 237, 241

Quintilian 101

Rainolds, John 195
rape 51–62, 75–76, 91, 99–102, 109, 144–146, 149, 152–153
repetition 7, 124
reproduction 17, 57, 125, 141, 165, 221–223
revenge 55, 59, 144, 148–153, 194, 233, 237
Rhetorica ad Herennium 97–98, 194, 197
rhetorical handbooks 97, 195, 197, 203

Sanchez, Melissa 4, 18–20, 76–77, 199
self-forgetting 123, 209, 239

self-shattering 241
Shakespeare, William *Antony and Cleopatra* 159–176; *Hamlet* 10, 30, 34–35, 147, 155, 159–160, 171, 175, 220–236; *Julius Caesar* 35–39; *The Merchant of Venice* 33–35; *The Rape of Lucrece* 52–56; *Romeo and Juliet* 129–143, 144, 150–151; *Sonnets* 43–50, 207–219; *Troilus and Cressida* 30, 35, 38–40, 54
Sidney, Sir Philip 69–70, 99, 238–239, 241
Sigo, Cedar 43–50, 242
sodomy 4, 134
Spenser, Edmund *Amoretti* 177–186; *Colin Clouts Come Home Again* 204; *The Faerie Queene* 81–111, 177–206, 240–241
Stanivukovic, Goran 180
Stockton, Kathryn Bond 60
Stockton, Will 3
succession 164, 222–223, 226, 235

suicide 51, 57–59, 148–149, 160
Sullivan, Garrett 5, 45, 55, 80, 107, 126, 164, 209, 210

tablets 30, 238
time 124, 216, 220–221, 228
tombs, *see* monuments
translation 44–45, 46, 69, 130–131, 133
Traub, Valerie 4, 7
Trojan War 11, 17–29, 38–39, 120–124

Virgil 11, 26, 43, 120, 238–239

Warner, Michael 123, 128
Webster, John 33
Willis, John 98, 194, 237
Wright, Thomas 38, 40, 208–209, 213, 216–217

Yates, Frances 5, 12, 98, 180–181, 194
  See also memory arts